Sara

Also available:

Sara
My Whole Life Was a Struggle
Sakine Cansız

"Surrender leads to betrayal, resistance to victory": Cansız with photos of Leyla
Qasim and Mazlum Doğan on the wall behind her, Çanakkale prison, 1990.

Sara

Prison Memoir of a Kurdish Revolutionary

Sakine Cansız

Translated and edited by Janet Biehl

PLUTO PRESS

Published in German 2015 by Mezopotamien Verlag as
Mein ganzes Leben war ein Kampf (2. Band – Gefängnisjahre)
First English language edition published 2019 by Pluto Press
345 Archway Road, London N6 5AA

www.plutobooks.com

British Library Cataloguing in Publication Data
A catalogue record for this book is available from the British Library

ISBN 978 0 7453 3984 9 Hardback
ISBN 978 0 7453 3983 2 Paperback
ISBN 978 1 7868 0492 1 PDF eBook
ISBN 978 1 7868 0494 5 Kindle eBook
ISBN 978 1 7868 0493 8 EPUB eBook

This book is printed on paper suitable for recycling and made from fully managed and
sustained forest sources. Logging, pulping and manufacturing processes are expected to
conform to the environmental standards of the country of origin.

Typeset by Swales & Willis, Exeter, Devon, UK

Simultaneously printed in the United Kingdom and United States of America

Contents

Translator-editor's preface

This is the second of three volumes of the memoir of Sakine Cansız, a remarkable Kurdish revolutionary woman leader. In the first volume, as readers already know, she described her childhood in Dersim, and her escapes from marriage in defiance of Turkey's patriarchal gender system. She recounts how she became a dedicated organizer for the group UKO, also known as Kurdistan Revolutionaries, advocating a socialist revolution in Turkey's southeast, where many Kurds live. In November 1978 she attended the founding conference of the UKO's successor organization, which would come to be known as the PKK some 18 months later. Sakine moved to Elazığ, a city near her hometown, to specially focus on organizing women. But in the spring of 1979, Turkish police began a crackdown on the nascent party, carrying out a wave of arrests of leading cadres as well as rank-and-file members. On May 7, in an early morning raid on a movement apartment, police arrested her along with two other members of the Elazığ group, Hamili Yıldırım and his wife Ayten. As Volume I ends, the three of them are in a police van en route to prison, in a state of shock and bewilderment.

At the opening of Volume II, no time has passed—they are still in the van, which takes them to a prison in Elazığ. That will mark the beginning of Sakine Cansız's 12 years of incarceration, the period covered in Volume II.

She entered the Turkish prison system at a perilous moment. A year and a half after her arrest, on September 12, 1980, Turkish generals staged a military coup and declared martial law. They abolished parliament, suspended the constitution, and banned all political parties and unions. Most significant for this memoir, they took control of Turkey's prisons and militarized them. Prisoners would now be overseen, not by guards and wardens, but by soldiers. In the days before and after the coup, PKK leading cadres, including central committee members, were arrested en masse.

Surely the most notorious post-1980 military prison was in Diyarbakir, the largest Kurdish city in southeastern Turkey. Within four months of the coup, more than 30,000 people were jailed here. PKK leadership cadre, as well as rank and file, were concentrated here. Sakine Cansız was taken here around March 1, 1981.

The goal of the militarizing prisons was to strip prisoners of their rebelliousness, and especially, to strip Kurdish prisoners of their Kurdish identity, and transform them into obedient, soldier-like Turkish nationalists. To this end, prison administrators ("the enemy," as Sara called them) showed no scruples when it came to violent torture.

Conditions at the Diyarbakir "dungeon," as the prisoners accurately referred to it, were the most dire of all. It was not simply that Diyarbakir was severely overcrowded. Between 1981 and 1984, the Diyarbakir dungeon became notorious for its barbaric cruelty, a "hellhole," as it was often called. The military administration inflicted horrific systematic torture on the prisoners on an unprecedented scale, with unparalleled methods, both physical and psychological. When detainees were admitted, for example, they were beaten until their skin was raw, then thrown into vats of excrement, so that their wounds would become infected. Then they were made to sing Turkish military marches.

The reader might well set this book down in horror, but that would be a mistake. While Sara refers to the barbarism, she does not dwell on it. Other survivors have written memoirs testifying of the barbaric torture (alas, rarely translated into English), but Sara prefers to focus instead on the dialectic of capitulation and resistance.

For in the spring of 1979 the nascent PKK had been blindsided. Its members had not yet had much experience in prison, and its ideologues and theorists had given scant if any attention to the subject, should its members ever be imprisoned. They had developed no theory of prison, no policy for how PKK members were to behave there—not even a clear analysis demarcating resistance from surrender. As a result, many of the young Kurdish detainees were understandably terrified and capitulated under torture, naming names, becoming informers, betraying the organization.

Sara wanted no part of capitulation, and she herself did not yield under torture. Instead, she closely observed the behavior of her comrades (or "friends," as the Kurdish movement calls them) and tried to discern the nature of their "weakness," as she calls it. From the outset she was determined to resist, and apart from an initial error based on misinformation, she never wavered. She fought back at every opportunity, snapping back verbally at Diyarbakir's torturer-in-chief, Esat Oktay Yıldıran, refusing even to scream under torture, so as not to give "the enemy" that satisfaction, and refusing to accept military rules. Above all she participated in the great hunger strikes and death fasts of 1980–1984.

By modeling unshakable resistance for those around her, male and female, she helped build their courage. By the time she was released, from Çanakkale prison in 1991, she was an acknowledged leader of prison resistance—and a legend.

* * *

This book is not only a powerful memoir but also a remarkable historical document. Sara wrote it (in Turkish) under difficult circumstances, in the mountains of northern Iraq, on a manual typewriter, sheltered from the elements by tents. She and her friends carried the pages in backpacks through mountain defiles. Thereafter the manuscript underwent some editing. It was translated into German, which is the version I used (I do not know Turkish). But to be frank, as I worked through the book, I found it to be in need of more editing than it had received—understandably, given the circumstances of its creation. The sequence was scrambled in places, at the sentence and paragraph level; episodes appeared to be out of sequence, and the narrative was too often interrupted by out-of-place inserted paragraphs. Important discussions were scattered. Chapter titles did not always correspond to chapter contents.

Eventually I concluded that a word-for-word translation (as in Volume I) would have been as frustrating for readers as it was for me. And not only did the book contain all these difficulties, Volume II was considerably longer than Volume I.

I am an editor by profession, having worked on manuscripts for New York book publishers for 40 years. As I worked on Volume II and noticed these problems, my editor's mind was inevitably working, and I could see how to fix them to make the book more readable.

But of course as a translator, I lacked the authority to do so. My brief was to translate, not to edit. Moreover, since Sakine Cansız is of enormous significance to the Kurdish movement, it would have been arrogant of me to change her text. Nonetheless, as a publishing professional, I wanted to ensure that her story was accessible to English readers.

So I created an edited version: I trimmed repetitions. I consolidated similar material that was scattered through the manuscript into dedicated sections. I corrected the placement of chapter titles, so they would correspond better to chapter text, and created new ones where needed. Where something essential seemed missing, I inserted words in brackets. I made numerous micro-cuts that have resulted in a shorter, more concise book. I did all this with the aim of editing the book's form without changing its content or altering Sara's meanings.

Readers may well disagree with this choice, but fortunately, Sara's original document exists in Turkish and German—it is on the record and available, not least for scholars who need the original. But I feel that by clarifying Sara's text, without doing violence to her content or to the book's overall integrity, I have widened her potential readership.

* * *

For background on Turkish prisons in the 1980s, especially Diyarbakir, I relied on several academic studies in English.[1]

Throughout the book, Sara refers to many people (often by first name only), political organizations (by acronym), and events, many of them recurring. I suspect that many readers will be unfamiliar with them. To provide explanations, footnotes and endnotes seemed awkward, especially when names recurred. So instead of notes, I compiled some lists: a list of the significant and recurring people in the book, a list of political acronyms and names, and a timeline. They are all at the end of the book. I strongly recommend that the reader use them.

I am grateful to Mezopotamien Verlag, the publisher of the German and Turkish editions, for permission to translate the book. Many thanks to Nazan Üstündağ for her careful review of the manuscript, which improved it greatly. Special thanks to Berivan Kutlay Sarıkaya, who is currently researching Kurdish women in Turkish prisons (and who once was one herself). Berivan, who is in contact with some of Sara's fellow prisoners mentioned in this book, afforded me important background information and advice, especially over coffee on a beautiful summer afternoon in Montreal. She read the early parts of the manuscript, answered my questions, and provided me with many academic sources. I can't thank her enough for help. For assistance with photos, I'm once again grateful to Inan Aslıyüce and Tijda Cansız, as well as to Mezopotamien Verlag itself. For help in identifying people in the photos, I am grateful to Hamit Kankılıç (who was with Sara at Çanakkale) and to Fuat Kav (who was with her at Diyarbakir)—Sara mentions both of them in these pages. Thanks, finally, to Metin Guven for translating some brief material from Turkish for me.

Janet Biehl
Burlington, Vermont, USA

Taken by surprise   The morning of May 7, 1979, was peaceful, with hardly any other vehicles in the streets, just the police van that had been part of the raid.

The van sped along the Malatya road to 1800 Evler, a prison on the outskirts of Elazığ, in one of the poorer quarters. Most of the residents were working-class families from Dersim, in temporary housing. We'd been active in this area, done educational work and held meetings, distributed leaflets, and put up posters. I'd been here myself. Our work had been meaningful to the people here. Young women had expressed interest in us, and students. Our resistance to feudal institutions and our use of revolutionary violence against fascism was especially appealing to young people.

But this morning my journey to 1800 Evler ended in secluded building on the periphery, under a large sign announcing "Agricultural Equipment Authority." Its walls were thick enough to muffle any screams, so they wouldn't be heard outside.

The police who'd arrested us were in a fine mood. They had carried out the raid without a hitch—there had been no shooting. Our traitors had given them information under torture, which had greatly simplified matters for them. This first phase of their operation was a success. Initially police arrested only a few of us who had been active around here, but later they would capture most. Later the police's "wanted" list would be leaked to us—and we saw our names on the list of cadres. So they'd been after us for a while.

We'd been arrested just as we'd been expanding our operations here. It was hard to accept. Oh, why had we used that flat as a meeting place, or stayed in this neighborhood at all! Obviously, these arrests weren't random. We'd talked about the dangers, but we'd taken no serious practical precautions, let alone followed them consistently. Now we were paying dearly for our negligence.

This thought weighed heavily on me. We'd made a grave mistake, and our recklessness was inexcusable. That we'd fallen into the enemy's hands so easily was horrifying. No amount of cursing on our part could help. Now the three of us would come face to face with the enemy. Even though storms raged inside us, however, we mustn't fall apart. A struggle lay ahead, and it was of paramount importance that we prepare for it deliberately and consciously. We'd just entered a war zone. From this point, everything we did would count: every look, word, grimace, tone of voice, and gesture. The enemy would notice everything, and wherever he found a weak point, he would strike.

No proof The van pulled up in front, near the gate. The police got out and bustled around. We heard a commotion—somewhere a celebration was going on.

They brought the three of us into a room where clubs, tires, and dirty strips of fabric were strewn around an uneven floor, amid puddles of water. There was a single chair. Clearly this was no ordinary waiting room. People were tortured here. The objects in the room were used for falanga [beating the soles of the feet]. The strips of fabric were used as blindfolds and to bind hands and feet. What the tires were for, I had no idea, but I was in no position to think about it.

I shoved my hands into my pockets and found a few notes I hadn't had time to destroy in the flat that morning—I'd stuck them there so I could swallow them when I got a chance. Now I tore them to shreds and dampened them in some wet cloth. Since no policewoman had participated in the raid, I hadn't been searched, but one could show up here at any moment. So the three of us gave each other warning looks, to take care of whatever we had on our persons.

Hamili was nervous—his temples were pounding. "Was there anything important in the apartment?" he asked. "Anything they could find?"

"No." Before opening the door to the police, I'd burned some things and thrown other stuff out the kitchen window. A copy of the *History of the Bolshevik Party* was all that remained in the flat, along with a copying machine, a typewriter, and a pile of tracing paper, colored paper, carbon paper, and regular paper. *Any normal apartment would have a typewriter,* I thought—*they can't charge us for having one.* Unknown to us, beneath the stack of paper was a flyer called "To Our Heroic People." But as far as we knew, the objects they confiscated would be no great problem.

But something else would be.

The enemy had made a direct hit on our organization in this district. The flat where we were captured had been exposed—apparently someone had broken under torture, which could lead to more arrests. Şahin Dönmez had been around, and other friends from outside the district might still arrive. But three people from the district committee were now in the enemy's custody. Hamili and I had been taken after Ali [Gündüz] was arrested, and a few friends from the subcommittees. Deaf Metin and Hüseyin Topgüder were still outside—Hüseyin had been transferred to [Gazi]antep. If they didn't take care, many more cadres could be arrested.

Even though so much had been happening, Şahin had seemed so relaxed. Normally he stayed overnight with friends. Anyone who wanted to expose one of the organization's flats would've chosen one of them.

A dangerous game was taking place. Within the organization there were people who caused problems, consciously or not, and so put everything at risk. First Antep, then Dersim—now certain people were trying to disrupt the organization in Elazığ. Would they succeed? The uppermost committee consisted entirely of cadres from elsewhere. Some people considered them "outsiders." Those who had problems anyway could easily latch on to this point.

I remembered my last encounter with Rıza Sarıkaya. Tempers had flared. Rıza had come to us from Dev-Genc and was an older cadre. But in Elazığ he hadn't been able to resign himself to playing second fiddle. His careerism led to competition and an alarming degree of infighting. We'd tried to discuss his errors with him, but he didn't change. Finally Cemil talked to him, which temporarily solved the problem. Rıza could go to another place where he was needed, we said. It would have been a good idea, allowing us to gain time so we could get to know him better, but he wasn't satisfied with that solution. And just at that point, he had been arrested. Maybe the enemy had caught wind of his discontent. There were many spies in Elazığ. Our groups operated as openly as possible, but that meant the enemy found out about everything right away. We weren't sure, but we had suspicions about what Rıza, after his arrest, had said in his statement.

[Hamili and Ayten and I,] by reminding each other what statements we'd agreed on, were expressing a definite concern. The outlook was grim. In a mass arrest, a sign of weakness or a mistake on the part of a single individual could encourage the enemy, who would then try to divide the arrestees and turn them against each other. A week earlier Hüseyin [Taze] had been arrested, then released—he had said something about this. All the arrestees were housed alone and interrogated alone, both to inflict psychological pressure on them and to induce them to turn on each other during interrogation and make statements that could be used as evidence. Such methods could be more effective than even the most brutal torture.

We could have got away! Back in the apartment, while the police were searching it, they'd asked who lived there. I'd jumped in and said, "It's my apartment. Sometimes my siblings come to visit. I've only just moved in. My family pays the rent. I'm looking for work. I've got nothing to do with politics. I'm just an educated, progressive-minded person." My calm, composed reply surprised the police. A few shook their heads, others smirked maliciously, as if to say, yeah, we'll show you who you really are.

Among them was a commissioner whose name I later learned was Zafer Karaosmanoğlu. He'd been calm too. He'd expected to find more people staying in the flat—he hadn't found everyone he was looking for there. The cops spent a long time counting the dirty glasses in the kitchen, looking for evidence of more people. Maybe they'd expected to find Şahin and some others.

During the search, they barked questions to test our reactions. The first impressions we gave them, our reactions to their tests and attacks, would be very important. The impression you make on your opponent will influence what comes later.

My first encounter with police had been back in Izmir, during the workers' resistance at Bornova.[2] I'd been arrested, along with many others. But this time was different—this hit had been targeted. And this time I was responsible for the organization. I had to protect it, to avoid doing anything that could damage it, and to adhere to my convictions under highly unfavorable circumstances. That would require hard work. The enemy would use every possible means against me. It wouldn't be enough just to assert my revolutionary will. The prison novels I'd read— *War of Resistance*, *Red Rocks*, and *Report from the Gallows*—depicted unimaginable torture and also unprecedented resistance, all of which was based on reality.

So it was important to assess the opponent correctly. Only then could we fight him properly and hope to prevail. Every moment that passed, every second, was crucial. Innumerable thoughts raced through my mind. Never before had I thought of so many things all at once. To understand this kind of situation, to get what we were feeling, you'd have to experience it yourself.

4

Could we have fled this morning? I wondered. *Could we have reached the building next door?* Was I imagining the impossible? Once, I'd tried to lay down a plank from the kitchen window across to the adjacent building, but it hadn't been stable enough. Then no one had bothered to look for a sturdier board. The people across from us were a nice young couple from Siverek. When I asked the woman if we could use the space between the windows when we had a problem—say, with the key— she'd said yes. So if we'd been better prepared, we could have held off the police long enough to disappear into the building next door.

And then there was the top floor. Dammit! I'd heard that police van coming! If only I'd got suspicious a few minutes sooner, or even seen it out the window—we could have run up to the roof and escaped that way. By the time the police climbed the stairway to our flat, we'd have been in the neighboring house already. We could have got some clothes from Gülay and scarves to wear as masks and slipped away.

But now it was too late. These were good ideas, and imagining them was very nice, but we had to face reality. We were no longer in the flat but in an interrogation room. It was useless now to imagine what might have happened. I was furious at myself. We just shouldn't have let ourselves be captured so handily.

In these first hours, the enemy's methods were already becoming clear. We had no time to ruminate. We had at most ten minutes to think and to compare notes. Time was as crucial for us as it was for the enemy. Every minute they allowed to pass [before questioning] was a chance for us to think and prepare ourselves and so was a win. Every second we used well could have positive effects in the days to come.

Capitulation, betrayal, and resistance   They took me in first, to a room at the end of the hallway, on the right side. It was full of police, including those who'd carried out the raid and search. They were sneering, as if they were about to fight a bull in an arena. Well, the observers and the bull stood ready. Only the matador was absent.

"Let's have at it," one of them said.

Another scoffed, "Just look at how she strides in here. You can see in her face how much she despises us!"

A cop sitting at a table shoved a transcript at me and said, "Sign!"

It was a list of the confiscated objects. I read it, then pushed the paper back to him. "I won't sign this," I said. "These things were not found in my possession. I already signed a list back in the apartment." That infuriated them. When they asked for my ID, I replied mockingly and arrogantly, enjoying showing them my contempt.

I wasn't following any particular plan, but from their questions, I could tell they'd obtained information about me from others. I pretended it wasn't serious. Certain points that seemed important to them—I acted as if they were trivial.

After this brief initial phase, the nature of the questioning changed.

We know everything about you. We know Cemil Bayık, Metin, and Şahin live in that flat. Yesterday evening you were all together. Judging by the number of used glasses, several people were there. Where have you hidden the weapons? You're one of the organization's leaders. Oh, you say you're an "educated, progressive-minded person"? Yeah, well, tell it to someone else! As for progressivism—no, your apartment belongs to the organization.

One question after another spilled out of them.

Clearly they didn't quite know what they were looking for. They were still trying to piece together the information they had to form a clearer picture of me. The actual interrogation hadn't yet begun.

Then they asked about the men friends who'd been previously arrested. They showed me the IDs of Zeki Budak, Rıza Sarikaya, Aytekin Tuğluk, Saim Dursun, Hüseyin Taze, and Ali Gündüz. Did I know them? I know none of them, I said. They taunted me, saying they knew who I was and what my role was. They'd spent a long time with Ali Gündüz.

"Maybe he knows me from Dersim," I countered. "Dersim's a small place—probably he heard my name there. That'd be normal."

They asked about Hamili and Ayten. I repeated that I'd known them in Dersim. Ayten, who'd been my neighbor, had come to Elazığ because she was ill. I spoke without hesitation and without contradicting myself, and soon they didn't know what to ask anymore.

It made them nervous to keep repeating themselves. Then they attached a cable to my finger and turned on the electricity. How much more they enjoyed my twitching and screaming! The shocks flung me against the wall. So that was what they'd meant when they'd said, "*Laugh now—soon we'll be the ones laughing.*" They upped the voltage while pouring water over me. My screams became more muffled. They took off my shoes and socks but didn't apply the falanga. They asked me more questions.

Finally they said I should think things over, and they took me into another room. It was a small cell, with a toilet and a double bed with filthy, blood-smeared blankets and mattresses. The windows were nailed shut and whitewashed.

Soon after that I heard a man's screams. Hamili was being interrogated. Time slowed to a crawl. The screams, elicited by electrical shocks, were interspersed with thuds of clubbing. I didn't hear Ayten's voice. I assumed they'd be more careful with her because she was pregnant, and torture would be risky for her. They requisitioned a woman officer to take her to a doctor to find out if she was really pregnant. The woman officer was delayed in arriving, so they brought Ayten to my cell. We laughed darkly about my statement, but Ayten was also uneasy.

The enemy had already interrogated people from many groups and squeezed information out of most of them by various methods. These initial encounters taught us which ones he planned to use on us. We had only just been arrested, and he didn't want to apply the most extreme tortures right away. He'd proceed according to a plan. Our battle with him wouldn't be confined to a single time or place. Rather, we would struggle at every moment of our lives and must never be deterred from the goal. Is that not the most important mark of a revolutionary life?

Earlier in the 1970s, as we vividly recalled, the state had repressed all progressive and revolutionary tendencies. Through its executions, tortures, and massacres, the state revealed its very nature. Whole books had been written about the interrogation system used around the time of the March 12 [1971 coup]. Some comrades had capitulated and betrayed one another, while others had resisted. Some betrayed even to the point of turning their family members over to the enemy. That behavior and its important consequences were discussed in schools.

Betrayal contributes to the defeat of a social uprising, but it doesn't account for it entirely. When someone betrays, the consequences depend on how organized the base is. The grassroots base of the resistance plays an important role. In Kurdistan in the 1970s, there was no avant-garde or organization, as the necessary conditions for an organized struggle weren't yet in place.

Historically, our struggle had had fellow travelers who went on to betray. In Antep, the actions of just a handful of betrayers had had a huge impact, but in Dersim they'd been punished. Tekoşin, [a PKK split-off,] had been such a betrayal. Celal Aydın had betrayed us in Elazığ and in Malatya. Letters that we intercepted showed that in Malatya, he had planned to wreck the organization, but his plan had been exposed and prevented. Şahin had driven to Karakoçan to pick up information, but he hadn't been involved any further. After the [execution of] Celal Aydın, Ali Gündüz was downcast for a few days. It was the first time he had killed a person, and he was struggling with himself.

Revolutionary vengeance requires profound class-consciousness. Hatred and revenge, anger and love, will be misdirected if they lack the correct foundations. Unless consciousness, emotions, and wishes are tied to an ideal, they have nothing to do with courage, virtue, and confidence.

The passion that united us Sharing circumstances with someone allows you to get to know them well. We all show various aspects of ourselves in various contexts. To understand someone, you need to know what just happened with them, then try to see where it could lead. But some circumstances reveal a person's true nature more clearly than others. In some situations you can no longer hide who you really are. All eyes can see you, and all ears can hear you. Your racing heartbeat and your pallor make obvious what you're feeling. Your body betrays you! Because by this point, [if you're a traitor,] you're nothing more than a shell of a human, with no personality.

When you're interrogated alone, you face the enemy alone. I could understand Rıza, and even Ali's behavior didn't surprise me much, but why had the others talked? These arrested friends were all from the district leadership. Every weakness they showed would have negative consequences on others. Their statements differed in length, and not all of them had capitulated entirely, but every single word, every short explanation, was an advantage that the enemy could use. Knowing how to exploit every weakness, the enemy applied group interrogation to them as well.

Meanwhile I had stuck to my statement that I was just a "progressive intellectual." The police had disbelieved me from the outset. They showed me what the others had said about me in their statements. Now they wanted to hear it from me directly.

So one morning they subjected me to a special kind of interrogation: the falanga. Aytekin, Zeki Budak, Rıza, Ali, and Hamili were all present— I recognized their voices—and maybe others were present as well. I was blindfolded, as they surely were too.

At first I didn't utter a word. It wasn't all that hard to endure the beatings. They clubbed my legs, between my legs, and my back. That kind of pain numbs the brain.

But when my fellow prisoners started to speak, I exploded with insults at them—of course, without political content. "You animals! I don't know you at all!" I shouted.

I only know Hamili because his wife lived in the same neighborhood as me! Dersim is a small city. Maybe Ali heard my name there, but there's no connection between us. You damn animals, you sons of donkeys, what are these allegations?

I was bleeding a lot, and finally I was taken from the room. Zafer Karaosmanoğlu, head of the district, was always present at my interrogations, performing the fatherly role as part of their psychological warfare. Now he sympathized with me, as if he hadn't been present at the torture, and he even brought me a clean undershirt to stop the bleeding. "There's no gauze here," he said. "Would you like to use this?"

But the police must have come to regret this tactic, since afterward, apart from Rıza, none of the others would repeat their statements. Clearly it's good to defend yourself!

My behavior had impressed the friends. When they were taken back to their cells, Aytekin said (so I later heard), "When they bring me in with *her* again, I'm not going to say anything more." Hamili was moved too. After this episode, I almost wished always to be interrogated with the friends present. Whenever the police showed me a statement that one of them had made, I demanded a face-to-face confrontation. That gave me a psychological advantage. And it gave me self-confidence, since the demands annoyed the police.

But I also learned things that depressed me in these confrontations: comrades whom I'd trusted really did betray organizational secrets. Not that I lost faith. I didn't despair—I considered it just a temporary weakness that wouldn't be carried too far. If anything, their behavior stirred defiance in me: *I will say nothing! They will get nothing out of me!*

Ayten was to be taken to interrogation after me. To spare her, I didn't tell her all the details. Statements had also been made about her. But she wasn't beaten. She was mainly used as a lever to pressure Hamili.

One day a commotion broke out. Car tires screeched, and inhuman screams were heard. New arrivals, we realized, were on the way.

I'd been taken to interrogation early that morning, which boded ill—they wanted the new arrivals to hear my screams, another effective form of psychological torture. A woman's scream has a different impact than a man's. It makes some people hate the enemy more, while it terrifies others to the marrow. Fear is the great precondition for defeat.

They let me go to the toilet, but I couldn't walk anymore. Ayten supported me on one side, and a guard on the other. As we shuffled forward, we passed an open door, and there, in another interrogation room, amid others, I saw Şahin. When his eyes met mine, he bit his lip, and his eyes widened in fear. I made my face impassive and continued on.

They must have left the door open on purpose! Were the police testing him, or were they trying to share with me the joyous news of his arrest? They'd always said they'd arrested all the friends—"Oh yes, we've arrested Cemil, Hüseyin Topgüder, Apo, all of them!"—as a way of dialing up the pressure.

Where, in what apartment, had Şahin been arrested? Not to know was itself like torture. I later found out that he had been arrested, along with Haydar Eroğlu, in the flat in the Fevzi Çakmak neighborhood. Once again, no precautions had been taken. Why had Şahin still been in the district at all? Hadn't anyone learned from our mistakes and fled? And why had he gone into an apartment that had long ago been exposed? It was unbelievable.

But the sight of Şahin shook me more than anything up to that point. Yes, it was bad whenever any of us, no matter who, fell into the enemy's hands. But Şahin's arrest was alarming. I had never sensed in Şahin any feeling of responsibility for the organization. I distrusted him so much that I wished they could have arrested anyone else. Had I developed an unconscious animus toward him? Was it right to feel so disquieted about his arrest? After all, other comrades I trusted had already talked. But no, I still trusted them, at least up to the point where their weaknesses didn't overwhelm them.

So I said to myself, *If his attitude toward the enemy is agreeable, then I'll be so disagreeable they hit the roof.* I didn't do it deliberately or think it through—it just happened by itself. As I passed the interrogation room, I had great pain in my feet, but the sight of him there made me snap to. I raised my head and proceeded with determination. His presence had the effect, reflexively, of enlarging my awareness of my own responsibility. His weakness meant I had to rise to the occasion. In a torture chamber, it is immeasurably important to avoid showing fear or indecisiveness. In a way, his presence made me feel stronger and more courageous than before.

Toward evening, he was interrogated in a room adjacent to Ayten's and my cell. The police called it "letting him sing." We could hear their voices. We pressed our ears to the wall, and I heard a rush of a clubbing and Şahin screaming, "*Abi!*" [big brother]. That was all! That was the entirety of Şahin's resistance! And then he started to talk.

I couldn't stand it and pounded my fists against the wall. Ayten said, "Stop—they can hear that!" That was probably the moment in my life when I cursed the most. There was nothing else I could do.

Comradely relations are like a fire that warms our hearts, and they create connections like nothing else. This fire, the basis of all our comradely relations, was what brought us all together. But I'd never really shared that fire with Şahin, never really befriended him—no honest, straightforward affection and respect ever developed between us.

I'd never trusted this swine, never liked him. As a member of the [Kurdistan Revolutionaries], he had belonged to the first organized group in Dersim, but we didn't have much to do with each other. [My brother] Haydar had thought Şahin had already been a traitor back then. After the bomb attacks, many people had been arrested and tortured at the police station, but Şahin had not been beaten and had called the police "*Abi.*"[3] Oh, my brother had been right!

I didn't meet him or get to know him till after I'd left Dersim.[4] I formed my impressions of him at the assembly in Izmir-Inciralti, and his later behavior in Elazığ and Bingöl reinforced my distrust—he had shown no awareness of responsibility for the organization. He was and remained a stranger to me—the heat of shared comradely fire never caught him.

Then Şahin had behaved strangely at the founding congress, and I was so disturbed that on the return trip, I told Cemil what I thought of him. Had the chairman [Öcalan] noticed his behavior? He'd been very patient. But the chairman was always calm and tried to understand. Surely the chairman had seen through him—surely he recognized Şahin's careerism and ambition.

Şahin had even been elected to the central committee! All of us were surprised. He had done nothing to earn it—it was just that all the other friends had withdrawn their names. I thought about this question often, and the conclusion I came to was that the chairman wanted to get to know him better through this important work—that was one way he interacted with people.

And now Şahin had capitulated at the first opportunity. With him, the enemy had no need for sophisticated methods. The enemy had had only to knock on the door. What happened to conviction, force of will, and the interests of the organization? No, his whole personality structure was geared toward treachery, with its fine line between revolutionary behavior and treachery. In the revolution, you have to put your abilities and strengths at the service of the struggle and apply them to the task at hand. Instead, he tried to suit the task to himself.

I had a splitting headache. In his statement Şahin described not only his own work but that of the organization in the Elazığ and Dersim districts. It wasn't that he had shown weakness in the face of police torture—they never really even tortured him, but he spilled everything just as if they had. He reported on what he had done in Elazığ, how long he had been here, when he had gone to Ağri, his activities there, and his return to Elazığ. It went on for hours.

I dearly hoped he'd stop there. If only Cemil had been arrested instead of Şahin! All this rotten coward did was encourage the enemy, who previously hadn't known much about us and couldn't even tell us apart from other leftist groups. They didn't know how to ask the right questions, so little information did they have. Oh, why hadn't this scumbag left Elazığ after the first arrests?

He kept on talking, even without the police asking questions. When he started talking about the founding congress, I flipped out and slammed my head against the wall. I could barely contain my fury. I wanted to scream, but [knew I] mustn't, so I bit my lips so I wouldn't make any noise. My throat burned. Ayten was shocked, even frightened. "Don't get all crazy!" she said, "If you do, these guys will pick up on it!" But she didn't realize the scale of Şahin's betrayal. She assumed he was just saying things under torture, but that wasn't it—he knew too much. As for the men friends, they didn't know what was happening— they couldn't hear Şahin from their cells, and other interrogations were taking place in different rooms at the same time.

He even gave the enemy tips on how to break certain comrades and who had which weaknesses. He made it so easy for them. And this was just the beginning—how much farther would Şahin's betrayal go? Because he spilled so much, the enemy left the others in peace for a few days.

One morning I heard voices coming from the courtyard. I climbed onto the bunk bed, peered out, and saw dozens of people standing in a row. The police were shrieking, "Take out your IDs! Empty your pockets. If we find anything on you, it will have consequences!" Everyone placed the contents of their pockets on the ground. I recognized Hüseyin Taze, Ilhan, Nail, and a few others. Then my eyes fixed on the last person in the lineup. To my disbelief, it was comrade Cemil [Bayık]. He stood calmly, with his hands loosely behind his back. He was wearing a suit, missing the tie. I felt joy and sorrow at the same time. Again I thought, *If only Cemil had been arrested instead of Şahin, he wouldn't have given the enemy all this information!* But that was nonsensical. Anytime a cadre ended up in prison, it damaged the struggle.

The police were absorbed in inspecting the IDs. One of them shuttled back and forth between the building and the yard. Some looked into the window of the adjoining room—apparently they were getting signals from there. Silently I prayed that Cemil wouldn't be arrested. The thought of Şahin drove me crazy.

After a while they selected a group, including Hüseyin, Nail, Ilhan, and Ercan. The others were ordered back into the vans, where the police would take them to the city center. What did that mean? Would they be freed? Apparently they hadn't recognized Cemil—he'd kept his face averted. Or maybe some twinges of conscience had stirred among the traitors, and they'd said nothing. Anything was possible.

The new arrivals had said they knew me, so I was taken back to interrogation later that day. The police were elated. "We caught them, both Cemil Bayık and Hüseyin Topgüder!" they crowed to me. "They sang like nightingales! You're resisting for nothing!" By then, as it turned out, Cemil had left Elazığ and gone into safety, but if I'd known that at the time, I'd have spat back, "You birdbrains, Cemil is long gone—and you let him go!" It would've been super, but I restrained myself. Now it was clear that they lied—they said things like that a lot. Still, even when I didn't believe them about something, I could never exclude it entirely, so uncertainty always lingered.

Pir Ahmet died in the hospital   The days passed with more interrogations and torture. The arrests didn't let up. Clearly the police were grabbing anyone who struck them as somehow suspicious. A name similar to that of a UKO member or a very distant connection was

13

enough. One day they brought in a guy just because his name was close to someone else's. They tortured him all day long outside our window, and not just with electricity jolts, hanging, and falanga. They did inhuman things to his organs and his whole body. They did everything that can debase and humiliate a person. Then they left him lying on the ground, wavering between life and death.

During this time people did die, but the police tried to avoid responsibility. For example, they freed one prisoner because they knew he wouldn't survive, but he died as soon as he got home. Later many such cases became known. [In 1977] Pir Ahmet Solmaz, a TİKKO revolutionary,[5] was tortured in prison till he fell into a coma—he died in the state hospital. But a doctor there called Musa Duman had certified him to be healthy, thereby absolving the police of all blame. Around the time of our arrest, revenge actions were carried out against this fascist torture doctor. They attacked and wounded him, then were arrested.

After Şahin's betrayal, the torture intensified. The interrogations were now based mainly on his statements. There was an interrogation room next to our cell, where people were tortured every day. Şahin was taken somewhere else, from where he could let the police know when he had forgotten something and wanted to be brought in again. By now the other friends knew about his treachery. Of course, everyone had squealed about something or other, so they could hardly pass judgment on Şahin, but there was an important difference: he had betrayed the organization not out of weakness, as the others had done, but out of malice.

Zafer Karaosmanoğlu came often to our cell to continue his "soft" interrogation. He kept referring to the concept of "progressiveness." It had already been established that I was a member of the organization's district committee, that I headed the women's committee and led propaganda and agitational work, that I conducted meetings, delegated tasks, and had participated in the congress. Yet I continued to insist that I was an "educated, progressive-minded person."

Hamili and Ayten had confessed a few things, but nothing too damaging. They had not confessed that they lived in Elazığ. Their apartment had been safe—no one knew about it except Hüseyin and Şahin. But I was worried. We racked our brains wondering if it had been exposed. The key had been found on Hamili or Ayten, but they'd said that they were from Dersim. When the police asked me about Ayten, I said I knew her from the neighborhood.

14

Ayten was brought in for interrogation from time to time, but [since she was pregnant] she wasn't tortured. One of the soldiers standing guard outside our window told me about it. Murat, who came from Cermik, told me he was Kurdish and slipped me a piece of bread through the window. I hardly ate anything in prison. Not because the food was terrible—it was—but I couldn't keep anything down. Anyway, Murat didn't contact me about food—he wanted to warn me [about Ayten]. A soldier from Serhat, also a Kurd, said, "Don't trust that woman, she's a spy. She's never beaten, not once. They give her tea and cigarettes. And they even let her meet her husband. Then she goes off and betrays you. Don't tell her anything!" The soldiers were very sure they'd interpreted their observations correctly.

Of course the soldiers weren't to be trusted, but a few might have been honest. When the two [Kurdish] soldiers Murat and Serhat had joint guard duty and I was alone, they took turns visiting me, one standing guard to warn the other. They didn't behave too badly, and my situation touched them. Many soldiers were upset by my screams during torture. Sometimes they couldn't hide their disapproval, snapping, "Those sons of bitches! What the hell do they want from you?"

For a long time I contemplated asking Murat to smuggle a message to the outside. Hamili and Ayten had an archive on the second floor of their apartment that absolutely had to be destroyed. I didn't have much hope that the friends outside would take care of it. Deaf Metin knew about the archive, but I doubted he'd do what was necessary. No, Nadire was best suited for the task. It would be easy for the soldiers to track down her address for me. Finally I did ask them to deliver a little message to my relative Nadire. They agreed.

The apartment was in the Razaiye neighborhood, so I wrote something like, "How is Aunt Raziye doing? Not too well, I imagine. Why don't you look in on her? Help her clean the apartment—she's sick, after all." I added a blank piece of paper, put a hair in it, and then sealed the letter, so Nadire would know if it had been opened. The soldier stuck it into his pocket. "Don't worry," he said, "I'll deliver it by hand and bring you the answer." That was a comfort. And the letter carried no risk if it were discovered.

Two days later I got my answer: "Don't worry about your aunt. We visited her and helped her. Metin went to the village. Don't worry about him either." What a relief. Now it didn't matter if the apartment was exposed.

One day after we were taken to the toilets, I went back to the cell while the guards were still waiting for Ayten. I had a chance to look through a window to the side where Hamili and the others were. The corridor was L-shaped. When the door was open, the men could hear, and they watched the area through a hole in the door and the window. Peering through the window, I spotted Aytekin and Hamili standing at their window. We said hello. They laughed, with restraint, then Hamili said, "After that day, we swore they'd never torture you again in our presence. But remember—you insulted us!" Aytekin added, "But that was good— your curses brought us to our senses." And Hamili admitted, "Our sister Seko may insult us in peace."

Both men were unshaven and scrawny. "Your apartment's been scrubbed, Hamili," I said. "Did you know?"

He was delighted. How did I know?

"I found a good soldier," I said breathlessly, "and I gave him a message, and then I got a response. By the way, Deaf Metin seems to have vanished."

They were shocked at how gaunt I'd become. "Take care of yourself, everything will be okay!" they said, and then I left. Just seeing them had been comforting. Despite all our mistakes, we still had the warmth and trust of comradely relations.

Such accidental encounters did me good. The police inflicted torture all night long, but sometimes in the morning it was calm. Another time we talked about Şahin. "We hear what he says too," they said. They told me they thought he'd been taken somewhere else. The police didn't want us to know about his situation. Sometimes they also attributed to others a statement that could only have come from him. Obviously they made use of him in any way they could. We had to stay alert.

Housecleaning By now almost everything about our district had been exposed. Şahin had told them everything he knew. Rıza had told them what the lower ranks didn't know. Most of those arrested were members of various committees and units. Their statements complemented one another—very useful for the enemy.

Yet I still stuck to my story about being a "progressive intellectual"— nothing had been found to disprove it, no writings or anything. Yes, they had Şahin's statement about me, but I could talk around that. But then on the eleventh or twelfth day, Hamili admitted he had an apartment in Elazığ. Police went to search it and found some writings secreted in the window frame, the stovepipe, and other hiding places. Among them were some of my handwritten texts. The police didn't show them to me right away—for a day or two, they just asked me what they meant and who could have written them.

Among the typescripts were the ones with my research on the social situation of women. We'd interviewed women in Çüngüş, Cermik, Siverek, and elsewhere, and students from those places had written reports. Our contacts in the schools would have been compromised— we'd written a list of their names—but fortunately we hadn't jotted down their surnames. If we had, the police would've used the list to drag those young women students in here. Under interrogation, some prisoners had told the police I was leading that research, so they wanted to get the information from me. But I was determined to prevent them from bringing in even one of these young women. I wouldn't give them the pleasure.

Sometimes the police pressured us psychologically, mentioning things they'd found in the flat. "The apartment of our seemingly innocent guests, including pregnant women, has been exposed. And what we found there!" they snickered. "Hey, we understood the stuff about oppression, but help us out—what are the three ways women are oppressed?" Okay, they'd read the manuscripts. Then they said, "We're gonna arrest all the girls from the women's committee. We've got some of them already, the ones from the neighborhood committee."

The police asked me for a handwriting sample. I made my handwriting crooked and stretched the 'a's out. A few of the letters in the manuscripts looked like mine, but most didn't. They mentioned various words they'd found in the manuscripts, but that didn't help them much.

Ayten told me everything she remembered that was in the apartment, and I tried to remember what I could. I didn't think we'd left that many typescripts there because of the risk, but I didn't know exactly. I'd handwritten lists of names and drawn organizational charts, but then Ali Gündüz had taken over that work. There was a rough drawing of the district committee, but it was more like a draft. Oh, what madness it had been to hold on to those documents! We could have forwarded them the central committee and held the content in our heads. It had been a mistake, due to our inexperience and carelessness.

In some ways the police were inexperienced too—they'd commenced interrogating us without any plan. If we'd been smarter, we could have prevented our weaker friends from making consequential confessions. It's important to understand the psychological aspects of betrayal, since the enemy benefits most from our internal weaknesses. But mostly the proceedings weren't very sophisticated—they relied on brutality and torture and asked crude questions. Over time it became more serious. The police formed new units to expand their investigations. Şahin served as their adviser. He told them everything he knew, including the people who would be most affected. He made it all so much easier for the police!

The arrest wave went on for 15 days, after which the police requested that it continue for two more weeks. Then they used the extension to threaten us. "We've got you in our clutches," they said, "and we're not gonna let you go till you've all sung like nightingales." They mentioned an operation in Antep and said they'd arrested the friends in Mardin, Diyarbakir, Urfa, Dersim, and elsewhere. Sometimes they named names to make their lies more plausible. "The UKO is finished. Oh, you wanna set up a Kurdish state? Well, we even nabbed Apo, him who you trusted so much." Another said, "You think Apo's gonna come and save you? Ha! He's living in a luxury apartment now, with women. How can you trust him?" So they blatantly contradicted themselves.

One day Ayten and I were brought into interrogation together. Hamili and Ali Gündüz were in the room. What game were the police playing now? I'd been arrested in the apartment with Hamili and Ayten but hadn't faced Ali yet. They'd brought me together with this group once before, but we'd given them nothing. I paused at the door and thought, *This is something new.* I wasn't blindfolded this time. I glanced at Hamili questioningly. The police were watching us closely.

Zafer Karaosmanoğlu was running the show. "Come on in. Oh, don't look so mad. The two men asked for this. Hamili wanted to see his wife, and Ali wanted to see you."

"Why should I talk to someone I don't know?" I said [referring to Ali]. "I'm just trying to figure out what's going on."

"But Ali knows you. Don't you, Ali?"

"Come on, Sakine," Ali said, "sit down. I want to talk to you."

I glanced over at Hamili, who sat as if frozen. Ayten looked surprised too. The situation seemed less like an interrogation than a visit. What should I do? Should I announce that I had nothing to say, turn on my heel, and leave? Or should I play the role of "progressive woman" to try to figure out what was going on?

Ali said, "I asked for this meeting." Then in Zazaki, "Come on, we have to talk."

I turned to the police. "What kind of game is this anyway? You're always bringing in new people who say odd things. I can't trust you." Reluctantly, I sat down.

Ali hesitated, as if he didn't know where to start. "Let's talk a little. You don't seem aware of what's been happening. Şahin has confessed. Actually the first to confess was Rıza. They found typescripts in the apartment. We said we were responsible for some of them. We had to admit a few things so they wouldn't do any further damage. But as far as you're concerned, everything has been told about you. I've told them you and I worked on the same committee, and that you were tasked with working mainly with women, and you'd only just started."

He continued in this vein.

What did he mean? How had this not been a confession? Hadn't he just confirmed Şahin's statement? I was seething. The police at the table tried to look nonchalant, but their eyes and ears were riveted on us.

"The police want to charge you with a lot of things," Ali continued. "They're not gonna leave you in peace. But we can admit to a few things and so defend the organization—"

"How is that defending the organization?" I burst out. "This is how you want to defend it? No way! I'll make a political defense. We've all been compromised by Şahin's betrayal. The enemy keeps saying the organization no longer exists, and many friends have shown weakness and succumbed to this psychological warfare. No, I'll defend the organization, and I'll do so overtly. Nothing else matters anymore. All its internal secrets have been betrayed. It doesn't matter if I'm on the committee or not. I don't care what's been said about me."

Ali thought I'd lost my mind. "As you wish."

The police looked dissatisfied. They'd expected the conversation to turn into a fight. I rose and said I wanted to go back to my cell.

Later, when Ayten returned, we analyzed the meeting together. The police had set us up, we agreed. What the enemy couldn't achieve through torture, he tried by more polite means. He wasn't stupid. Of course he'd tried to use Ayten, as Hamili's wife, against him. The police often threatened rape, their most important weapon during interrogation. By now I was used to hearing their threats to "poke in a stick."

Ayten said Hamili had admitted certain things. He hadn't been in Elazığ much—he'd moved around, while Ayten had worked under my leadership. Hamili didn't know anything about the texts that had been found in the apartment—only Ali, Metin, and I had known about them.

The goal wasn't to get out of here. From now on my goal would be to protect the organization and the friends.

Defending the organization The police gave us a questionnaire and demanded that we answer it by handwriting a statement. Were we going to be taken to the prosecutor's office? I wondered. Were the hearings going to start? No, it seemed more like a continuation of the interrogation phase. Raids and arrest operations were still under way. Most arrestees from other [political] groups were released promptly, like some students and teachers from Hozat and Çemişgezek. The police concentrated on our people.

Their questionnaire asked about our families, our siblings, our position within the organization, the organization's goals, who we'd recruited, and so on. The statement I wrote would be binding, so I had to think carefully about my testimony. The police mustn't be able to use what I wrote against us; at the same time, I wanted to defend the organization. It seemed safe to handwrite it—that way they couldn't alter or add anything. At worst, they'd tear it up. But so what. I would use this written statement as an opportunity to defend the organization's goals and make clear that I was a revolutionary.

For my résumé, I wrote briefly: "My father is a worker in Germany. My siblings go to school and to university." They asked why I'd divorced my husband. They'd already asked me verbally several times, insisting, "The organization made it happen, so you must be very important in the organization." I said I'd married on the wishes of my family, then lived with my husband for a while in Izmir. I finally broke up the marriage because we didn't get along. Latching on to this point, the police had asked Izmir for my criminal record. That was how they found out I'd been arrested twice, because of the workers' strike, and that I'd spent time in prison. Well, I'd said I was a progressive person. That just meant I defended myself against injustice.

Anyway, to the question, "How long have you been with the UKO?" I answered in such a way as to deflect further questions.

I went to Izmir, then came back to Dersim for the divorce, when I stayed with my mother. I got a flyer for the Kurdistan Revolutionaries. The murder of Haki Karer influenced me most, as well as the fact that he wasn't Kurdish yet supported the Kurdish cause. So I developed sympathy for them. I went to public forums. Since I showed interest in them, they took an interest in me. Ali Haydar Kaytan talked to me. I left Dersim in April and went to Elazığ and rented an apartment of my own. Then Ali Gündüz found me.

I wrote it all down the way we'd talked about it. It had to be credible. We'd rented that last flat sometime in March and had been there off and on. If the police asked the landlord about it, his answer mustn't contradict our statements.

I continued writing my defense, saying that I'd read books and also *Serxwebûn* ["Independence," a UKO/PKK newspaper]. "I haven't been in this district for very long, so I don't know it or the people well. I got to know Nadire and her family because they're related to Metin Turgut. I made a condolence visit." I had to mention his name since they were always asking me about him. I concluded that out of all the people I'd worked with, the police knew the names of only these few. As for Ayten, I said she wasn't a revolutionary, had no interest in revolution, and that I knew her only a little.

Since I'm a woman, it suited me to work on women's propaganda. I was just getting to know the district, so now I've been arrested without having done anything. The organization's goal is to establish an independent, united, free, democratic, and prosperous Kurdistan. Our country is at present a semifeudal colony. That's why we want a democratic revolution against Turkish colonialism and its local collaborators. It will be carried out by alliance between workers and peasants. The working class will play a leading role.

As I wrote, my excitement mounted, and I felt like shouting my convictions to the enemy and to Şahin: "These are our goals, and they will one day become reality!" I wished they would ask me more such questions.

They did. "Do you believe in the goals of the UKO?" they asked. Other questions seemed intended to provoke: "What do you think of the Turkish republican state? About its security forces?" The questions flowed. "Where does the organization get its money and weapons? How many people lived with you in the organization's apartment?" The most interesting question was the last, very conscious one: "Do you regret anything?"

I responded, "I've done nothing I regret."

I kept my statement to this general outline. I admitted my connection to the organization and avoided saying anything that could damage it, the friends, or myself.

I finished [and handed it to them]. Later they came back and said from the door, "But you said you were just a progressive person! We've known all along who you are. But you haven't told us anything. We tore up your statement. We're not stupid." These were cops responsible for brutal torture.

The police who conducted the interrogations behaved more warily. Zafer Karaosmanoğlu and a cop named Mehmet wanted to discuss things with me. They told me they'd read *Serxwebûn* too. They had difficulty pronouncing the name, or so it seemed—they pronounced it incorrectly in odd ways, as if to trick me into saying it correctly. But I had problems with pronunciation myself. The friends sometimes laughingly called my way of speaking "elegant Kurdish."

The subjects of discussion with the police changed over time. Mehmet the cop said he was impressed by my ideas but didn't understand some of them, and would I try to persuade him? He was trying to determine my degree of consciousness. That was so dumb! As if that were still important! I couldn't care less anymore what they thought my role in the organization was. It didn't change anything. I discussed openly with them, without trying to persuade them. When they felt challenged, they insisted the organization was no more. In their eyes, it had consisted mainly of Şahin, and his betrayal had smashed it. They always played that card, even when they knew better. We were at war. They knew how to use their advantageous position, while we had only our ideology and our convictions. I didn't hesitate to articulate them every chance I got.

I no longer reproached myself, as I'd done during those first days. Instead I tried to keep my spirits high, as the situation required. Yes, Şahin Dönmez had betrayed us instantly, had confessed everything he knew about all our organizing work. It depressed many friends, but many other cadres continued the struggle. Betrayal, confession under torture—such weakness could disrupt the organization but they didn't threaten it. When you're a prisoner, you have to figure out how to live, how to arm yourself, how to keep the revolutionary spirit alive. You have to choose between fighting the enemy and betraying.

I held firmly to my belief that the friends outside would take all necessary precautions from now on. Of course I was still worried—Comrade Cemil had almost been captured. Maybe there had been arrests in other places too, although no arrest wave could be as bad as the one in Elazığ. In reality, the only alternative was to stay strong and not collapse.

I scrawled a quotation on our cell walls and on the covered-over windows. Comrade Fuat [Ali Haydar Kaytan], while in prison, had written a good analysis of the poem "I Was a Man," which I'd learned by heart. One passage I remember in particular:

> It's true, we're creatures who emerged from weakness and are capable of propagating and developing. But you who claim to have arisen from virtue—you're sterile old maids, you're rotten. We swear by our martyrs, and even if we're only a tiny group, we'll fight until Kurdistan gains independence.

Our movement often used this oath, writing it on prison walls, using it in flyers, reciting at forums. Many friends memorized it. Even if we couldn't read the words anywhere, it did us good to be able to repeat them, to refresh our belief in them, to take their meaning to heart and to inscribe them somewhere as if shouting them. That helped us gather our strength in this revolting place. These quietly immortal words were laden with hope and fighting spirit.

"You're fighting for nothing" The interrogations continued.

"[The 1970s revolutionary hero] İbrahim Kaypakkaya sang like a canary," one of the cops told me, "even though the propaganda had him saying he'd rather die than betray. Don't you want to be like him? Oh, we know everything about you! We've even arrested Apo—he's down in the basement. We can bring him up here if you don't believe us! He's sung like a nightingale. So why are you still playing the heroine?"

"Okay, bring him up here," I said.

"What'll you do when we really bring him in?"

"I'll be strengthened and inspired," I said to the cop. His fake friendliness and triumph gave way to contortions of anger, and he pressed his lips together. *Now they'll come after us again*, I thought. Oh, so what? It felt great to annoy them. Let them do what they wanted. The club hit my head, and I staggered. They slapped me. "Look at that bitch," said the cop. "She wants to threaten us."

"Stop insulting me!" I snapped.

Zafer Karaosmanoğlu interjected, "Now, stop insulting Mrs. Sakine." That's what he usually called me, "Mrs. Sakine," playing his good cop role.

Another said, "You're fighting for nothing. What're you still trying to defend? The organization's over and done with! Yeah, a few of your people are still outside, but once we grab them, it'll all be over. We're on their heels now."

"Even if everyone here betrays," I said, "even if you arrest everyone, even if only Apo remains, that will still be enough for me." Silence, as they all looked at me strangely. Then decided not to take me seriously—another tactic.

One of the cops read aloud from a sheet: "The meeting took place in the village of Fis. Those who participated were Haydar, Duran, Resul—"

"Wait a minute!" another interrupted. "She's just a sympathizer and kinda new in the organization. She only just started doing propaganda work with a few girls. She can't understand this at all." They guffawed coarsely as they mocked me.

Zafer Karaosmanoğlu watched me intently for my reaction—they still cared about this issue. Presumably the investigation would continue in this vein. Şahin must have included me on the list of participants at Fis, even though the cop didn't mention my name. They seemed to be waiting for me to show weakness and remained cagey about the extent of Şahin's betrayal.

One day a commotion arose in the building, when a rumor spread that someone in the basement had tried to commit suicide. The guards and soldiers screamed at each other. Fearfully, I looked over at Ayten, both of us wondering who it could be. Had they tortured someone to death and were now passing it off as suicide? No, no, surely it wasn't Hamili! Was it Aytekin? If not, who? Such moments of uncertainty were like torture.

"The basement is overfilled," said the soldiers. People from other leftist groups had been arrested and brought in: from HK, Kawa, TİKKO, Dev-Yol, and Dev-Sol. Some journalists were arrested as well, from *Aydınlık*, including Adil Turan. At that time the PDA was at war with us, obstructing the distribution of our newspaper in Siverek, Hilvan,

Batman, and other places, and generally behaving like the colonialists' errand boys. We analyzed every piece of information we got.

Even from a cell, it was important to try to see through the enemy's machinations. You could tell from the enemy's actions that Şahin was the source. Putting it together, we thought the enemy had been deliberately spreading a rumor about Şahin—that he had supposedly resisted in some way, then attempted suicide. A few of the journalists had done propaganda for Şahin in the past. Had they been brought here to report on his supposed resistance and alleged suicide attempt? Did the friends [in the men's ward] know what was happening? I wondered, concerned they might believe the rumor about Şahin.

But that rumor was nonsense. If Şahin had really tried to kill himself, he'd have succeeded. More likely, the enemy wanted to assess the value of his information and use him in an operation to arrest even more friends. His confessions had been extensive, but Elazığ's organizational structure hadn't been entirely wiped out.

The enemy had obtained the information he needed. He was now familiar with our organizational structure and with our contacts—that was a hard, momentous blow. Optimism would've been inappropriate. Physical destruction isn't the only kind of loss—the organizational structure itself was threatened. I was worried. Şahin knew how the friends normally behaved. If they'd taken no precautions, then the results could be catastrophic. The enemy had discovered our structures and our future tactics too quickly, too easily.

Yet not for one second did I lose hope or confidence. Never did I get so pessimistic as to think, *It's all over*. Şahin wasn't everything, and one region wasn't everything. Hope that we would survive this phase kept me going. For me, it made no difference whether it was day or night—I could hardly sleep or eat anyway. I felt remarkably agile. Was that just empty heroics? Was my self-assurance a symptom of folly? No! My very loathing gave me strength, and my fury kept me on my feet. It didn't change anything, but at least I didn't give the enemy what he wanted.

I hadn't the slightest doubt about Şahin's villainy, but the interrogations were somewhat confused. The torturers labored like shift workers in a factory. The night shift turned the interrogations over to the day shift.

But one night a strange interrogation took place, as a new torturer had arrived from Ankara. The guard who came for me looked strangely anxious. Normally he stomped on the floor and ripped open the door, making a huge racket. When we first arrived, there had been only one door, but then they'd added a big door with iron bars, like in a giant castle, so now we could hear when the two doors were opened. Sudden door-opening was one of their more beloved forms of torture. In order to psychologically pressure us and never leave us in peace, they sometimes barreled in, throwing open the first door with a huge clash, then went away without opening the second. But this time it was different.

When I arrived in the room, the new torturer was pacing back and forth. He told the guard, "Leave, and shut the door." I saw a mattress on the floor but no other torture instruments. On the table was a pile of handwritten manuscripts.

What would happen at this interrogation? A chair stood at the ready, the defendant's chair. It might have been an electric chair if it had a magnetic field. But no, I thought, one person couldn't manage that alone. Someone had to regulate the electricity jolts, while another asked questions, and a third ran the cables over the person's hands, feet, and other body parts.

"Why did you shut the door?" I asked in a steady voice, trying to quell the fear mounting inside me, trying to sound like someone demanding an accounting. Meanwhile I was assessing him.

"What, are you afraid?" the man said. "It's chilly—that's why the door's closed."

"No, it's not chilly," I said. "Leave it open. And why would I be afraid?" I kept my voice steady.

"Let's talk a bit. I'd like to get to know you better," he said, inspecting me from head to toe. His dirty grimace told me he was drunk. He came closer, reeking of raki. Then he paced, observing me from the corner of his eye at every turn, evidently gauging my reaction.

I still didn't understand the purpose of this nighttime interrogation. Finally he crossed to the table and read aloud some paragraphs from some typescripts, about the meeting in Ankara-Dikmen, about Ağrı, about the suspicions around Mehmet Turan, and about Celal Aydın. These were Şahin's statements.

"Do you know about this?" he asked.

"Nothing to do with me," I said.

"Want to hear the parts where he talks about you?"

I pretended to be indifferent, but inside I really did want him to read on—of course I wanted to know what was there. But he didn't read anymore and instead stretched out on the mattress. Then, leaning on an elbow, he looked over at me. He asked if I was married and began to play with his penis. Then he lay back down and asked, "Do you miss it?"

My scornful look discomfited him, as I'd hoped it would. Yes, they often threatened to rape me or "poke a stick in there." He didn't say those words, but I braced for a sudden attack.

But this torturer turned out to be a scaredy-cat. "What's going on here?" I said, heading him off.

I'm a revolutionary, and I choose my convictions deliberately. They are what constitute my honor. You're not going to achieve anything through curses, torture, and rape. If you think otherwise, you're mistaken. Do whatever you want! But you know, you can't interrogate me alone. And besides, you're drunk … I know all of you, Zafer Karaosmanoğlu, Mehmet Yilmaz, Kerim …

I rattled off a few other names that I'd memorized from the list on the door.

As I did, the torturers panicked. "We're not gonna let you live! You're as good as dead!" they shouted. "Don't forget—you're in our hands! You'll rot here for years. You have no friends to avenge you."

Suddenly, since I'd used their names, the nature of the interrogation changed. Some of the torturers became friendly. Even this new guy tried to placate me.

Hey, don't misunderstand. We were just talking in a friendly way. Can't you tell when someone's trying to be nice to you? I haven't done anything. I'm not a torturer or whatever, I'm a civil servant. I stand with the Republic of Turkey. I have opinions too. If you don't like them, too bad.

I was pleased with myself. Once you understand how these idiots' minds worked, you can work the situation and set your own boundaries. If you start by showing the enemy he won't be getting everything he wants, it impresses him. But when he sees that he won't easily lure his prey into the trap, he becomes fearful. You can get them to hit you instead of doing other things—or you can even prevent any blows at all. But if you leave the initiative to the enemy and then sit back and wait, you've already lost. Bowing your head in defeat makes it all so much harder.

How many hours did it last? I don't remember, but when I got back to the cell, I saw that Ayten was in far worse shape than me. Exhausted, she was sitting on the mattress with her head buried in her knees and her arms wrapped around her legs. She leaped up and grabbed me, then looked me over. Nothing had happened—I was still standing! "What's happened?" she cried. "What did they do to you? I was so afraid for you." Of course I didn't look great, as I could see from the gritty mirror over the washbasin. My lips were dried out, and I had circles under my eyes. I told her about the interrogation. "Those devious bastards!" She hugged me in relief.

Nurse Elif The episode with Celal Aydın resulted in more arrests in Malatya. In his notes he had mentioned Elif Kartal, who turned up as one of the new prisoners here. She was a nurse from Gölbaşi, in Adiyaman province. Her family were typical Kurdish villagers. She had thick eyebrows, swollen black eyes, and a snub nose, wearing no makeup. She moved and spoke clumsily.

She was brought to our cell first. She seemed like a civil servant, like state personnel. Working in forensic medicine in Gülhane, she was accustomed to interacting with the military and police. We weren't thrilled about her but tried to be helpful. We impressed on her the importance of not being intimidated by police methods.

Without going into detail, we hinted that we knew Celal was a traitor and that she shouldn't make any mistakes. "The enemy tries to exploit our internal conflicts," I told her. "Maybe you know some people, but don't betray them. That'll only make it harder for you. And it's not right to harm anyone."

Irritated, she snapped, "Why didn't those who betrayed me think about that? I've got nothing to do with the organization, but they're asking me a lot of questions. Celal wanted to use me. What's going on? I don't understand any of it."

"Okay, some things may be hard to understand at first," I said, "but you'll catch on. What counts is your attitude. The police will want to pin things on you. You mustn't accept it. You're a nurse—you have to do with a lot of people and you were just doing your work. Tell them as little as possible. The less you say, the better."

Elif didn't stay long in our cell. The police, understanding something about the human psyche, suspected that we would influence her. Of

28

course they asked her what we'd talked about, even though they had a pretty good idea already. She dropped a hint, and I thought, *Oh dammit, let her do what she wants—even if she just makes herself ridiculous.* Fortunately she was transferred.

Transferred—to an individual cell. In the mornings she strolled to the lavatory in a nightgown, toothpaste and her personal soap in hand. Her food was different from ours. She was allowed to move around freely and ambled into the interrogation rooms unperturbed and smiling. Celal Aydın, who'd betrayed us, and Elif! How had it happened? Elif had acted more brazenly than Celal, but under interrogation she'd broken immediately and settled in here.

At first we couldn't blame her, as we had no organizational ties with her. We hadn't given her anything and expected nothing from her. She was just a nurse. The police could have let her go immediately, but they wanted to use her, and she'd offered to be used.

In the absence of female police, Nurse Elif took on a police role. And she entertained the male cops. It was really disgusting. A few friends, not knowing her background, actually thought she was police—she laughed in the torture room, while others were being tortured. It made them furious. She was a Kurd who denied her own heritage.

Dreaming of escape   The second 15-day period since the arrest was nearing its end. Of course no one really placed any hopes that the enemy would respect the legal deadline, but we were concerned that an extension would mean he wanted to dig out more facts.

At the time of our arrest, the party had not yet announced the founding [of the PKK]. Up to now we had been called UKO, and we still used that name publicly after our arrests. But the new name was to come with the announcement. Had the friends outside done it yet? The announcement was to be accompanied by actions, but had the arrests inhibited them from making it? What were the friends outside saying about us? The uncertainty tormented me, since all threads ran through Şahin. Was his betrayal only recent, or had it been going on for a while? New questions kept arising. How could I make contact with the outside?

Was there any way to escape from 1800 Evler? The windows and doors were barred. Could the friends attack the prison and get us out of here? Three to five of them, armed, would be enough. The enemy wouldn't expect it, since he was preoccupied with torture. Would that do it?

The thought of escaping was perhaps illusory—but no, it wasn't impossible. The guards here were locals. Some of them must have a conscience, a sense of honor, and be ready to take a risk—and then it would be very easy. The military posts outside would present no great obstacle. The prison was on the city's periphery, and all around lay open field, so we could disappear into the darkness. I loved such daydreams.

Nothing left to betray?   The [two-week] period was extended again. The interrogations continued, and written statements were taken. Maybe they really had torn up my earlier statement, I don't know, but they asked me the same questions and typed out my answers. They also asked some new questions based on the statements of others, parts of which they read aloud. Rıza's were very detailed, but many others had also made statements about various meetings.

Someone said I'd organized several meetings. That was false, I said—there'd been only one meeting. Who participated in them? they asked. Those who participated had already said they were present, I said I refused to name names and tried to say as little as possible. They threw some names of people, events, and places at me. I said,

> You're making everyone into a UKO member. The prisoners are just giving you those names because they're afraid. You ask them for names under interrogation, and they'll mention anyone they know from the neighborhood, or the street, or school. Their statements are fiction.

They asked me about Celal Aydın. "He had the kind of personality that made him hostile to the organization," I said. "It's the job of the organization to detect such personalities. We discussed the situation at the regional level, but no decision was made about punishment—that was outside our authority."

The police wanted to arrest as many people as possible, and they wanted confirmation for the statements of Şahin and the others. Şahin had reported about the episode with Celal Aydın, and the police had taken his statement seriously. But Şahin could only guess about our work because he didn't know those details, although he himself had himself proposed the central committee's punishment.

I resisted: "Why are you asking me, if you're so sure about what others have said? Well then, in that case, I'm not going to make any further statement."

Şahin and Ali had both described the founding congress in Fis, I knew, and they had said I was one of two women there. So the police asked me about the meeting at Fis. But I made a very limited statement, mentioning only myself, knowing they would drag me back into interrogation. Even though everything had already been told about the founding congress, it was still wrong to talk about it. Party discipline and silence were more important in prison than outside, even if the enemy already had information.

In a place where treachery and betrayal ran so deep, it irritated the police that I, as a woman, defended the organization. They realized they wouldn't be getting what they wanted today and brought the interrogation phase to an end. They had everything they needed, really— there was nothing left for me to protect. But now that my position in the organization had become known, I wondered one thing: Suppose, I'd admitted from the beginning that I was a Kurdistan Revolutionary, then been silent about everything else. What would have happened? It really didn't matter whether I came out of here alive or not. But it would've been the right response to the betrayals and the counterattacks. It was too early to talk about resistance, but it would've been an important form of practical action.

"Is this a courtroom or an interrogation room?" Şahin's betrayal had damaged our organization and the enemy could count it as a success, but it hadn't eradicated the organization. Most of the cadres were still outside. As a result of the police's arrest, some districts now lacked cadres, but this blow had also been a warning. Both inside prison and outside, the sense of defeat was widespread, but it wouldn't last long— the struggle would continue. Every attack by the enemy would give rise to a counterattack. At the forthcoming trial, the betrayals would be front and center. We suspected that the media were already mounting a propaganda campaign.

Inside the prison, talking to the men friends, Şahin tried to have it both ways: he rationalized his double-cross, and at the same time tried to bury all hopes under a pile of capitulation. "If you ever get out of here," he told them, "you'll move back to a village and live simple lives. You'll keep cows and chickens. This revolution is over. I'm the end, and it's all over."

But the enemy was more realistic, as you could tell from his interrogation methods. What was really over, and how deep did the defeat go? The revolutionary movement had the capacity to reverse the setback. It would figure out how to prevent more damage and which precautionary measures to take that would last a long time.

The taking of statements was almost over, but the prison administration wasn't going to leave me in peace. Guards still brought me into the interrogation room every day, the one just across from the men's block. I asked them to take off my blindfold, and they did so promptly, as if I were in charge. During the interrogation, I sat across from them and so I could see them close up. Good—they made that concession. It was a victory for me. Calmly I made it clear that I wasn't going to leave the initiative to them.

"You make it hard for us," they said, "because you never tell us anything. Yet we've got so much evidence against you!" My admission that I'd taken part in the Fis meeting boosted their morale, even if it wasn't the full account they wanted. I'd limited my account to generalities, but I still felt bad about it. The police, for their part, were jubilant as I sat tied in the chair—they sent jolts of electricity into me that drove screams from my lips, sometimes muffled and broken, sometimes shrill. The interrogators thought they were just the normal screams people made under torture, but Zafer Karaosmanoğlu noticed I was crying. The men friends in the nearby cells assumed I was being raped, they later told me.

Zafer Karaosmanoğlu not only participated in my interrogations but also came to our cell. "Why are you crying?" he asked. "Because you admitted you participated in the Fis meeting? Yes, surely, now your friends will say you didn't resist us. That hurts your—how do you call it? Ah yes—your revolutionary pride!" He'd hit my sore spot, then drilled deeper.

"My compliments!" he said.

You're the only one who defies us, or as you put it, you're the only one who struggles against us. You consider us enemies, you call us fascists, but we're only doing our jobs. We're not especially happy to do it. Frankly, I respect you. Have you ever heard me say anything negative about you?

His words contained a grain of truth. The man was a wolf, using a method that let him wage war yet feign innocence. He asked more questions, but composing myself, I said with calm determination, "If

you ask me anything more, I'll withdraw my statement. I've already said
I took part in the Fis meeting. I won't say more than that, even if you
continue the interrogation for months." I meant it seriously. I wanted
them to work only on me and leave the others in peace. My words had
an impact. They didn't come back that day.

I braced myself with my new determined attitude: *I won't say anything
more. If they ask questions, I'll refuse to answer.* Thereafter, when I was
interrogated, I limited myself to making propaganda for the party,
knowing that a political defense disconcerted them. "Would you
really say that to the court?" they said. "That you want an independent
Kurdistan? Then you really will be executed." They considered it a
defeat if someone left the interrogation still defending their convictions
and willing to do so to the court. Their goal was to bring broken and
repentant people to court. "Do you really want to say to the court what
you said here? Then you'll be brought right back here," they said.

The next day they came to finalize my statement. They wrote down
exactly what I said. If they altered any wording, I objected. Their last
line was interesting. Without consulting me, they wrote: "She shows no
remorse." This sentence delighted me, even if in their eyes it counted
against me and would increase the punishment.

We were still in 1800 Evler. The third 15-day deadline arrived. Every
day we were taken in a van to the military court in the city center. On the
way I talked to the men friends. The soldiers kept breaking in and saying
talk was forbidden, but we didn't care. Şahin rode in a separate vehicle.
Once we were in the courthouse, we were all brought to the waiting
room for defendants. One soldier read the list: "Şahin Dönmez, Ali
Gündüz, Sakine Polat, Hamili Yıldırım, Aytekin Tuğluk ..." I was happy
about the sequence, although I wished I could have been first. The police
announced that if we didn't repeat our interrogation statements to the
judge, we would be taken back to 1800 Evler. It was an effective threat.
The torturers were in the courthouse, standing around the corridors.

The men friends made such a sorry, feeble impression in that waiting
room. My conversations with Aytekin and Hamili weren't especially
warm, as I was furious at all of them. I talked to Hamili and Ali Gündüz
a little about Şahin's betrayal. "It's obvious what he's doing, but what's
with you two?" I asked. Ali lowered his head. "We've also betrayed,"
he said. "You can call it weakness or confession, it doesn't matter. It's
inexcusable." Hamili gestured at Ayten, saying, "These dirtbags used

33

her against me, threatening to rape her. So I told them a few things."
His words made me furious. "What kind of honor do you think you're
upholding? The police always make such threats! We have to give
priority to the values of the party." The men friends around us could
hear the discussion. Rıza kept his head down.

Then Şahin emerged from the prosecutor's office, saying, "We'll be
taken back to interrogation if we don't make exactly the same statements
here." He wanted to bring down the others, as if his own betrayal weren't
enough. Then I was called in. Passing him, I said, "I know what I'll say
about the statements of this scumbag."

I stormed into the small room in a fury. A fat man with glasses and a
red face said, "Come in, sit down. Sakine Polat, Cansız." He was Cahit
Aydoğan, the lead prosecutor, as I learned later. "Hm," he murmured,
"do you know Şahin Dönmez, who was just here? He's Apo's right-
hand man. He's explained everything wonderfully, that there's no more
organization, and the UKO is over. Ah, but you're still defending it, is
that right?" He was supposed to ask for my statement, but he didn't care
about the rules of the court. He just wanted to find my weak point and
see what I knew. He was a higher-level investigating authority.

I wanted to show him I knew what was going on and at least get on
his nerves. "Is this a courtroom or an interrogation room?" I demanded.
"All the police who've tortured us are in the building." Then: "Go ahead,
ask me questions. I have a lot to say."

Surprised, Cahit Aydoğan smirked arrogantly. "You're quick to anger.
You realize you are now in the office of the military prosecutor. Why are
you talking about interrogation and torture?"

"During my interrogation, the police referred to the statements of
Şahin Dönmez. You're doing the same thing here. Şahin is no one's
right-hand man. He's a traitor. Through his betrayal, he has destroyed
himself, but not the UKO. Even if everyone here betrays the movement,
it will still continue. Apo alone is sufficient for that."

The man looked perplexed. "Ah, yes. You were interrogated?
You're going back to 1800 Evler." Dismissively, he looked down at my
identification, noting my two surnames.

"I was married and then divorced," I said. "I was detained before I
could change my name on my ID."

"Did the organization demand the divorce?" he said.

"No, my husband and I didn't see eye to eye, so we separated."

"Was it a political divorce?"

"Yes. I'm a Kurdistan Revolutionary. He was opposed to that, so I left him."

"What was your position in the organization?" he asked.

I said I was a sympathizer and refused to say anything more. "I'll speak in detail before the court," I said. He asked more questions, but I saw no point in answering. An arrest warrant would be forthcoming. Whatever I had to say, I'd say to the court.

Back in the waiting room, I said to those who were after me in line, "Don't give him anything and withdraw your statement. They're threatening to continue the interrogation."

My eyes fell on Hüseyin Morsümbül, who I knew about from Bingöl but had never seen before. While I was in with the prosecutor, he'd been telling the men friends about himself. Now he was sitting next to Şahin, who was telling him, "It's all over. Even before they detained me, everything was exposed."

I couldn't stand it anymore. "You scumbag!" I took off my shoe and threw it at him.

It's all over—for you! You're just trying to distract us from your own betrayal. And you, [Hüseyin,] you're listening to this traitor? Oh, he knows he's getting out! Now he's trying to twist everything. But we know what you are!

My voice could be heard outside the waiting room. The soldiers ordered me to calm down, saying, "This is a courthouse!" Then they went to Şahin to escort him from the room. "Good," I said. "All he did was undermine our morale." On his way out, he sniped at me, "You're playing the hero for nothing, you know. It's all over. What are you trying to defend?"

After he was gone, I said to Hüseyin Morsümbül, "Şahin's lying. He's told them everything he knows. Now he's trying to gloss it over. He acts like there's no difference between his deliberate betrayal and the weakness of others under torture." I couldn't allow the men to think everything was over and there was nothing left to preserve.

There wasn't time for the prosecutor to see everyone that day—Şahin had been in with him for so long, as had Ali Gündüz. Now Ali looked weak and dejected and didn't speak. Apparently he had stuck to his statement and felt guilty. But Hamili, Aytekin, and a few others did withdraw their statements.

Back to the torture chamber   Back at 1800 Evler, we were put in the basement, in three iron-gated cells close together. Ayten and I were in a cell together again, without Elif.

Ayten's statement had been accepted, and very likely she'd be released, but no one could be sure till it happened. "Don't admit anything in court," I advised her. "Then they'll let you go, and that would be great! You can tell the party about everything, so they'll know what to do. They may not even realize the extent of Şahin's betrayal."

Aytekin and Hamili were together, pacing back and forth with rapid steps. At one point Aytekin came over to the gate and joked, "We've finally found work. If we get out of here, we can go into the village and breed cattle. That was Şahin's advice."

"How could you stand it?" I said. "Şahin, Rıza, Ali—what's going on with them? How can they just drop their convictions like that? Is betrayal becoming normal?"

"Not everyone can throw their shoes like you," said Aytekin.

At midday Şahin was brought from wherever he'd been. I threw a plate of food at him, shouting, "You slime bucket, what the hell are you doing!"

Okay, it was kind of pointless. Throwing shoes and plates is not an appropriate reaction to betrayal. It was just a way I tried to break through the general indifference that was allowing treachery to be considered normal. The soldiers removed everything from my cell that wasn't nailed down and forbade me to go near the door.

Şahin wasn't brought back after that. The interrogations would continue, and just thinking of it was stressful. No one came to our cell door. Sadly, everyone except Aytekin and Hamili avoided even looking at me.

Every day for about a week we were taken to court, to make more statements, and then we were brought back to the basement. The sounds of torture from the upper level were unceasing. It was part of the enemy's psychological warfare.

Suddenly, on the third day, Ayten was released. As we parted, I whispered to her, "The friends should be careful. Absolutely you must get in touch with them. Don't talk to all the friends, just the trustworthy ones." We hugged. She hugged Hamili and said, "Take good care of yourself." Her eyes were brimming with tears, and her face was twisted in pain. She left—she was lucky. But we were sad to be without her and perhaps never see her again. I was also somewhat relieved—it would be good for Ayten, and it would be easier for me to fight the enemy alone.

That day, outside the prosecutor's office, I ran into [UKO attorney] Hüseyin Yıldırım. When I turned the corner, there he was, across from me, carrying a briefcase and wearing a judicial robe. "Sakine, my dear, is that you? Look at you! I hardly recognize you!" He glanced around the waiting room and saw the others looking miserable. He was scarcely recognizable himself. As he strode over to me, the soldiers stepped in: "You need permission to talk to them." He stepped back without objection. His deference to them, his obvious fear, and his interest in us—it all seemed odd to me. Of course, it was good to see a lawyer after so long, but I would have preferred someone besides Hüseyin Yıldırım.

Later he told me,

I've taken over the brief for you, Hamili, and Mustafa ... You're getting out, don't worry. Your families are here in Elazığ. Do you need anything? But you have to be careful. Mr. Celal was astonished, he said he respects your beliefs, but it'll be better if you don't say radical things—they'll be used against you.

He was giving me advice! Well, in an emergency, the devil eats flies. I didn't like him personally, but it was good to have a lawyer, since at least it meant contact with the outside world.

After Ayten left, I was alone in the basement cell, wrapped in a filthy blanket, trying to warm myself. The plumbing from the upper floors ran through my cell, so the toilet stench intermingled with the damp and cold. I was lost in thought when all at once I heard a voice at the small window by the bunk bed: "Sakine! Sakine!"

I leaped up and raced over, my heart pounding wildly. *The friends— the friends have come!* I thought. It was dark outside, but I could make out the head of a soldier. It was Murat from Cermik. *Dammit!* My excitement subsided.

"How are you?!" he asked. He had been withdrawn from the outer security area and was bringing me food. So that was why he'd abruptly disappeared. I guessed someone had noticed he was a Kurd.

Excitedly he said, "I have a pistol I can give you."

"A pistol? What kind?" I was astonished. "Do you have it on you?"

No, but he could bring it to me if I wanted it.

Did this mean I could escape? "Leave the pistol with the friends on the outside," I said. "The ones in Cermik—you can give it to them. But when the time comes, help me get out of here."

Murat looked around nervously. "The comrades are waiting for me in the car," he whispered. "I just wanted to see you. This window's barred—otherwise we could drive you away now."

"Dammit, too bad!"

"I'll visit you, no problem," he said. "I'll be there." He asked if I needed anything, then disappeared, as if my spontaneous suggestion had frightened him.

Murat hadn't been able to do anything for me, but I was excited at the prospect of escape. Imprisonment, it turns out, gives rise to an extreme desire for escape. I started thinking about it seriously. One fantasy led to the next, as I concocted wonderful plans.

I tried unlocking the gate with a bobby pin, wrapping my handkerchief around the bars to muffle any noise. It didn't work, but I could open handcuffs with a bobby pin. I'd have to pass through two doors: my cell door and the one in the corridor. Then there was the outside door that led to the grounds above, the open field around the building. How hard would it be to slip past the guard on watch? I knew people in the neighborhood—would I be able to find them? Ah, there it got difficult.

After the prosecutor finished the interrogations, we were taken to court, placed under arrest, and sent to prison. As for Şahin, the court announced that—at his request— he'd be separated from the other prisoners for his own safety. This sleazeball! I'd thrown a shoe and a plate at him, and now he thought his life was in danger? He and the enemy were both so concerned! But then, he knew UKO well enough to realize his betrayal wouldn't remain secret for long.

I'd openly accused him of treason, even though we were in prison. It was good that he was afraid—of UKO. But it was also irritating that we weren't rid of him. There were certainly friends who could take care of that. If he hadn't been separated from us, we would have found a way.

Then we were moved to another prison, on the road to Harput [in Elazığ province].

Harput schools became our prison It was a two-story gray building that stood apart, surrounded by a couple of barracks. It looked more like an apartment building than the prisons I'd seen so far. The upper story had a balcony. The windows were of normal size but fitted with bars or barbed wire.

Our handcuffs were removed, and I was separated from the others. Elif got out of the jeep ahead of us, no handcuffs. Why hadn't she been released? Was she being held as a witness because of the episode with Celal? Or to get on my nerves? And she did get on my nerves.

One officer shouted, "Women on this side!" At first I thought they were going to put us up in the barracks. Once we were inside the building, people stared at us.

The officer called, "The men can come in now." The handcuffs were opened one by one, and the men were brought inside and taken to the upper story. Prisoners from Dev-Sol, TİKKO, the HK, and Dev-Yol were all put in the same cellblock as the [UKO] men. I watched them nervously, and they looked at me. Aytekin's look was questioning, as if he wanted to know where they were going to put me. I signaled that I didn't know. We heard that some right-wingers were staying on the lower floor. So we were to be in a prison with fascists? How was that supposed to work?

They brought Elif and me into a room on the ground floor. We could see that a cell had been set aside, with new doors. Men's voices were coming from the other side of a wall, some of them clearly audible. The fascists. Between us and them stood only a wall. It felt bizarre to be so near fascists.

I didn't speak to Elif, just glared at her—she looked horrid to me. I still didn't understand why there'd been an arrest warrant for her. Hadn't she been useful enough, with her petit-bourgeois background? People like her respected police as important state officials.

Someone came for Elif, then for me. "Mrs. Sakine, you're in a cell with Mrs. Elif," a police captain said. "But Mrs. Elif says she's afraid of you, that you must be angry at her. In this prison, we have only this one cell for women. There are no other options."

I refused to share the cell with her. "I don't know her at all. I don't know if she's police, a nurse, or something else. During interrogation, she was separated from us and moved around freely. She even sat as an observer at torture. You really should release her."

"That's for the court to decide, not us," he said. "But suppose we did put you in a cell together—would you hurt her? Hm, you don't look like you would."

"I didn't say I'd kill her," I spat. "I just don't want to be in a cell with her, and I've said why. If she does something that violates my principles, I'll react accordingly." I was taken back to the cell.

Elif was away for a long time, probably as they conferred with a judge. Finally, they decided she had to stay with me, and she was brought back. Was it her job to monitor me? If so, that was a kind of warfare. For a long time, we didn't speak to each other unless we had to. Once or twice, she was called to the administration office, ostensibly to get money and stamps. Was she still letting them use her? The suspicion wasn't outlandish. She watched everything I did. When I talked to someone in the exercise yard, she strained to hear, even as I tried to stay out of her earshot. I was sure she was observing me.

Finally, she said she wanted to talk to me. She [said she] knew Aytekin from Malatya.

[I asked Aytekin about her.] Whenever we went to the exercise yard, I'd converse briefly with the men friends. Aytekin was upbeat about Elif, saying, "She wasn't a bad sort in Malatya. Celal is to blame for this. Probably she's afraid we're going to influence her. You're kind of tough, but she's a woman—talk to her. Influence her."

Me, tough—really? But I didn't want to drive Elif into the arms of the enemy. Maybe I really should talk to her and try to help her. Oh, I had, at first, advising her how to behave toward the police—then she'd gone off and told the police about it! She might do the same thing again.

But gradually I began to talk to Elif, which made her happy. Without going into her situation, I gave her examples of the methods that the enemy used against us directly or indirectly. I asked her how she'd been arrested and how her interrogation had gone. She sketched it out for me, and I understood her better.

Things that we needed daily, we got from the men. Their letters did me good—they told me not to smoke so much. Hamili and Aytekin always addressed me as "Seko." Just hearing this name strengthened my feeling of closeness and connection with them. Outside, such things hadn't been as important. Of course, certain comrades had often shown love, respect, and connection. Every comrade had value, but in some cases the value was very concrete. In this sense, I loved Hamili and Aytekin very much. Outside we'd always tried not to show that and behaved appropriately. But in prison our sense of mutual connectedness, in defiance of the enemy, grew enormously.

Although some events had created a certain distance between Hamili and me, I still loved and respected him. Outside we'd called him "Kara." In a report I sent to the outside, I talked about the events before and after our arrest. I described how the prison administration had used Ayten against Hamili and how it had weakened him. He'd told me about it himself, but when he found out I'd written it, it hurt his pride. A few rare times we talked about honor and property.

Our visitors gave us information about the situation outside. Aytekin's mother, Nail's mother and sisters, and sometimes sympathetic young women gave us fragmentary news. The arrests wave, the confessions, and especially the betrayals had had negative consequences. Understandably, people we'd drawn in now left, although much was misinterpreted. Still it would take a long time to rebuild the organization. The friends outside stayed in contact with us, as we smuggled our reports and assessments out to them.

My family had been coming to visit me since the interrogation period. I was glad they stood behind me. My mother Zeynep, her eyes filled with

1 Cansız family members. *Left to right:* Ismail (author's father), Ali Akgün (brother), Zeynep (mother), Cansız, and Hasan (brother), 1990.

41

tears, talked ceaselessly about her dreams and premonitions. In April, when I'd been in Dersim for the divorce, she had complained, "My son has moved away too." Then: "Aren't you afraid of Allah? Other people do revolutionary work without leaving home, but you're both gone. That's just wrong." She always thought about us, she said, so we were always present in her dreams. She'd told a friend, "She [Sakine] had better take care of herself. The other night I had a nightmare in which she was still in trouble." This woman had a sixth sense! What she'd feared all along had happened. Her bad dream had come true.

[My elder brother] Haydar said he was proud of me and made the victory sign when he left. Ali and my younger siblings knew what had happened—and their love and connectedness to me had grown along with their hatred of the enemy's actions.

Şahin was here [in Harput]. This prison had two separate blocks, and Şahin was in the one for prisoners who were considered not dangerous. He was still trying to influence people who weren't aware of the true situation. A few idiots still babbled on about how he had made his confessions only under torture. I explained to Metin that he and his fellow prisoners must be on their guard. They should organize to keep new arrivals from falling under Şahin's influence, it was more important than ever. This rat just wouldn't stop—he wanted to bring down the organization with his exit. The organization outside still didn't grasp the dimensions of his betrayal.

Nail's mother and sister came to visit and brought us information. When they visited Nail, they came to see me as well. His mother had shed some of her traditional values, so we'd been able to use her home for meetings and for educational work—she took an interest in it herself. She and her daughter felt close to Nail. His father had no interest, even though he was a teacher—he was more of a Kemalist. The family had come from Mazgirt to Elazığ, to the Istasyon neighborhood. They were furious about the arrests and the betrayal. They kept asking, "Will Nail be convicted?"

I asked Nail's mother to stay hopeful. At a time like this, it was important to look out for the people and keep the contact going. Many people in Elazığ were in a similar situation. Our relationships with most of them were only recent, but our circle of sympathizers was really large. Inevitably the vacuum created by the arrests would become noticeable. Those with enough consciousness would find a way to keep the connection going, but the others would need support.

I urged Nail's mother and sister, "Don't let your connections to people be broken. While we're sitting here, you have to take over our tasks." The mother gave me a pained look: "I wish I were here in Nail's place." This wasn't easy.

Aytekin's mother visited. She listened to what her son told her and sometimes brought news of other friends. I'd had good relations with her outside and now was often present when she visited. But she was frightened, as she kept asking, "My girl, have they tortured you much? It must have been horrible with Aytekin, but he won't tell me about it. His feet still haven't healed, and he refuses to show them to me." Then she broke down and cried.

The administrations treated the fascists differently, openly preferring them. This unequal treatment angered the visitors and stirred them up against each other. It even came to open threats. On visiting days, there were always clashes at the prison gate. Finally the administration set different visiting days for the groups, but that didn't solve the problem, as some families had members on both sides.

Nor was it easy inside. When the [UKO] friends were in the exercise yard, the fascists screamed abuse at them from the windows, and vice versa. They also ran into each other en route to the administration. In a space so small, run-ins were unavoidable. Some in the administration, both commanders and soldiers, had direct ties to the fascists and protected them.

We got to thinking that the accommodations had been arranged this way deliberately. After all, the jail had two buildings. We steeled ourselves to resist provocations, but it was obvious when something was going on. The enemy acted against us in various ways. When one thing didn't work, he applied different kinds of pressure. The many prohibitions alone result in a tense atmosphere. We wanted to proceed in an organized way and wondered what to do. The prisoners had to arrive at a common position, to show the enemy that we wouldn't let him push us around.

During interrogation, the enemy had tried to exploit every weakness. At first he seemed mainly to deploy brute force, but with time he used diverse methods to try to grind people down. Now the shock of interrogation and torture was over, but we pondered, discussed, and analyzed it. Mistrust reigned, and mutual recriminations. The torture period had revealed who stood where. Some had submitted out of sheer terror, while others gave up their convictions, then blamed the party instead of their own weakness. Still others tried to analyze the events and their own behavior and to stand up for the party.

At first we evaluated things superficially and incorrectly. It had been hard to hold out when confronted with the enemy. The situation had been so serious, yet many things got mixed up. Such difficult times made clear the importance of conviction, connection, and strength of will.

The enemy's intentions and machinations weren't to be underestimated. They made it all the more important for us to defend the organization, to advocate for it, and to draw a clear line between betrayal and resistance.

The friends whom the enemy had arrested were those in charge of the Elazığ region. He had hoped thereby to deliver a heavy blow to our movement. Maybe he hadn't planned the attack or foreseen its course in detail, but he must have regarded it as the first step in a long-term plan. He had sensed weakness in us and decided it would be worthwhile. Nothing happened by chance.

He had chosen Elazığ because the movement had important organizational structures here. And with its connections with all the other regions, it had strategic significance. At the same time, the fascists were well organized here in the state institutions. Elazığ's social structure resembled those of Bingöl, Malatya, and Erzincan, and its connections to them meant they too could potentially be brought under control. By attacking Elazığ, an institutionally fascist center, the enemy sought to suppress the development of our movement in Dersim, Amed, Hilvan-Siverek, Batman, and elsewhere.

Moreover, the chairman and other leading cadres had often held meetings in Elazığ. Except for those in Ankara, our most important assemblies had taken place here. The Kurdistan Revolutionaries had made their name here. Elazığ was home to groups of the Turkish and Kurdish Left—as well as agent organizations directly tied to the enemy. So the foundations for a radical transformation were in place here. All that was needed was organized leadership. To play that role, many cadres and cadre candidates had come here. The organization needed to develop a working system that, in addition to widening the base, ensured a deepening ideological content. The preconditions for practical development in this direction had been in place since the founding congress.

But the leadership cadre hadn't been ready for it. We were still amateurs. We lacked the ability to address these events with the requisite professionalism. We failed to position ourselves at the right time in the right place. Our way of working was too schematic, too narrowly conceived, too oriented toward meeting daily demands. How had the enemy known that? Did he really know everything? It was hard to say. There were some indications, but the consequences of our own mistakes and weaknesses were obvious.

In the report I sent to the outside, I assessed these events from different points of view. I could name most of our failures clearly. The arrests and their consequences had been a defeat. The betrayals had been a coup [for the enemy]. I didn't assume, however, that the whole organization was threatened. I still had great faith in the party and in the chairman. I believed that in reaction to the betrayals, we could develop a more determined position. But it was also possible that the betrayals were being kept secret, especially in Bingöl, Elazığ, and Dersim, and that not even the cadres had been given precise information about them. I didn't know for sure what the friends outside thought about them, or how they evaluated them, and not knowing tormented me. In the end, no resistance emerged that corresponded to the spirit of our movement.

2 Cansız with brother Metin Cansız, at Diyarbakir, c.1984.

Meanwhile the enemy used the betrayals to attack our movement. I kept thinking there would be more arrests. Şahin had said that Hayri and even the chairman might be in Mardin. At the end of April my brother Metin had been arrested, along with Doğan and Mustafa Yıldırım—Hamili's brother—in Erzincan. Then the three were transferred to this prison in Harput.

Rıza behaved as he always had outside. He tried to hide some of his statements from us and made excuses for others. His behavior had resulted not only from weakness but from anger at the organization, which had already caused us problems outside. No one wanted him to become clay in the hands of the enemy. His family had to be informed about our problems with him, and if they were really committed to the organization, they would have to take a position against him. The friends outside stayed in touch with the family, to keep them on our side, so that they could influence him. In a certain sense, it was good that he was with the friends. As long as he didn't surrender to the enemy, he might be saved. But the friends found him exhausting.

Mustafa was now in charge here [for the party]. It wasn't obvious that he would hold an official function, and no one expected he would, not even him. He rarely took the initiative, just observed and assessed the situation, without really controlling things. But messages from outside were now forwarded to him. From the messages and from visitors' news, we learned that the friends on the outside distrusted the whole Elazığ group. They thought we were all guilty, even if they were unclear about who'd played what role. Just the fact of being arrested had been an offense—it interrupted the work and destroyed the local organization. We all knew we carried that burden of guilt and were ready to accept the party's punishment. The situation was very serious.

Exercise yard took place mornings and afternoons for about an hour. The time was limited, since the fascists used the same place for their exercise. Our written and verbal complaints to the administration about it were always rejected. One morning [the friends] arrived at the exercise yard first. Aytekin and Hamili were running laps together, while Elif and I worked out on the balcony. We couldn't use the space in front of our cell, since that was near the fascists. And the part of the yard near the barracks was where the soldiers were housed. So we used the balcony, from which we could see the men friends and talk to them. Yes, our conversations were always interrupted, but we didn't care.

[That morning] Aytekin was nervous, pulling at his Mao cap. He tried to hide his anxiety when he saw me, but I could tell something was up. Hamili seemed the same way—even from a distance I could see his temples pounding. Suddenly chaos erupted, as the friends raised their fists against Rıza. Prisoners from other groups jumped in.

Rıza couldn't do anything. He just wiped the blood from his nose with his hand and turned pale. The soldiers didn't see what was happening. They just stood at intervals around the barbed-wire-bounded square, their rifles at the ready. The tumult lasted only a few minutes, and then the situation calmed.

Aytekin and Hamili went back to running laps. I watched them curiously and nodded to them in approval. They smiled. Sometimes you had to take a position. On principle I was opposed to beating, since brute violence in my view is mostly senseless and impractical. But if it was used to define a specific position, it could be important.

Still, I didn't take Rıza as seriously as I did Şahin, whose very existence drove me insane. He was still trying to influence new arrivals to the prison! We'd warned the party outside about him, but how could we get to him ourselves?

Just letting him live was an offense. Every day I made plans to eliminate him. It became an *idée fixe*. Imagining it gave me relief, even if it didn't change anything.

Hunger strike   We were allowed to have only certain books in prison. Some just weren't available outside, or the relatives were afraid of buying them. But there was a list of banned books, and the Marxist classics stirred particular fear. As for newspapers, except for trashy tabloids, we were allowed none. The papers often reported about us nowadays. Aydınlik ran a series about the UKO, publishing not only photos of us but our names and addresses. And it denounced revolutionaries in the name of the "proletarian revolution." The enemy made use of this open polarization, but the series also had the good effect of exposing the PDA's true colors. No longer could it deceive people with its revolutionary veneer.

We talked about the problem of books and newspapers with the administration—the prisoners from different groups chose representatives who functioned as speakers. Sometimes we petitioned jointly. Yes, we were prisoners, but we didn't want to be at the mercy of the enemy. After all, we were political prisoners, so books, newspapers, and radios were necessary for us. The prisoners' families would bring them, but the administration didn't accept much of what they brought. The guards scrutinized everything closely, even seams and zippers. Sewing needles were forbidden. We were insistent so that our problems didn't dim into forgetfulness.

We began a two-day hunger strike, to demand that the administration regularly provide us with books and newspapers, separate our visiting days from those of the fascists, and ensure security for visiting family members. Elif didn't participate officially, but she hardly ate anything anyway. It was interesting how hard she tried to show the enemy that she had nothing to do with us. She believed his promise that she'd be released. Actually, she should have been released long before, but they were using her as a witness. We still treated her with suspicion. Hardly anyone supported her. Even the soldiers disdained her [for not participating]. She hardly dared raise her head.

The hunger strike began on a visiting day. We refused to receive visitors. As the families gathered at the checkpoint, we shouted "Long live the resistance in the hunger strike! Down with the repression!" My too-high voice could be heard above all the others. It was our first collective action in prison. It gave us a feeling of unity, not only ourselves but also the families outside. And it annoyed the administration. Some prison staff said, "You're only hurting yourselves. If you'd filed an application, the thing could have been settled. Or did the organization coerce you to do this action? Did you get an order to do it?" Others were more sympathetic, saying, "It's a shame."

During the hunger strike, we drank only water and, once or twice a day, took a fixed amount of sugar water. During the hunger strike in Izmir, we'd also drunk tea, but here we were careful to follow the rules. Others might do it differently, but we didn't care. A friend was chosen to represent the prisoners and negotiate with the administration. We had previously decided which demands were non-negotiable and which could be flexible. Members of other political groups took part, but we [UKO] were the majority. The administration considered our representative to be the negotiation partner. It was natural and had nothing to do with the majority question. It was enough that we were from the PKK, although back then we were still called UKO, the name that was still used publicly after our arrests. The image was important.

Our lawyers visited at defined intervals. In addition to Hüseyin Yıldırım, there was Mahmut Bigili, whom the friends had retained, and some from the bar association in Elazığ, also hired by the families. Having several lawyers made sense to us, since they at least could publicize the events. Hüseyin Yıldırım had taken charge for most of the friends. He said he was active in other prisons too, but we got no further information from him. He wasn't very well liked. Those who knew him from Dersim said he was a drinker. Still, it was positive that he was working on our behalf.

Mahmut Bilgili, from the Ankara Bar Association, was married to the sister of Hasan Serik. I'd met her once in Tuzluçayir, and she'd seemed to have potential, but then she got married, which doesn't promote much development. But we regarded Mahmut as a friend. There was no separate room for us to consult with our lawyers, so we used an administration room—where the enemy could listen in. At every visit Mahmut brought us up to date about the outside. What Hüseyin Yıldırım told us was less credible—in fact, highly questionable—and seemed more like his own interpretations. Frankly, he seemed to lie all the time. When I shared my reservations about him with the men friends, they found my suspicion excessive and said I'd prejudged him. It's true that I had no concrete evidence against him. But my memory of him in Dersim, as well as his extreme behavior, aroused my mistrust. I kept my distance from him.

It had been naïve of me to tell the friends about my mistrust of him, but then they were just as naïve, if also well intentioned, in telling him that I mistrusted him. Probably he had complained about my coldness to him, and they wanted to fix the problem. I still got annoyed. Had they boldly said to him, "Sakine doesn't trust you. She says you lie"? That must have taken him aback.

He tried to talk to me about it. "I don't understand some of your descriptions," I explained.

> Maybe you mean well and are trying to spare me because I'm in prison, but that's no good. I'm not a child, and I want to know what's really happening. If you try to prettify reality, you'll only make things worse. That's all I meant.

With that evasion, I tried to put an end to the discussion. But he continued to be overly rosy during his visits and was more energetic than the other lawyers. His lies gave the families hope.

Fantasies of escape   Harput was beautiful in the morning when sunlight fell on the hillsides. The prison buildings stood on bare ground, but between the checkpoint and the spring, there were fields and fruit trees.

Our cell had neither a washbasin nor a toilet, so we had to go to the spring to get water, to use the toilet, and to bathe. The spring water was wonderful. Mornings, afternoons, and evenings, I always lingered and played with the water like a child. As I washed my face and hands and brushed my teeth, the soldiers were astonished that I took so much pleasure in it—prison was supposed to be a place of unbearable deprivation. So they became curious about me. *Who is this woman who committed such felonies?* every new one asked. Their superiors had portrayed me to them as a monster and assured them that guarding me would require their utmost diligence. To prevent the solders from developing sympathy for me, the administration drilled them: "She's a terrorist, a murderer. She wants to divide the fatherland and form a Kurdish state. Be careful—it's forbidden to talk to her or interact with her under any circumstances. Just carry out your orders." Still, a few of them wanted to get to know me, and sometimes they deliberately overlooked things. When I talked to the men friends in the exercise yard, they didn't intervene, and they brought us greetings and messages from the other prison building. They often asked me if I needed anything. And they let me linger at the spring.

I observed the soldiers closely. Some of them came from Kurdistan or from a large city with a more democratic and progressive culture. Meanwhile the fascists among them did everything to make our lives harder. One soldier, Murat, came from Manisa and seemed very interested in me. He reminded me of the soldier from Cermik who I'd thought could become a revolutionary if the friends ever reached out to him. I don't know what became of him. But with Murat, his town Manisa is near Izmir, where I had lived, so we had a basis for a conversation.

Certain aspects of this prison building seemed promising for a breakout. Our cell had two doors, one of wood and a gate of iron bars. The wooden door was seldom locked—usually we closed it from inside. The iron gate could be removed from its hinges. The door was a hand's width shorter than the frame, and the lock wasn't stable. The constant opening and closing had worn it down. I'd pounded on it during our hunger strike, which had helped. Whenever Elif was away from the cell, I used a spoon to scrape away at the concrete foundation. It was wonderfully exciting. I realized the bedsheets were olive green—I could easily make trousers from them. The shirt wouldn't be so important, since at night the soldiers sometimes walked around in white underwear. I could see them as they entered or left the barracks. I cut my hair in a short military haircut. When someone asked me why, I explained that my hair was falling out. My escape plan wasn't anyone's business—I'd mention it to one or two friends when the time came.

Meanwhile Murat from Manisa was so impressed by me that, despite his fears, he did everything I asked of him. He came from a working-class family and was very emotional. "Many people in this prison," he said, "have no sympathy. It's a man's place. I have sympathy for you." He disliked Elif because of her good relations with the administration—police from our interrogation period even came to visit her! Since we were the only two women in the prison, the soldiers watched everything we did with great interest. I tried to avoid doing anything that would arouse their notice.

During daylight hours, I studied the prison grounds. The best point of departure for an escape would be the spring—it was guarded by soldiers with only a watchtower. Two rings of barbed wire surrounded the grounds. When we went to the spring in the daytime, two armed soldiers usually escorted us, but at night only one came with us. He was invariably annoyed to be dragged to the toilet at night, since he was tired and it was cold. So nighttime would be ideal for an escape, especially if Murat was on duty.

I could make my way to Kirkdutlar or Esentepe within an hour. It would be harder for them to get hold of me out there. Baskil would be a good place, or Kellek, a village where families from my uncle's village had settled years ago. I'd been there once. People there would hide me. Just the thought of hiding filled me with rapture. But I mustn't be hasty. I had a tendency to rush, and too often that had done me in. I must wait patiently for the right moment and plan what to do if anything went wrong. The enemy wasn't stupid, and he didn't trust us at all. Every day he tightened security, so in that sense it would be better to act fast. Clearly this prison couldn't accommodate women—maybe the administration didn't want responsibility for us, or maybe we annoyed them, but I was afraid they would transfer us at any time. The friends didn't want us to be transferred. "Don't talk about it," I warned them. "If you press them about it, they might do just the opposite."

The [1969] novel *Papillon* [by escaped prisoner Henri Charrière] inspired me. All day and all night, I worked on my escape plan. Of course the enemy expected escape attempts, but not from women. They didn't think women would try it. And even though the soldiers were constantly told how dangerous I was, they weren't all that watchful.

One day we heard some wonderful news over the radio. Kemal Pir, who'd been arrested after the founding congress, had escaped from prison in Urfa. I shouted for joy. Did the men friends know? Just at that moment I heard a racket from above. In their cellblock, news spread fast. If they spoke in a loud voice, we could hear them in our cell. During the hunger strike, we'd communicated by shouting. And now we all shouted the news together, as if we'd coordinated it. Aytekin cried, "Seko, did you hear?" And "Have you heard? Pir has escaped! Hurray!" Then the prison personnel showed up, and we stopped. "Oh, nothing's going on," I said. "It's okay. We won't talk anymore."

Yes, Kemal Pir had escaped! It was superb. He had previously escaped from Ordu prison—Rıza and others had got him out. Pir's vibrant personality just couldn't be caged. He'd once said that for a revolutionary in prison, the greatest action was escape, and now he'd done it. This news validated my own plans. Soon they'd be saying, "Sakine has escaped!" I could hardly think about anything else. By now all the men friends in the prison were probably thinking along the same lines.

Our trial had not yet begun. The date was still unclear. Attorney Mahmut said, "I've heard a rumor that all the trials are to be consolidated in Diyarbakir. It might well be true." Several well-known cadres and hundreds of sympathizers were already imprisoned in Diyarbakir, so I actually hoped to be transferred there. Şahin wouldn't be able to move around so freely there. But the enemy seemed to want to drag out our proceedings to detain us longer; many families were nervous about the prospect of our transfer to Diyarbakir.

In his statement, Şahin had said the official announcement of the party's founding would be accompanied by a series of actions. Had he also mentioned the specific actions? For months we'd been waiting anxiously. Finally in late July [1980] the party announced its founding. Instead of "UKO" or "the movement," we were the PKK, Partiyê Karkerên Kurdistan, the Kurdistan Workers Party. Şahin had disclosed the name under interrogation, but I hadn't mentioned it.

At the same time, [on July 30,] the party carried out an action against the Bucak clan. Within Kurdistan, there were complicated social contradictions. Local feudal landowners collaborated with the colonializing institutions, which in turn supported them. In [Siverek and Hilvan], the Bucak clan supported colonialism. In order to organize the people for the national liberation struggle, we had to eliminate these treacherous collaborators, who characterized our movement as feudal banditry.

[The head of the clan,] Mehmet Celal Bucak, was injured. Comrade Salih Kandal and many other friends, among them Ahmet and Cuma Tak, lost their lives. I knew them all. We weren't accustomed to such a high death toll. The loss of such valuable comrades was painful, all but unbearable. We all felt only sorrow and shared our memories with each other.

But the actions continued, which gave us strength. As far as we could tell from the news, the mass protests and clashes were spreading. That rat Şahin had propagandized that our organization was done. No! The party continued, Chairman Apo was still outside, and Pir had escaped from prison. We were suffused with hope. Many revolutions experienced temporary setbacks and betrayals. If we held on to our belief in the revolution, it would continue.

It was intolerable to have to sit in prison while so much was happening outside. *Dammit, how could we have been so careless?* I berated myself again. *And now, of all times!* The fascists were losing followers, and the other [leftist] groups were silent, apparently cowed by the state of emergency. If we'd been free, we could have pushed things further in Elazığ.

From now on, our ways of working would clearly have to change, to include armed actions. We'd often discussed weapons training in preparation for guerrilla war, but now it became essential. If only we hadn't been arrested, we could have made a difference. Since the arrests, we'd been busy processing what had happened and questioning ourselves, but by now we just felt empty. We'd been plucked from the battlefield. My god, it was too much, we so wanted to be there!

New arrivals More and more of us were now in prison. Of course, it's not good for prison numbers to grow, but it did us good to see new faces, and every new arrival meant we got new information. Word spread quickly as to who had arrived from which group.

A woman named Atiye arrived. We had both been active in Elazığ and had sometimes met in the street or during family visits. I had seen her in a few demonstrations, too, like the one where she covered herself with a black cloth to avoid being noticed. She adhered to Dev-Sol.

Atiye was Circassian, a beautiful woman who looked older than she was. She smoked a lot—so much that it discouraged me from smoking—and had a strange ruling-class hauteur. Her people's history was marked by massacres and betrayals: during the Crimean War, the Abkhaz [a Circassian subgroup] had been betrayed, and then the Turkish state had been responsible for their massacre and genocide. Yet they'd deeply internalized social chauvinism. I couldn't understand Atiye's Turkish-chauvinist feelings. At our first meeting she'd seemed ice cold. It wasn't because she belonged to the Turkish Left—many people on the revolutionary Left were our friends and comrades. But Atiye behaved like the daughter of a general. She'd lived in Ankara and worked as a civil servant, so that meant she was bureaucratic and egoistic. Still, we talked a lot about the state of emergency, the [1978] Maraş pogrom, and the events in Elazığ. It did me good—I had a need for substantive conversations.

Elif and Atiye seemed to like each other, even though I warned Atiye about Elif. It was typical of the Turkish Left to be friendly to the people we had problems with. *My political values are flexible,* Atiye said. "We're all in prison, so we can't exclude anyone, otherwise we'll drive them over to the enemy." Theoretically she was right, but Elif was allowing the enemy to use her. Atiye wasn't trying to change her behavior, but if she somehow managed to influence Elif, that could only be good. Elif might join Dev-Sol—she could do worse.

Another new arrival was Sevim Korkmaz, from Dersim. She didn't fit any template. In Dersim she'd associated with Turkish leftist groups. Now in prison, she found Atiye's views reactionary: "Dev-Sol rejected the arguments you're making here long ago. They're based on social chauvinism." Atiye got angry and explained to us the difference between Dev-Sol and other groups.

Sevim Korkmaz was pretty, lively, and well versed in theory. She'd completed Teachers School and passed the university entrance exams. She hoped to leave prison soon and continue her studies at the university, but that was for her also a means to an end. She was glad to have left her family behind, even if it took her being arrested to do so. "I often wanted to run away from home. They pressured me a lot," she said. Her father, Hasan Korkmaz, was mayor of Dersim and alienated from his own culture. He was inclined toward Dev-Yol and categorically rejected his daughter's revolutionary efforts as a UKO member. But her arrest frightened him. "In a way, it's a good thing I was arrested," Sevim remarked. "Maybe now he'll understand what the state is about." Someone from the Elazığ group had probably mentioned her name under interrogation—there were many young women in the organization who were more important than she was.

The months sped by. Most people assume that time stands still in prison and every day must feel like a year, but it's not so. It was awful to be cut off from the struggle, but there was no need to waste a single moment complaining. Friends sometimes said [affectionately], "We wish you weren't here—you make it hard for us." I expected that from the families, but the friends' complaints seemed funny to me. The enemy had captured us and wanted to make us feel that we were imprisoned at every moment. Precisely for this reason, we refused to let it get us down and forced ourselves to keep on living even in prison, to keep our world of feelings and thoughts alive. For revolutionaries, that was essential. People who face the enemy incessantly develop unexpected strengths. The higher your ideals are, and the stronger your convictions and willpower, the better you'll be able to assess the enemy. If you fall into his hands, your loathing for him will become boundless.

Fascists For months we had been asking not to be housed in the same prison as the fascists. These cadres, dogs, murderers, brutally attacked revolutionaries in schools and universities, as well as normal people. Who knew how many they had on their conscience? But the state protected them. They controlled Firat University—most of the faculty and staff were fascist. It was obvious why the prison administration housed us all together. The fascists did everything to make our life more difficult and were champing at the bit to attack us. Finally, what we most feared came to pass, completing the administration's plan.

It started on a visiting day. Aytekin's mother visited him, then me. Aytekin had a "present" for me, she said, and wanted to give it to me at the next opportunity. What could it be? I wondered. Most likely a secret message from outside. "Okay, I understand," I said. "He could have just given it to you." Usually secret messages from outside were smuggled into the prison, hidden among useful objects. But apparently that hadn't been possible. I was impatient.

The next morning the [PKK men] went to the exercise yard first. On the way, they passed our cell. The wooden door was open. Sometimes I waited there in case someone wanted to give me something. The next door led to the fascists' section, and soldiers were usually stationed there to prevent clashes.

On this morning some of the fascists passed us on the way to the administration. They were in a good mood, elated. Raif Cicek glared at me and made some insulting remark. I shouted, "You fascist murderer! You've killed 60 people!"

While the first group was with the administration, a second group was brought in. So I had to stay in the cell. I protested to a soldier: "Tell your superior we want to go to the exercise yard." And I pounded on the door.

The officer in charge heard the noise and came over. "Why haven't we been taken to the exercise yard?" I demanded.

"We had other things to do," he said. "Lawyers for some of the right-wingers were here. We wanted to prevent them from running in to you."

This officer had a gentle manner. He was here temporarily, a TKP member, and sometimes he talked politics with us. He seemed to know nothing of the ongoing intrigues. He behaved respectfully but sometimes paid too much attention to the rules.

Two of the fascists hadn't yet come back. At our urging, Elif and I were finally taken to the balcony. We greeted the men down in the yard. Aytekin was in a good mood, fingering his Mao cap. He was standing with Hamili and Sadi and Zeki Budak, if I remember correctly, and they were talking and laughing mischievously. I made a questioning gesture. "We'll tell you later!" they said. But we rarely had a chance to speak up close. Sometimes I was allowed to talk to Hamili—I claimed he was my cousin. We had to speak in whispers through the barbed wire so the soldiers couldn't hear us. It was better to write.

Aytekin [and Sadi] were running laps, while others were sitting along the edges or talking in groups. The windows of the block where the fascists stayed were fairly low. Whenever we were all out in in the exercise yard, two friends kept an eye on those windows.

Suddenly, as we were trying to tell each other something, shots rang out. It was unclear where they came from. Panic erupted, people screaming. The soldiers released their own safety catches and shouted, "Stop or be shot!"

Some of the men friends had fallen and were lying in their own blood. "Fascist murderers! Murderers! Fascist administration!" I cried. Some of the men tried to hide under the windows, while others tried to escape through the barbed wire. They were in the line of fire, wounded.

The soldiers were ready to shoot. An officer screamed at the top of his lungs, "Stop, don't shoot them! They're just trying to get away from the shots! Let them out, then surround them outside! Don't shoot them!"

It was terrifying. The soldiers were panicking. Maybe some of them were even involved. The plan was for the fascists to attack us from inside, and then the soldiers from outside. Perfect. They were going to massacre us, out of revenge: in March at Newroz, some fascists had been killed.

"Restrain those soldiers!" I shouted. "We see through your plan! Don't let the friends go just so you can shoot them!"

"Okay, calm down," the officer said. "We'll stop them."

I was crazy with anger and worry. We went back inside the building, where along with some of the men friends, we chanted slogans. But they were locked in the cells.

On our way down to the basement, we ran into two fascists—I later found out they'd been getting haircuts. As soon as I spotted them, I grabbed a chair and hurled it at them with all my might. It hit one of them in the knee. He screamed, "You Communist!" and I shot back, "You fascist dog! It was you who fired those shots!" I glanced around but didn't see any more objects to throw.

The soldiers led the fascists quickly toward the barracks. We went to our cells. There had been shooting in our direction too. A few of the men had run in our direction, without noticing it, when I called out a warning to them.

The captain and the other officers hadn't intervened at all. They deliberately stayed inside the building. The officer on duty and the sergeant had panicked and didn't know what to do. Much later a smoke bomb was thrown into the building, and the fascists were told to hand over their weapons.

The soldiers tried to force us to go to the barracks, but we defended ourselves. I reached for the officer's pistol. He cried in fright, "My pistol, my pistol!" More soldiers gathered around. I tried to grab a weapon from a soldier. If I got my hand on it, I'd have pulled the trigger right away. "You're murderers, you did this!" I screamed.

The officer swore, "No, that wasn't us. I didn't know anything. I have nothing to do with right-wingers."

So it continued awhile longer, until the captain and the other officers came. "You fascistic murderers!" I screamed at them. "You've killed our friends! How many people did you kill?" I asked the friends who'd been in the building if they'd seen anything. "How many people were hit?" They hadn't been able to tell amid the tumult.

I couldn't stand still, and then the captain ordered, "Handcuff her in the back and take her away." I retorted, "Stop these murderers! Why aren't you putting handcuffs on them? Why aren't you taking their weapons away? Oh yeah, right—you gave them the weapons yourselves. You won't even give us a sewing needle! We can't get needles, but you give revolvers to the fascists!" Finally they dragged me away.

I don't know how many hours passed, but after a nerve-wracking period of waiting, some of the men friends were brought back on a military bus. They'd had to lie down on the open field with their faces to the ground, under guard. Some of them had carried the wounded into the military hospital. I tried to find out how many were wounded and dead. Many of the men weren't there. I asked about Aytekin, Hamili, Adil, Zeki …

Mustafa said, "Calm down. No one was killed. Only one friend was wounded. They have flesh wounds from the barbed wire. A bullet hit Aytekin in the shoulder, but he's okay. Don't worry."

I didn't believe it. "How is Aytekin? Tell me the truth, right now!"

Later another group came back, Hamili among them. He said Aytekin and another friend would be taken to [a hospital in] Malatya.

So Aytekin's wound was serious! Suddenly my knees got weak, and the blood froze in my veins. *Aytekin, Aytekin* … I saw him before me, his mischievous smile that morning, playing with the cap, his joyous, rambunctious ways, his quick, decisive stride. … I felt terrible foreboding, even though Hamili kept saying it wasn't serious. Hamili and Mustafa mentioned that in the confusion at the hospital, they could have escaped, but they'd passed up the chance.

The shots had come from two sides, but the fascists had handed over only one pistol. Obviously they had further plans. One fascist was taken to court as the suspected perpetrator. No one was transferred, so [Elif and I] found ourselves once again in the same building with them. The men friends in the other building started a hunger strike in protest. We decided to join and wrote a letter stating that the administration had contributed to the incident by introducing weapons into the prison and not taking any precautions. They were still doing nothing to provide security for us. The hunger strike was a warning, better than keeping silent. We asked the families to help.

A few days later Hüseyin Yıldırım arrived. The legal conversation took place, as always, in an administration room. The officer on duty was the same one as on the day of the incident. Hüseyin had nothing new to report, except that the PKK trials had been combined—Metin's and Doğan's were now combined with ours. "I've talked to Mr. Cahit. He told me he was trying to change this decision, so that the trials of the Elazığ group can take place in Elazığ." By "Mr. Cahit" he meant the military prosecutor.

"Aytekin was seriously wounded," I said. "How is he?"

Hüseyin hesitated, then said, "We've lost Aytekin."

I leaped up and slammed my fist on the table where the officer was sitting. "You murderers! You've killed him! You brought this weapon into the prison!"

The officer stood. "Calm down. It wasn't me. I had nothing to do with the weapon."

Hüseyin Yıldırım added, "Sakine, my daughter, please calm down. He is after all an officer."

I grabbed the officer by the collar. "You're guilty! How often did we warn you? But you never even conducted a search! We couldn't even get a sewing needle from you. Where did these weapons come from?" Then I ran outside and yelled, "Aytekin is immortal!"

The men started chanting, "Down with the fascists!" They called to me asking what happened. I told them Aytekin was dead. I sat in the corridor, while the men sang revolutionary songs. Then the door to the men's block opened, and they were allowed to come in. Normally the administration never let us get so close. Astonishingly, they were behaving gently. We chanted slogans and sang fighting songs into the evening.

I saw Hüseyin Yıldırım leave the grounds, accompanied by two soldiers. Obviously he was disgraced because he had told me the truth.

Later we learned that Aytekin had been murdered at the hospital. Apparently the nurse had pulled the IV out of his arm or stopped its flow.

Had it been an act of revenge for Celal Aydın? It was Aytekin
who'd intervened in Malatya and sent Celal to Elazığ. Celal had never
returned. The fascists in the prison were men Aytekin had known from
his neighborhood. Surely it was they who'd shot at him. Outside, too,
several attempts had been made to murder Aytekin.

His death shook us all up, deeply. After all the torture he'd undergone
in prison—to be shot! Several times he'd said he cheated death, but
death finally caught up with him in prison. The fascists had targeted him
first. As I write, I still see him before me, the way he was outside, under
interrogation, and then on that last day. I'll never forget his vivacity,
his warmth, and the revolutionary beauty of his soul. The pain hit me
deeply. Well-intended people advised, "You must not be so emotional,
you can't let yourself go, you have to get used to it, you must be
strong." But their suggestions left a stale aftertaste. "That's too simple,"
I said.

A few days later Mustafa told me,

Don't be angry, but on the day of the incident, I destroyed the secret
message that was intended for you. I had to. I thought I could toss it to
you when we passed by your door, but I couldn't because the soldiers were
standing there. After the incident we were detained outside for hours. I
still had it on me, and I thought they would search us, so I destroyed the
message without reading it. I wish I'd read it first.

In another message from the party, intended for us, they said they'd
received our reports. The party considers our arrests to have been a defeat.
And they said something about Şahin, something he was supposed to have
said—it was very different from what was presented. They said everything
had already been betrayed before he was arrested, and he had been forced
to admit a few things.

The secret message had come directly from the party! How could I
not be angry? What had the friends written to me? How could this have
happened? The unbelievable incompetence preoccupied me for a long
time. At least they'd received our reports, but I couldn't forget what they
said about Şahin. Should I write to them?

Rumor had it that everyone except the fascists were to be transferred
to another prison. If I were to escape, I had to do it before that happened.
I decided it would be too conspicuous to sew myself a pair of pants, but
at night colors wouldn't be discernible anyway.

Then came another disaster, a stroke of bad luck. The officer on duty was standing in the doorway talking to us, with his foot pressed against the doorjamb. I'd been gradually hollowing out the concrete foundation with a spoon. The whole frame wasn't stable, and the lock was loose. While the officer was talking, he knocked the lock with his hand—and suddenly found himself holding it. He gave a start. "What's this?" he asked suspiciously. "How can it have been so loose?" Then he examined the door and discovered the hollowed foundation. He tried lifting the iron gate and saw that it came easily off its hinges.

He yelled to the soldiers, "How can you not have noticed this? You open and close this door every day!" Then he ordered a welder to come at once. While the welder worked on the door, the soldiers gaped with amazement. The men friends upstairs got curious when they heard the noise.

The officer turned to me. "Mrs. Sakine, you weren't planning to escape, were you?"

"Looks like I missed my chance," I said. "What rotten luck! If only I'd noticed it!"

The man was a fox, in the mold of Zafer Karaosmanoğlu, with a knowledge of human nature that wasn't to be underestimated. They'd zeroed right in on me. Oh, this was bad. Now they'd keep a closer watch on us. Dammit, why had he come over here? I was ready to try and escape that very night! But now all the guards were suspicious of me. It was so inconvenient.

I didn't want to go to another prison. This one hadn't even been built as a prison but as a military installation. The security had many weak points. Did the friends outside in Elazığ know about it? The organization there had been destroyed, maybe no one was left. I knew I was right—a prison break would constitute an action taken against the enemy. If I'd been able to use the opportunity, it would've been a good hit. Probably I was too optimistic, but this dream was just too beautiful.

Now I had only Murat from Manisa. I asked him bluntly, "Help me escape. My father is in Germany. I'll make sure you can go abroad. You don't like military service anyway. You're a worker—your family is working class just like mine. I know you don't want to do anything against me."

He looked surprised for a moment, then: "I expected this. You know, it's not only prisoners who think about escape—soldiers do too. But what if we're caught? It wouldn't be so bad for you—they'd just throw you back in prison. But me? I swear, they'd kill me."

"They won't catch us—trust me."

"I'll think about it. When should it happen?"

"That's easy. At night, during the watch," I said briefly. I didn't go into detail, in case Murat turned out to be untrustworthy. But no—he was honest and had good intentions. He hesitated a little, worried about what would happen afterward.

"Look, on this side the barbed wire is really low," he said as we were walking to the toilet and the spring. "Here's where the patrols pass. It'd be a practical route," he said. I'd thought of that spot already. So I'd observed correctly. The thing could succeed, if only I could persuade Murat. "I'll think about it," he said.

The next day we were all transferred to another prison [in the vicinity]. So this plan too came to nothing. What awful luck!

* * *

The new prison was a two-story building with tall windows. The administration and the military were housed on the upper story, [the prisoners on the lower one]. A long corridor separated our level into two blocks. Hüseyin Güngöze was put in charge of one block, Mustafa the other. Each block had many cells, with doors leading onto the corridor. The iron doors were thick and large. I was no longer segregated from the men. I could converse with them through the window to the yard and through cracks in the cell door.

The toilets were near the entrance, where food was also distributed. In the visiting room, the prisoners could sit in booths that separated them from their visitors with iron bars, barbed wire, and a pane of glass. The exercise yard was divided in half by barbed wire.

The prison grounds were a military zone, dotted with military installations, including a military court a few minutes away. From the prison we could see the Kirkdutlar neighborhood. The road to Harput rose above the building.

The prisoners were diverse. Reso, who'd joined us from the MHP, was here—he'd been arrested with a pistol. He was a Zaza from Palu, with the soul of an anarchist. I'd talked to him soon after he joined us and had been impressed.

The prisoners who'd been in the hospital came back. "Sadi is doing well," they said. He had been running laps with Aytekin that day, and a bullet had grazed his forehead. [My brother] Meto had been hit in the knee during the shooting, and the bullet hadn't yet been removed.

And then Baki Polat arrived in the prison and was put in the second block. I ran into him in the exercise yard. He said he wanted to talk to me. I adamantly refused and warned him to show some maturity and respect my boundaries. *But we're relatives*, he insisted—*it's only natural that we'd talk*. He just didn't understand. Once or twice he called to me from the yard, "Sakine, Sakine, talk to me!" "We have nothing to talk about," I'd respond. "If you've got something to say, talk to the friends." He was a total nuisance and pushed me close to the edge. He asked to be transferred to my block, but I told the men friends under no circumstances to transfer him.

We arranged transfers between the two blocks ourselves, internally. We tried to create a balance. We put more of our own people in the block that was closer to the street and left a few token friends in the other one. We were thinking about digging a tunnel, or possibly using the sewer system as an escape route.

And there was something else. Şahin was in the second block, along with the token friends and some prisoners from the Turkish and Kurdish Left. He came over to visit our block a few times, but I shouted from the window, "Don't you ever let that scumbag come in here again, ever!" I criticized the men for allowing it.

The friends passed a resolution to punish Şahin, and we wrote to the party outside recommending that it punish him, but so far we'd had no answer. They still hadn't officially recognized his betrayal. Didn't they believe us? It infuriated me. Even if they felt they didn't know enough, we had the best information about him. We knew exactly who he was and what he had done.

On some points the party was still in a fog. Sometimes in an organization, you can't always wait for an order to come from above. One individual could have taken responsibility. Many friends here would gladly have done so, finding it unbearable that a traitor walked among us. It would have had positive effects both inside and outside.

But then, none of us had the right to execute a punishment on our own initiative. We were part of an organization, after all, and waited for approval from outside. "We'll do what the party says," I told Hamili.

"They will criticize and maybe even punish [him]. Meanwhile we're all feeling guilty because we got arrested and made statements. We have to be honorable. Whatever the party decides, we'll accept it and carry it out."

But what was the party waiting for? Its attitude toward traitors was more or less known. I couldn't understand it. I was sure it was a mistake to fail to punish him, so I persisted in our proposal. Hüseyin said he'd forwarded it, but the times demanded "patience."

* * *

Ali Gündüz had not stayed strong under the brutal torture. Initially, he did, but after a while he began to lose his convictions and his confidence, as his statements revealed. The content of a person's confession didn't matter as much as the mindset created by the act of confession itself. Ali was teetering on the brink of capitulation. He couldn't bring himself to betray, but he also couldn't free himself from this emotional state and return to resisting. He was deeply troubled.

I knew him and understood what was happening with him. I read something he wrote, saying he was in a depression, and he cursed his own weaknesses, considering them treacherous, yet he couldn't find his way out. The enemy was never going to leave him in peace. If he couldn't extricate himself from this condition, he'd crack for sure.

I was worried about Hamili too—his pride was hurt that two other friends had been put in charge of the prison blocks. Hamili and Ali had a friendship that seemed unhealthy to me. They brought out the worst in each other. Ali's defeatism blended with Hamili's hurt pride. I confided in Hamili about my concern for Ali and, frankly, my mistrust. "He doesn't bounce back quickly," I said. "His attitude is dangerous. Try to influence him. Don't let him turn into a problem."

"Ali is thinking about asking to be transferred to another prison," Hamili admitted. "He told me about it." Ali wanted to run away? How had he reached that point? Had the enemy made him some kind of offer? Or was it something else? Maybe he was uncomfortable with the men friends. No, that couldn't be the reason. Their behavior toward him was natural, if ineffectual, which irritated me.

"You're out of your mind!" I said to Hamili severely. "If Ali is even thinking about such a thing, you have to take a strong stand against it!

You have to bring him to his senses. And why did he mention this to you and not to anyone else?" A wave of fear swept over me. Everyone makes mistakes—you have to own them if you're ever to be free of them. If Ali ran away from his, it could become a crisis.

Then I spoke to Ali himself through the crack in the door. "If you get yourself transferred to another prison," I said, my heart filled with rage, "it will mean you want to cross over to the enemy." That was harsh, but I forged ahead: "Your attitude only encourages the enemy. You have to get rid of it, otherwise you're heading for capitulation."

Ali was ashamed. He reddened, and his eyes filled with tears. That's how we parted—it was our last conversation. Later the friends quietly passed me some of his notes and poems to read, in which he had openly expressed how he felt. He was afraid of his own reality—that was the real danger.

* * *

In Dersim there had been a shootout with Tekoşin members. Haydar Alparslan (Kemal Zap) was shot in the ambush but was only wounded. The friends joked, "You've got nine lives."

Around this time Hasan Aydın arrived. He'd been arrested in a skirmish between Pertek and Çemişgezek, where two very valued friends died. In Dersim, Hasan Aydın had been head of the Teachers School and had propagandized against us for the HK. Now he was in prison with us, on a murder charge. We had to do something. We couldn't live with a murderer. We talked about it, reached a consensus, wrote a proposal, and forwarded it to the party outside. It was the only correct position, and we wanted to implement it right away. But we needed a weapon. How could we smuggle a revolver into the prison?

While the others were out in the exercise yard, Meto, Memo, and Daimi cut iron bars from the bunk beds and shaped them into spears. They showed me one—it was sharp like a spear. Their decisiveness emboldened me. Prisons are battlefields too. A revolutionary has to be ready to carry on the struggle, even with the limited possibilities available in prison. Otherwise prison is unendurable. The enemy tries to dominate your whole life and crush your struggle. You have to fight him with all the might that your will and your convictions can muster.

The other HK members here protected the murderer and wouldn't let him out of their sight. We agreed on a plan. When Hasan went to the toilet, friends in several cells would ask to go too, at the same time, and while the soldiers were busy unlocking doors, the friends would attack Hasan. One night I heard screams and realized what was happening. My fellow prisoners didn't know anything about it and got frightened—they thought someone was being tortured. "Calm down, it's nothing," I told them. We were highly sensitive to the sounds of torture, screaming slogans and pounding on doors whenever we heard the slightest cry, but this time, if we made that racket, it would only alert the soldiers.

Hasan had gone to the toilet, and the men had grabbed him and stabbed him seven times. But he survived. This dirtbag too apparently had nine lives. He was taken to the hospital and later released from there. The enemy knew how to protect his own people.

We issued a text, explaining that Hasan Aydın had been an agent, a provocateur, and a murderer of revolutionaries. We called on other groups to dissociate themselves from him. We demanded that the HK-ers remove the agents and provocateurs from their ranks, but instead the HK members got together with other groups to form a social-chauvinistic bloc, as they had on the outside. What were the principles on which it was based? Unclear. People glibly spoke of "disagreements among revolutionaries." Meanwhile we exchanged messages and had conversations with members of Kurtuluş and Kawa, who acted more circumspectly.

Mehmet Yıldırım confessed to attacking Hasan Aydın. He was brought to court, where his statement was taken. He explained he'd known Hasan Aydın in Dersim and couldn't bear his provocative ways. He mentioned no political affiliation.

After the [Hasan] episode, Atiye actively inflamed the group infighting. As a [Dev-Sol] cadre from Ankara, she was a rhetorically skilled speaker. She was also calculating and sly. We found her suspicious due to her contacts with people outside her group and with the administration. She was allowed to have visitors in the administration rooms. Sometimes she was taken to court alone, even though others from her group were in prison too. She had her own cash box and a voracious appetite, devouring milk, honey, eggs, cheese—even cookies!

Hüseyin Yıldırım once asked me about Atiye. "Whenever she's taken to court, she talks only with the prosecutor. That's suspicious. Hm, I can find out more about her." He was in a position to know, so I said, "Sure, you can do that."

I'm not always easy to get along with, but if someone has an attractive quality and exudes a warm desire for a revolutionary life, then I feel respect and commonality. If such a person takes one step toward me, I'll take ten. But egoistic Atiye lacked all the qualities of a revolutionary: she was careerist, vague, irritable, unfriendly, and bureaucratic. I found her unbearable. In fact, none of us thought well of her. Even Elif steered clear of her now. Atiye even urged her comrades to take positions against us. Whose interests did that serve? The friends criticized me for being harsh toward Atiye, but I criticized them for ignoring what was going on with her. Still, I tried to find commonalities with her where I could and to create the conditions for a common front against the enemy. Objectively, we were on the same side.

New arrivals were tortured, but some betrayed no one. Mahmut Aktaş, a friend from Adıyaman, was arrested in Elazığ for trying to murder a PDA journalist. During his interrogation, they hung him by his feet for a long time, so afterward he suffered from constant headaches, and his eyes were bloodshot. And Haydar Karasungur was arrested with a stack of leaflets in a bus. After his torture, his condition worsened every day. He was wasting away. Finally he was taken to a doctor, who examined him, and soon thereafter he was released. Later I learned he had tuberculosis and his condition was critical. The doctor's certificate had contributed to his release. I was comforted to think he could find medical treatment outside and regain his health.

Sometimes people become mistrustful in prison. When Haydar Karasungur was released, [some wondered] if the enemy had let him go to make it easier to get at his brother Mehmet, the teacher [and PKK central committee member]. But Haydar was also a valuable comrade. He and Mehmet had much in common, but Mehmet had a sharp sense of humor while Haydar was much softer, with a natural modesty that was as attractive as a calmly flowing river.

* * *

The enemy inspected packages addressed to us very carefully. At least once a week they searched the cells, often while we were in the exercise yard. For the women, policewomen went through our clothes and such, while soldiers inspected the rest of the cell and checked to see if a hole had been dug or something was hidden in the mattresses. He always thought of someplace new to look.

Many of us were thinking about escape. A barbed-wire fence stood a few meters away from the block opposite ours— Hamili and Hüseyin wanted to dig a tunnel to the fence, then cut the barbed wire. Someone else had an iron saw smuggled in—they could cut the bars on the windows with it. I got a package that contained some new slippers with heels. The men friends told me to remove the soles, and I found revolver parts inside! I was delighted. But a few parts were still missing. How could I get them? Another package containing slippers would be too conspicuous.

I developed a new escape plan: I'd get out through the hospital. Not the military hospital—I'd make sure I was taken to a civilian hospital. I told [the prison administration] I needed a gynecological treatment and paid for the medical insurance. I told the friends [outside] about my plan and gave them my estimated date. They issued approval. "I'll be outside before you are," I bragged to Hamili and the others, cocksure as I was.

I gave the friends outside the precise date and the time, and I said goodbye to the friends in prison. A pair of soldiers and an officer escorted me to the [civilian] hospital, and since I was a woman, they didn't pay much attention to me. There we encountered a great crowd of people. The soldiers studied the crowd nervously. The officer examined my papers. Everyone was staring at me. I looked around—right now would be a good moment. I told one of the soldiers my handcuffs were tight—could he loosen them a little? In the examination room, they'd be removed entirely. Inconspicuously I tested them to see if I could pull my hand out. *I could!* My heart pounded wildly. I was practically home free.

Surely among the doctors, nurses, or some other personnel, there would be an acquaintance who would help me.

"The doctor isn't here," the officer told me. "How about seeing a different one?" I agreed, "Yes, please find out if there's another doctor I can see." The escape time that I'd given the friends arrived, but the friends were nowhere to be seen. Had something gone wrong? Much to my relief, the officer said, "There's a private doctor downtown. We can go there to his office." Downtown! A lot was always going on there, and I knew my way around. Dr. Aysel Dağdevirin's office was right next to the stop for the communal taxis going to Hozat. If no one from the party came to get me, I could try a taxi or just vanish into the crowd. Maybe I'd even find the friends there. One idea after another raced through my mind.

We drove downtown in a jeep. As we stepped out, some men sitting in a coffee house stared at us. Their faces looked familiar. The officer muttered nervously, "Where are we?" and called over two nearby military police. We climbed the stairway. The doctor's waiting room was full, and the receptionist said, "You'll have to wait." The officer got even edgier. People came and went from the office. A young man glanced at me as he left the waiting room. *Now it'll happen*, I thought.

After a few minutes more, I was examined. I asked the female doctor to write that I had to come back and be checked again. "The soldiers don't understand anything," I said. Smiling, she agreed and wrote a prescription for me. I really was sick, which made the whole thing more credible. Then we left the office.

As we went down the stairs, I slid one hand from the cuffs and covered it with the other so no one would notice. There was a crowd in front of the door, and the officer ordered them to disperse. The jeep drove right up to the door, with military police still inside. If I ran for it, they'd catch me. So I gave up my plan.

I was distraught. Where were the friends? I looked around, but the soldiers were pushing me into the car, and we drove off. Then through the car window, I saw Bilge and two other friends rushing toward the doctor's office. Bilge's skin was very bright, and her cheeks were flushed. I wanted to shout to her but contained myself. The sight of them blackened my mood even further. I was desolate.

Back in prison, everyone eyed me curiously. Hamili's look spoke volumes. Later I explained, through the crack in the door, what had happened. The friends tried to comfort me: "Ah, what bad luck. Okay, next time it'll work. Don't be sad."

Later I learned that the friends had reached the hospital at the right time, but they'd been delayed getting to downtown. By the time they arrived, I was gone. This failed escape attempt depressed me no end.

Other plans misfired as well. The missing revolver parts never arrived. We repeated our request that the party punish Şahin. By now we'd been waiting almost six months for an official decision. And then the attack on Hasan Aydın so frightened Şahin, he was transferred to a nearby military prison for his safety.

The first exile   The administration was sending some prisoners back to interrogation, and once there, they were interrogated along with or before the newly arrested arrivals. We had to take action against this outrage. What form should our action take? Various groups offered suggestions, and some supported our ideas. We wrote a joint petition against it, and we protested by blocking off the cells, so that when the soldiers came to take the prisoner to interrogation, they would have to use force to remove us first.

We prepared for a [hunger strike] and wrote a text for it that we shared with the other [political] groups. Our main demands were that prisoners were not taken back to interrogation, that our trial begin as soon as possible, and that we be given the materials necessary to prepare for our trial and mount a defense. We also demanded permission to receive the consumer goods and books that our visitors brought us.

For our own purposes, we wrote a text about prison itself: about what it meant to be there, the enemy's goals, how revolutionaries must resist there, and the goals of our own prison policy. To avoid discovery, we kept only the one copy, which we took turns reading. My turn came last, on bathing day. My cellmates Sevin, Atiye, Elif, and I were to go to the bath together. Before we left the cell, I hid the text in the radio's battery compartment, which had never been inspected in previous searches. As we were leaving, the men friends, Hüseyin and others, asked me were the text was, and I told them. We then went to the bath.

On the way back, Sevim and I stopped a little while in the yard, while Atiye and Elif went on ahead. When I got back to the cell, the text wasn't there. Strange. This text was the only thing missing from the cell. The previous day, Atiye had been taken to court and had spent a long time in the administrative section. Had she betrayed something? Or Elif? Who else could it have been? Or had someone overheard me telling Hüseyin where the hiding place was? It was puzzling. The men friends had no idea. I suspected Atiye.

But now the text was in the enemy's hands. That meant we had to start the hunger strike right away, before he could do anything to obstruct it. We hadn't yet decided how long the strike would last. I suggested a week, others wanted a few days. We agreed on five and kept that limit to ourselves—in our petition to the administration, we'd said the strike would be open-ended, that we'd continue it until our demands were met.

Once again we started the action on a visiting day. We told the first group of visitors that we were going on a hunger strike and why, then refused any further visits. At intervals, we chanted slogans so our relatives outside could hear.

We negotiated with the prison administration through our representatives and those of the other various groups. The administration always told the reps,

> The PKK-ers are whipping you up because they want to control you. And you're falling for it! No one's oppressing you here, everything's fine. They want to stir up discontent and send a message to the outside. We know who's behind it.

And they said they had proof.

On the fifth day, the administration met our demands, and we ended the hunger strike. The next day I was called to the administration. Ali, representing our block, accompanied me, and we were taken to the office of the prison director, Major Ali Duman. A captain and two other officers were present. "By order of the commander," Duman said to me, "you're being transferred to a civilian prison."

I was astonished. "Why? What for? We're a group here, and our trial is supposed to start soon. What's the reason?"

"That's not our concern," the major said. "We're just carrying out the order."

I was furious. "Oh really?" I shouted. "You can't claim there's a space problem for women—there are other women here. I want to know the reason right now. And I demand to see the written order. Until that happens, I refuse to take one step from here.

"Besides, in civilian prisons, the fascists attack people like me. They stab someone in those places every day—including many of our friends. Why am I to go to such a place—so the fascists can attack me? One of our friends was killed just a little while ago. Dozens have been injured. Isn't that enough?" They were clearly sending me into exile because they saw me as the ringleader.

"Don't make trouble, or we'll drag you out of here," they threatened.

"Oh yeah? Sure, who'd expect anything else from you. But I'm not going."

Then Ali Duman burst out, "First you stir up discontent in the prison, then you refuse to leave! You just want to cause trouble, to provoke the other prisoners! You know men react a certain way when a woman is handled roughly. We've found your writings—we know your methods." Drops of spittle flew out of his mouth.

"What writings?" I shouted. "Oh, what amateurs you are! Here everyone has their own will. There's no single person deciding things. If you think sending me away will make a difference, you're seriously mistaken."

Our confrontation continued in this vein. There was no written order, they explained. "Oh, really," I said. The major made a phone call and told someone I wanted to see a written order. I couldn't hear the answer, but afterward he said more mildly, "Look, this is above my authority. Don't cause any trouble."

"I'm going to my people now," I said. "All my stuff is downstairs." They agreed. They could just have packed me off then and there, but in the cellblock I could ask the friends what they thought. Maybe if they refused to let me go, the decision could be altered. At first, the friends didn't want to let me go, but since the enemy could use my very presence as an excuse to attack, I had to. The other [political] groups agreed. But the friends too worried that fascists had the civilian prison under tight control—the personnel there were all fascist cadres.

I scooped up my things, and as I departed, I swallowed hard. "Take care," the friends said. "We'll get you lawyers and your family. We'll get you out of there." Suddenly I felt very alone. We'd been in prison, but at least we'd been together. Okay then, that was part of the struggle. I had to be strong. What was beautiful was to keep on living and fighting in defiance of the enemy. I balled my fists and swore that if they considered me so dangerous, then I'd just have to cause them a whole lot more trouble.

A car pulled up in front of the military building. The officer in charge got out and then came back with some papers. We drove to the civilian prison. I had to wait in the car for half an hour. Finally, I told a soldier to go get someone responsible. After a long time, he came back and said, "The commander is coming right away." When he finally arrived, I asked why it had taken so long. "I want out of this car, I don't like it here. And I've got to use the toilet. What, are they preparing a welcoming ceremony for me?"

"Lady, I can't do anything about that," he answered. "The director and the prosecutor are inside. They'll come out and get you. I don't know why it's taking so long."

Another half hour passed. When they finally let me out, soldiers were lined up by the door. Behind them were people in civilian clothes who looked like prisoners. I recognized a few of them right away—fascists. Why were they there?

Surrounded by soldiers, I was brought into the director's office. He locked the door from the inside. Some women guards were in the room too. He went to his table and rifled through some papers. "Look, I don't take sides," he said. "I just do my job. You're angry that you had to wait, but have you ever seen a director lock his door from the inside? I have to do that to ensure your safety. This paper says I'm supposed to protect the prisoner." A murder was committed almost every day in these prisons, and the fascists were in control of this one. And this director intended to protect me by locking the door!

Nervously he turned to the window and sucked on his cigarette. "It's better if you stay away from the exercise yard."

"Why?"

"I'm the director here, and if prisoners can come into my office ..."

It was clear now. Okay, the man had good intentions. After a while I was taken to the women's block, surrounded by soldiers. I wasn't wrong—a "welcoming ceremony" had been prepared for me. The fascists called the shots here.

Despite the director's warning, I did go to the yard. The guards and the other prisoners hung blankets from the window as a screen, but the fascists insulted and threatened me from the window anyway.

I had to take the situation seriously. My cell door wasn't very secure, and the women guards were under the influence of the fascists. One night I saw a women guard creep out of a cell wearing a nightshirt. I followed her—she didn't go to the toilet. The door to the yard wasn't locked. I opened it a crack and could see through the guardroom window that she was in there in a hideous position. The man she was with was a fascist arrestee. The other women had told me how women here were used.

The next day I asked this guard, in the presence of others: "Where were you last night?"

"I was sleeping," she answered in surprise. "I'm a guard, I can come and go as I wish."

"No, you're no guard," I shot back. "You're a woman who sells herself to fascist prisoners. Are you going to open this door tomorrow and let these dogs into my cell? You're not going to stay overnight in the women's block anymore. In every prison, guards have their own rooms. I don't trust you."

Encouraged by my words, the other women pointed out which women were selling themselves. The next day an inspection took place. The director used it as an excuse to talk to me. How was it going? he asked. I said I wanted books. And I said in a loud voice that the women guards weren't to be trusted: "If they open the door at night and meet with the fascists, then they're also in a position to let the fascists into the cells."

Helplessly, he answered, "What am I supposed to do? The best thing would be to hand in my resignation." What a miserable guy.

I didn't stay there long. The director and the prosecutor, concerned about my safety, put in a request that I be transferred. Almost every night murders were committed. One night two people were stabbed—I knew one of them. Two days after my arrival, I talked to [the lawyer] Hüseyin Yıldırım though the director's window. He said he'd been hit at the gate.

Aytekin's mother came to visit, and to avoid arousing suspicion, she announced herself as the visitor of another prisoner. It was the first time I'd seen her since her son's death. She cried during the whole visit and could barely speak, but she managed to tell me that before he died, Aytekin had said to her, "You're Sakine's mother too. Just as you do for me, you must take care of her." She wanted to fulfill her son's wish despite the circumstances. But it was too dangerous for her here, so I asked her not to visit me often. It would be the last time we saw each other in Elazığ.

The prison director came to our cell window to talk to me. Placing his hands around his mouth, he whispered, "Get ready—you're going to be transferred. They've granted our request. You're going to Malatya."

I was to be exiled again! At this rate, I'd be touring all the prisons. Annoyed, I shot back, "Is that the solution? People are killed here every day, and the same dogs are in Malatya."

"I can't take responsibility. I'm told they want to kill you." Yes, that director was really miserable.

Ten minutes later, once again escorted by soldiers, I was taken outside. It was nerve-wracking, but I was proud of myself. The enemy had revealed his own powerlessness. He didn't know what to do with me. Every sign of powerlessness or aggression on the part of the enemy bolstered my resistance and gave me strength. How beautiful it was to cause problems for the enemy! It helped to be infused with the spirit of the PKK. One individual alone is weak and has only limited efficacy. One person alone can't change anything. But those who work with others, are open to reality, and are true to themselves can endure even isolation.

No lack of confrontations   I always associated Malatya with fight songs that memorialized [THKO founders] Sinan Cemgil and Kadir Manga [who were killed by soldiers in 1971]. I remembered that when the Left and Right were clashing at the Teachers School in Akçadağ, the Turan Emeksiz gymnasium had been moved to Malatya.[6] And now the prison! My associations with Malatya were unforgettable.

A few days before my transfer [from the fascist-run civilian prison], a new woman detainee arrived from Malatya-Doğansehir. She had been arrested for supporting the PKK. I left my things behind for her, since she had no visitors, and no one had shown any concern for her. In the commotion before my departure, I hardly had a chance to speak to her but managed to warn her, "Get yourself transferred to the military prison. Tell your lawyer when he comes." The civilian prisons were horrible, especially for women.

When we reached Malatya, it was evening but still light. Once again they made me wait in the vehicle for a long time. I felt sick after the drive—car travel always makes me ill. I wanted to get out, but the soldiers refused. Suddenly I saw movement at the control point, at the entrance to the grounds. Guards were running around. "What's going on?" I demanded.

The soldiers said they didn't know, and one of them asked a guard, who said, "It's a brawl between rightists and leftists. The rightists attacked the leftists." So I was right! These violent clashes followed me everywhere! But I was glad there were leftist groups here. On the other hand, there were also aggressive fascists. What they failed to accomplish on the outside, they tried to achieve in prisons. And look, they would attack in several prisons almost at the same time. That couldn't have happened without someone ordering it.

After a while I was called in. The admission formalities were brief. The prison seemed overfilled, and I could hear voices coming from the cellblock. A woman guard was summoned, Mother Hatice. "This woman is a political," they told her. "Inspect her things inside—there's too much happening out here." That was good, since I was tired and feeling ill.

We entered the women's block. The wooden door was full of holes, presumably so the prisoners could peer outside. The block gave the impression of neglect, like an old bathroom. The wooden pillars in the sleeping room were blackened and rotten. Spiderwebs hung everywhere. Wooden bunk beds took up the length of the walls, with only a narrow path between them. Bags and bundles were hanging everywhere, and wet laundry, and clothes stuffed into pillowcases. The yard was small.

At the wooden door stood a vivacious young woman, Ayşe. She wore makeup and was carefully dressed. From time to time she glanced through the holes in the door. "Mother Hatice, where did she come from?" she whispered to the guard. All the young women called the guard "Mother Hatice."

A middle-aged woman wearing a *salvar* [traditional Kurdish pants] hugged and kissed me and said very warmly, in a Malatyan accent, "My revolutionary daughter, I welcome you. Mother Zeynep will take care of you!" Coincidentally, she had the same name as my mother. "I have two mothers called Zeynep," I said. Everyone laughed.

The other prisoners came over to look at me curiously. They had lots of questions, so I explained in one breath who I was, what organization I belonged to, and what I had been through recently. They were impressed and kept asking questions.

We talked for days, or months actually. Every woman's story was like a novel. There were adulteries. Young women raped by their brothers, fathers, or other relatives. Mothers locked up for theft. Women who killed their husbands because they were "betrayed." Fights over property.

A beautiful woman with clear skin came over to me, wearing a *salvar* and carrying some knitting. Her name was Güzel Dağdeviren, and she was from Doğansehirli. She extended her hand, saying, "You're very welcome here."

She told me she'd been here over ten years, which astonished me since she seemed so vibrant and cheerful—clearly her connection to life hadn't been severed. With the kind of patience that testifies to much life experience, she told me about the many different prisons she'd seen, the "politicals" she'd got to know, the guards she'd fought with, and the dirty businesses they'd tried to draw her into. We would become good friends.

Hatice was an Alevi and a widow. Her children were in school and were involved "with politics." They lived in Cavusoğlu, a neighborhood where many leftists lived, so it was called the "Communist quarter." It impressed her that I was Alevi and had ties to a particular political orientation. She showed respect and kept asking if I needed anything. She brought me the daily newspapers promptly.

A second guard, Mother Zöhre, was somewhat older and more withdrawn. She tended toward the right politically, I was told, but wasn't too conservative. Güzel told me all about the guards, the other prison personnel, and the prisoners, so I quickly got an overview of the situation. Right away I got messages from the other blocks, asking if I needed anything. People from other [political] groups also showed this kind of concern for me, which was heartening. One message came from [PKK] friends—during a shift change, they'd given it to a guard, who passed it to me. These friends were from Akçadağ and Yeşilyurt.

[The friend] Fuat Çavgun had been transferred here from another prison. I was really lucky. I got to know Fuat Çavgun here. He had been arrested in Urfa and was the brother of Halil Çavgun, who had been working with the resistance in Hilvan. Halil was killed, a year after Haki [Karer]'s murder, by the Süleyman clan. Halil's and other friends' revolutionary work in Hilvan and Siverek was a model of the people of a region taking their fate into their own hands. And in Hilvan, women formed the front line of the armed demonstrations.

The enemy wanted to make life hard for me by shipping me around from one prison to another, but I was enjoying the tour. I met new people and relished the new questions they raised. It was never boring.

I soon made contact with the party outside. It was a special joy to receive messages from them. Delil Doğan was now in charge of [the party in] Malatya. It had always been an important area—first Aytekin, then Bozo Süleyman had been here. Presumably they'd returned after the arrests in Elazığ.

The prospects for a revolutionary uprising were usually better in places where the fascists were organized. Changes in large social structures occur only slowly, but once the foundations are laid, organized work can proceed quickly. And the fact that the enemy thought he had just destroyed everything made the work all the more gratifying. A few friends had spent time [at leftist training camps] in Palestine. Delil was one of them. Weapons training had by now become indispensable, since the enemy attacked directly.

Books I'd requested arrived, as did many flyers. Nor did Hüseyin Yıldırım abandon me. He had taken on cases in Ankara and Kayseri, but while traveling there, he always stopped to see me and ask if I needed anything. He gave me a mattress and, at every visit, some money. Of course, my father reimbursed him for his expenses. I didn't know what he charged, but some lawyers' fees were exorbitant. The repression had become a good source of income for them.

I didn't trust Hüseyin Yıldırım any more than I ever had. He always wanted to know if I'd had contact with the outside—he drove me crazy with that. "No, I have no connections," I said. "But how can that be?" he asked. "The friends wouldn't leave you in the lurch!" He complained several times that he had something to share with the friends but couldn't find them.

One day he arrived very excited and out of breath: "The fascists shot at me! I barely escaped!" He whirled around dramatically, as if they were still behind him. At that time Malatya was in a state of chaos because of an assassination attempt on the mayor, Hamido, but that wouldn't have made Hüseyin Yıldırım a target of attack. Why did he always tell stories that put himself in the limelight? Was he trying to gain my confidence? No, that couldn't be it. He was just a liar, and afraid of being in the crosshairs.

"Did Şahin say something important about you?" he asked me. "He can retract it." Sometimes he claimed, "It looks good for you and Mazlum [Doğan]. If you weren't making a political defense, you'd be free now. You'd be outside. I've told Mazlum the same thing. Some of the others confessed to taking part in actions, even though there are no concrete statements about them. But that's not the case with you—you're only charged with making party propaganda. Since you've already served some time, you could be released immediately with the minimum penalty."

I refused even to discuss it. "We've made our decision. Of course I'll defend myself politically. It's wrong to talk about it as if it were some kind of tactic."

Another time he read me a letter to Mazlum that was supposedly written by his sister, but she obviously wasn't the writer, because all it did was repeat suggestions made by Hüseyin Yıldırım himself! That man was a pest. He persuaded prisoners' families to put pressure on us, since of course our families wanted only that we get out of prison as soon as possible. He pretended to be acting out of sympathy for me. When he said, "You'd be outside now," it was pure hypocrisy. He was associated with Kawa, but that didn't really explain his behavior, since Kawa couldn't have cared less if we made a political defense and then had to sweat it out longer in prison. So in whose interests was he acting? "You're in the enemy's hands, you have to bend," he'd say, expressing a thoroughly Kemalist logic, the logic of a coward. He was absolutely terrified, but why? I was glad I could see through his lies, since it confirmed my doubts about him.

I wrote to the men friends [I'd been with] in the Elazığ prison, hinting at my attitude toward Hüseyin Yıldırım. They wrote back. They hadn't escaped yet. They had no news about Şahin—we were still waiting for him to be punished.

Ali was faltering and threatening to take others down with him. Hamili, in an intense letter, admitted that I'd been right about him. "If I'd gone with Ali," he wrote, "everything would've been much worse." Good—it was important to notice when someone was gravitating toward betrayal. Hamili understood that now and was fortified against it. I told him what I thought. This correspondence did me good.

* * *

The year [since our arrest] had seen many important developments in Turkey.

Fahri Korutürk was president [of the Turkish Republic], but the government and parliament existed only for appearances' sake—it was the military that actually governed.

The workers' and students' movements were both getting stronger. Hardly a day passed now without demonstrations and violent clashes. In the city of Fatsa, revolutionary people's communes were founded. The revolutionary movement took over the municipal administration, and people chose their own representatives.[7] In retrospect, in its degree of organization and its readiness to fight, Fatsa resembled Hilvan and Siverek.

There had been factory occupations in Izmir-Taris, and they were echoed in many other places. (I'd applied for a job in Taris once, but they'd considered me suspicious, so they didn't hire me.) Several leftist groups had been organized there; Taris also had a fascist organization.

What was the enemy planning? After the Maraş pogrom, he had declared this state of emergency and carried out mass arrests. But in Hilvan, Siverek, Batman, Mardin, and elsewhere, we were fighting, and the people stood behind us. In Hilvan a people's council was elected. The former mayor asked the people for forgiveness. Women were elected to the council. We targeted the enemy's fascist strongpoints within Kurdistan with revolutionary violence. The media reported much about the "Kozik war" [the conflict between the PKK and the Bucak clan in Siverek].

Now we heard constant denunciations of groups that sought to violate "the indivisible unity of the fatherland and the nation," and declamations against "anarchy and separatism." The newspapers and TV babbled constant propaganda about national unity: "The leaders of the separatist terrorists must be crushed, while they're still few." The crackdown in Siverek, Batman, and elsewhere was becoming more severe. Even the smallest development in Kurdistan was suppressed bloodily. In Batman, Edip Solmaz, a Kurdish patriot, had been elected mayor [in 1979], but the enemy murdered him. In Siverek, funerals turned into a political demonstrations. The enemy fired weapons into the crowd, killing people.

The government extended the state of emergency to ever more provinces of Kurdistan, including Malatya. State operations [against leftist groups] continued, and there were many more arrests. I heard that Hayri [Durmuş] and [Kemal] Pir had been arrested. What would happen? The commander of the state of emergency and the general staff gave one explanation after another.

But the PKK would not be easily demolished. We were evolving into a political force, and the arrest wave couldn't put a stop to it. The Kurdish freedom movement was expanding so rapidly. After the arrests of [Kemal] Pir and others, the PKK made plans that, if implemented, would pose a great danger to the state. The enemy would have to respond comprehensively. The documents that he had confiscated from us frightened him: they were about founding a military council and carrying out a revolution. We would initiate the guerrilla struggle in Kurdistan, which would speed up revolutionary developments in Turkey. We discussed and analyzed these events—after all, the revolution in Turkey was closely tied to ours. We saw that they were driving the enemy to reorganize himself, to avoid the revolution at all costs. We followed and analyzed these events, even though we had access only to very general information and limited contact with the friends outside. We could hardly discern the outlines, but the day seemed to be approaching.

Malatya Prison Six months sped by. Every day in the prison, routine problems arose, gratuitous bickering and squabbling. Meanwhile, I listened patiently as the women described what they'd done to others, how they'd been raped or cheated, and how very young girls had been turned into prostitutes. Their stories showed how this society treated women. I wrote letters and petitions on their behalf. "I'll write a novel about you all," I said. Although the social reality was familiar to me, their individual fates were tragic. My pride and joy in being a revolutionary were all the greater. Many of the women envied me, saying, "I wish I were political."

Over time their squabbling diminished, as the prison administration noticed, impressed: "It's good that Sakine came. We were always busy managing conflicts among the women prisoners, but now it's much better."

It was a civilian prison, even though political prisoners were also detained there. Visitors who traveled a long distance were allowed to visit in the mornings as well as the afternoons. The guards on duty were in charge of deciding whether prisoners could touch their visitors in greeting. Usually they could. Sometimes we could even offer our visitors food or tea. Atiye was released [from the other prison], and now she came to visit, saying she'd been with friends in Malatya. I wasn't thrilled, especially after what Hüseyin Yıldırım had said about her.

But many people came to visit me—they'd announce themselves as visiting the men friends, then come over to me. Prisoners who lived in Malatya sent their visitors over to me. Fevzi Kara, arrested on charges of shooting a fascist, was from Doğansehir [a district in Malatya], and relatives were here in Malatya. They visited him regularly—and me too. I also got visitors from almost every leftist group, and packages bearing the names of their associations or groups. This solidarity was gorgeous.

I shared my gifts with the other prisoners, who were even happier than I was. The guards enjoyed it too—they delivered food to the prison, and it was customary for the prisoners to give them something back. We gave the best parts to them. Sometimes they got so much food they could take it home with them. Sometimes the guards even brought stuff in and offered it to the prisoners. It was almost like a family.

My passion: escape! All the while I concentrated on one thing: escape! I'd failed before, but this time I wanted to pull it off. Opportunities had slipped through my fingers. I'd have to try it again without expecting help from outside.

The circumstances here weren't so bad. The women's ward was to the left of the prison entrance. On the upper story was the director's apartment, reached by steps that ran above the yard. The external wall was high and topped with barbed wire, but that could be overcome. At the gate and on each side of the wall was a guard post. The soldiers walked back and forth. A road ran directly in front of the prison. I'd have to wait for the right moment. If a lot was going on out there, I could make a dash for the street and disappear.

The other possibility was, again, the hospital. I could be taken there for inpatient treatment, then escape. My doctor had prescribed medications for me, saying that if my condition didn't improve, "you'll have to be treated awhile in the hospital." In this prison they weren't suspicious of me yet. Most important, the women guards liked me, as did the prisoners.

But I had a problem: I didn't know Malatya at all. It was a big city. I'd have to rely on the friends outside. I wrote a message to the party outside with my proposal, sure that they would accept it. My letter was forwarded, I learned, and I was told I shouldn't worry. But I heard nothing for a long time.

Later I found out that Mazlum Doğan had also been planning an escape at the same time. [On November 27, 1979, he] had been arrested, along with Aysel [Çürükkaya] and Yıldırım [Merkit], in a car while driving to Urfa, with papers that identified him as İbrahim Şenol. His true identity wasn't revealed at first, but there was a real danger that in prison someone would expose him. The enemy liked to smuggle agents, alleged revolutionaries, into prisons just for this purpose. If Mazlum were to run into Şahin, for example, Şahin would identify him right away. So he had to get out as soon as possible, and my escape was delayed so as not to endanger his. I had to be patient—Comrade Mazlum Doğan's escape was more important.

Mazlum did break out, but he was caught. He'd hidden in a dumpster. Soldiers were standing nearby, so he had to hold still for a long time buried in trash. He'd accomplished the most difficult part, but then the friends who were supposed to pick him up arrived late.

What had gone wrong? Didn't the friends on the outside realize how hard it was for a person in prison to find the right opportunity? This action really had to succeed, at any cost. I'm sure they made plenty of excuses, but what good were they? Mazlum was back in prison, and a fine opportunity had been squandered. And in the process, his true identity had been exposed. Thereafter Mazlum admitted he was a party member and defended its goals.

All day every day, I fixated on escape. One day I saw Necmiye in the bathroom, watching her friend in the men's block through a stovepipe hole. Necmiye, who came from Malatya, had killed her husband and her friend; she'd been in prison for five years and faced possible life imprisonment. From her I learned that you could look through the hole and see the exercise yard and the kitchen of the men prisoners. This toilet was broken and wasn't used. The wall was rotten and thin—it'd be easy to widen the hole.

I'd heard that the men friends were planning to escape too—Fuat Çavgun and others. In a secret message, I asked him if he and the others used the yard, the one visible from the toilet, for their exercise. I wrote my message in a crossword puzzle in a newspaper and sent it to them. We'd done that before without anyone noticing. I handed the newspaper to a guard, who then delivered it personally. He'd chat with the men friends, who often asked how I was doing. This display of concern impressed the guards, who wanted to show that they were treating me well.

I finally got an answer to my message: *yes.* They'd already guessed I was planning an escape. Probably the friends outside had suggested such a thing during a visit. So Fuat's hopes rose, and he wanted me to keep working on it.

Maybe I could break out with them. I began to think about a group escape. The group shouldn't be more than three or four. I got hold of a spray that could knock people out. At the moment of escape, I'd spray it in the cell. If it was nighttime, that would be no problem. We'd definitely need a weapon, since things could get tricky at the exit. If necessary, we could take a guard hostage. As for the soldiers at the exit, it wouldn't be hard to put them out of action. Then if a car was waiting for us, we could be long gone in just a few minutes.

This plan seemed doable. I ruminated about it, almost like an obsession. I never thought about legal ways to get out of prison. Why was that? Did I have a desire for adventure? Or is it just inherent to imprisonment that everyone dreams of escape? In my view, any revolutionary in prison must have escape as a goal. For revolutionaries, every dungeon is too small.

I trusted my fellow prisoner Güzel. Without letting her in on anything, I asked her about the prison layout and security. She gave me information about the surrounding neighborhoods. She was an intelligent woman—she realized I was asking for a reason. *Why didn't you ever try to escape?* I asked her. She told me she was already on half-day release.

> And where am I supposed to go? They know where my father's house is. My husband is dead. His family is hostile to me. But you have many friends who'll help. If I were like you, I'd have escaped long ago.

She was right about that. She also knew Fevzi's family, which strengthened my confidence in her. Still, I was cautious.

I sent the [party] outside a message with the new plan and the use of a revolver. They approved it. I sent Fuat and the others a few questions along with the message that the party outside should send friends to come [and pick us up]. Fuat and his friends got impatient. "Let's get going, before someone gets transferred or something else happens," they wrote. We could have made more plans, but it was more realistic to finally carry out the best plan instead of always making new ones.

Pistols were smuggled in inside two boxes of chocolate. Fevzi's mother carried one of the boxes, and a 9-year-old child held the other. Fevzi's mother hugged me, gave me the boxes, and whispered in my ear, "There's something inside." Then she said, "A friend of yours gave me these. He'll probably come to see you too. At the moment he's in the men's block."

Usually when visitors brought little gifts, the guards took them straight to the men's block without inspecting them. Hatice was more or less leftist. She was on duty that day. Wanting to be helpful, she offered to take the boxes. I gratefully declined, and so as not to arouse her suspicions, I carefully opened one box and offered her a piece of chocolate from the top layer. [Grandmother] Ayşe said, "Give them to me—I'll take them in for you." I said, "No, let them be." She was savvy—the weight of the packages would have told her they contained more than chocolate.

After Fevzi's mother left, another visitor had arrived for me. Hatice opened the door, and he and I shook hands. "I see you don't recognize me," he said. "I've known who you are for a long time. We forwarded your message, and we're still awaiting an answer.

"Delil [Doğan] was here [in charge of Malatya], but he's gone now. He's been sent to Karakoçan [a district in Elazığ province]." He said he and Delil hadn't agreed on certain things, and he complained that Delil was "sectarian."

It irritated me that [this party man] had said so much right away: "You should have worked it out between yourselves. It makes no sense to talk about it now."

He changed the subject. "Something's gone wrong. In the men's section there's a friend who's waiting for an answer [to his message about the revolver]. We suspect that a message has been intercepted. That'd be awful, since it mentioned the revolver and its destination."

My head was spinning. "What? What message? How could the revolver have been mentioned? And it was intercepted—where?" He stayed calm, but I was distraught. "If that's true, then I'll call the woman back and give her back the boxes. I'll tell her we don't need that much, and she should take them to the men friends."

Clearly the group escape plan had been compromised, but I would stick to my own. The more people got involved, the greater the risks anyway. I asked him to draw a map of Malatya and send it to me.

Before he left, he asked if I recognized him. "I'm Haydar Eşiyok from Karakoçan. I know you from the Teachers School. I want to tell you more, but there's no more time now. I'll write to you." Then he left. Later, I remembered who Haydar Eşiyok was. He'd been in prison and was beaten on the head. I'd heard that the effects of this injury made him a problem.

After a while Fevzi's mother returned, and I gave her the boxes. "If you don't find anyone, hide them in the village," I said.

She was worried: "Please don't start such dangerous affairs with us. Our families have been through so much already."

I was sorry. The whole thing had gone wrong.

On the next visiting day, a young woman brought me two letters in the same handwriting [from Haydar Eşiyok]. One began with "Comrade," the other with "Sakine." In the first, [official] letter, he wrote: "Something went wrong, so I had to leave quickly. With Fuat

85

and the others, there'll be nothing for now. Your suggestion has been answered: positive." A little farther on, he said the "first region" had to settle something urgently, so the friends wouldn't arrive for a while. I should make preparations, and the correspondence should continue. Finally, he said the affair would surely succeed.

I was delighted—this official message showed that the outside was taking my escape plan seriously. But what matter did the "first region" have to settle so urgently? I racked my brains wondering.

Then I read the second letter: "Sakine, I was so happy to see you again, even in prison." He lavished much praise and assured me he felt great respect for me. He'd been interested in me since we first met, he said, and had never forgotten me. Now he wrote about his magnificent love for revolutionaries and other nonsense.

As I read this letter, I fumed. *How dare he? Is he crazy?* Well, maybe mental illness could explain it. My god, and this friend was in charge of the region!

I wrote a short reply asking him to show the necessary seriousness and to respect the intentions of my letter.

But after I sent it, I couldn't stop thinking about it. Maybe he wasn't really a comrade. What game was being played here? He'd said he was Haydar Eşiyok, but I hadn't recognized him. Yes, I'd heard the name before, but I didn't recall this face. The escape plan had fallen through! I hadn't even been able to touch the revolver. I couldn't figure out the purpose of this letter. I was almost convinced it was a trap.

Then [in another letter] Haydar wrote that I must have something against men in general, because of my failed marriage. I'd hurt his feelings, he said. He'd known me for years and always been impressed by my revolutionary commitment, which inspired him. My failure to recognize him had upset him. It went on in this manner. Clearly I'd injured his feudal pride. He was a total pest who always thought he was right.

It was just too strange. All those guys who supposedly loved me so passionately tended to idolize me. They hardly dared love me, they said, because of my goddess-like nature. But with their clumsy, unbounded, disrespectful, and cheap declarations of love, they essentially smashed an idol that they'd created. Their emotional world contained a drive to dominate others. Where did their woolly feelings begin, where did they end, what were they based on, and what were they good for? On the one hand, these men were secretive, egoistical, and individualistic; on the other, they were crude, exuberant, and absolute. At any moment their supposed love could flip over into a desire for revenge.

Did Haydar even know me? Even if what he'd written was honest, he had to be aware of my current circumstances, what I was trying to do, and why. Only an idiot could fail to understand that.

I tried to calm myself. I wouldn't stoop to his level. Escape was the only thing I cared about. How could I get him to understand that? Now that Delil was in Karakoçan, this guy was the only [party] leader in Malatya.

Finally I wrote back:

> I don't want to hurt your feelings, please don't misunderstand me. But I've sent you an important proposal, and you should give it top priority. I don't hate men. Of course my experiences have left scars, but my behavior isn't the result of insecurity. In your letter, you used a few expressions that you should be careful about. I'm not a woman who dresses up and sells her feelings. If my revolutionary attitude really impresses you, then you shouldn't cheapen it this way. If I ever get out of here, we can talk about it, but I'm looking for [escape] routes now. Hüseyin Yıldırım says I might be transferred to Diyarbakir soon. If you delay, I'll have to find another way out of here.

I was trying to get him to take my escape plans more seriously, yet convey that I wasn't beholden to him.

Then something extraordinary happened: while I was painting the cell, I found a set of keys. I tested them, one at a time—*and one of them actually opened the door.* I was doing handstands in excitement.

Escape from Malatya Given Haydar's attitude, I had no great expectations [of getting help from the party outside for my own escape]. I asked only for an address where I could go if I managed to slip out, since I didn't know Malatya. Strangely, I was told to go to a coffee house in Seyranbağları.

Quietly I gleaned information from my fellow prisoners. I memorized the addresses of short-term prisoners who'd been released. Presumably I'd be looked for there first, but they could still be useful. The Cavusoğlu neighborhood was full of Alevis and leftists. Güzel was well known throughout the city. If I revealed my plan to her, she'd help me, but I held back because secrecy was a principle for me. Finally I confided in her. She asked almost no questions and offered to give me her ID.

Hüseyin Yıldırım showed up with a new story: he'd got hold of the secret file of Özden Mızrak [of the HK].

The HK is saying I should give it to no one and threatening me. I've told them all that if I give it to anyone, it'll be to the PKK, but I can't find anyone to hand it over to. If I could find Ali Haydar, I'd give it to him.

I asked him to give it to me. He said he didn't carry it around with him, which made sense, but I was highly skeptical. "So where's the file now? How did you get it?" "I know a good prosecutor. It's a very important file, it's got to stay secret." He rattled on like this. I'd had enough. I wrote a message to the party leadership, reporting my observations and suspicions. I'd already informed Haydar, and the friends in Elazığ knew too, even if they hadn't taken my ideas seriously.

Meanwhile Hüseyin Yıldırım said we'd be transferred in August, which was coming soon, so I told the friends outside that I wanted to take the next good opportunity to escape. I redoubled my planning.

Now I could unlock the door from inside, but some of the prisoners slept in the yard, which could wreck everything. Roma women liked to sleep out there with their children. The yard was small—there was only about one step between the door and their mattresses. In the cells there was no fixed sleep time. Many prisoners stayed up late talking, while others wandered around sleepless, and some, to beat the heat, got up to run cold water over their hands and feet. A few times I stayed up all night to figure out the best time for an escape. Only ten meters lay between the outside door and the control point. The guards' room was right next to the door, and next to it was a waiting room with a large window. Guards slept in both. When it was hot, they left the windows and doors open.

I watched the guards' behavior. They took different shifts every week, which was very convenient for me. They often left the prison to go shopping for the women prisoners. They seemed ready to help. Sometimes they went out 20 times a day to pick things up. Zöhre's mother, who lived near the prison, was ill. Zöhre fixed meals for her in the prison and took them over to her. Sometimes she went there in the middle of the night. The prison was like her second home.

The outer gate at the control point consisted of an iron grille and had two wings. The soldiers walked back and forth between them, sometimes stopping at the control point. Across the busy street from the prison was a Tekel plant [a tobacco and alcoholic beverage company], and during the shift changes, when there was a lot of commotion, the soldiers liked to watch the young female workers. The guards worked in two shifts. The best time for an escape would be the factory's nighttime shift change.

I observed it and memorized the time. But one or two prisoners were always still awake then. I confided in Güzel. "You shouldn't hurry," she said. "Let's figure out a place outside where you can go. I'll help you. We'll do it soon." I told her I was supposed to be transferred on August 20 and couldn't wait any longer. If only that cursed bastard hadn't told me the date, I'd have been more patient.

Güzel gave me her ID. We didn't look anything alike, but that wouldn't matter in the darkness. Women's IDs usually weren't inspected anyway. I had some pamphlets, brochures like "Capitulation Leads to Treachery, Resistance to Victory," "Ideology and Politics," "The Maraş Pogrom," and "Serxwebûn." I sent them over to Fuat and the men friends, so I'd have nothing written on me.

"Wait for me outside in a suitable place for a few nights," I wrote to the friends outside. "We'll only need a car."

Lately, Zöhre had been arguing with the chief guard—they didn't see eye to eye. Incredibly, she'd tell us about such things right away, and about what was going on outside. She and Hatice liked us, and they told us everything that might be of interest to us.

And the door to the women's ward had those useful holes! Ayşe stood there most of the time. She was from Adana and had worked as a prostitute in a casino. She'd been in prison for more than six years but still looked young and beautiful. Many of the guards were after her, but all the prisoners and personnel knew she had a relationship with one of the guards. Day and night she peered through the holes in the door. She'd given up some other behaviors, but she still couldn't tear herself away from that door. Some of the prisoners noticed I'd been looking though the holes a lot recently. I said I was expecting a visitor, and also my possible transfer to Diyarbakir was being tossed around, so "whenever I hear an engine, I worry they're coming to get me." They believed me.

And Zöhre rarely wore her uniform—she put on the jacket only for official events. The rest of the time she dressed like other women, wearing a skirt, pants, and a black scarf around her head. That was good. And even though there was a guardroom, at night she slept with us in the women's ward, usually dozing off in front of the TV. She'd been doing that for years and saw no danger in it. She left her clothing in the guardroom or hung it on a peg. If it was warm, she put on pajamas or a nightgown.

The night [of August 20, 1980] arrived. It was getting late, and I had to resort to various tricks to get the Roma women to go to sleep, but finally they did. Then I took Zöhre's clothes from the peg and put them on in an empty room. Zöhre was tall and stocky—her clothes were much too large for me. I put on sandals with heels, so I'd be closer to her height. I tied a cloth around my waist to keep the skirt from slipping down. As Zöhre sometimes did, I tied her embroidered headscarf around my head and pulled it low over my forehead, so my face would be in shadow, then wrapped the ends around my neck. Most important, I had to imitate Zöhre's gait, and of course her voice, although since she'd been fighting with the other guards, I could skip words of greeting.

I wanted to swing the keys in my hand the way Zöhre did. I carried a tray with a cut-up melon and vegetables, the way she did. Just as I was about to leave the guardroom, I saw Grandmother Ayşe climbing down from the bunk bed, groaning. Of course, she was going to the toilet right now! I stepped back into the room. The light was off, it was dark. My heart pounded wildly. What if someone happened to come in? What if one of the Roma women woke up?

Grandmother Ayşe finished her toilet ritual with many prayers and returned to her bed. As soon as she lay down, I was off. I couldn't have waited a second longer. I grabbed the key ring and opened the lock. I didn't put the clasp back in but left it hanging—I'd meant to ask Güzel to close it for me. There was a danger that the wind might blow the door open, but I continued because just then I saw the soldier at the gate talking to a guard who'd pulled up on his bike. I didn't want him to come over to me at the door.

I held the tray in one hand and waved the keys back and forth with the other, the way Zöhre did. I was about to slip through the gate when I heard a voice behind me: "Mother Zöhre, Mother Zöhre ..." It was the chief guard. I rattled my keys, muttered something, and went on.

The soldiers outside had heard him, so they didn't check to see if I was really Zöhre. The head guard, still standing by the soldier, teased, "Mother Zöhre's still mad at us." *Perfect!*

My heart raced. I hadn't worn shoes with heels for a long time, so walking was hard, but I did my best to imitate Zöhre's gait. A soldier was walking back and forth along the wall. Suddenly he slowed. I watched him out of the corner of my eye and continued.

Prison walls can be endlessly long.

I made it to the factory, then rushed off in another direction. I careened into a blind alley and whirled around—the side streets were empty. I went back to the main street. I needed a car to get to the address Haydar had given me in Cavusoğlu. Sunrise was only two hours away. I spotted a patrol car and pivoted in another direction. I'd been outside for a quarter hour already. In front of me were a few houses with lights burning. Was this the way to Cavusoğlu? Could I risk knocking on a door in the middle of the night and asking? But it'd be just as risky to wander around without knowing where I was going.

Hesitantly, I knocked at a house where the door was ajar. An older man in pajamas appeared. "Good evening," I said, trying to speak like an old woman, to match the way I looked.

The man seemed surprised. "Yes?" An elderly woman joined him.

"I need to get to Cavusoğlu but got lost in the dark. I've just come from the hospital, where I was taking care of a sick relative. He's a man, so I couldn't sleep there overnight. Now I need to get my relative's house in Cavusoğlu. She's a nurse. She told me how to get there, but I can't find her house."

"What's your name?" they asked.

"Sekine," I said, inexplicably not using a different name. People in Malatya say Sekine instead of Sakine.

While we were talking at the door, I heard sirens in the distance and a loudspeaker blaring announcements. I thanked the couple and trudged off in the direction they'd pointed. The husband called after me, "Sister, why do you want to be alone in the middle of the night? That's not right. Come on in."

When I reached the street, I broke into a run. My escape had already been discovered, and I was still near the prison. I ran to the end of the neighborhood. Beyond lay the main street, which I wanted to avoid. I crept into someone's yard and found a dark corner to think and to change my clothes. I took Zöhre's off and stuffed them into the cloth I used as a bag.

My initial excitement gave way to joy and confidence. The hardest part was behind me! Now I just had to get to safety. I was furious that

Haydar had only given me an address instead of a reasonable map. And I'd asked the friends to wait outside for me for a few nights—they hadn't done that either. Okay, I'd see them soon and hold them accountable.

From the yard, I looked over at the house. Someone inside coughed—elderly people must live here. Should I knock on their door and ask for help? Lights were on in some nearby houses. This neighborhood was known to be leftist. Would I get help if I said I'd broken out of the prison? Maybe they'd have sympathy for me since I was a woman. Maybe I'd happen on a revolutionary, patriotic family. Maybe their children would be active revolutionaries.

I couldn't decide. I heard engines roar. I got up to look around and saw a police personnel carrier slowly turning the corner. I sat back down. The engines and the lights were coming closer. The quarter was being searched. I heard the voices of soldiers and police. Fortunately, my hiding place was off the beaten track. How could they have noticed my nighttime escape so quickly? Had the guards been suspicious? Maybe they'd called Zöhre and seen the open door.

After a while it got quieter, but the personnel vehicles were still driving around. I was waiting for sunrise. I thought about crossing the main road and disappearing into the dark poplar woods on the other side. Uninhabited areas would offer the best protection. But now it was too light for that. A young man walked by—I thought of getting up and asking him for a vehicle but quashed that idea fast. Finally I got up and walked after him, my bundle in hand. He disappeared, maybe into a house. I turned left. Ahead of me stretched a long street. Soldiers were standing at the end.

One of them shouted, "There she is! I recognize her! It's her!" Instead of turning and bolting, I stood next to a car and acted like I was waiting for someone. Maybe I could fool them that way.

But they kept coming toward me, so I sprinted away. In my heeled sandals, I didn't get far. One of the soldiers released the safety on his weapon, while the other grabbed me.

"What's going on? What do you want?" I shrieked.

"Aren't you Sakine? Of course you are—I know you! I drove you to the hospital a few times."

I said confidently, "Here's my ID."

The soldier inspected it and said, "It's Güzel, from the prison." He whistled and fired a shot to tell the other soldiers. I made noise too, to try to draw nearby residents from their houses. Maybe they'd make a commotion, and I could flee. Or maybe some revolutionaries would try to free me. But only a fearful face or two peered out from a balcony.

"Don't shoot," I said to the soldiers. "I haven't seen you, and you haven't seen me. Look, I'm an innocent person who's been in prison for almost two years. You're soldiers, you're children of the people. You just haven't seen me. I can give you money. My father's in Germany. I'd never forget your kindness."

One soldier, from Kars, seemed inclined to help but whispered to me, "I can't do anything. I'm not alone."

The other was a fascist. "You're trying to trick us," he said, firing another shot.

Two minutes later police cars pulled up. They hadn't left the neighborhood. Faces in houses watched us curiously. The police roared into their walkie-talkies, then bickered with the soldiers, who said, "The state prosecutor ordered us to bring her right back." But the police insisted on taking me to the commander of the state of emergency.

In the police vehicle, cops insulted me. "This daughter of a donkey's son! See? She doesn't care about anything. Girl, we almost ran out of gas searching the neighborhood all night. Look at us!"

I didn't say anything. It hadn't yet sunk in that they'd caught me. As we drove past the prison, they called out, "Heads up, we've got her!" I saw my bedding and other things piled outside the gate. Dammit, in the prison they'd thought I'd made it!

We reached the public prosecutor's office, where journalists were refused entry at the gate. All the police who'd participated in the search gathered around me like a pack of hounds and gawked. Among them were a team of reinforcements from Elazığ. During the night my photo had been circulated everywhere, and roadblocks had been set up. They'd worked fast.

One cop tugged at my headscarf and said, "She put this on so we wouldn't recognize her." I swatted his hand away: "Behave yourself!" The cops wanted to let me have it, so the prosecutor broke in, "Officer, I'm in charge here. Please step outside. Where's the chief of police? His teams must withdraw to their positions. The woman is under our supervision. We'll take her statement."

"But Mr. Prosecutor," said the police chief, "we're under orders to bring her back to the commander of the state of emergency in Elazığ."

"I'm not going to discuss that with you," the prosecutor replied sharply. "Please don't try to negotiate. I know my job."

The police left the room. The prosecutor had the secretary call and order tea, "also for Mrs. Sakine." He gazed out at me from behind his desk. "Bravo! You escaped, and a woman at that! You seem very proud. I must say frankly, I respect you."

Tea was served. When I turned it down, he acted like he was offended. "I have stomach problems," I said.

"You even turn down the tea!" he said. This short, portly man looked at me as if hurt, shook his head, and then smiled with sincere benevolence. "How did you escape?"

I explained everything matter-of-factly. I pulled the keys from my pocket and handed them over. Then everyone was called into the prosecutor's office—the guards, soldiers, Zöhre, Hatice, the head guard Sexo, the man on whose door I'd knocked and asked the way to Cavusoğlu, and even women from the hospital who had names close to Sekine or Zekiye.

At first the prosecutor didn't believe me. "You couldn't have escaped without help from the guards. You promised to pay someone a bribe. Your family must be in Germany."

I'd had no help, I insisted—"otherwise I'd have succeeded." Zöhre and Hatice were brought in, both looking awful from crying. I repeated that they'd known nothing, although it became a problem for them that they stayed overnight in the women's ward. "I stole Zöhre's clothes. I pinched Güzel's ID."

Zöhre nodded at me gratefully. Both had been terrified about what I'd say, but now I'd saved them. The inquest ended with people being fined. The judge asked the chief guard Sexo, "How could you have mistaken Sakine for Zöhre? Look at her! How could you miss it? Come on, admit it—you got money for this!"

"Your honor," Sexo answered, "she really did look exactly like Mother Zöhre. And Zöhre and I had an argument, so when I called out to her, it wasn't odd that she didn't respond." Everyone smiled, including the judge.

Back in prison, Fuat Çavgun and the others had jumped for joy when they heard about my escape. Up to the moment I was brought back, they didn't believe I'd been caught. The friends in Elazığ had broken into dancing too, at the sight of the newspaper headline "Sakine Cansız escaped." Now a friend read the next sentence, which abruptly ended their joy: "She was captured."

Before the escape attempt, when my family had come to visit, I hadn't let on about my plan, saying only, "Don't worry, I'll be out soon." My father read the newspaper on the plane from Istanbul to Germany. He too saw only the first part initially and yelped in delight like a small child. If he could, he would've stopped the plane and got out. Then he read the rest and burst into tears. I wished he hadn't known anything about it.

For three months, I couldn't get over my failed escape attempt. I couldn't stop analyzing my mistakes—after succeeding at the hardest part! The letters I got from outside and from other prisons made it worse. Almost every day someone from Cavusoğlu visited and said, "Why didn't you come to our place? If only you'd let us know, we'd have freed you, whatever it took." Even some TİKKO and HK members said, "If only we'd known, we'd never have let them get you." The Roma women said, "God in heaven, our tents are under the poplar trees, only a hundred meters from where they captured you. We'd have dressed you as one of us and hidden you. We'd never have turned you in!"

All these well-meaning remarks only made my pain more acute. I heard that some people from the Seyranbağları neighborhood got into a fight with people from Cavusoğlu in a coffeehouse. The ones from Seyranbağları said, "You always say you're Alevis and leftist, but you couldn't even rescue this girl. If she'd come to us, not even an army could have retaken her!" Oh yes, everyone wanted to be my savior!

Haydar and the others wrote me: "We were in the area a little earlier that night. The night before, we sent someone. You shouldn't have acted so hastily. Probably you're angry. Don't let it get you down—we'll try another time." I wrote back criticizing them and explaining that I had to rush because Hüseyin Yıldırım had said I was being transferred to Diyarbakir in August.

The prosecutor had asked me if I would try again, and I'd said, "I'm a revolutionary. Nobody wants to be in prison. The state is holding us by force. If I get the chance, I'll try again." I would, but of course prison security would be tighter now.

Hatice and Zöhre had been having nightmares about my escape. Every night now they checked several times to make sure I was still there. One night Hatice woke up from a nightmare and shrieked, "Sakine is gone!" All the prisoners burst out laughing.

It took the two guards a long time to recover from their shock. I was under more intense scrutiny than ever, even as I kept an eye out for another chance. I hadn't given up on the hospital idea, but I'd need help.

But after the military coup, my contact with Haydar and the others came to an end.

September 12, 1980: a turning point in Turkey   On the morning of September 12, 1980, we awoke to the sound of racist, fascist marches and generals giving speeches over the radio and TV. Hatice turned deathly pale: "Have you heard? The military have taken over!" A military coup! I thought of the juntas in Greece and Argentina, and previously in Turkey.

General Kenan Evren explained that he had taken over the government to ensure the unity and intactness of the fatherland and the perpetuation of the state.

> Separatist bandits in the east and a few terrorists in the west are rioting in the streets every day. They're dividing our workers and our youth, our neighborhoods and streets. They want to turn our beautiful fatherland into a bloodbath. Citizens, these bandits won't achieve their traitorous goals. Our armed forces have everything under control and stand at the service of our citizens.

This speech was rebroadcast every half-hour.

The junta banned all political parties, abolished parliament, and imposed martial law. New decrees were issued hourly, and their precise observance was mandatory. "All privately owned weapons must be turned in immediately at the nearest police station. Anyone who does not comply within three days will be subject to legal consequences." *Legal*—that was funny: which laws were they talking about?

The TV showed people standing in long lines to turn in their weapons or themselves, and the heads of political parties being arrested. Demirel, Türkeş, and Ecevit all looked pale as they were carted off from their offices in Çankaya. The military procedures were followed exactly. The junta tried to project itself as mature, modest, and neutral. The coup had been well planned.

In this way the military managed to suppress every revolutionary or democratic opposition movement. But it knew from experience how to hit the weak points of the revolutionary opposition. The junta used its tactics like a pesticide spray against the people.

The state of emergency had been proclaimed after the Maraş pogrom, and now the military had carried out a coup. The arrests in Elazığ had been just the beginning, and afterward our party had taken some precautions. Many cadres were already in [the Beka'a Valley in] Lebanon for guerrilla training [at the PKK camp there]. We took the arrests as a warning, and the party leadership had left the country. Subsequently all cadres were directed to leave as well. Not everyone could manage it. Those who stayed behind, like people in Hilvan, Siverek, Batman, and Mardin who had been resisting for a long time, had to dig in their heels and continue the struggle, even if it meant arrest.

The spirit of capitulation spread to every corner. It was unbelievable. Where were the thousands who'd taken to the streets to demand their rights? Where were the workers' resistance, the student movement, the peasant rebellions? What about Fatsa? All those revolutionary groups—they had to do something! They couldn't just go quiet!

The junta used every tool at its disposal for counterrevolutionary purposes. In Kurdistan, it deployed never-ending violence. In Turkey, it wiped out the revolutionary democratic opposition and arrested countless revolutionaries. Some opposition members fled to Europe. The counterrevolutionary propaganda got shriller by the day. The TV and newspapers showed images of people who'd been arrested. Some were forced to confess to their alleged crimes to the cameras. The military junta used every technique to show that all of Turkey was submitting.

Clearly the United States was directing the junta, and many imperialist states supported the coup. Internationally the junta was praised as "moderate" and the military as a "savior," although contrary voices were also heard.

The military coup had extreme effects in the prisons, both military and civilian. The junta issued a decree: "Every prisoner is a soldier!" Turkish flags were hung everywhere. And prisons now had to adopt military discipline. At Malatya prison, the guards, their role transformed by the coup, gradually turned into soldiers. The prison administration inflicted new methods of repression on Fuat and the other men friends. Every week they raided the cells arbitrarily. They confiscated books. There was a list of approved books, and all others were whisked away—a sign of things to come.

The friends in the Elazığ prison described in their letters how the inspections, the exercise yard, and social activities were all now subject to

SARA

strict military discipline. "Every prisoner is a soldier" and "Every citizen is a soldier" became the slogans. Friends who showed a lack of "respect for the flag" were brutally beaten. The prisoners were divided into two groups: those who showed respect for the Turkish flag, and those who didn't. Some knuckled under right away. A sense of panic was spreading.

Then my contact with the outside was broken. Haydar wrote me a brief letter, saying he had to leave the area and would be out of touch for a while. I was in a state of limbo, with so much unknown.

The whole society was to become militarized! Chauvinism and racism were running rampant. We gradually realized that the junta was trying to instill fear in the whole society in order to legitimize violence. Its slogan "Against both right and left" gained broad support.

In early March [1981] I was ordered to get ready to be transferred. In the administration building, a civilian guard handcuffed me to himself. I objected, but he said, "It's for security reasons—it's an order. You can curse all you want."

"Isn't there enough security?" I asked. We sat next to each other in the car, and I held my arm up the whole way because I didn't want his repulsive hand to touch me. It was uncomfortable for him too. After a while both our hands were swollen, and he released the cuffs.

Celalettin Can was in the car too. He had shaved, and his clothing was clean. Only two days earlier his mother had visited him in prison and brought him clothes. I turned and greeted him with my eyes, but he didn't respond. He had been shown on TV, over the headline: "Horrific confession of a Dev-Sol leader." He'd made statements that were useful to the enemy. To appear on TV was a serious offense since it had such a bad influence on the population.

In the car, the cop tried to get me to talk. First he said to Celalettin, "You were in charge of the east. You said, 'Revolution is the only way.' But nothing's left of that, eh? You're gonna go to Europe when you get out of here, huh?" Celalettin muttered some words of assent. I glared at him furiously, and the cop noticed it. "What—you don't like that? You know him?"

"It's not a question of whether I know him, but ..." I didn't finish. Celalettin was visibly unwell. My very presence was making him feel ashamed of his own weakness.

I asked where I was being taken, but they said it didn't concern me. I expected to be back at 1800 Evler, among new arrests. Or maybe, as a result of my escape attempt, my case was being transferred to the commander of the state of emergency.

Celalettin was taken to 1800 Evler for interrogation, but they took me back to Elazığ prison, where I was reunited with Hamili, Hüseyin, Mustafa, and Meto. Everyone was getting ready to be transferred. There was a crush of people, and we couldn't talk much. Overall, the friends' attitude wasn't negative. The other [political] groups had abandoned them, and those who still resisted were isolated. The administration divided the prisoners into two groups, "dangerous" and "less dangerous" and tried to mix fascists in with them.

The men friends received a message from Cetin (Semir) asking them to accept new [militarized prison] rules. Then a message arrived from outside: "Some rules may be acceptable, but kissing the flag and such is out of the question."

This letter should have clarified the enemy's goals for us and explained how we could wage a suitable resistance. Instead, based on this letter alone, some of the friends took the easy path and submitted at the first attack. We talked about it and decided that in the next prison, we would reject the rules laid down by the military junta. We would carry on there as the friends we were.

To Diyarbakir as prisoners One day a militaristic captain came in and read names from a list. The first was Şahin Donmez. "Get over here and stand at attention! You're a soldier—face forward!" Oh, just the sight of that scum stoked my revolutionary rage. That loathsome dirtbag, who'd surrendered all his humanity and debased himself to the most miserable level. That coward, with his meaningless life—he even avoided eye contact with me.

Then came more names—Ali Gündüz, Hamili, Sakine, Mustafa— about 75 of us. We were told to pair off, get in the van, and sit on benches with a soldier between each of us. We climbed in. Şahin and Ali sat together. Elif was next to me. Would I never be rid of this woman? I still didn't know her real position.

We were all together again for the first time. En route we tried to guess where we were being taken. Presumably it'd be a new prison. Most friends were incarcerated in "fortresses," military prisons, distant from each other. There was a new prison in Diyarbakir, the enemy's most secure military prison.

SARA

We fell silent, each wrapped in our own thoughts. No one really dared speculate about what exactly lay ahead. Many of those who'd joined the struggle hadn't really ever thought about [the possibility of facing] repression. Many were surely wondering about the destination, or hoping to be released after the trial. I was thinking about the friends we'd see in the new prison. This silence didn't bode well—in fact, it should have been a cause for concern.

We knew the enemy would try to intimidate us, isolate us, cut us off from the outside world, and exploit our weaknesses. And we knew that somehow we'd resist. But in general, we had insufficient consciousness about the significance of prison and the enemy's prison policy. We knew the military coup had intensified the repression, but we neither anticipated nor understood the nature of this junta, or its goals, or its attacks on the movement, or the function of its prisons. And our organization had no clear political policy on how to behave, over the short and long term, in prison.

Prisons had already played an important role in the revolutionary struggle. In the past Sheikh Said and dozens of leading Kurdish resistance fighters had been imprisoned, sentenced to death, and executed. Details about their imprisonment weren't well known. We had previously been in awe of those who'd spent years in prison. How could they have stood it for so long? Now we'd been in prison for over a year ourselves. We'd had many new experiences and witnessed countless episodes, but we still didn't know how to interpret them. The meaning of an individual's imprisonment couldn't be reduced to the number of years. Only later would we develop an analysis of prison and its significance, both for the revolution and for the enemy.

I held on to my optimism and my confidence because I believed in the party. Even if some individuals should betray or capitulate, I knew the party, with its ideology, would ultimately win, and that the enemy's repression would come to nothing. Nothing and no one could shake my faith, even for a moment. Of course, negative events sometimes depressed me, and often I failed to adequately uphold the party line. But my convictions gave me the strength to continue. I liked this part of myself and held fast to it.

As the vans pulled up in Diyarbakir, we found ourselves in a neighborhood that looked like a slum with vacant lots. Across the way was a multistory building that looked like a pyramid, with many windows.

100

This prison was bigger than the one in Izmir, bigger than a factory. Was it taller than Diyarbakir city walls? The enormous iron gate swung open, revealing military vehicles in the inner courtyard.

We were told to bring our things and filed out of the van. "Let the women through," someone said. At the entrance our admissions were processed, as officers stood by. We were steered through a second door and then had to wait on a staircase landing. From there we could see into a long corridor. Every 10 or 15 meters there was an iron gate. Soldiers were lined up along both sides of the corridor. A few held clubs, while others gripped leashed dogs. All were tall and strong and wore the uniforms of commando troops. We saw right away what was to happen. They were like a pack of wild animals awaiting their prey.

It all happened very fast. The men friends went in two at a time, and suddenly the soldiers were clubbing them from both sides. There was screaming, and the barking of dogs. Many friends collapsed in the onslaught. Then they were ordered to strip and lean toward the wall.

I stamped my feet and screamed, "You bastards!" Yes, they were trying to intimidate us. Oh, I wished they'd beat me too. Elif looked on in terror, her lips pale, her face taut.

Suddenly an officer appeared next to us women. Where had he come from? What was his rank? What a face he had, with malicious bloodshot eyes. He smirked sadistically, grimaced inhumanly. Sometimes a person's appearance gives the wrong impression—a person with a humane face can turn out to be sadistic. But with this guy, his past had left its marks on his face. You could see at a glance what kind of beast he was.

He planted himself before me. "What's your name?" "Sakine." "Are you Turkish?" "No, I'm Kurdish."

He slapped me, hard. Coming after the wearying journey and the clubbing in the corridor, this was too much. "What's that supposed to mean?" I shouted. "What is this?"

But he had already turned to Elif. "What's your name?" "Elif." "Are you Turkish?" "Yes, I'm Turkish."

The torturer snorted contemptuously, "Bravo!"

This was my first encounter with Esat Oktay Yıldıran in the Diyarbakir dungeon. No one wants to get a slap from the enemy, but to be honest, it lessened a bit of the agony I felt for the men friends. Their torture in the corridor continued as Esat joined in the melee. It was horrifying. Most of the men were naked except for underwear. A few still lay on the ground, and screams and moans filled the corridor. Elif followed the order to "turn around!" and lowered her head. I stood off to the side, not wanting to see the friends in this situation.

Another officer ordered us, "Bring your bags and follow me. No, don't look over there—lower your head," then ran ahead. I didn't care what he said—the men friends were still being beaten. Anyone still clothed was forcibly stripped. In the tumult, it was difficult to make out individuals. The soldiers were assaulting the men as a group.

They took us into a long, narrow corridor. "We'll inspect the suitcases," said one. "And we'll inspect you," said another.

"No way," I said. "Aren't there any female employees here? You are *not* going to search either us or our things."

"Lift up your jackets." This soldier just had to have his way. "What have you got on you?"

"Nothing," I said, lifting the lower edge of my jacket. Elif took hers off, and her suitcase was searched, but I still refused.

"It's an order. We've got to search everything," they said.

"Then I'd like to speak to whoever gave this order. I insist on female staff."

"Okay, I'll only look from above," the soldier said, fearful that his superiors would hear about his incompetence. In the end these soldiers were only instruments in a torture machine. Some of them, recent draftees, were participating in this reality for the first time. Military culture was pervasively racist, chauvinist, and fascistic, and independent thinking was forbidden. Unlike the self-chosen and doctrinaire fascists, the ordinary soldiers just carried out orders as they were being forcibly integrated into the Turkish military system.

After a while Esat returned. "I searched for you in the wild beauty of the mountains of Tunceli [the Turkish name for Dersim]. Now I have you in my hands. You were in Tunceli, weren't you?"

"No, I was arrested in Elazığ," I responded.

"Here I make the rules. Everyone who comes through that door has to obey them. Here everyone is a Turk. UKO, Kurds, and such—none of them exist. Right, Elif? You're Turkish, right?"

"Yes," Elif said.

Esat snorted derisively again. "You killed Celal Aydın, right?" he said, in Elif's hearing. So he knew we'd punished him, which meant the various institutions coordinated.

He turned, took a few steps, then turned back around and tapped the palms of his hands with his club. To the soldiers, he said, "Take Elif upstairs. Female police will search her." A blond policewoman was waiting by the door with bowed head. When she heard Esat, she hopped to.

Esat turned to me. "Are you Turkish?" he said with another slap.

"No. I'm a revolutionary. In the revolution, one's ancestry plays no great role, but I'm a Kurd. If I were a Turk, I'd tell you."

"Oh my, oh my!" Esat became serious. "I don't want to hear anything about Kurds. Put her on the ground!" he ordered. The soldiers did so promptly.

Then he clubbed my feet. I mentally counted the blows … 1, 2 … 15… 20… The policewoman turned her back to us while Esat beat me. She clearly couldn't stand to watch—her face was twisted in pain, as if she could feel the clubbing herself.

Esat warned, "If you don't say you're a Turk, I'll grease the club and shove it into you." It was no empty threat, and this was no ordinary prison. What was going on here? An affirmation of Turkishness was being demanded of us. "You just have to say it once, 'I'm a Turk,' and it'll all be over," Esat said.

As the clubbing moved up my legs, I stopped counting. At some point, I heard a distant voice ask, "Is she dead?" Esat lifted my eyelids and said, "No, she's still alive." I must have passed out.

After you undergo the falanga, you absolutely must move—otherwise gangrene can set in. But my legs were numb, and I couldn't walk without support. As the policewoman held my arm, I hobbled a few steps.

In my first encounter with Esat, he'd slapped me, and in the second, he'd delivered the falanga. What more was there? To be hung on a hook, electric shock, nakedness, rape … ?

I heard voices coming from the yard, Esat's among them. Then I heard the voices of women, reciting weakly in chorus, "I'm a Turk, I'm honest, I'm hard-working …" Were other women prisoners being held here, women besides us? Whose voices were they? Surely Elif's, but I'd heard several. Had these women prisoners been here before us, or were they new? Looking through a window, I could make out women in the upper level. They were peering through windows down at me. Elif must have told them I was here.

Finally I was taken to a cell at the end of a corridor and locked in. The windows were shut tight and whitewashed so I couldn't see anything. I listened awhile, then managed to crack open a window, and again I saw women on the upper level. They saw me, and we greeted each other. One pushed to the front. She looked familiar, but I only recognized her when she put both hands around her mouth and called out, "I'm Aysel!" It was Aysel Öztürk, who I'd first met in Zeki's apartment in Bingöl, along with [her husband] Selim [Çürükkaya]. They were living in Ali Güngör's flat. "Come and visit us in our petit-bourgeois apartment!" they'd invited me. I'd done so, briefly. Aysel had complained that gossip was denigrating her lifestyle and her marriage as petit bourgeois. I said, "If that criticism is meant for the apartment furnishings, who cares? The apartment belongs to the organization, not to you. But if marriage is more important to you than revolutionary work, then you should take the criticism seriously."

Aysel had been one of the early ones to be arrested, along with Yıldırım Merkit and Mazlum Doğan, on the road to Urfa. Now she hand-signaled me that she'd send me a message during the night. I was impatient to hear from her.

Soldiers came into the cell, beat me, and left. They were curious about me—they were different ones every time. It was cold, it was March, and I had only a blanket in my lower-level cell. I could hear the sounds of clubbing and screams of pain coming from all sections of the building. As I peeked out my window, I saw more soldiers.

Sometime during the night I awoke to a rhythmic tapping on the heat pipe, coming from above. I tapped back in the same rhythm in response. My window was open a crack, and outside hung a plastic bag on a cord. I grabbed the bag and detached it. The cord was pulled back up. In the bag were some food and a letter, which I opened quickly and read:

We seven were down there where you are now, for a while. We were transferred up here just today. Generally, as a tactic, other wards accept some rules. Accept the "I'm a Turk" rule, so you can get moved up here. Then we can talk in more detail. Greetings, Aysel.

I expelled a curse: *May God punish you!* What tactic was she talking about? So much was at stake in saying "I am a Turk." They didn't ask if we belonged to the revolutionary movement, let alone to UKO. They just asked if we were Turkish. But even if we said we were Turkish, it wouldn't all be over, despite what Esat said. No, they wanted to break our Kurdish identity itself. Back in Elazığ, prisoners had been required to kiss the Turkish flag and to pray.

How had the decision been changed so fast? Aysel had enclosed a pencil so I could write back. Since I had no paper, I wrote on an empty space in her message:

> I don't understand your message. On the way here, the men friends and I all decided we wouldn't accept the rules. Have they lost their minds? You speak of a tactic, but it's the other side that's using a tactic. Have all the men friends accepted the rules? Has there been an instruction [from the party outside]? I must know and await your answer.

I tapped on the heat pipe, the cord was lowered, and I inserted the message into the bag along with the food they'd sent me. The bag was pulled up. I made sure there was nothing in my cell to indicate this contact had happened.

The answer came back quickly: "It's generally accepted, as we were told. When you come up here, we can talk."

I was baffled. Accept the rules *tactically*? What?

I knew Aysel and trusted her. I wasn't angry at her or the other women friends. Surely they hadn't decided on their own to accept the rules. The question was who had. Was it the men friends from our group? Or had others, who'd been transferred here before us, made the decision? But why? We were in a dungeon, so decisions didn't necessarily reflect a common will, but in here, each of us had to represent the organization.

The organization. The advice in Aysel's message must have come from the organization and not from individuals. What should I do? I had to figure out what was going on. How could I communicate with the outside from in here? There must be some way. If the advice came from the organization, I would heed it.

But if the advice didn't come from the organization, I'd resist indefinitely. But what was resistance? What further rules would the enemy set? If we accepted some rules but not others, would that amount to resistance?

My mistake In the morning, during exercise, the male prisoners were forced to sing military marches nonstop. The din penetrated into my cell, along with the sounds of torture. Before the enemy could do anything more to me, I said to a soldier, "Call your superior in here."

"Who do you think you are?" he answered. "We don't do what you want—you do what we want!"

The soldier didn't dare to deliver my request to Esat and told an officer about it. The officer visited to "get to know" me, which once again meant beating me. "Why do you want to see the captain?" he demanded.

"I want to see someone in charge. It doesn't matter who."

"Then it's me. What do you have to say?"

"I want to talk to my friends upstairs."

"We don't let anyone up there who hasn't accepted the rules."

"You want me to say I'm a Turk. Okay. You know very well I'm a Kurd, not a Turk. And besides, I'm a revolutionary."

The man gaped uncomprehendingly. Had I just said I was a Turk, or had I been discussing the illogic of the rule? Shaking his head, he left.

Soon Esat hurried in, panting like a dog. "Do you know who's up there?" he asked.

"I know they're women but not who they are."

"Why do you want to talk to them?" Malice slitted his eyes. What celebration was he planning for me now? He patently relished the prospect of torture. It would bring him joy. "The voices of women are like music to me," he once said.

Why did it bother Esat that I wanted to go upstairs? I wondered. Didn't he want me to follow the rules?

"Come on, let's go out into the yard," he said. "Are you a Turk?"

"You know I'm not a Turk. But you want to force me to say I am. It makes no sense. I'm a revolutionary, so it's not important whether I'm a Kurd or a Turk or belong to some other nation."

"Enough! I'm not here to argue with you. Who's pressuring who here?"

"Now I want to say it on my own, but ever since I got here, you've been trying to force me to."

"Do you know the oath?"

"No."

"Didn't you go to school?"

"Yes, I did."

"Then let's say it together. Say it after me!"

At that point I should have said, "No, I'm not going anywhere or saying anything." Esat would've blown his stack. Dammit, was this about resistance or capitulation? The enemy forced you to say a few words, and then he had you in his hands. Such methods were intended to break a person's will and convictions. If you said one sentence today, the enemy could hope you'd say more tomorrow.

He repeated the oath a few times and demanded that I speak.

I refused. "Before, you just wanted me to say I'm a Turk. Now you're asking even more of me."

Finally he ordered me to be taken upstairs.

I felt miserable and could barely drag myself up the steps. Anyone could have seen right away that I'd been tortured. I don't mean the physical torture—that was long forgotten. My pain came from feeling that we'd let ourselves be defeated quickly. The friends called it a tactic, but why had they thought it necessary?

When I reached the upper level, Aysel [Çürükkaya], Cahide [Şener], Hava [unknown], Gönül [Atay], Fatma [Çelik], and dozens of other women hugged me. A few came up to me shyly. Some were aged mothers. There were so many women up here.

After we exchanged greetings, I could no longer hold back: "Who was it? Dammit, why did the men friends make this decision? Or was it the organization that decided?" Now I asked the women friends: "Tell me— how was this decision made?"

Aysel lit a cigarette and inhaled deeply. Gönül stared straight ahead. Fatma lay down, saying she was sick. Some of the other women had straggled out.

Aysel said, "We've had no contact with the men friends for a week or more. The prisoners in the big cell next door sometimes send us things, and they told us everyone in the whole prison, including the Elazığ group, had accepted the rules. We don't have more information. A few women friends are in the hospital—maybe they'll come back with news. The message to you was only our own opinion—"

Fatma interrupted, "I wasn't there—speak for yourself. I'm ready to go back downstairs. I would be even if Sakine hadn't arrived."

Gönül jumped in: "Fatma, cut the crap. Then why haven't you done it already?"

Aysel, looking stricken, spoke softly, as if making a confession: "For a week, there were nine of us in the cell. We were tortured constantly, all day long. At first we all refused to accept the rules. The soldiers organized marches in the ward. They stayed there at night, even Esat. He ordered each soldier to get into one of the women's beds. The torture and the psychological pressure—not everyone could withstand it. We were only nine, and most of us are very young. Soon they stepped up the torture. We heard the Elazığ group was coming. Esat named you in particular. He wanted absolutely to break the resistance."

I'd interpreted Aysel's message as conveying the official decision of the party; it had induced me to give up my resistance, at a time when the enemy hadn't expected at all. I had actually called in Esat myself to accept the rules. I was mortified.

I couldn't stand it. "Oh, so that's why he wanted me in a cell by myself. If you'd held out for just one more day, we would all have been together!" I roared at them. "Then at least we could have made the decision together. Oh, how could you do this! Why didn't you tell me it was your own opinion?" I was seething.

Aysel chain-smoked. The women on the bunk beds and in the corridors listened intently. The atmosphere was tense. A lot of prisoners were in here, and whenever the door opened, more arrived. Most were from the PKK, and most of those from Halfeti, Batman, and Siirt were very young. The ones from Hilvan and Siverek were of various ages. A few women had children with them.

What, was I to go back now and say I made a mistake? But then I realized that it was significant that it hadn't been the enemy's torture and pressure that had brought me to this state. That was important, since it meant I could change my position at any time. I could reverse myself—it wouldn't even be hard. But it was a tactical defeat. "I won't stay up here. Even if I'm alone, I'll still resist."

Meetings with other prisoners They shaved off the men's hair and beards and cut the women's hair as well, five or ten commandos for just a few prisoners. "A few were shorn like sheep," Gültan told me, her face pained. [Gültan Kışanak had been in Diyarbakir prison since the summer of 1980, before the military coup.] At first only a few friends were here. We had been resisting the new rules since November, [she said.] Now they've bent a little, but their spirit of resistance hasn't been extinguished.

"At first we women were isolated," Gültan continued, "and in no position to analyze the events fully, but our anger at the enemy was unbroken. We discussed what he might be planning, knowing his goal was to destroy our organization. We knew he tried to induce us to revolt, so he'd have an excuse to eliminate leading cadres. We held seminars, and our magazine *Hawar* appeared regularly. Most important, we cared for prisoners coming from interrogation. Some broke under torture, but the organization could reclaim them. At first the wards could communicate with one another. We could talk to each other, exchange messages. Sometimes Mazlum [Doğan], Hayri [Durmuş], or [Kemal] Pir came over here to the women's ward. We could talk through the door slot.

"In January [1981] the repression intensified. The KUK, *Özgürlük Yolu*, the DDKD, Rizgarî, and others bowed to the rules right away. But we went on a hunger strike. Not everyone participated, but TİKKO, Kawa, and some of the other groups joined us. Over time, though, the resistance crumbled. The wards were brutally attacked, and a few prisoners were isolated. Nowadays we don't get any good information at all. More and more people have ended up here. We were told that they all accepted the rules. The prisoners from the next ward said our resistance was pointless since everyone else had given up—"

Gönül interrupted, "Mümtaz and the others advised us to be reasonable."

Gültan continued evenly, "During the hunger strike, they misinformed us. And they said no one would be surprised if the Apoçu women got impregnated by the soldiers. They considered the enemy's repression to be fated. Resistance was futile and dangerous." Of all the women's descriptions, Gültan's seemed to me the most realistic.

Gönül, who seemed unwell, kept whining about how isolated she'd been. Whenever she spoke, I noticed, many prisoners looked at her disapprovingly, scowled, or whispered among themselves.

I'd first met her in Tuzlucayir and was less than impressed by her immaturity. Now she made me uneasy, the way Elif did. She said she was looking for her fiancé, Rıza. [A few months earlier Ayşe Dişkaya, who'd previously been imprisoned with Gönül, told me: "Gönül got special treatment, even during torture. She can't be PKK." And: "She went around in a low-cut nightgown. Apparently she has a fiancé. The police kept asking about him. She'd told them a little. Probably they let her move around so she'd go to him."] Did the enemy want to use Gönül to find Rıza? Maybe. She'd said she was looking for her fiancé. Maybe by saying she was looking for her fiancé, she was trying to misdirect the police. But for the enemy, it was like an offer. The more I got to know the enemy, the more mistrustful I became. Could Gönül damage us?

Aysel took a dim view of Gönül.

> When we were downstairs, she kept to herself. She complains a lot about how isolated she is—it drives me crazy. She always elbowed her way to the foreground and called attention to herself, so they isolated her as the ringleader. But a few officers were always with her. Some of us mistrust her. She doesn't seem to consider the enemy her opponent at all. She hasn't been tortured very much. Fatma says she resisted during interrogation, but we don't know how much she really did. Now she tries to capitalize on it. When we talked to Mazlum about it, he advised us to give her what she wants and not cause any problem. Here in prison there are many strange people we have to get along with, and it's hard. If he hadn't said that, we'd have stayed away from her.

Cahide had arrived in prison while I was on the lower level. On the first day she'd supposedly said, "I don't belong to the party. They isolated me, didn't try to draw me in. I'm independent and do what I think is right." And she'd taken the easy route and said right away, "I'm a Turk," so she'd been transferred upstairs. She kept her distance from the others. When I was brought upstairs, she hugged me and cried.

[I met members of] the Batman group who were interesting. As Gültan explained,

> The whole group was arrested—there were nine of them, all very young. All had leading positions in the neighborhoods or in the woman work but had little idea about the values and politics of the party. Many blamed the party. The enemy used women to break them. He served them alcoholic drinks and showed them videos with sex scenes. It went very badly for them. The police also tortured them sexually. They snapped and confessed quickly in terror. We women wrote about it in a report, naming the individual cops. Then the police came here and threatened to take us back into interrogation if we didn't withdraw our statements. I think the enemy will make more use of this situation.

Some of the women prisoners from Hilvan and Siverek had been arrested arbitrarily and were terrified by the interrogation, by the threats and the torture. The police stripped them and inspected their breasts and their most intimate places, looking for PKK tattoos. They threatened the women with rape and tried to get them to inform on each other in their statements. By all these methods, by preying on prisoners' personal weaknesses, the enemy tried to individualize people from almost every group.

Many people from the Turkish and Kurdish Left ended up in a state of total psychological defeat. They considered resistance to be nothing more than an excuse for the enemy to inflict further attacks and torture. And their groups' continuing antipathy toward the PKK, even in prison, also benefited the enemy.

I had trouble living with my mistake. My defeat tormented me. I'd acted rashly, without forethought. I punished myself for it. I could still reverse what I'd done, but I couldn't resign myself to the fact that I'd done it at all. After all, the first encounter with the enemy was so important!

But I also knew I couldn't resist alone. I'd made a strong impression and forced the women friends to take sides, and some had picked mine. It would've been better if I'd resisted all the rules from the outset and never accepted a single thing. But I knew I wouldn't capitulate or lose my nerve again, and my determination eased my conscience a little. That would have to be enough.

The enemy's goals   I had become acquainted with prison in Izmir, but despite some similarities, the situation here was very different. Above all we had to try to understand what prison meant for the enemy. This prison wasn't like the others, [I saw.] Here the enemy proceeded treacherously and deliberately.

First we had to acknowledge Turkishness and the indivisibility of the fatherland. Sometimes he made us beg for food: "*Bismillah irrahman irrahim* [in the name of God most gracious and compassionate]. Bon appétit. Praise Allah, may our army and our nation remain."

Then he told us that we were not prisoners anymore—we were soldiers, and "if you want to live, do what we tell you." He made us do a military count-off "for security reasons": we had to stand at attention and count off one by one. Later we had to say our own numbers out loud.

Then the enemy made everyone swear an oath to the Turkish flag and sing the national anthem. He made prisoners sing military songs as they marched through the exercise yard. Prisoners sometimes had to stand outside barefoot for hours in the heat or lie in the rain and snow for the falanga on the icy-cold concrete, screaming. Men prisoners had to crawl naked on concrete, or wade in sewage up to their necks, while singing Turkish marches ... they had to sit in water contaminated with shit, razor blades, and chemicals, ... the malice of making us recite lines from freedom songs and mixing them with ugly insults ...

He purposefully let time pass between introducing new rules, so they wouldn't stir up opposition, and so they'd build on each other. He went about it systematically over the long term. He constantly threatened, "You'll never get to court, we'll crush you, you'll all die here alone." He'd say, "I have you all in the palm of my hand, and I'll smash you like flies."

To the enemy, anyone who had revolutionary convictions was guilty, anyone who carried the spirit of the PKK or had been influenced by it in one way or another. Of course, he attacked some of us more harshly than others, to divide and isolate us, to bring us to their knees. He sought to entrench the feeling of defeat. When talking to other prisoners, Esat repeated at every opportunity, "There's no more organization, no more PKK. You're in our hands ... Your leaders have all become Kemalists, and soon they'll become soldiers. Your organization doesn't exist anymore." He'd point to me and say, "She's the one who brought you here." And he said to me, "Apo, the one who put you here—he's now living it up in a luxurious apartment with women, while you're here scrounging in misery."

We discussed these rules and these techniques. When Mazlum visited our ward, he warned us,

> The enemy wants to exploit our weaknesses by separating us from each other, individualizing us. He wants to prevent us from organizing, until we're just a crowd of people who've lost our fighting ability and are ashamed of our own weaknesses to the point of helplessness. He'll use all the time it takes. Then he'll attack us. So we have to protect the organization.

As time passed, we understood they weren't merely about acknowledging Turkishness or begging for food. The enemy was worried about this newly awakened Kurdish identity, and he was trying to eradicate it. By bringing us into line step by step, he wanted to militarize us, "Turkify" us, make us manageable so we would lose our Kurdish identity.

You might tell yourself that saying "I'm a Turk" isn't the end of the world. You may even make fun of "Turkishness" while you're saying it. The enemy is trying so hard to steal your identity, so you make a joke about his holy "Turkishness." *What's wrong with that?* you think. *I'm still a revolutionary.* But these are the first signs you're no longer yourself.

And it's not over, either for the enemy or for you. For the enemy, it's about breaking your will.

Some of the women wondered, "What have we done that we're being tortured so cruelly?" Many came from places where our struggle was well developed, but for others consciousness of Kurdish identity was new. They had siblings, husbands, or children in the struggle and had only just begun to develop political consciousness themselves. They'd helped with the educational work or joined women's groups, or neighborhood committees, or they'd worked with students. They weren't murderers or thieves—most had never even handed out a flyer. So they couldn't understand why the state was proceeding against them so brutally. *I haven't committed any felonies, they thought, so I'll be released. Yes, I admitted a few things to the police, but then before the prosecutor I withdrew them. And I confessed only under torture. So I should be released on the first or second day of the hearing.* Sadly, their expectations didn't correspond to reality. It wasn't about whether someone's crime was major or miniscule. It was about robbing us of our convictions. Here women too were to be militarized.

Here we were in a place where we could hear thousands screaming and see fear in their eyes. Every day someone cracked, defected, informed, dragged his own values through the mud. You observe the human drama of those who have become so alienated from themselves that they lick the boots of their torturers. The prisoners in the ward next to ours capitulated promptly and gave the enemy everything he asked for in the form he wanted. We heard them singing military marches, and we shouted, "You bastards, you've surrendered. Now you're singing fascist marches? Have you no shame?" As later prisoners accepted the rules to a certain extent and lost their will to resist, our insults continued.

Because surrendering was dangerous. The struggle wasn't over yet—in fact, it had only just begun. The enemy had benefited from being able to attack us before we could organize ourselves in prison, and we had bowed to the rules. But we hadn't surrendered our convictions. Our confidence in the justice of our struggle was unshakable, and we wouldn't let go. Confessions under torture happened all the time. What was important, after the torture ended, was to find your way back quickly. The setback was only temporary.

It was out of the question that we would give up. Resistance gives you self-confidence and initiative. You forget your worries and savor the unbelievable pleasure of prevailing on even one point. You have to work on every single person. Everyone's behavior—their attitudes, convictions, and fears, their courage, confidence, and mistrust, their anger, everything—depends on your own behavior. To attend to the foundation and at the same time fend off the enemy's attacks means you really have to give all. A solid organizing effort also ensures that the movement will continue without particular individuals.

Sometimes waters quietly shift beneath the surface until they surge, and at other times a great wave generates a sudden current. In either case, you have to throw yourself into it. You have to find balance between the strength you actualize in yourself, and the strength of the foundations.

In a normal war, a certain balance prevails, as conditions change. But this war was one-sided and was waged ruthlessly. The torture ground us down and divided us, so much that any resistance became an act of heroism and strength.

If anyone expressed doubt that things could change, we objected strongly. We just couldn't lose hope. Not the PKK. If you lost your convictions and hope, you couldn't be PKK or call yourself a revolutionary. The enemy might have been stronger tactically, and we'd accepted some rules, but that didn't mean it was all over. The friends outside would surely think of something, and if we could stay in touch with our men counterparts in prison, things would surely change. We were sure of it.

The men begin a death fast, January 4, 1981   We [PKK] prisoners now numbered about a thousand in total, including both leadership cadre and members. Many other groups capitulated in the first days, in effect withdrawing from the battlefield, meaning the enemy had fewer people to attack. But for our people, the PKK embodied their convictions, their commitment, their hopes, their yearnings, and their common identity—they held on. In some prisoners, torture actually eased their fears. The more the enemy tortured, the greater our hatred and anger. He insisted on humiliating us, but that made the path to a dignified life all the clearer. We knew he tortured because he was afraid, and his fear dissolved our fears.

[On January 4, 1981, the PKK leadership had begun a death fast to show that they would refuse to obey military rules.]

We got the news that the men had begun a resistance, a group of leadership cadre. They had started a death fast. The main demand, we learned later, was an end to the torture.

At the time a death fast was still a new phenomenon. It differed from a hunger strike in that during a hunger strike you could drink water and at certain intervals even sugar water. And you set an end date. Yes, you risked death, but that depended on the extent of the demands being made. A hunger strike didn't take you up to the edge of death. But in a death fast, the demands are different—life-and-death matters. The enemy has attacked by every means, he has deprived you of the right to any other life. He permeates every aspect of prison existence so that life itself becomes torture. For prisoners in such a situation, the death fast is their best way to induce the enemy to grant them a little air to breathe. *You're forcing us to die? Okay, some deaths are worthwhile!* In a situation where everything is organized to make every moment of life a moment of torture, the death fast demonstrates the strong will of every cell in your body to resist in a way the enemy hadn't anticipated. The enemy forces you to experience hunger, thirst, and sleeplessness, he forbids you to speak or even to see. But death fasts would change some people's attitudes, and those who entered them, while some died, would become legends.

When we heard about the men's death fast, I wanted to join right away. But you don't start a death fast without organization. We hadn't even done a hunger strike yet. Hunger strikes had to be coordinated and make the unified demands. We discussed the conditions in which this principle was true or false. Didn't we have to draw our own conclusions from events? And under our current conditions, how important a role did support from the organization play?

The enemy's actions were unbearable, but our uncertainty was even worse. [Our prison communication system, between the women's ward and the men's, was all but impossible.] It depended entirely on luck. We were in the same building, but you can't communicate with the people on the other side of the wall or even in the next ward.

Organizing in the women's ward   In prison, standing strong against the enemy on one's own is important. A revolutionary will converges in you. You feel conviction, determination, a pure desire to fight. The revolutionary struggle is the most beautiful of all. You will not swerve, and by the very force of your personality, you will rip the enemy to shreds. It's not just about you—he sees his own reflection in you. In your resistance, he recognizes his own helplessness.

But although I was also prepared to fight alone, I was convinced we all had to resist together. In prison, it's necessary to organize the resistance. Occasionally, I would find myself isolated or in a small group. If the enemy felt I was dangerous or if I went up against some rule alone, I'd end up back in the isolation cell. But resistance in prison has to be organized. The enemy was tactically strong and deployed every possible means, so first we had to make sure that all the doors were shut that might allow him entry.

Talking to the women friends about it all, in small groups and one on one, helped mitigate the fear and tension. I decided we needed to marshal our forces and mount a resistance. I would work to transform those from whom the enemy hoped to gain the most. *The enemy won't get what he wants from these women,* I thought. *He won't touch any of them or use them against the revolution, not even the most difficult and undisciplined.*

Gültan and Zeliha were elated, the others felt better too, and we could talk to members of other groups who might be open to it. Between ourselves, we discussed which women friends to approach and how to divide up the tasks.

Internally we divided up the short- and long-term tasks. Gültan, for example, was to communicate with the other groups and try to win over friends who didn't want much to do with the organization. She drew no special attention to herself but was astute about the enemy and relations among the friends.

In prison, communal life is essential. We organized daily social life in the women's ward as a commune. It provided an occasion for communication even as it represented a high ideal value. We shared our tasks so that our daily needs could be covered in only one place. We developed routines to avoid sowing antagonism or drawing the enemy's attention. We wrote a common shopping list, then divided up purchases to groups according to the list.

Many members of other leftist groups had been individualized—they'd lost almost all sense of community. But our insistence on forming a commune impressed them, and we were able to develop some commonalities with them. Some of them were valuable friends who possessed revolutionary pride, and we shared much in common with them, even if their organizations had a different orientation or they'd proved weak and helpless under torture. The enemy couldn't destroy that revolutionary commonality. Often when he tried to recruit spies and informers, it didn't work out, because people in other groups, influenced by our behavior, told us with embarrassment about the enemy's recruiting efforts.

Our commonality made it easier for us to work with them on other things as well. We bought and used at least the basic staples together. It didn't matter how much money anyone had—we wanted to break just that orientation. We distributed our money among several friends in case the enemy should separate us. Many people got no visits from families, so drawing them in had a positive effect on them.

The women behaved differently from the men. The men had to stand with their faces toward the wall and salute on command by clicking their heels together in military fashion. But such behavior wasn't imposed on women. The enemy wanted to make us beg and such, but we said, "No, we don't accept this rule," and so obstructed implementation. At the time we didn't realize that we might be treated more mildly than the men: if they treated us more harshly, we might have joined the later death fast. But we didn't realize that till the action had already ended.

For Esat, probably one of the most beautiful moments in his life would have been to break the women's resistance. He was always irritable and irascible and offensive, like someone who can't do what he wants to do. Every time he entered the ward, he said: "You beastly descendants of beasts! How you enrage me!" The curses he came up with were remarkable. It may seem strange, but having an enemy can strengthen a person. His insults, his rages, actually bolstered our self-confidence. If the enemy reacted to us that explosively and viciously, after all, it meant we still lived and resisted, we were still standing, and we were strong. True, we'd made some concessions, but he hadn't achieved his goal. He'd claimed he could squash us between his fingers like flies, but he really couldn't. Nor had he reduced us so that we fit in his hand, and he knew it.

He assigned some new prisoners from the TKP the tasking of spying on internal communications within the women's ward. He pumped Elif for information. He wanted to know names, and whether we were organizing and holding meetings. She said she didn't know anything. The beatings, the torture, the hearings after her arrest—they all terrified her. But since she was a state-employed nurse and a broken woman, the enemy welcomed her. We told Elif frankly,

If you tell them anything, it won't be good for you. All this time with us, you've let yourself be used. Why don't you stand up to them, finally? If you want to live here with the rest of us, then kindly act a little bit like a human being. Otherwise you'll just be hated.

We were careful around her because we considered her a spy. Even the soldiers didn't like her.

Throughout these overwhelming events, I kept thinking about escape. The doors stayed open until late evening. Soldiers weren't always around. They arrived in big groups if someone was to be beaten or if there'd been an incident, but otherwise there was only a guard, a soldier, and a petty officer for the whole ward. Was it possible to climb out over the roof? I talked about it with Gültan, Aysel, and others. A few thought me delusional that for thinking about escape. "It can't work," Aysel said. "The building is tall, and it's in a military restricted area."

"Let's go up to the roof and take a look anyway," I said. Gültan wasn't against it—she had kind of an anarchistic soul, but a peaceful, moderate anarchist! We considered making a rope out of bedsheets. Then we tried a clothesline, but it chafed our hands. When it was quiet in the corridor, we tested the exit door, but we couldn't budge the lock. We tapped on the walls. There was a guardroom, but guards hardly ever stayed there. Maybe we could break through a wall. But it seemed hopeless. We had some pieces of iron to use as tools, but the outlook wasn't good. The situation changed every day. The exercise yard was available only at certain times. Sometimes the guardroom was used for interrogations. My dreams of escape began to seem illusory.

I did tell the others about my earlier escape attempt. We kept the past alive by telling each other our stories of struggle. Recounting such moments always made us feel better. Our memories were like books, poems, novels, well stocked with comedy and tragedy, love and sorrow. They gave us strength. We told the same stories over and over, especially ones about certain friends or about the chairman, or about an action we'd carried out or a difficulty we'd overcome. We listened breathlessly, as if we were hearing it for the first time. Such storytelling balanced out our pain, so we didn't have to repress it.

A Lebanese and a Frenchwoman   Sarah and Monique arrived in the women's ward. Sarah came from Lebanon and Monique was French, a doctor. They'd gone into South Kurdistan to help the Kurds. But their medical work brought them difficulties: when they tried to return north, they'd been arrested at the border because of their support for the PKK.

They were segregated from us, on the lower level, their windows painted over, and their doors locked. We exchanged messages and became close emotionally and intellectually. Reyhan Saribal of TİKKO knew English and translated our correspondence.

They were very alert, as these were perhaps the most intense moments of their lives. Sarah was highly emotional, highly affected by her surroundings. The sounds of beatings and torture drove her to stay in bed, Monique explained. Monique, for her part, refused to eat one day, to protest pretty much everything being done to us.

They intended to report on conditions here once they were released. Monique scraped paint from the windows to see what was happening. She taped the sounds of torture with her audiocassette recorder (it was later spotted and confiscated). We wrote some reports about the enemy's procedures and prison policy for them to give to people on the outside.

As she was leaving, she raised her fist and shouted, "Kurdistan!" Then at the last minute, she shoved all of our reports back at us—carrying them was too risky. But she said, "We saw everything, and we promise, we'll let people know about it everywhere!"

Cahide Prison is a horrific war zone, where personalities are tested harshly. If you have shortcomings, you can't hide them—they'll be exposed. You are deprived of every means of fighting, you are fully under the enemy's control, and your life is subject to his whims. At every moment he confronts you with your own naked reality. You are tested: what are you trying to run away from, and how far are you willing to run?

Quite a few prisoners nurtured a secret animosity toward the organization. Under interrogation and torture, they'd capitulated to the enemy, but now they regretted it. They were angry at themselves for their weakness, and now they expressed their regret in different ways, some by keeping their distance from the rest. But they all shared one thing in common: anger at the organization. Here was their logic: the enemy had attacked them in prison—because of the organization! "If you were with a different organization [besides the PKK]," the enemy said frankly, "we wouldn't be doing this to you." Members of the other

3 Cansız with Cahide Şener, at Diyarbakir, undated.

groups were "smart," the enemy said, precisely because they didn't belong to the PKK, and they were beaten less brutally.

[I think this problem afflicted my old friend] Cahide. [She] was not doing well—she stayed in bed and cried and chain-smoked. I couldn't understand it at first, even though I knew her well. Her work in the school and later in Siverek had always been praised. In Elazığ, she had worked well. What had happened? Why was she so angry at the party?

Cahide grew up and attended school in Siverek. Her character was the product of her childhood and her family circumstances. Her father worked as an agent for seasonal workers. The family had also been involved in smuggling, and the father was a gambler and a drinker. Of all his children, she was closest to him. Her proletarian mother manufactured candy and worked hard to fulfill her daughter's petit-bourgeois desires.

Her family moved to Urfa, but Cahide and her sister Nevin stayed behind in Siverek and dedicated themselves to revolutionary work there. Cahide worked hard and was much respected. As a revolutionary, she had many talents that she could use brilliantly. She was clever, resourceful, and eager to take the initiative. She was active during the fighting in Siverek and was deeply involved, even using weapons. She had procured weapons and ammunition, and she ensured that certain useful people had careers in senior government positions. She even shot someone from the Bucak clan [enemies of the PKK], which proceeded to put a bounty on her.

She got engaged to Süleyman—but their engagement created problems. They were the only friends [in Siverek] to get engaged. Kemal Pir and Mehmet Karasungur, who were in charge of the local organization, approved the marriage, but Siverek is a small place, and they were closely watched. Once when Cahide felt sick, she picked up a prescription from the hospital for pills to regulate menstruation. The label listed the medication's possible side effects for pregnant women. The daughters of the house where she was staying and some friends saw the word *pregnant*, and the rumor mills ran amok. It was even rumored that she had had an abortion.

The rumors distressed her greatly, feeling like an attack on her honor. In a place like Siverek, rumors can endanger your life, but even the friends considered the affair "a matter of honor." Finally, one internal discussion got so heated that friends drew weapons on each other. Cahide wrote a report to the party central committee, about the men's reactionary behavior, and demanded that it hold them accountable. But Hasan Şerik. "didn't forward my report," she told me. [The local party] shunned her, and she had to give up revolutionary work. Then Süleyman was arrested. She risked visiting him in prison with a false ID, even though she was wanted too. Then she was arrested.

After all her revolutionary successes, she had experienced a period of defeat. Defeats are inevitable. If you've been beaten in a fight, you can get up again and try again. But if you haven't fought back, defeats are dangerous. Defeat that takes place in the soul and takes possession of your feelings, thoughts, and will, always make you susceptible to betrayal.

Sobbing in fury, she told me she blamed the organization. She refused to consider that she had behaved provocatively, instead of taking care not to harm the organization. She saw herself as entirely in the right. That's how she justified her weakness during interrogation and in prison, telling me, "It was the only thing I could do." After that deep first conversation, she continued to ruminate about these events. Her anger and distress disheartened other women friends.

Cahide's deep sorrow was that she hadn't been able to defend herself against the enemy's attacks, and yet she couldn't get away from the prisoners whose presence contributed to her misery. She was stuck, and in these circumstances, her state of mind was dangerous, because Esat greatly wished to recruit a woman informer.

One day a guard summoned her. It wasn't a court day—presumably it was for a lawyer visit. Cahide was away for a long time. Lawyer conversations usually lasted only a few minutes, sometimes only seconds. Normally, whenever any of us left the ward, the rest awaited their return in silence. Whether it was for a court date, a hospital visit, or a lawyer conversation, a trip to the outside was always a difficult moment. Anything could happen. They could drag you to torture or to a lineup. Every path out of the ward involved torture. And waiting for Cahide to return was torture of another kind, since her psychological shakiness made her not especially trustworthy, and because her behavior gave the enemy hope.

When she reappeared, she avoided our eyes, hung her head, and went for a cigarette. Everyone had their own opinion, but I knew her best— yes, clearly she had sunk even further. When she looked at me, her eyes welled with tears. She was so ashamed of herself. For a while she stayed away from me, feeling guilty, and I was careful not to make any sharp remarks.

[When she was ready,] Cahide explained to me what the enemy had asked of her and what she'd said. She didn't hold back—if she'd omitted even a word, I'd have noticed.

> I can't keep anything from you. You get to the bottom of everything. Even if you don't ask me, I'll feel compelled to tell you everything. You created my revolutionary self. Sometimes I get so angry at you and wonder why you have such influence on me. I trusted the party because of you, but also the anger I feel now. Why can't you leave me in peace?

She sobbed for a long time.

I was amazed by my own patience. I'm actually a very impatient person. Did my impatience make patience necessary?

The enemy knew Cahide was having problems with the organization— she'd admitted it during interrogation. And he knew she was feeling her personal concerns more strongly than her concern for the organization. In fact, she had said the organization had "finished" her.

This time the enemy had interrogated Cahide—and brought in her father, Koç Ali. Nevin [Cahide's sister, who was also in detention,] became a bargaining chip. If Cahide would confirm to the court the statements she'd made under interrogation, Nevin would be released. Then Koç Ali gave the police some money, in return for which they promised that Cahide would be tortured less and Nevin would be released. The police asked her to write a letter to the party outside that her father was to deliver to Mehmet Karasungur. The police assumed she knew who stayed where and who was connected to whom. She gave them false information, she told me, and warned her father in Zazaki to stay away from the police.

Where would Cahide land with her unstable behavior? If she didn't regain her balance, she would do damage Either she'd return to the resistance and try to find herself again, or else she'd give herself over to betrayal. Patience has its limits.

"A lot of us have put our lives on the line for the struggle of our people," I told her, "but you've let it slide and are thinking only about your rights and the restoration of your supposed honor. A lot of us have problems with isolation and other punishments. But no one else has become so angry. Is what others say about you really so important? The party, after all, approved your engagement to Süleyman. You could have got married. You could have an abortion or others could have believed you did. So many important things have happened, but for you, none of them are as important as defending your own honor. That's all you care about, and the enemy takes advantage of it.

"Even if people had made statements about you, even if police had found your name in reports they confiscated, or even if completely different accusations could have been made against you—none of that would justify your behavior toward the police. You knew the police were looking for you, yet you went and visited Süleyman [in prison]. And you got so involved that Nevin became a bargaining chip. Maybe your father brought money, but you wrote a letter and now you speak of giving false information. You've capitulated. Right now you aren't in the party, because you've set yourself against it.

"You've finally got to choose: either you resist or you betray. Remember our past. You always used to say how great the revolutionary life was, how appealing. So get unstuck now. It's in your hands. Maybe you won't do everything they want now, but you've given them hope. The enemy won't let go of you, because you've encouraged him. He'll keep on making demands of you—he'll want every bit of you. He'll try to use you even more.

"But if you adopt a consistent position, if you stand up to them, they'll stop calling you in. You've seen for yourself that all the prisoners are pressured to act like spies—except the men friends [cadres]. Once we speak with someone and they start behaving consistently, the enemy leaves them alone."

Sometimes my voice rose in anger, but I tried to keep it even, as I appealed to her memories of our shared work in the past.

"But it was different back then," she cried. "The party was different in Elazığ. In Siverek, comradely relations were sacrificed for personal considerations. The values were different. They just stood me in front of people. I couldn't look anyone in the eyes anymore," she sobbed.

"Pull yourself together! All you do is lie in bed and cry and smoke. Get a grip! This whole problem goes back to your own weak behavior toward the police. You haven't got over it. But it's not too late, it's still in your hands. All you have to do is tell them not to call you in anymore because you don't have anything more to say. If they call you in anyway, too bad. They'll keep coming around all the time, torturing and threatening. You are capable of resisting, and you won't be alone. But you've got to get over yourself, do you hear me?"

"Yes, okay."

"Promise?"

She smiled, tears still hanging in her eyes. "I promise."

"Then snap out of it."

She rose, and the next time I saw her, she was more cheerful. She ate, moved around, talked, and so returned to the land of the living. It made life easier for the other friends too, although a few still didn't trust her and regarded her as unstable.

The trial begins, April 13, 1981 The torture escalated. Every day, every night, every hour, there was torture. Every day dozens of soldiers on duty came to the ward tortured and beat us as part of their daily routine.

But the messages we got were contradictory. Some said all the wards had accepted the rules, and resistance continued only in the isolation cells. Sometimes we gave credence to the most negative news, and sometimes the messages affected us so powerfully that we couldn't judge the situation anymore. Some said it would be good to die.

Cut off as we were from the outside world, we had no idea what was happening there, what the situation was, or what the friends were coming up against. We could only make vague guesses. We had no radio, no newspapers, and no visitors to pass on news to us. Sometimes we saw a newspaper that was full of hostile propaganda and lying reports. Then it was taken away. Sometimes they also gave us tabloids, but they had no news value.

When [our lawyer] Hüseyin Yıldırım visited me, they would bring me to him out of isolation, escorted by an obese policewoman. In the visitors' booth, the policewoman kept her eyes fixed on our eyes and dared not blink lest she miss anything. She was so fat, her feet were on top of mine. "Why are you so thin?" Hüseyin Yıldırım asked me. "Are you ill?" "No, I've been in isolation," I said. "Insomnia and such take their toll." At that moment the policewoman stepped heavily on my foot, warning me not to tell him about anything that was really going on. Hüseyin Yıldırım caught on, and the conversation didn't last long.

Our lawyers tried to get our [Elazığ group] trial transferred to Elazığ. I assumed I'd be able to interact with the men at the hearing, but once in the courtroom, if we even exchanged looks, we were beaten and insulted. Even the men who sat just to my right and left didn't dare look at me or respond to my questions. Their sad, careworn faces drove me crazy. We too were tortured and forbidden to speak, and we too would be beaten when we got back to prison, regardless of what we did here. But we had to at least greet each other, if only with our eyes.

One or two of them managed to croak, "We're okay," just that. The men on the other side, sitting farther away, at least smiled. The soldiers beat them only a little, but they clubbed those near us on their tied-up hands. The handcuffs stayed locked until the judges entered. The men friends wore black jackets that were part of prison gear, with civilian clothing underneath. Zeki Budak and Hüseyin Güngöze were sitting nearby—I overheard them whispering that a trial in Elazığ would be better for us.

[Our lawyers] failed—[our trial was still] merged with the PKK trial in Diyarbakir. This court ruling delighted no one more than Esat Okay. After the hearing, he rubbed his hands together and crowed, "I'm giddy with joy." After that, I agreed with Zeki and Hüseyin and said, "Dammit, if only ours had been transferred to Elazığ!"

Şahin's betrayal had been a bonanza for the enemy—based on his information, they charged dozens of leadership cadre, in Elazığ and elsewhere, including Mazlum, Hayri, Pir, Karasu, Rıza, and Muzaffer. They had him talk at the trial—we guessed, as a way of undermining our morale.

The men had long ago decided to make a [political] defense and developed a plan for it, which they'd sent to the party outside. They'd sent a copy to the women's ward before I arrived. The women friends had hidden single pages in various secure places, but it was risky to try to retrieve them, since we could be watched, and they might be discovered during a search. So I had to wait for the right moment to go get them and then hide them away again. If they were ever discovered, I'd say they were my notes.

I prepared my own political defense. But I had a problem: without the approval of the party, could I even mount one? During my interrogation, I had acknowledged my connection to the organization and defended our ideology. At the first court hearing I had made a clear [political] defense, not imagining anyone would have a problem with it. But it would be better if I could inform the organization.

And should I call myself a sympathizer or cadre? I wasn't sure. If only I'd been able to communicate with the men, they'd have advised me, but absent that, I'd call myself a sympathizer. I might have mounted a more comprehensive defense as a cadre, but what right did I have to call myself cadre? You couldn't just designate yourself—only the party could do that.

Finally, I decided to ask Mazlum and wrote him a message. A month later I heard nothing from him, and the message came back to me. I tried several times, always with the same result. I didn't destroy the message, though, because I wouldn't give up hope. But he never got it.

[The PKK's main trail (with 591 suspects) began in Diyarbakir on April 13, 1981. It was the fortieth day of the still-ongoing death fast. Inmates arrived at the courthouse pale and exhausted.]

Since we in the Elazığ group had been arrested first, we figured we'd be tried first.

The death fast ends During the death fast, the enemy intensified the torture to force prisoners to capitulate and to betray. This was a form of action on the part of revolutionaries who felt responsible for many prisoners. The men showed that one can survive for weeks and months on only water and air—and in the process develop an iron will. The families spoke about Mazlum, Pir, Hayri, and the others publicly. The media didn't report on it, but it wasn't ignored. It was a beginning, a warning.

[To end the death fast,] Esat Oktay gave his word that he would limit the torture and the isolation measures. But he didn't keep his word—the changes he made were only temporary.

[The death fast that began on March 4 ended 43 days later. During that period attacks on prisoners had increased. In the negotiations, Esat Oktay had promised to end torture, allow inmates to make political defenses at the trials, allow family members and lawyers to visit inmates without beatings, end forcing inmates to beg for food, end the use of excrement for repression. In exchange, inmates agreed to stand at attention, military style, when they saw the guards, and to go to visits and trials in single file. Some refused to read the Turkish oath and the national anthem, and refused to refer to the soldiers as "commander." Esat Oktay soon stopped respecting the agreement and resumed practicing torture.]

By May, our gloom was oppressive. Torture continued for days on end. Esat came into the ward and cursed us until he foamed at the mouth. Naked men were forcibly brought into the women's ward as part of psychological warfare. Esat loved hearing women's agonized screams—to him, they were like a beautiful melody, and he showed his love by inflicting the falanga on us for hours on end on the ice-cold concrete floor. The inmates in the next ward must have been wincing. Then he'd shriek, "I'll have you sterilized! I'll wreck your fallopian tubes so you can't have any more children, and your people will die out!" He wanted to extinguish the Kurdish people.

At other times this sadist would show his special love for women by snarling, "Wish we didn't have any broads here!" and "Soldiers gonna knock up those PKK girls." And he'd beat us with a club between our legs till we bled, then threaten to "shove the club inside." He pulled our lips till they tore.

[On May 24, 1981, the last remaining resistant leadership cadre finally agreed to obey the military rules.]

One day Aysel was called away, and when she returned, she was distraught. She'd seen [her husband] Selim. His ward had resisted accepting the rules until that very day, when they'd finally given in. "The torture [the men friends underwent during the death fast] was merciless," she said. "They were naked. Mazlum was there. When Selim was brought in, Esat told him he was going to rape me. Selim accepted the rules. Then they dragged him away."

For seven months, prisoners had been waging a desperate resistance. We women all believed that one day we too would refuse rules that were forced on us. The men were showing us "how to pull ourselves out of this," we told each other. So Aysel's news [about the leadership cadre accepting the rules] came as a hard blow. The resistance had been broken, in unequal conditions and with the cruelest methods. It caused us more pain than our own situation did. No one wanted to believe it. The knowledge that we'd left them to act on their own made it even more painful.

Although the defeat demoralized the prisoners, most considered it only short term. Most expected that conditions for a far wider resistance would be created, when developments were more favorable and new forces could be gathered. It wouldn't be all that hard to win back those who felt weak and helpless, unless they were really traitors. Knowing that, the enemy went all out to prevent us from reconstituting our forces.

The corridors echoed interminably with screams of agony. The enemy was trying to create a new human type, one who had been stripped of everything human and drilled into absolute submission. That was the core aim of the enemy's prison policy. And he wanted revenge, so he attacked savagely at every weak point.

The Nazi camps had reduced people to silent naked bodies whose eyes showed no traces of hope and who moved only when it was time to die. Were there other such places in this world? You didn't have to look far—your eyes could stop at Diyarbakir.

Yet Diyarbakir was also different. How to describe it? It was a place like any other, yet it was unparalleled in its use of torture to nakedly annihilate every trace of humanity. The prisoners screamed their souls out of their bodies. They sang fascist marches, then felt ashamed of it. Even as the enemy enjoyed his victory, however, he was consumed with fear. The prisoners mourned their defeat, but they also had a lifeline that terrified the enemy, and that was their own secret reservoir of hope.

"Don't let it get you down" The trial was deliberately delayed. The enemy could imagine what subjects [we would bring up]. So he wanted to obliterate in advance every bit of strength, every spark of will that we might show in the court.

Esat told us, "I've crushed your leaders like flies. Now they're all Young Kemalists [an authoritarian group within the Turkish military]. The PKK has no more central committee, only Kemalist Youth. Communists, Kurds, and PKK no longer exist—they're all my soldiers now." Most of the prisoners refused to believe that the resistance had been annihilated. Those who did believe it used it to justify accepting the rules. But the leadership cadre, as we saw on drives to the courthouse or the hospital, acted differently from other prisoners. They refused to stand with their face to the wall, and when the soldiers insulted them, they refused to respond with "Yes, my commander!" They were carefully segregated from the other prisoners.

One of our leadership cadre was Kemal Pir[, a Turk from the Black Sea area]. The Laz and other prisoners from that region regarded him as a living legend. An aura surrounded this man that was hard to explain. His words and his unflinching attitude, even toward high-ranking officers, deeply impressed even the soldiers and guards. They had been trained to see him as a separatist murderer, and they tortured him, but they didn't get to his secret core. All his encounters with Esat were like battles in a war. Soldiers recounted in amazement the time Esat offered him a rope, and he said, "This rope couldn't hold me—it would tear." Everything he said was profoundly meaningful.

In anticipation of November 10[, anniversary of the death of Atatürk, founder of the Turkish Republic], Esat made a special plan: the "Young Kemalists"—that is, the prisoners—were to participate in a memorial ceremony to honor Atatürk. Further, a poetry, writing, and speaking competition was to be held.

Prisoners were brought from every ward [to participate]. Some were outright traitors, while others had tried to resist but shown weakness. Some participated in the ceremony voluntarily—their fear made them canny, and they considered themselves clever. Oh, they'd already sunk into the muddy swamp anyway, so what difference did it make if they sank a little deeper? Gönül was chosen from our ward and felt she was extremely clever. She wasn't the enemy's first choice, but none of us wanted to participate. They could beat us to a pulp—none of us would go voluntarily.

But the enemy had no great interest in people like Gönül anyway—he had in mind [leadership cadre], as Esat announced over loudspeakers that had been installed in every ward:

Everyone who once served on the central committee of this or that organization, and who so misled many poor people and tried to divide the fatherland, is now in the hands of the state. Their regret now makes them eager to enroll as brave soldiers of the state.

During the ceremony, Şahin's voice came over the loudspeaker. He recited the principles of Kemalism, with all the intonation of a traitor reading a prepared text under supervision. All the women cursed him. "That scumbag! He squawks like an animal! Now he's a Young Kemalist? What's next, will he change his name to Atatürk!?"

Then Esat announced: "Next, we'll hear contributions from … Mehmet Hayri Durmuş, Kemal Pir, and Rıza Altun." We couldn't believe our ears. I assured the other women, "It's another scheme. These bastards have found some snitches to speak in their names. They're trying to manipulate us. Don't worry about it."

But inside I was tense. Was it possible [that our cadres had capitulated]? I hated to think about it even for a moment, but I had to be prepared and if necessary prevent this propaganda show from demoralizing the women friends.

Gültan and I paced anxiously. "Are they really going to have the friends speak?" she pressed me.

"They could," I said. "The enemy is trying to make it seem that all the prisoners without exception have given up their ideals and are just a meek mass. It's a plot to destroy the confidence that the rest of us have in them. But even if the friends do speak, it's just a tactic. They accepted the rules, but only tactically, because they're considering the whole situation."

Then suddenly as we were talking, Hayri's voice came over the loudspeaker. Someone exclaimed, "Ah! It's Comrade Hayri!" Everyone rose to their feet out of respect, as if Hayri were actually standing there across from us and telling us some very different things. His was a voice we'd longed to hear and that carried our hopes. We listened in a profound silence to the words he was speaking now. Some held their heads in their hands and stared into space with pain-filled eyes and sighed deeply, consumed with fury and anguish. Aysel pounded her fists against the wall. Durre cried.

Then Pir and Rıza's voices came on. No one was listening to their words anymore—they were as empty as taking the oath to the flag or singing the national hymn. What was meaningful was the sound of their voices—they sounded different from those of Şahin and the other traitors.

I left the room and went to the toilet so no one could see my tears. If I wept or broke down, I'd never be able to face the others. No, at least one of us had to assess things correctly and clarify the enemy's goals. The episode was unbearable, unexpected, and contradicted our ideas, but it had to be evaluated in terms of the nature of the struggle and the prevailing conditions. I must not give in to sorrow or rage.

Aysel was cowering on her bunk bed, groaning, moaning in a way that reminded me of Esma back in Dersim, whose younger son had drowned in the Munzur—she had wailed nonstop. It had been unendurable, like Aysel's moaning now. It was a form of torture in its own right. [Aysel] was capable of producing a whole range of dirgelike tones to express misery and helplessness and longing for death. Helplessess overwhelmed any overtones of anger and hatred.

"What are you doing?" I snapped at her. "Stop it! Really, this is just what the enemy wants. He's trying to shake our faith in our leadership cadre. He's trying to say, *Here are your leaders—no point in supporting them anymore!*"

Why did people who are depressed and anxious take to their beds and stay there? In prison it was because of psychological problems. But as they lay under the covers, their thoughts would go around in circles. Some women fainted, had nervous breakdowns, or tore their clothing. Usually the rest of us tried to bring them back and took care of them, talking to them, even begging them.

No, Aysel, we have to hear something else in their voices, in their names, in their breath. You know, when I listened to them, I thought I was hearing Comrade Hayri talk about the revolution in Kurdistan, and I thought I heard Pir ordering an entire army to press forward. See? We have to translate their words into different terms, otherwise we allow the enemy to achieve his goal. Of course, it's difficult to hear them sing fascist marches, but it must have been even more painful for them to sing them, to turn on their own people this way. The friends won't go on like this for long. People can bend only so far.

They're trying it with us [women] too, singling out individuals who will influence the others. Just a little while ago they called me in because I hadn't sung along with a march. They wanted me to sing it alone. But I lowered my voice as far as I could. Finally they threw me into the cell.

I deliberately don't sing along, so they try to coerce me. Just remember, accepting a few rules is not the same as giving them everything they want. This is an important point. Now after this supposed victory, the enemy will try to influence the prisoners and will report it in the media. Of course it will do damage, but mark my words, no one on the outside will fall for it. They know as well as we do that it's all just an enemy scheme.

Gönül came back to the ward. She'd been able to see the men friends, at least from a distance, so that was good. Gönül told us, "The men were fine. When Pir walked by, all the soldiers were gazing at him. None of the friends looked defeated." Rıza had greeted her and even said, as he walked by, "Don't let this get you down—it will pass." Everyone cheered up right away.

Gültan seemed encouraged too:

The enemy is very nervous now. He must know we're going to react to this. Esat surely realizes that an explosive resistance has to follow. But let's not you and I react so emotionally—I've come to understand this. You're right to be angry, but we have to be careful to avoid demoralizing the other women.

Esat Oktay, enemy of life and beauty The number of women prisoners kept growing, reaching around 100. Both women's wards were filled to capacity. Many came from Siverek and Viranşehir, even whole families. The older women cried together all the time. Durre's son, Ali Yaverkaya, was in prison, while her daughter Hanim was in the mountains. She was proud of her children but also sad. When she cried and beat her breast, we suffered with her. It was as if all the suffering in history could be found in those tears and that wrinkled face. She symbolized the pain and hatred of all Kurdish women.

Esat shouted, "Here there are no women or men—only soldiers!" And the soldiers beat us. At other times he mocked us, saying that as women we should be sure to keep our ovaries warm. Another time he told the soldiers, "My son, here we have women—you understand. Bring them cotton and newspapers." But then he would take our newspaper-wrapped tampons and throw them into into a torture chamber, to damage our "honor" and embarrass the men prisoners. That shocked us when we heard about it, and we took to hiding our tampons in the other trash.

The mother of Mazlum [Doğan] arrived here, along with Mazlum's sister Serap, and her daughter Baran. Three generations of women, all arrested and interrogated together! Kabire [Mazlum's mother] glimpsed her son in the interrogation room:

> I was afraid Mazlum would be interrogated again, but I was also glad at least to be able to hug him, if only for a minute or two. I wish it could have lasted longer. If only I could be with him all the time!

She cried until she had no more tears. Thinking of her sons Mazlum and Delil always made her sing sad songs.

Serap hid her joy, pain, and longings. A quiet woman, she spoke only with her eyes, which were coal black, like Mazlum and Delil's, and just as bright and sharp. Esat couldn't look into Serap's eyes, since eyes express the truth. Serap's hatred for the enemy burned in her eyes. That was too much for him. Her daughter's eyes were like that too, even as a child.

Yes, as a child. We had three children here now: Baran, Ali, and Hêlîn. Baran, at 5 or 6, was the oldest. Esat replaced her [Kurdish] name Baran with [the Turkish name] Bahar. He seemed to have a weakness for children, making inexplicable strange displays for them. When he took Baran by the arm, she'd shudder, repulsed by his touch. She had witnessed torture and was terrified of him. Could a sadist love children? we wondered. Didn't he have any children of his own?

Baran and Ali were afraid of the enemy because he tortured us, but they were also afraid of us because we *were* tortured. They both had a mother, a father, a homeland, and ID papers. At least they had a place of birth and an address, even if it was in the Republic of Turkey.

But Hêlîn was born in prison—she'd heard the screams of torture in the womb. Unlike Baran and Ali, she knew no other life. Her existence wasn't recorded anywhere. Her only address was the dungeon. Hêlîn, whose name was Kurdish, grew up in this torture chamber, often hungry and feverish in the ice-cold spaces.

Her mother was Emine. Hêlîn didn't know the word "mother," she just said "Emine." Whenever Baran and Ali used the word "mother," Hêlîn found it strange. Emine had brought her into the world, but she thought of the rest of us as her mothers too, since we all took care for her, changed her diapers, fed her, and tended to her, so she was part of us all.

4 Cansız with Emine Turgut (mother of Hêlîn), at Diyarbakir, undated.

Hêlîn learned to walk without crawling first. She had no toys, knowing only bunk beds and concrete walls. She knew the sky was blue and what clubs and falanga were. She learned to walk and sit in excrement. So she really was never a child. Pain, misery, and longing for beauty forced her to grow up quickly; I'd never seen a child grow up this way. But she was greatly loved. In this hateful and inhuman environment, she was the purest and most beautiful part of life. Hêlîn was one of us, sharing our sorrows, fears, pains, and joys. If one of us was sad, she was too.

Hêlîn didn't know her father, but she wasn't looking for him. Most of the men she knew were torturers. Whenever she saw Esat, she would wail, "Enough, stop torturing!" But he thrived on her hatred and anger. He was an enemy of life and of beauty, his heart barren of love.

She knew about the men friends. We women loved her, visited her, and taught her her first word—"Apo." She interpreted it as a synonym for "good man" and from then on she spoke of "my Apos." She listened to the Apos' distant voices, sometimes for hours, with her ear pressed to the wall or her face to the door. Sometimes she mistook the soldiers' voices for those of the men friends and almost shouted for joy before stifling it. And sometimes she heard their screams.

Esat was inhuman—he made even affection for children into a means of torture. In this case, he tried to use Baran to pressure Mazlum. He would take her by the arm and bring her to Mazlum. He finally succeeded in alienating Baran. When Mazlum tried to pick her up, she burst into frightened tears and refused to let him take her into his arms—much to Esat's joy. Perplexed, we scolded her: "Why won't you let Mazlum hold you? We don't want to talk to you." We all gave her the same reaction. We frightened her—it was terrible of us. "Why aren't you talking to me?" she screamed at us. "Okay! I promise I'll let him hug me next time!"

The next time … the next time … there would be no next time. If only she'd let him kiss her beautiful eyes! Everyone in the dungeon had unforgettable experiences, but little did Baran know, one day she would yearn to embrace her uncle. It would be her strongest memory of the Diyarbkir dungeon.

Esat Oktay had no human feelings. His whole emotional and intellectual world was oriented toward the fascistic system, and his actions all harmonized with it. He was inhuman. To look for a spark of humanity in this malevolence would mean betraying all of humanity. He had made the Diyarbakir dungeon into a little Nazi empire with himself at the pinnacle. He tried to extinguish all yearnings, all wishes, all enthusiasms. Even his own child died young.

But unlike the Jews in the 1940s concentration camps, we were organized. We had already organized our resistance for years [before prison]. We'd founded a party that would lead our people to freedom. Although we were imprisoned, hundreds of cadres outside were carrying on the freedom struggle. So the enemy couldn't commit genocide on us, as had been done to the Jews, the Armenians, and—in 1938 and earlier—the Kurds. Instead Esat's goal was to get us to deny ourselves, to renounce our own thinking, to so alienate us from ourselves that we surrendered totally. In the Diyarbakir dungeon, Kemalism, with support from traitors, tried once again to efface Kurds who dared to raise their heads and demand freedom.

The PKK fought to reconstruct society, with an ideology based on Kurdish identity, humanity, and socialism, and it succeeded in awakening people to the possibility of a new life. The enemy might hit us someplace, but new life would spring up elsewhere. Our movement wasn't like the traditional Left or like traditional Kurdishness, both of which were familiar to the enemy. All previous uprisings in Kurdistan had been beaten down, the various movements and their leaders stamped out. This new Kurdistan resistance movement might be weak, but it had made a good beginning. Would the enemy succeed in bringing it to a tragic end in the dungeon?

Restoring Cahide　In prison you can't hide your state of mind—it's impossible. Our eyes were like cameras that captured everything and everyone. We all watched each other, even if it made some of us a little self-conscious.

Aysel had tuberculosis. In prison, the risk of infection was great. The filth, inadequate nutrition, and airlessness were prime conditions for the spread of pathogens. The enemy contributed by giving us contaminated food. We tried hard to protect ourselves.

Aysel lay in bed sick—she needed surgery. Her ovaries were infected with tuberculosis and had to be removed. Her malady was infectious, and here we were all crowded into the ward together. I took care of her while trying to keep her dishes and laundry separate from ours. Some friends thought my caution was exaggerated, but Aysel herself didn't take the issue seriously enough, and her indifference to personal hygiene bothered others as well, paralleling her seeming indifference to life.

Prison was like the depths of hell, but we had to preserve cleanliness and order even there and squeeze as much beauty as we could from life. The leadership cadre washed and dried their facecloths carefully and kept their clothes clean and orderly. Mazlum always looked clean and vital. Why did others neglect themselves? Aysel wasn't to blame for her illness, but her poor mental health caused her various ailments. She whined and cried incessantly. I was constantly fighting this regrettable side of her.

Aysel was taken to the military hospital, so she couldn't try to make contact with the outside through the staff. After all, she was with the PKK, the enemy reasoned—anything was possible! We were proud that he saw us that way, and it bolstered our confidence in the party.

Then a soldier called for Cahide, I got suspicious, as I knew her psychological condition was seesawing. Esat's intrigues with her must not succeed. I pulled her aside and said sternly, "Cahide, you have to take a stand this time. No matter how little respect you have for yourself, don't let them make you into their instrument."

She was to go to the military hospital to keep an eye on Aysel. While she was in the enemy's area, she made a weak attempt to object, but Lt. Ali Osman yanked her nose and growled, "I'll destroy you." Cahide recoiled in fear. Finally she was taken to the military hospital, where she advised Aysel to be careful.

Two days later Cahide insisted on being released and was. She came and told me everything. She knew she couldn't put anything over on me. The enemy was part of her life, but so was I. I represented her bond to the party—we had got to know each other when she'd first joined the organization, and it wasn't a memory she could simply ignore.

I told her,

The question isn't whether you've done anything harmful. The issue is that you still let yourself be used. Why didn't you refuse? You could just have said, "No, I'm not going." They might have tortured you a little, but that's all. You're still waffling, still on the fence—and they still beat and humiliate you. At least hold your head high when they beat you! Come on, hold on to some dignity. Why can't you decide? Are you afraid of the beatings? Of death? If you don't want to be Cahide, but would rather be someone else, then just go!

She cried again. Some of the women found my efforts with her annoying. "She's obviously gonna cross over to the enemy," they said. "Why are you trying so hard with her?" But others supported me in my efforts to extricate Cahide from her situation.

Cahide fell silent for a few days, then finally made her decision—and seemed to come back to life. Now whenever Esat or Ali Osman came into the ward and asked her about some technicality or other, she coolly refused to respond. That was new. They didn't want to crack down on her around the other prisoners, so they pretended they didn't care. Most of us welcomed her transformation, although some still didn't trust her.

One day in the exercise yard, Cahide was wearing clean, neat clothing and had her hair tied on one side. She was moving energetically, even aggressively. Her face, previously tense, cold, and helpless, now gave the impression of decisiveness. Then she went upstairs before anyone else.

Soon Gültan and Zeliha called out me frantically to go to Cahide, and in a few leaps, I was there. Cahide lay in bed with foam around her mouth. She was still alive.

"Cahide, what have you done? Tell me!" I had to get her to talk.

"I wrote it all down," she whispered, pointing to her pocket. It contained a letter addressed to me. I took it and shoved it into my pocket. Later I read it—she's written that she didn't blame us, but her situation was unbearable, and she lacked the strength to stand up to the enemy.

Finally, Cahide admitted she'd drunk insecticide. Before we could ask anything more, soldiers barged into the cell, Esat among them. How had they found out about it so fast? we wondered. Who had told them? Apparently they'd noticed the commotion. They took Cahide away immediately. Even Esat looked unsettled, as if he were very angry or afraid. He was responsible for what had happened.

Everyone was shocked and frightened. Later, Ali Osman turned up and asked, "Who saw anything? What was that insecticide doing here?" He turned to me: "Or did you tell her to kill herself?"

He was testing me. I glared back at him.

"You goddamn animals!" he exploded. "There's no suicide here under our supervision, you hear? We're the ones who decide whether you live or die. No one else cares if you kick the bucket. Get real! You're all guilty in the eyes of the state, that's why you're here. The court decided on your punishment—not us. Our job is to keep order and see to your safety." Then more softly: "Don't make it harder for us than it has to be!" And he stalked out. The suicide attempt had rattled him—not because Cahide's life was important to him but because of the possible consequences.

The doctor said she'd have died if we'd found her only five minutes later. She stayed in the hospital for a while, then returned. As she slowly came back to life, she wrestled with her weaknesses and defeats. I don't know if she overcame her fear of death, forgot her personal sorrows, or demolished the bridge to betrayal. But she needed our help. We had to do everything possible to bring Cahide back and persuade her to take a clear stand in court against the enemy. She had to feel shame that she'd not lived up to her own standards, and she had to understand the consequences of her individualized rage and her narrow concept of honor. As long as betrayal is even a slight possibility, the enemy will try to exploit it at every opportunity. The women friends agreed to help. Later she promised that in the future she'd take a stand in court.

Esat so wished for a female informer and tried hard to recruit one, but none of the women in our ward would become turncoats for him. A woman from the Izol tribe told us in detail what information he had asked of her, and about whom. "You've been good to me, so I didn't do you any harm," she told us. Esat's wish would remain unfulfilled—let him choke on it! But then he always lied to the men friends, saying he'd turned one of the women and she'd be on TV the next day.

Others who had also been undecided and broken under interrogation watched Cahide's case closely. We discussed the need to create a communal feeling and eliminate weak links that the enemy could benefit from. We had so many internal conflicts. Every single friend had a boatload of problems. The enemy's pressure, the strain of torture, egocentric behavior, moodiness, pessimism, lack of political analysis ... all made it harder for us to adhere to generally accepted principles. But the friends were determined to resolve internal conflicts without the enemy being aware of it.

Mazlum's Newroz, March 21, 1982   The days leading up to Newroz were tense. This would be my second Newroz in the Diyarbakir dungeon. The previous year had seen death fasts. Now we were isolated. Interrogations had continued throughout the prison, and betrayals were rampant, especially in the Elazığ group—the band of traitors around Şahin, Ali Gündüz, Erol Degirmenci, and Yıldırım Merkit validated the enemy's prison policy.

New prisoners arrived in our ward and were taken to interrogation. I knew some of them personally, others only by name. The enemy coerced prisoners into writing statements, where they responded to dozens of questions and declared regret for their past behavior. If the enemy didn't like a statement, he had them write another. Some arrestees had decided in advance to betray, and they freely allowed the enemy to use the statements. When someone well known defected, the betrayal was shocking.

We observed the new arrivals surreptitiously. When they went to the toilet and had to wait in line there, we'd rummage through their trash and sometimes find torn-up confessions. It was good to read them. We kept the paper scraps, reassembled them, and hid them so we could use them later in court if necessary. We didn't let all the friends read all the statements, and we didn't tell everyone the specific names.

Near our ward, a former guardroom was transformed into a torture chamber, equipped with hooks, electroshock, and other instruments. Women newcomers were interrogated there before being brought to our ward. None of the torture instruments there were unusual, but it was all abnormal.

"They're preparing this torture room for us," I told the other women prisoners. "Maybe for special interrogations, but there'll be torture every day. The enemy is trying to force everyone to defect, even us. He'll probably start by singling out certain people."

"They'll isolate certain prisoners and try to get them to inform. Maybe rape them. We can't sit back. If we don't defend ourselves, he'll rape us all." Everyone said with determination: "Then we'll kill ourselves. These repulsive bastards aren't going to touch us." Up until now women had been raped only during police interrogations, but now they would presumably start in prison. We wouldn't allow it. We'd resist together. This wasn't a decision for the men friends. If women were going to be coerced in special ways, we'd take special action against it.

We discussed what action. "We could do a mass suicide action, through self-strangulation. Or we could beat our skulls against the wall until they break. That's our only means of resisting an attack." Everyone agreed. We shared our decision with a few honest women from other [political] groups. Then as if we'd made a pact, our spirits rose. We all put on thick socks and sweatpants under our skirts. But then, because of the falanga, we mostly did that anyway—Esat took special pleasure in clubbing naked legs.

In the next days, the guardroom was quickly emptied out again, so it looked as it had before. The doors to the corridor weren't even locked. What was going on? Had someone died during torture? Or had we been overheard? Had we disrupted the enemy's plan? We speculated excitedly. Strange, how fast our moods could shift! State of mind is so important in confronting the enemy. We could spite him just by holding firm to our lives and convictions.

We absolutely wanted to celebrate Newroz, knowing the party outside would also do certain actions. But there was so much we didn't know. We weren't allowed to have even the slightest contact with the men.

"The friends must be planning something," we guessed. We trusted them, they were our hope.

We wrote a Newroz declaration. Cahide painted a symbol for the New Year festival, and we hung it on the wall in a spot where it wasn't visible through the door slot. It was about the size of two pages. We brought out some candles we'd hidden and cut into small pieces. We arranged them on the floor so they spelled "*Biji Newroz*," and we had enough to write "*Biji PKK*" too. We lit the candles, took a moment of silence, then read our declaration aloud. Then we danced *halay* in a half-circle.

A few friends stood watch at the door so the soldiers couldn't see anything through the slot. We didn't care if they came in after the celebration. But it was Newroz, who could stop us? A few people from other [political] groups took part in the celebration. Others slunk into the other ward, afraid the enemy would storm in and beat them. That was sad, but we let it drop, so caught up in the excitement were we. More and more people joined the *halay*, and the half-circle got wider. Afterward a nice theater piece was performed. It was an important celebration.

Despite the huge racket we made, no soldiers came to take a look. Why? Something seemed off, but what? Had there been actions outside? Why else would the enemy leave us alone on such an important night? Newroz without beatings—it just couldn't be! Or maybe someone inside the prison had done an action. Had the men started another death fast? Oh, this time we absolutely would join.

We pressed our ears to the door but couldn't hear anything from the corridor or the nearby wards. Bedriye pounded her fists on the wall and chanted, "*Biji Newroz, biji PKK!*" But only a weak echo answered her.

The silence lasted for days, dead silence, even during the evenings. Had the daily beatings become so routine that their absence now unsettled us? Had some disaster happened? Dammit, we women didn't get any news—it was like a prison within a prison. The uncertainty was nerve-wracking. We knew only what we heard from the next ward over, or from some individual prisoner en route to the hospital. Sometimes the friends even welcomed defectors, before realizing what they were. We tried to find out about other prisoners from the guards.

New prisoners were also our main way to get information from outside. The friends who distributed food would take it down the lower ward, escorted by a guard to keep them from talking to each other. One day we arranged with the ward leader that during food distribution, if the soldier-guard tried to come in, she would stall him at the door. Meanwhile Gültan would ask a new prisoner, Bezar, for any news.

I waited on the stairway from the upper level. The minutes dragged by, the wait was interminable, and I feared the worst. Then Gültan emerged and stopped at the foot of the stairway. Something wasn't right. She seemed to be limping, her head was hanging, and she was sobbing. "Gültan, what's going on? Tell me!"

When she raised her head, I saw tears in her eyes, and she was deathly pale. My heart stopped. Whatever it was, it had to be bad.

I followed her into the small kitchen, which stood empty. We often came here when we wanted to talk and didn't want others to overhear. She was still crying.

"What's going on? What happened?" I asked again.

She hugged me. "Mazlum."

My arms fell, my heart seemed to want to escape my body, and I froze, my eyes brimming with tears. *Mazlum? ... Mazlum? What's happened?*

Gültan managed to choke out, "They say he hung himself on Newroz."

"What! Hung himself? He'd never do that! The enemy's lying! The enemy murdered him, then called it suicide. I guarantee that's what happened." I choked up too, as hatred welled in me. How far would the enemy go? Would he kill off the whole leadership cadre? We had to do something!

Later Aysel came in, crying uncontrollably. Word got around. Mother Durre beat her chest and wailed so bitterly, it must have been audible outside.

Just before Mazlum's mother, Kabire, was released, she had said, "If only I could see Mazlum one more time." They hadn't alllowed it. And Baran couldn't give him the hug she'd promised. Mazlum ... Mazlum ... Mazlum ... No one wanted to believe it. Time stood still.

That evening we held a memorial service. Everyone participated. I gave a eulogy, and after a moment of silence, we sang militant songs. Mazlum's action filled our hearts with hatred but also brightened them and united us. It shamed those who'd shown weakness.

What had been Mazlum's purpose with this action? Many couldn't understand it at first. Earlier he had written: "Surrender leads to betrayal, resistance to victory." Slowly we realized that he'd intended to send us a Newroz message: *Resistance is life!*

When Hayri learned that Mazlum had hanged himself, he immediately saw it was "a political action of great significance." Last May the resistance had been broken. Since then, the enemy had intensified his brutal campaign to induce all the prisoners to defect, and it was showing results. The leadership cadres knew something had to be done. Mazlum understood that prison life as a totality was organized to destroy people's personalities, to annihilate their individuality. He had seen the danger and tried to prevent it. Aware of his historical responsibility, he had paid the price alone. Here where we all breathed the same air, his splendid fire had burned right next to us. He had commemorated Newroz in an action that hit the enemy directly. He ripped away those ever-tightening snares, warned us against delay, and succeeded in halting the betrayals for a time.

At first, many didn't grasp the secret of his heroism. That was natural—not everyone can use death to give life meaning. Not everyone can find beauty in harsh conditions and still look death in the eye. Many feared life as much as they feared death and died a thousand deaths even while living.

And we were still pressured, knowing this one action wouldn't stop the betrayals altogether. I felt it deep in my heart. But surely the necessary action would come.

We hadn't done justice to Mazlum during life. Now in death, he defined the word *dignity*, and his Newroz action would have ripple effects. It would revive the spirit of freedom and unity. Now we would discuss new forms of resistance, and our subsequent actions would mutually enlarge and complement this one.

These events affected us women deeply, and we awaited a signal for action. It didn't occur to us to get active ourselves. But then, what were we supposed to do? We'd always assumed a party decision was required before we could organize resistance. "The organization has to start anything," we thought. And how could we do anything if the men were quiet? But it was horrible to just wait all the time, and we got impatient. The preconditions for an uprising were more than ripe.

In the wake of Mazlum's action, all the prisoners searched their souls. Not just the leadership cadre but everyone connected with the party looked for how to proceed. Mazlum's action became a milestone event for PKK resistance. From now on, we would all measure ourselves against his commitment. On one side was the infamy of betrayal in a situation of terror; on the other side was the greatness of Mazlum's heroic act. He had opened a new horizon, and hearts that were already flowing toward it wouldn't wait any longer.

The disintegration of Yıldırım Merkit Normally the enemy tries to find your weak points. Your revolutionary duty is to arm yourself against it, and to express a certain attitude. A person who shows doubts, who behaves ineffectually and ambivalently, encourages the enemy, opens a door for him, gives him home. The person who signals a reluctance to fight usually ends up a traitor. In prison, that inner attitude leads to capitulation. Such a person is irretrievably lost.

Fear is one of the first steps on the path to betrayal. All rulers work with fear, since it transforms people into easy victims. The enemy protects himself from his own fears, using actions that play to our fears. But fear can also enable a person to overcome danger. If you transform your fear into strength, you can terrify the enemy and even freeze his activity.

Yıldırım Merkit had been arrested along with Mazlum, during a traffic inspection [in November 1979]. And Yıldırım had panicked. Why had he been so afraid? Had he felt responsible as a leader? But in his fear, he overlooked the fact that Mazlum was with him, and no one was more concerned about the organization than Mazlum.

No, Yıldırım's fear was mostly for himself. Here in prison the enemy was everywhere, but he was so afraid of the enemy that he made things easy for him. For a while, influenced by friends, he suppressed his fears or kept them under control. But over time his weak personality surfaced. His very demeanor projected fear and defeat.

Before Yıldırım came to [the PKK], he and his family had been with the PDA, which had a veneer of representing the "revolutionary proletariat," but it had no use for revolution or the Kurdistan Left and never contributed to a democratic approach. Its orientation was basically Kemalist. A group's class character doesn't necessarily determine its attitude toward Kurdistan, but the Merkit family's initial adherence to the PDA was no accident—its Kemalism suited them. Later they were attracted by the Kurdish freedom movement's struggle, but then they chose to betray it.

Esat sensed Yıldırım's fear and exploited it. Torturers can quickly spot those who, like themselves, are consumed by fear, and they know they're easy prey. Şahin and Yıldırım were the best examples. Their betrayals stemmed from fear, and fear robbed them of all their humanity. In Esat's hands they achieved a state of total humiliation.

Yıldırım's betrayal apparently began when he looked through a door slot and saw Hayri [Durmuş] alone in a room, writing. For a long time, the enemy had tried to prevent us from seeing even Hayri's silhouette from a distance. But in the case of Yıldırım, the enemy pointed him out—"Look, there's Hayri—even he is writing a confession now."

Actually Hayri had been writing his defense. He had told the court he wanted to write a defense and had requested paper and pencil.

Our current circumstances aren't suited for the preparation of a defense. We don't have the necessary materials, not even paper and pencils. We have nothing but torture. In this court, we're charged with belonging to a certain movement, so we have the right to say something about that organization. I want to prepare my defense in writing.

The court had approved the request, and Esat had seen to it that it happened. But underhandedly he had taken the opportunity to show Hayri to other prisoners, saying he was writing a confession.

Every one can make mistakes, show weakness, and suffer defeats. They're understandable. But to believe that Hayri had given up, and to conclude that therefore one must also commit betrayal, was to lose all logic.

In any case, this episode alone wasn't the only reason for Yıldırım's betrayal. But the enemy kept trying to exploit his weak points, and he had so opened himself to it that this small manipulation was enough to induce him to cross over. Ruled by his fears, he went his own way.

The rest of us mostly refused to be dragged down to that level. Many who showed weaknesses and were on the brink of capitulation triggered sympathy in others. But toward Şahin and Yıldırım, they felt only hatred and anger. Even those who'd been close to them and whom they'd brought into the organization now felt contempt for them.

One day during a trial, I was sitting in the van waiting to be taken into the courthouse, when I saw Hayri, sitting among other men friends. His hands were chained behind his back, and his big body was bent over. I was sad to see him this way and burst into tears. But the very sight of him bolstered my strength for months. He showed concern for the friends around him—he really was a leading personality with an awareness of responsibility. His posture remained upright, and it would've been unjust for me to be disconcerted by the sight of him chained. After all, that was what the enemy wanted—to deprive us of our confidence and our convictions.

The Elazığ group in court [In October 1981 our attorney] Hüseyin Yıldırım was arrested, as I later learned from my father. Something seemed fishy about it. The jerk had barely participated in our hearings. He was frightened and spoke only to request our release. Now he'd been arrested—why? Someone must have had their eye on him. So which ward was he in now? Other lawyers had been arrested—was the enemy trying to intimidate lawyers to keep them from representing us in court? Possibly, but I was uneasy. Later, when I asked someone about it, I got beaten up. Esat forbade the flow of information between outside and inside, and my lawyer's arrest constituted a piece of information.

The main trial against the Elazığ group started, prosecuting three men from the central committee. The enemy pulled Şahin and Yıldırım out of the trial, and they would be the main witnesses [for the prosecution]. Şahin was the Elazığ group's most important traitor and had been most often used in prison, as when he insisted to the Elazığ group that the organization was dead. The trial would put his betrayal on display.

Only Şahin and the other traitors were given the right to speak at the trial. In fact, it became a showcase for them. The enemy's goal was to turn the courtroom, like the police interrogation rooms and the prison itself, into an arena for betrayal, where no one would dare defend the organization. There were also secret sessions. In every hearing there was a chief traitor. The courtroom would be a theater of war.

Şahin talked nonstop. He described the PKK's founding and distorted the facts to cast the chairman in a bad light, down to how he took his meals. He debunked the party's ideological goals from a Kemalist viewpoint. He was vindictive and aggressive—strange how much effort he put into it. For years he'd ranted with hostility, but that apparently wasn't enough for him. Now he lashed out at everything and everyone and snarled that the PKK was doomed to failure.

But Şahin was right about one thing: the enemy really had decimated the Elazığ group. All the Elazığ friends had been brutally tortured. Day and night the enemy, supported by the traitors, had pressured them to repent and go to work for the enemy. He reminded them constantly how they'd buckled under interrogation. To grind them down, he even made use of the party's criticism: "Your own organization hasn't stood behind you, not once," he pointed out. "It says you're all traitors. It's all over. What are you still trying to defend?" Dozens had defected, abandoning their convictions. Some had shown weakness, and some waited helplessly for a signal. Only a very few stood by the party openly.

It was true that the party had made a [negative] assessment of the Elazığ group. The party had to hold them accountable, especially those who had failed to resist. Even our failure to take precautions, such that it had led to the arrests, was an offense to the party. Undeniably our level was far from that of the PKK cadres. But even before the party criticized the defectors in the interrogation phase, the defectors had written a report to the party confessing that they'd failed and agreeing to be held accountable.

All the charges against the defendants were based on Şahin's statements and on information extracted by torture and beatings, which the soldiers called "Apo's Book." Under the laws of the Republic of Turkey, if they were found guilty of the crimes they'd been charged with, they would be executed. Executed! The word didn't pass easily over one's lips, but in prison the torturers dropped it constantly: "You'll all be put to death" was one of their favorite sentences. Esat joyfully read aloud to us from the indictment, naming who had behaved how during interrogation, who had said what to the magistrate, and who played what role in the party. Before the trial opened, "judicial hearings" had been role-played in the prison. The torturers played the role of judges and meted out torture according to the person's alleged role in the party. They charged a few friends with 20 or 30 murders [and found them guilty. To others they said, "You haven't done anything. If you're smart and don't cause trouble, you'll get off." But they were really interested in the "hard cases." Absurdly, even the pettiest torturer was looking for a big culprit.

Prison is the grimmest of all theaters of war, and we were novices. People betrayed right before our eyes, even in the courtroom. Could we be silent about it? But wasn't the goal of all the enemy's machinations to silence us? No, this was precisely the moment when we had to make a stand for the party. Mounting a political defense was no simple matter, but it was the party that was on trial here. Instead of allowing the enemy to exploit our weaknesses, we had to turn our weaknesses into strengths and denounce colonialism in the courtroom.

Throughout that first day of the trial, the men friends remained silent, including Hamili—none of them spoke up. What were they waiting for? I wondered. Or was I too impatient? Should I wait my turn? But if Şahin was going to distort the truth, I wanted to break this appalling silence. Someone had to expose his lies. The friends had told me that in other proceedings, most prisoners had stood by the party and affirmed its principles. They defended the party's ideology and policies, the nature of our revolution, the nature of our struggle, the necessity to go abroad, our concept of socialism, the character of the enemy, our goals and allies, the social and political structures of our base, and the importance of the chairman. They'd affirmed their love for Mazlum, whose action had been a stand against betrayal.

I was determined to speak this way as well. But when I rose, the judges denied me: "You'll talk when it's your turn." Then Şahin mocked me for playing the heroine. In his view, everyone had surrendered, and I was just trying to inflate my own importance.

The court stenographer wrote down only Şahin's remarks. Our lawyers didn't say anything either, they just looked tragic and called for the release of some of their clients. The few family members present sobbed. Terrified by their prison visits, they hardly dared even look at us. So went the first day of the trial.

And Esat continued his manipulations during the trial. Once I was sitting in the big prisoner transport van with some of the men. At first I was thrilled by the unexpected chance to talk to them, but then I noticed that many were defectors. They were lined up facing forward, and strangely, none of them looked at me. Among them were [my brother] Metin, Doğan, and Mehmet. Our eyes met briefly. I couldn't believe it and shook my head questioningly. Why were they behaving so oddly? Metin seemed to try to tell me something with his eyes. Only later did I understand that Esat had put me in this van with them deliberately to destroy my morale. When I got out, I said to Metin, "What are you doing with these scoundrels? After all this misery, are you going to become a traitor? Idiot! I'll see you when you get out of here!" He tried to answer, but the soldiers stepped in and pulled me away.

The trial continued, but I don't remember how I managed to sit in the courtroom, given the betrayals. I didn't pay attention. I kept thinking of Meto with a lump in my throat—it just couldn't be true. That scumbag Esat was trying to use my brother to finish me off. A few times I looked over at the defectors. Meto looked back at me. Then I looked to the other side, where Hamili, Selim, and Sadi were sitting together. They didn't return my questioning look. We couldn't even use our eyes to communicate anymore. Metin later told me that after that day, "I've never cried so hard in my life."

The torture continued during the trial, uninterrupted. Even as we were shuttled to and from the courthouse, the sessions continued. But no one stood up in court and said, "We're being tortured." When someone mentioned torture anyway, the judges said, "What happens in prison is of no concern to us." Sometimes we women were clubbed downstairs, before they let us go up to our ward. The men were beaten even in the courtroom. The soldiers were trying to create the impression to the court that the women prisoners were treated well, but that enraged us: *The men friends must think it's all going brilliantly for us.* The neighboring wards heard our screams, but our voices didn't penetrate to the other wards.

At the next day of the trial, Meto sat somewhere else. It was another one of Esat's manipulations—to seat different prisoners among the defectors every day. He had found the Elazığ group's weak point.

Finally [sometime in the next days] Hayri rose and said, "The inhuman torture and pressure are creating the silence." Then he turned to the other prisoners and said, "I believe that someday you'll all defend the party. Those of you who confessed will withdraw your confessions. You'll beg the party and the people for forgiveness."

But Şahin shot back, "They let themselves be persuaded to join the organization. They were young, so it was easy for the party to seduce them. You can't blame them, but now they recognize the truth. They don't think about the organization anymore, only about getting out of it as fast as possible—"

I interrupted: "They were silenced through torture and pressure." Then I swung around and said to the men friends, "Why don't you say anything?"

Silence.

"They'll talk," I continued. "And when they do, they'll explain how during the interrogation phase, Şahin Dönmez tried to break our convictions. He called us all cowards, because he himself had been cowardly enough to commit treason. This court isn't following its own rules. It's Şahin Dönmez who's guiding these proceedings. He speaks for days while we can't utter a word."

The judged bellowed, "Sit down, or I'll throw you out!"

Finally it was my turn to argue my defense. Hamili, Selim, and I all made political defenses, unlike others who acknowledged they were party members or sympathizers. I had written a comprehensive defense, sticking to the earlier plan. Our speaking time was very limited, but they didn't even let me read my declaration to the end since they considered the content punishable. So when I tried to defend myself, they stopped me. Later my declaration itself became the occasion for another indictment. I was charged with making a statement—but I hadn't even been permitted to read it aloud! Comical. This court was political—and to defend the party and adhere to principles was a crime.

Hamili and I also made a joint statement. The friends had written it, and Hamili and I signed it. Hamili was able to read it aloud.

Overall the courtroom struggle boosted our morale. After each session, we joyfully celebrated those who'd defended themselves politically by passing around messages with their names.

The situation was so contradictory. The prisoners, while in the wards, followed the enemy's rules and sang Turkish marches. But in court, they made speeches denouncing the enemy and colonialism and defending the party's ideology and politics. In court, we always advocated for the party, and even though we were the "guilty" ones on trial, we prosecuted colonialism. We voiced our convictions, declared our respect for the martyrs, and swore to do right by the party, even if we'd previously failed. Our mistakes and offenses were as much a part of our reality as our unbearable and debilitating situation in the prison, which we cursed every day.

The Night of the Four, May 17–18, 1982   Then the main trial was adjourned until an undetermined date. Trials, it seemed, took place only when the court and the prison administration decided they were necessary.

In May, the guards brought me from the ward for a hearing. They were behaving strangely. They were on time, but the prison corridor was empty. They put me in the van. The soldier next to me was silent, tapping his legs and hands with his baton, apparently lost in thought. What was going on? My heart raced, and my throat burned.

The driver was Laz, as I could tell from his dialect. In the past he'd talked a lot—he was in charge of external security and spoke more freely than the soldiers inside the prison. "How many died in the fire?"

he asked the soldier next to me. "I saw the one who was taken to the hospital. Oh, he was bloody all over. Horrible."

The soldier next to me didn't react. Maybe he hadn't heard.

The Laz repeated his question.

The soldier was uncomfortable that I was listening in. Guards never talked of such things in our presence, knowing that we were to have no access to information. But then without looking up, he said, "Yeah, man, they have some strong principles. The guy was a fiery blaze, but he was still chanting slogans. Incredible."

I gasped audibly, then tried to compose myself, but they didn't say much more. The Laz said only, "The one in the hospital is in critical condition. Probably he's dead too."

The van sped on without my noticing—I didn't care if the sky was light or dark. My eyes were full of tears, and I was in pain, but I didn't dare cry around these bastards.

Some of my comrades had set themselves on fire—that much I'd understood. Who and how many, I didn't know. I let out a sob. Should I tell them I was sick and had to go back to prison? Trial sessions usually dragged on for a long time—it would be like torture to sit in the courtroom all day. But maybe one of the men friends would stand up and say something about it to the court. Someone had to. I wished Hamili and the others would do it. But maybe Hamili was one of the ones who …

Normally when Hamili and I saw each other, we acknowledged each other from afar with our eyes. For all of us, it was a beautiful moment to be able to smile at each other. Back in the cell, we would analyze it in detail. "And what happened then?" the women would ask eagerly. "He laughed and greeted me." I answered joyfully. "Oh, if only we could have seen him too!" they said.

Today when I entered the courtroom, I looked around. Hamili and others from his ward were there, except for Sadi. When the court checked who was present, someone told the stenographer that Sadi was ill. Then who could it have been? Was it leadership cadre again? The judge said something inaudible. I prayed to the gods that today's session would come to a quick end.

The proceedings were [not] interrupted. No one said anything! Did they perhaps not know?

Afterward I was brought back to the transport van, and so were Hamili and the others. Good. Yes, their heads were bowed, and they'd said nothing, but at least I could see them. The soldiers repeated that no one could raise their head and talk.

Hamili couldn't hear me. I kicked him, and he jumped a little, then smiled broadly.

Next to him sat Rıza Bozyel. "Has something happened?" I whispered.

"No, why?" asked Rıza.

"Fire," I whispered.

Hamili turned slightly in my direction and looked at me from the corners of his eyes, trying to understand.

"Fire," I repeated.

"We're doing okay," he said.

I was astonished. Had the soldiers that morning made up an incident and deliberately had me overhear it? But it hadn't seemed like an intrigue—they'd seemed shaken up.

Back in prison, I managed to climb the stairs with effort. The guards looked as if they hadn't yet overcome their shock. Normally the guard responsible for our ward never missed a chance to abuse us, but today he was quiet. I entered the ward. Everyone waited nervously for news. I told them what I'd heard that morning. A sorrowful silence spread. No one dared venture any guesses.

Not until a later court session for the Urfa group's trial did we learn exactly what had happened, when men friends spoke out during the proceedings about prison conditions. They announced their commitment to the party and sought to mount a political defense. Then Fuat Kav stood up and said, "Four of our comrades set themselves on fire. Mahmut, Ferhat, Esref, and Necmi left behind a letter. I'd like it to be entered into the record." Then he read the letter.

On the night of May 17–18, the anniversary of the death of Haki Karer, they had set themselves on fire. Later we were told they'd said, "Don't put out the fire—fan the flames!" One action gives rise to another—the Four had responded to Mazlum's appeal.

We women had found out about Comrade Mazlum's death very late, and now the same thing happened with the action of the four. We held a memorial service for them, where the women who'd known them shared their memories.

Gönül: a stranger among us Every death brought us closer together, but a few prisoners lost all hope, and we constantly had to shore them up. When the torture was intense, people turned inward. During concerted attacks, we temporarily suspended internal conflicts, but once the situation relaxed again, they became intolerable.

The soldiers were always breathing down our necks. They become ever more sadistic and attacked us like animals, sometimes sexually, when a prisoner appealed to the soldiers' primitive instincts with her looks or behavior. It was only occasional, but we hated it and warned against it. Most of the women prisoners united against it, but to some, we had to explain categorically that for a woman to debase herself this way was unacceptable. Whenever the soldiers insulted us, we snapped back, even if we got beaten for it. If they attacked a woman who'd prostituted herself in a casino, we intervened and took her in. We resolved that a rape or similar assault would lead to a rebellion, so we included all the prisoners and channeled individuals' rage. A concerted reaction to the enemy's aggression would intimidate him. If Esat came to us half naked, we reacted with disgust and revulsion. Usually he met only with the ward leaders or called Gönül.

When times are hard, when the enemy attacks, prisoners have to unite. Some prisoners are ground down or knocked off course, while others refuse to be discouraged and bounce back every time. It's a meaningful distinction. In a revolutionary life, there are no secret fears, feelings, or wishes. The nature of the revolution isn't veiled—it's stark naked.

That's why Gönül was like a stranger among us. My first impression of her had been spot on: phony, selfish, and shallow.

Soon after I arrived at Diyarbakir, women friends had explained to me that Gönül sometimes chatted with the officers for hours, then rejected being criticized for it. When Esat Oktay took over, the administration tortured ward leaders, but Gönül [our ward leader] was taken to isolation instead. Everyone who resisted was beaten, but Gönül emerged unscathed. Rumors swirled around her. Gönül was like a stranger among us. No one liked her much. She was high-and-mighty and much impressed with herself. Since she was more educated than most of us, she thought she was special.

We were trying to help prisoners who suffered from inner conflicts, but Gönül undercut our efforts, depressing them further, strengthening the doubts of those who just drifted along.

It really wasn't hard to see into her psyche. Back in Ankara and Tuzlucayir, she'd joined the revolution the way a stage actress joins a play. It had little to do with political consciousness, and she rarely got involved in the organization's internal affairs. She lacked any real feeling for the revolution or even the natural enthusiasm of youth. No, she just reveled in her petit-bourgeois know-it-all attitude and enjoyed the flattery and compliments.

Esat deliberately fueled our mistrust of her. Whenever he came into our ward, he'd ask for her. If he didn't see her right away, he'd shout, "Where's Gönül?" When she rushed in, he'd put his hand on her shoulder and ask her confidentially things such as, "What do the women need for their periods? We'll give you newspapers, you can make pads from them." Or "What does Hêlîn need?"

He always emphasized, "Gönül knows such-and-such, she's smart." By saying "Gönül knows, Gönül understands, Gönül is smart," he stroked her psychologically. She loved flattery, even from Esat, as we well knew—she even regarded praise from him as her due. Whenever Esat or Ali Osman called out her name, he was targeting her weakness. And when the rest of us heard it, we scowled in worry and anger. We all looked over at Gönül in wondrous unity.

Esat was our enemy, administering a system designed to break our wills and strip away our personalities. But none of this bothered Gönül. Before our very eyes, she catered to his whims, even knowing how we would react. She acted toward him like an employee toward her boss.

Her behavior drove me nuts. "That's enough, Gönül!" I'd say in front of everyone.

This scum is toying with you. Why do you go along with it? Doesn't it bother you? Esat knows your behavior demoralizes the rest of us—that's why he keeps it up. What he can't accomplish by torture, he hopes to achieve this way.

Sometimes I was severe with her. Then she'd cry or rage that I'd judged her all wrong, but her behavior didn't change. We were fighting a real war of nerves with her.

We really didn't want her to cross over to the enemy altogether. "If nothing else, look at Rıza's ring on your finger," I'd beg her.

At least respect that relationship. Who knows what Esat is telling Rıza about you? Pull yourself together, and don't always stand to attention when Esat comes around. If you've got something to discuss with him, do it in the presence of other friends. Otherwise you raise suspicions. If you'd stick to a consistently rejecting attitude toward Esat, he'd leave you alone.

I tried to bring her to her senses this way. And we brought her in to one of our committees when decisions were to be made. Sometimes we gave her tasks, like writing something or doing some educational work. We tried to dispel the mistrust around her, but her own behavior didn't help.

Whatever became of the young women from Dersim?   A new group arrived from Elazığ, and among them were [my girlhood friends] Fadime K. and Nimet [Kaya]. Earlier arrestees from Dersim, under interrogation, had named them in their statements. The group's trial was consolidated with that of the Elazığ group.

Fadime had been in my very first group back in Dersim and got involved with the movement right away. "This ideology attracts beautiful people," we'd both said. We did educational work in Dag together. She was not talkative, but what she said made sense. Temperamentally she was calm, upbeat, and mature. "She's dedicated and hungry for action—she'd be a terrific militant," we said of her. She didn't suffer fools and reflected before she acted.

After the first arrest wave in 1979, Fadime's group from Elazığ fled to the mountains, where they stayed through the [1980] coup until their arrests. Among them were Çiçek Selcan and also Azime Demirtaş, who died fighting the enemy and entered history as our first woman martyr.

Deaf Metin had been there, [she told me,] where he caused a lot of problems—he stirred up conflicts, behaved erratically, was either too dogmatic or too passive, and mostly looked out for himself. And he bothered women. "He's the most repulsive creature I've ever known!" Fadime told me.

How did you ever work with him in Elazığ? In the mountains, no one could stand him for a second. He picked fights with everyone. He didn't listen to anyone else and pranced around like he was the party. He really had it in for Hüseyin [Eroğlu], who was engaged to Çiçek Selcan. That irritated Deaf Metin, so he talked terrible trash about them, spread all kinds of dirt. He hit me a few times. Once I panicked and hit him back and threatened to shoot him. That scared him, so he left me in peace afterward. Just as I was leaving, he came on to me. But then he got afraid I'd report something about him. Oh, I hope he didn't go abroad! What would he tell the party there? Now Hüseyin and I are both arrested, and he's the only one from the leadership who remains outside. I know he'll try to make Hüseyin look bad. If I ever get out of here, I'll hold him accountable, and I'll tell the party everything.

Recently she had been trying to leave Turkey with Hüseyin and others but was arrested on the road to Mardin. She had been interrogated in Dersim, then taken to Elazığ prison and finally to Diyarbakir. She was tortured with electricity—but didn't scream. You know, when electricity is applied to your body, you just have to scream. I could endure beatings without screaming, but not electrical torture. People produced every possible sound, but not Fadime. The police were stunned. "We've never seen that," they said. "You're abnormal." And they told the story everywhere. When Fadime told us about it, we laughed and said, "Now you're famous." During her interrogation, the police read aloud statements that others had made about her, but she had not confessed, saying something only about the courier she'd been arrested with.

I knew so little about developments since I was arrested. What were our people doing anyway? Fadime caught me up. Kiymet and others had gone to Ankara. Perihan had withdrawn from the work in Hilvan; one of her younger sisters had a relationship with a soldier. Nimet was here in prison. Türkan Cakmak was isolated, having sacrificed her abilities in favor of a screwed-up femininity. Cemile Merkit was married to Ali Haydar Kaytan. All this news bubbled out of Fadime. "Stop!" I cried. "I get it."

[She told me more.] Sevim [Kaya, sister of Nimet,] was no longer active. Nadire had gone to the mountains. Yıldız Durmuş and Kadriye had been released from prison. Gönül Tepe had jumped from a balcony during a house inspection in Bingöl and injured her back. Erol Değirmenci was married to a comrade and had a child—in Mazgirt, they violated our principles for revolutionary comradely relations. Erol's stepsister, Özden, was with the HK and seemed untrustworthy. Nurhayat, in Ağri, had been arrested on the expectation that she'd turn informer. She'd spent time at Diyarbakir, then been released.

Almost nothing was left of the young women from Dersim. "What happened to the young one from the Teachers School?" I asked. She'd been sent to Hilvan. What about Fadime Y.? No one knew—

presumably she had taken another path. A person's initial time within the organization was formative. Then difficult times showed who was weak and couldn't organize even him- or herself.

Finally, Fadime and others from Elazığ prison told us that after Mazlum's death, some of our leadership cadres had been shot, both inside and outside prison. It was devastating, unbearable that these important people had died! Maybe if they'd been more distant from us, we could stand it, but we were close to them all.

Dreaming of Esat's death I used to plot Esat's death. Oh, how I'd brooded over plans, for days on end! I'd swiped one of the iron skewers used to break up ice in the exercise yard and hidden it. Fadime and Aysel asked me about my plan and wanted to work with me. It was best to minimize the number of friends involved, but I brought them in.

The iron skewer wasn't very sharp, but it was heavy. I'd sharpen the tip and make use of its weight. Hiding it in the cell was risky, so I'd tie it to my back. I'd wear a sweater, so I could whip it out at the right moment. He'd die faster if I struck him on the neck first. He'd be reading my petition, I'd whack him with it, then stab him lethally, before the guards even noticed anything.

"But how, and where?" Aysel and Fadime asked. I'd figured that out too. We'd bring Esat to a rear cell. I'd tell him I wanted to talk to him about an application—alone. He wouldn't expect an attack. After the guard on duty announced his arrival by saying, "My captain is here!" he would arrive accompanied by several guards. I'd have to say the matter I wanted to speak to him about was confidential, so he'd send them away.

Between the two wards stretched three long, narrow corridors. This part of the building had an L-shape. To reach the rear cell, you had to turn left twice. It was like a labyrinth. We figured out how to prevent the guard from hearing what was going on in the rear cell: the ward leader would strike up a loud conversation with him, maybe by the staircase at the main entrance.

After I killed Esat, I'd get rid of the document. I'd say he'd attacked me first and had hit back in self-defense. That way I'd stay alive long enough to be tried in court. There I'd take responsibility for the action and say, "I killed him because he murdered dozens of friends." I'd either get the death penalty or die by torture, but I was ready for both.

Planning the action, just talking about it, made us feel great, as if we'd already carried it out. But Esat didn't visit us as often as before. The longer we put off the action, the more doubts surfaced. Aysel said,

The soldiers are really going to lose it when they see you've killed their captain. They'll slaughter us. Do we really want to risk that bloodbath? And we should inform the male friends in advance. It's a very serious matter.

And should we delay in order to get [party] approval? But why? Probably this was a reflex hung over from earlier times, when every procedure had to be approved. But it now had the effect of blocking activity. What was wrong with using a good opportunity for revolutionary creativity?

We'd already had to decide many things ourselves— we'd been on our own for more than two years and settled a lot of things. We'd moved from weakness and capitulation to resistance. Maybe not consistently. But when the soldiers insulted us for refusing to say "Yes, my commander!" hadn't we decided to defend ourselves? The soldiers had demanded that we beat each other up, but we'd refused. And we didn't permit disparaging remarks about the martyrs. If we managed to spread this defiant attitude and then delivered a death blow to the enemy in the women's ward, where no one expected it, the whole prison would rebel.

How could we play a leadership role in that rebellion? "We could get the men prisoners to join our active resistance," some said. "If we women united to start an action, word would spread fast, and we'd gain support."

But killing Esat, I pointed out, would call up a whole different reaction.

Can you imagine the delight outside when the party and the people hear about it? They'll say, "The women did this thing even though they're in prison, where their hands are tied, and here outside it's so much easier." Oh, we'd get everyone moving!

Pir, Hayri, Akif, and Ali [A month after the Night of the Four, in June 1982, male PKK prisoners entered a death fast. Participation was limited to leadership cadre. On the 55th day, July 14, 1982, Kemal Pir, Mehmet Hayri Durmuş, Akif Yilmaz, and Ali Çiçek died. Their martyrdom is considered of significance equal to those of Mazlum Doğan and the Four.]

The actions of Mazlum and the Four were extraordinary. Although much of the organization had been destroyed and the prisoners were constantly surveilled, the enemy feared further actions, which made him even more aggressive toward us. He never left us in peace. After the Night of the Four, he forced the men prisoners to sing marches around the clock. That and raw torture, at intervals, kept the prisoners from sleeping. He used isolation cautiously, or so we deduced from what reached our ears.

But then came a loosening. We had to sing marches, but not always, not so that it took up our entire lives. But in some wards, the men prisoners had so internalized the enemy's regimen that they sang without even being asked. If the soldiers who supervised them were in the mood to do some beating, they announced the singing wasn't loud enough or good enough.

Starting in July, Esat didn't show up as often, but one steamy hot day, a soldier-guard stepped into the ward. "My commander is coming—are you ready?" he trilled, referring to Ali Osman. What nonsense. Normally they didn't care if we were ready or not, although sometimes they informed us in advance. In the past we'd insist on advance notice, saying, "This is the women's ward! Yet people come and go at all hours. Why aren't we told in advance when someone's coming? We don't accept that."

Once Lieutenant Ali Osman came silently to our cell, stood at the door, and glared at us with hatred in his eyes. Clearly he wanted to tell us something.

I always enjoyed using eye contact to push back at the enemy—I'd meet his hateful soul by glaring back at him. It heightened his fears and undermined his supposed strength as he tried to mask his own helplessness and weaknesses. And what a delight to witness directly his animosity toward me.

On this visit to our cell, Ali Osman said, "Those sons of bitches Kemal Pir and Mehmet Hayri Durmuş are dead. Have you got that? Dead! I'm told you've howled and torn your hair about them. You keep saying they still live, they're immortal—such nonsense. Sakine Polat, you get on my nerves. What are your moments of silence for? Who are these sons of bitches to you? Talk!"

After a pause, I said, "Stop insulting them. They were revolutionaries. No one's torn their hair—"

But before I could finish, he clubbed me on the head. Then he left without a word, presumably before turning any more of the prisoners against him. His visit served a warning to us: someone had told him about our memorial service for them. And yes, it was true that some had cried—Mother Durre had broken out into loud wailing. Maybe that had been heard outside.

Pakize casts blame We opposed and loathed all forms of torture. The enemy tortured systematically and brutally, attacking not only revolutionary ideas but human values. We women refused to bow to the enemy's will without putting up a fight. Internally our own rules applied, not the enemy's. We discussed everything, from the enemy's facial expressions to his courtroom behavior. Representatives that the enemy chose had to adjust to representing our will and not his—we insisted on that from the outset. Sometimes it didn't work, but usually it did. Despite the torture, we didn't lose hope or our convictions.

We reacted against behavior that betrayed humanity, our own comrades, and women in general. We forbade any woman in the ward to reveal weakness before the enemy—it only encouraged him—it was unpardonable. If someone cried, wailed, or pleaded, they got dark looks. Of course they sometimes did anyway. Many women in prison were still stuck in a traditional mindset. For them, tradition was more important than their identity as Kurds or as women. So internally we had the most problems with them. When women seemed to go different ways, we tried to bring them around by talking to them; with others we were tougher and imposed punishments. We punished behavior that encouraged the enemy and betrayed other prisoners, if only symbolically. That was probably a paradox. What angered us was weakness, a mindset of enslavement, and reactionary behavior.

The soldiers, for their part, kept an eye on prisoners, noticing those who had a problem, or avoided the others, or seemed depressed, or showed weakness. In the enemy's system, everyone spied on everyone else. The soldiers even spied on each other. They were especially alert for any prisoner behavior that seemed potentially dangerous and interpreted any activity as they saw fit. Sometimes their interpretations were right. They speculated about who was weak and who was strong-willed. Oh, we knew each other well. We learned to interpret the soldiers' behavior too, although we sometimes erred, especially when we let our wishes and expectations guide us, which could lead to more pain.

Pakize, from Hilvan, had been pregnant when she was arrested, and had a miscarriage under torture. She agonized at this loss. Sometimes she directed her rage at the enemy, insulting the torturers with screams that tore through the air, shaming the male prisoners in the next ward.

But more often she blamed the party for the loss of her child, turning on us like a madwoman. If only there had been no party! If only she hadn't been Kurdish! If only she hadn't opened her home to the friends or participated in the work! Her life would never have come to this! Now she refused to follow our routines, and went her own way. If we pushed back, she'd go to women from other [political] groups and cry on their shoulders. She found the other groups less threatening, since the enemy wasn't as hard on them as he was on us. According to her, those groups were smarter than we were: we couldn't keep our mouths shut, which gave the enemy reason to keep torturing us.

She didn't participate in our meetings, but she did participate in our communal cashbox—and always insisted on extra expenditures for herself, as if we owed her something and had to cater to her wishes. She had been imprisoned for her ties to the PKK, so the PKK must be guilty of causing this pain she endured; therefore we had to accommodate all her wishes!

Esat tried to use Pakize against her husband, who was also imprisoned, bringing them together a few times. She'd expected to be released during the trial but wasn't. Some prisoners from her area were released, but she had to stay. It all put her in a bad mental state. So she became a danger to us, since in prison the enemy welcomed any conflict with open arms.

Pakize complained to the soldiers about her situation. After she went to the hospital, she kept telling the soldier she had to go back to get medication. Did she see her husband there? Was she becoming a spy? We didn't know. We had a rule among ourselves that no one spoke to the soldiers alone. All the friends were very observant on this point. Anyone who broke this rule was presumed to have malicious intent.

We watched Pakize closely. Had they promised her something? What were her motives?

Esat also tried to use Nimet. One night she awakened from a nightmare screaming "Apo-terrorist!" referring to us. But we still helped her and talked it out with her. After that, she ignored him. She was straightforward and open with us. By the time she left prison, she said she had much to thank us for and would never forget us.

5 Cansız with two unidentified women, at Diyarbakir, May 1987.

We are moved downstairs Torture was subsiding during this time, and things were relatively peaceful. Court hearings took place less often. Recently the Urfa trial had ended, and now only the trials for the smaller groups were going on.

One day later Ali Osman turned up at the door again. "Sakine Polat, Aysel Çürükkaya, Gönül Atay. Get ready to go downstairs," he barked, then left.

We froze, then suddenly burst out at once—"What! Where do they want to take us?"

Gültan, Fadime, Nimet, and a few others wondered, "What do they want from you? Surely they'll throw you into isolation or take you to a men's ward. Okay, we'll come with you."

We said, "Transfer to a men's ward? Oh that'd be great—we could finally talk to the men friends! If that happens, we'll send you messages. Look for pieces of paper in the clothes we send you." The prospect was strange but delightful, as we swung between joy and sorrow.

Aysel said, "When he told us to get ready, I thought he meant for the falanga. I almost fell over." Once they actually had put us through the falanga before we were moved, to terrify the other prisoners.

He'd said to get ready, so we gathered up our things. But why were we being moved this time?

Gültan asked the soldier-guard, "Should the friends bring all their things?" The soldier answered, "They should do what my commander said—go downstairs. I've opened the door. They should bring their bedding." So we were to be segregated to the lower level. But why?

Ask me what the worst form of torture is, and I'll tell you: uncertainty. We could only speculate. We hugged and kissed each other goodbye, and some cried.

"You're in charge now," I told Fatma, Fadime, and Gültan. "Keep everyone's spirits up. Keep an eye on Pakize, and talk to her. The friends from Hilvan know her—they should take care of her. And try to help Cahide. We're just downstairs, we'll be in contact. Be careful with written messages. At night, you can drop a string from the window, but only in case of emergency. You can also hide messages in food. As soon as we hear any news, we'll share it with you. If one of you goes to the hospital or to the courthouse, tell the men we've been separated. I trust you."

Gültan and Fadime looked dejected but said calmly, "Okay."

Fatma said, "I want go down there with you! Why can't I?"

I laughed. "Unfortunately that's not up to us. You're needed here. Don't make the same mistakes as before—coordinate with the men," I told her.

"Oh, just go then!" she huffed, offended. "I know what has to be done." She didn't seem to care what the others thought of her. Sometimes I wasn't sure if she was one of us or not.

Although we didn't know the reason for our isolation, we decided to interpret it positively, a precaution taken by the enemy because he sensed danger. So in a way, it boosted our confidence and fanned our fighting spirit. What indescribable pleasure it gave us to disturb the enemy! This was exactly where our struggle lay. Our joy and pride grew when both sexes struggled in an organized and systematic way.

In the new cell, everything was iron and concrete: the bars on the windows, the giant doors, the bunk beds, the chains and the handcuffs. Once there, we listened to the noises around us, peered through the door slot, pressed our ears to the walls, trying to figure out what had happened. We could hear voices from the next ward, normal conversations, but only as a murmur, hard to understand. Once we heard a guard open the door and call the name of a prisoner. We heard one ask for a pencil, another cough like a tubercular person.

"Be sure to use only your own dishes," I said to Aysel. "And wash your clothes and your towel. And you know, you smoke way too much—if you don't stop, you'll be sick." She glared at me but sighed helplessly. She moved her body like someone in pain, who'd been defeated by life and was waiting for death. When she smoked, she inhaled deeply, as if she were trying not to waste even the tiniest bit of poison. But she was poisoning her lungs!

In prison, our addictions were an excellent point of attack —the enemy sometimes punished us by depriving us of tea, cigarettes, visitors, or exercise yard for months. When he confiscated our cigarettes, many women took it hard. Some were slaves to their nicotine addiction. Losing cigarettes enraged them—even more than when their highest values were attacked. Some took to smoking dried tea dregs rolled in newspaper.

I smoked cigarettes but without pleasure—I abhorred them. The more they were banned and the friends couldn't satisfy their cravings, the more I stayed away from them. During times when we had cigarettes, I campaigned for us all to quit together. But quitting was hard, and I was usually alone by the end.

We all drank tea, it was a normal part of cold weather and conversations. But now it became a form of pressure, even torture. The tea we got tasted bad—it smelled like the plastic cups and often caused diarrhea and fever. Maybe they added something to it, but we never found out. But no one wanted to give it up.

In the exercise yard, we could get some air and move more freely. Seeing the sky made a great difference. In the yard, you could spend time alone thinking or walk around with others. Yes, the concrete floor wasn't soil, but it was still beautiful to walk on ground affected by sun, rain, and snow, by nature. It was especially beautiful in the rain. But the yard also meant dancing *halay*, having snowball fights, and enjoying the shoots of green that grew in the cracks. It meant discovering beauty amid hatefulness.

But now that we were isolated, we weren't allowed in the yard anymore, and the others could use it only at certain times. The enemy tried to restrict our mutual contact as much as possible. Esat sometimes preferred that the soldiers deliver beatings under the open sky, while he watched from a window.

Visitors were now our only connection to the outside—they gave us news about trials. Our family ties were very strong. Families outside worried about the prisoners and vice versa: *Are they still alive? How is it going with them?* Visiting us in prison was the only way to get an answer. Our families gave us everything they had. But family visits were supervised—even family members were pressured and tortured. As the arrests and detentions continued, the families felt the repression—the patriotic families of revolutionary children were constant targets of attack. So the prison walls were extended outward.

Most of the lawyers acted like brokers. Desperate relatives would try to do the impossible and to influence a verdict with cash. The state happily took their money—as well as their hope and their humanity. Everything was under state supervision, be it having visitors, or getting information about the trial, or conferring with a lawyer.

The big old cell   Directly across the corridor from us was a big old cell—its peephole was directly across from ours. This cell was as large as ours and the next ones over combined. Prisoners had been brought here to write their confessions, but recently the room was rarely used. Once while a friend was mopping the corridor, she opened the door slot and peeked in—and met the eyes of a defector sitting at a table writing. The defector, having already abandoned all human qualities, choked with fear that a prisoner had dared to look through the slot—it terrified and shamed him. And she likely hadn't expected to find anyone in the cell, and the sight of this dehumanized snitch horrified her. She slammed the slot shut: "Bah, may Allah punish you!" which surely added to the defector's fear and shame.

Shame is part of human nature, but it's absent in traitors. It's actually more accurate to speak of them as shameless. In fact, committing crimes against humanity actually strengthened the perpetrators' shamelessness. It was simply disgusting!

Whenever we heard a door open or close, we peered through our peephole and through the peephole directly across from ours. The distance was short—the corridor was narrow—and the peepholes were big, the size of a circle formed by the thumb and forefinger. So we could see what was going on there—or at least the prisoners' heads—it was a lot. They sang marches, sat on the upper bunk, or paced between the beds. The guards often peered in at us through the peepholes. Sometimes when they were cleaning, we could even exchange written messages through the door slots.

On Newroz and on May 1, we tossed declarations through the slot into the other cell. What the inmates would do with a message, or think of it, we could only guess: "They must have got scared and torn it up unread," we supposed. "No, they must have read it, they've heard our voices and know it came from us." Whenever we sent a message or called something out to them, their mood seemed to improve.

Once we finally met the eyes of one of the inmates in that cell, through our peepholes. Finally they'd noticed us! Using hand signals and gestures, I tried to ask him what was going on in the rest of the prison. He gestured back that he didn't understand my question. I took a piece of bread, showed it to him, then closed my mouth with my hand—to ask whether a hunger strike or a death fast was under way. Again he didn't understand. Or did he think *we* were on a hunger strike? For days we signaled intently back and forth, but neither side understood the other. My god, how patient we were!

As for the cell next to ours, we beat our fists against our common wall. Sometimes we said our names and said we were in isolation. We asked for news but got no answer. They reacted to our pounding with knocks. I cursed in fury. "How much fear can one person have!" We would've been crazy with joy if they'd talked to us.

Letters to German Ralph   We first spotted Ralph through the window. One day when he was taken to the toilet, we had a chance to greet him. He had heard our women's voices and looked pleased to see us. Since there were no soldiers around, I explained using hand signals that I wanted to write him a message and that I would leave it in front of the toilet window. He understood right away and nodded. In the afternoon, as a test, I wrote a note in the margin of a newspaper, a few sentences in German: "What's your name? Where are you from? We're Kurdish women." Then I watched him retrieve the scrap and wave to us.

The next day he wrote back in Turkish, with the help of a dictionary:

My name is Ralph Braun. I'm from Germany. I live in a village on the Swiss-German border. I'm a tour guide. Almost every year I go to Akdamar in Van, where there are many historical places related to Armenians, as I explain to the tourists. The police charged me with belonging to ASALA

[Armenian Secret Army for the Liberation of Armenia] and brought me here. I don't know my way around. I'm glad to see you. Yours, Ralph.

We took to writing regularly, hiding the letters in different spots in the toilets. We were very creative that way, evading the notice of the soldiers on duty. I wrote to him about the PKK, Kurdistan, the prison, and the events up to now. He showed great interest and asked many questions. He wrote about the countries he'd visited, most recently Afghanistan. We discussed the Afghan revolution and Soviet policy.

He wrote about how hard the torture had been for him, and what he'd seen and felt here. "I wish we could use another language besides Turkish to communicate," he said once. "These guys are so repulsive, I even hate their language." We told him about Mazlum's action, and the Four, and those martyred in the death fast. We assumed he'd keep our letters as documents, or at least memorize as much as he could, so later he could pass the information on to the outside.

He was alert and sensitive, explaining what he'd learned in prison, what he'd gleaned from the soldiers' conversations, and even his dreams.

Ralph became one of us, even though we didn't really know each other. We wrote to him about the frequency of our beatings and our visits to the court and the hospital. We told him about our joys and sorrows, our hatred and our anger. We ate the same food and drank the same tea. He ate only a little so we could have more. If there was meat, he hardly took any because he thought we needed it more, as he wrote to us.

On Christmas [1982], he offered to share his celebration with us. His mother had brought him pine branches, candles, and cake. He hid some of it at the bottom of the trash bin in the bathing room. Then he wrote to us, "Look in the trash tonight." We found the cake wrapped in plastic, cut it into thin slices, placed the candles between the pine branches, and lit them. So we celebrated Ralph's Christmas in friendship. We sent him a Christmas card, sharing what the New Year meant to us and where our hopes lay.

He wrote back that he'd spent hours with a dictionary trying to understand our letters and that we'd become a great source of strength for him: "You're my window into life. I find vitality with you, and I like you very much."

He promised to remember what we told him always: "I'll talk about it everywhere. My mother is a journalist, and I'll publicize everything."

When he was finally released [after about seven months], we felt bereft. The corridor seemed so empty. In a dungeon, human contact is very important, which was why the enemy went all out to prevent it. When a person feels alone, it's easier to finish them off.

According to Diyarbakir prison records, Ralph Braun, from some city in Germany, was a member of ASALA and then became a Turk. But the real Ralph became a witness to cruelty inflicted on humanity. He had seen what Hitler's SS and Esat Oktay's Turkish imitators were capable of. He experienced misery and torture in the Diyarbakir dungeon, but he also had the good fortune to get to know the PKK and to breathe the same air as our martyrs. His friendship was internationalist in spirit. We have only good memories of Ralph. And he kept his word, just as Sarah, Monique, and other prison tourists did.

A near betrayal by a woman   Pakize hadn't taken part in our memorial service for Pir and Hayri, but afterward she asked angrily,

> Why didn't you tell me? I was sleeping in the other ward. I was sick. Don't you trust me? I've suffered so much, but you don't give me any consideration at all. Well, in the future I won't let anyone interfere with my affairs. I'm done with the commune. I don't need it, I'm not alone, my family cares about me.

She blathered on a while longer.

In her confusion about the death fast, she turned to the enemy. She gave a prescription to an officer and said, "Get me this medicine." We normally paid for everything we needed out of the communal fund. Pakize with her single request made clear that she was moving away from us and toward the enemy, but how far would she go?

Some of us had seen her talking to a guard that day, so we observed her closely. That evening she went to bed before roll call, saying she was ill. Just before roll call, I said, "Bring Pakize here. Even if she's sick, she can stand up for two minutes."

The ward leader Ismahan went and brought her to us. She was moaning. "You don't believe me. I'm sick," she complained. "What do you want from me?" She said it loudly and tearfully, evidently so a guard, waiting on the staircase, could hear. "Just because I didn't participate in the memorial service, you think I'm an enemy. But others didn't take part either. And not everyone present was there voluntarily."

We cut her off and smacked her. "What are you saying—are you crazy? Do you want to betray us? What did you talk to that officer about? Are you selling out in order to meet your husband?" We said a lot more and covered her mouth so she couldn't scream.

At that moment the solider said the officer had arrived—the one to whom she'd given the prescription. One of us said to Pakize, "Hold your tongue. If you say one word to the enemy, you'll see what you get." She got in line with us, and there was roll call. Afterward the officer asked her, "Are you sick?" and she said yes.

Ismahan jumped in, to prevent her from speaking further. "Women's complaints, it's nothing serious. We'll buy the medication. There's a prescription."

The officer was surprised. He'd probably thought we didn't know about the prescription.

The next day Pakize stayed in bed and told the officer she'd been beaten.

"No, that's not true," said the ward leader. "She's lying. She's crazy. We bring her food and wait on her. She's just pretending to be sick."

The officer didn't know who to believe and left the ward, shaking his head. A short time later Pakize was taken to isolation. They wanted to frighten her, get her to talk, use her. She'd already told them about the memorial service and the meetings. Although she considered herself clever, she didn't know Turkish well and mixed a lot of things up. But she wanted to ingratiate herself to the enemy.

The next day we heard Pakize's wails coming from the cell. The enemy had left her alone, without food, on the cold concrete floor. Her effort to butter him up had failed. Now she was in a dilemma. The enemy didn't take her seriously, the soldiers thought she was loony, but she couldn't decide about us. Her constantly shifting moods rendered her ineffectual. She'd smeared us, yet she was now in isolation. We'd held fast, and our unity had awed and frightened her.

Finally she opened the window and cried to us, "Forgive me, I messed up, I know. Get me out of here!" She was weeping. Pakize wasn't the only one with extreme mood swings—we all had them. That was why, given the enemy's constant, systematic pressure on us, it was so important to stay connected to life, and to fight hopelessness, tension, and distrust.

We told Pakize through the window that her previous behavior had made her guilty. She promised to change. "I wish I hadn't done it," she admitted. "You've been worried about me for two years. I know it's no better for you than for me—you've been tortured even more. Well, if you can stand it, then so can I."

We gave her something to eat and warm clothes. Finally the ward leaders explained to the officer, "Pakize's from a village. Her trial hasn't gone forward, and she lost her child through torture. She's psychologically damaged. Isolation is dangerous for her." It was a good move—we wanted to avoid the enemy recruiting a prisoner and using her against us.

There simply must be no betrayals in the women's ward. We wouldn't give Esat the satisfaction.

Pakize now denied to the enemy what she'd said before, saying she couldn't remember. Meanwhile the enemy had reservations about returning her to the women's ward, but there was no place else for her, so finally she came back to us. For a while we limited our social contact with her. Only certain friends talked to her much. She made a self-criticism and promised not to repeat her behavior. But for a long time she wasn't allowed to take part in official meetings. Once her trial finally began, she was released after a few days.

We women were angry at this near betrayal by a member of our own sex. Whatever, our shared reaction was meaningful and soothing. This small incident was no great victory over the enemy, but it showed how personal weaknesses and unresolved conflicts can resurface and lead to bad consequences if we didn't stick together.

Gültan is released Around this time, Gültan was suddenly released. I'd rarely been so happy about anything. It was almost as lovely as the thought of Esat dying. Gültan had experienced and witnessed everything in prison and resisted consistently. Her commitment to the party was beyond question. She'd report everything to the outside objectively. She could even explain our Esat plan [to the party and get its approval].

Through Serap, I sent a message to the outside about the various ways Gültan could get the reply back to us. It would take a while. "I hope you won't make us wait too long," I said to Gültan. "Esat might get transferred out of here—so we need an immediate answer. If you can't get it to us in writing, then verbally." We agreed on a code and memorized it.

"Okay, don't worry. I'll find a reliable contact," said Gültan. "Maybe not the exact day I'm released, but I'll take care of it right away."

I handed her the indictment from the main trial to take with her, along with documents about how the prisoners had behaved under interrogation, how the enemy viewed the PKK, and how the courts functioned. She took it with her, but we never heard whether the prison administration actually allowed her to take it outside.

"It's so hard to leave you here," Gültan sobbed as she left.

"Hug the chairman for me, kiss him on the eyes and forehead," I said. She was one of us, leaving us. It was crucial that she report to the outside about what was going on in prison. And of course we were also concerned about her.

For months we waited for the message from Gültan. Our excitement rose with every visit and every package. Whenever new clothes arrived, we didn't let them be distributed to the prisoners until we checked them. We took every package into the cooking area and inspected it, sometimes for hours. We were especially careful with things that we'd prearranged with Gültan. We never gave up hope that she'd send us a message, maybe even from abroad. (When I met her again, eight years later, we got into an argument about this episode, and I yanked her hair.)

"The path of Mazlum, Hayri, and Pir is our path"   The enemy had hoped to quietly strangle the PKK behind prison walls, so it would no longer be a bearer of hope for the people. He had organized himself toward this goal. He created new laws, executions, and prohibitions to break the Kurdish resistance. The trial was to supply a judicial verdict that would punish the Kurdish people for their very identity. To achieve all this, the enemy had to break the PKK's spirit of resistance in prison.

But we not only endured, we redoubled our commitment to the struggle. The PKK had shown a vibrant spirit of resistance, and its level of prison resistance was unprecedented. It had a strong ideology, capable leadership, and creativity in revolutionary organizing. Based as it was on this stable foundation, our defeats were only temporary; we could still hold its ground and build its revolutionary network, challenging both history and colonialism.

Mazlum, Hayri, and Pir had shown us how to transform a temporary defeat into its opposite. They had known which methods of struggle were effective and how to rebuild resistance—all while affirming the importance of life. They had advocated that the organization withdraw from Turkish state areas, both to protect the cadres and to carry on the revolutionary struggle outside its borders [in Lebanon and Iraq]. Their revolutionary vision strengthened our confidence in the work the party was doing outside.

"Surrender leads to betrayal, resistance to victory," they had said. Hayri, one day in court, had turned to the other prisoners and said, "I believe that someday you'll all defend the party. Those of you who confessed will withdraw your confessions. You'll beg the party and the people for forgiveness." And Pir had said, "Today I face death. Tomorrow it will be someone else. Everyone will be ready to give their lives for our cause." Their spirit of resistance lived. By daring to say, *We'll decide on our own deaths*, they were attacking the backbone of the fascistic junta.

In the past, the men friends hardly dared raise their eyes and look at us, since it meant risking torture. Back then I'd have given anything for a hint of a smile in their eyes, so profound was my yearning, but only rarely had we dared greet each other with our eyes or a slight nod of the head. But nowadays we could exchange looks, whisper messages like "Don't worry, it can't go on like this forever," and even converse. We spoke loudest in our defense speeches.

[In July 1983], a year after their deaths, we expressed our feeling of connection to the martyrs in our political defenses before the court. At every hearing, we reaffirmed our fidelity to Mazlum, Hayri, Pir, and the others. "If things continue like this," people often said, "we'll welcome death. We don't accept life without dignity. Death is better than an inhuman life. The path of Mazlum, Kemal, Hayri, and Ferhat is also our path." We infused our defense speeches with quotations from them—they provided both the framework for resistance and its core, with the words, "Long live the PKK! Long live an independent and unified Kurdistan! Long live Apo!"

[Mustafa] Karasu was a model of prison resistance. Everyone thought of him as in a class with the martyred comrades. He had survived the [1982] death fast, but perhaps he'd rather have died along with Hayri and Pir, and Akif Yilmaz and Ali Çiçek, whose youthful enthusiasm he admired. Probably he suffered more from survivor's guilt than we women suffered from not having participated in the death fast at all. As it was, he, Fuat Çavgun, and other friends had developed long-term health problems as a result of the action.

Many who had previously confessed under torture now recanted. In court, they declared, "I ask the party and the martyrs for forgiveness" or "This statement was made under torture. I did an injustice to the party. If the party gives me another chance, I won't waste it, even at the cost of my life." Hundreds of prisoners were caught up in this spirit.

The martyrs had taught us that what was unbearable was life without resistance.

To truly follow in their footsteps, however, we had to carry our defiant courtroom attitude over into prison itself. We had to use our positive foundation to convince the prisoners of the need for future resistance, to organize them anew, and prepare for it, step by step, in mind and spirit.

The departure of Esat Oktay, September 1983 Esat had regarded the deaths of the martyrs in the 1982 fast as a victory, and he had even referred to them as "sacrificial lambs." But as a result of their deaths, he was removed from Diyarbakir prison.

Nor had he foreseen the effects of the death fast on the party outside: it was determined to do justice to the martyrs' resistance by carrying on their work.

Once he was gone, we placed our hopes [for his death] outside. We believed the party would avenge the martyrs' deaths, and we ached to hear news of it. He simply mustn't be allowed to live. There was no place for him in this world, he had forfeited any right to it. That he still breathed and walked the earth with his accursed boots was a crime in itself. And we had to bring about his death. It is never pleasant to kill a human being, and I had condemned it several times, but sometimes it was necessary for the class struggle, of which I was part. But Esat had drunk human blood for so long, he reeked of it. It would have been terrible even in an animal.

To punish Şahin Trips to the courthouse were always a special torture. We had to ride in that hateful transport van, sometimes even a hearse. Then after we arrived, we had to stand around for hours waiting. Once the session began, we had to listen to the judge's nonsense. Usually we weren't allowed to say anything or we'd be thrown out of the courtroom. It was horrendous.

But the worst part of all was the sight of Şahin and his cohorts. During the proceedings, he sat in front of the judge's bench, on the left side.

He'd always been ambitious, driven by careerism. Now he made every effort to be the best possible traitor. I made sure my contempt for him showed on my face through every hearing. If I had to walk past him, I'd spit, "Despicable scumbag." I spoke to him only to revile him. But this duel of words and looks wasn't satisfying. My heart ached for revenge.

After Esat left or fled the prison, my thoughts turned to taking revenge on Şahin. I imagined killing him in court in front of the judges, who themselves were merely an extension of Esat. To me, Şahin was a greater enemy than the whole Turkish state, worse than Esat and the other torturers, worse than all other Kurdish traitors. He embodied the ugliest sides of all of them. He was a rotten, contemptible traitor without backbone or personality. Oh, no words for him satisfied me.

I still had my iron skewer. [Normally before we went to court, we were searched.] There were no female guards, but sometimes there were policewomen, repulsive creatures who'd condone the torture of other women. One torture policewoman, Nuray, would sit with her legs crossed and laugh artificially to goad the soldiers on. She chain-smoked and probably took a sedative. But policewomen didn't last long. Even Nuray couldn't stand it—she lasted only two weeks, then vanished—transferred or left the force, we didn't know. Anyway, whenever a policewoman was on hand, she'd search us before we were taken to court. We resisted being searched between our legs and inside our underwear.

My plan was to tie the skewer to my upper leg, so it wouldn't show under my skirt. Then once we were in the courthouse I'd feign nausea, so I'd be taken to the toilet. There I'd pull out the skewer and slip it up my sleeve. Back in the courtroom, I'd strike. My chances of success weren't bad, although probably the soldiers would overpower me or shoot me.

I had to attach the skewer in such a way that I could still sit. It absolutely mustn't slip off. But every time I tested it in the cell, something always went wrong. And it was hard to walk with it tied to my leg, and the cloth ties cut off my circulation.

One day I finally succeeded in bringing the skewer into the courtroom. But on that day of all days, the vile Şahin wasn't there.

I sat frozen as the judge issued some ruling or other. Up to now Şahin had *always* been present. Why not today? Did he suspect something? I cursed my bad luck—it just wasn't possible! This one thing would've brought me so much happiness. How often I'd dreamed of it!

Was fortune toying with me? Or was my bad luck my own fault? Probably that was it—I failed to make good use of my opportunities. But after that I never had another courtroom encounter with Şahin. It was maddening.

At the end of the day, once again, I failed, just as I'd failed back in Elazığ prison. That still pained me. The friends had passed a resolution to punish him, then waited for approval from outside. It never came. I could have insisted till the friends took care of it—my influence would've been enough. But I could also have done it myself. The party would hardly have criticized me for punishing a traitor. But no, our mistake had been to expect permission to come from somewhere else.

This time I'd developed a specific plan, and yet I never got beyond a certain point.

I wanted to scream with rage. The action could have had such good effects! Oh, I felt like a failure. I wasn't strong enough. I wasn't calm enough. I was too rash and too angry to achieve my goals. My ineffectuality tore at me. I hadn't even been able to discharge my anger. All I did was devise new plans—and thereby waste time and strength. I failed to bring my dreams into reality because my struggle was unfocused.

The women friends I'd brought in lost confidence in me, saying my dreams were beautiful but impractical. That was bad. Yes, I lived in an exorbitant fantasy world, but the actions I fantasized about were doable. The question was, should we take risks and allow ourselves to dream, or avoid risks and reject dreams? I always preferred to take risks, and that was the choice I made my whole life.

I didn't want to wait anymore. The martyrs had spoken unequivocally: they had ordered us to act. No one could fail to miss this order, not anyone who still had a little humanity, a revolutionary conscience, and their convictions, who hadn't given up and wasn't ready for an ignominious death. Was there anyone who hadn't heard the order? *The path of Mazlum, Kemal, Hayri, and Ferhat is also our path …*

Fadime and her group were transferred to Elazığ. We wrote a message for her to take to the friends there, telling them about our resistance actions, their outcomes, and our current situation. *Don't believe the enemy's counterrevolutionary propaganda*, we wrote. *Expect positive events.* We ended with the words, "The path of Mazlum, Hayri, Pir, and the others is our path." Fadime made sure the message was delivered.

Later Samil would tell me that the letter had triggered consequences that made it worth the effort. After years of isolation, I know what role letters can play—a small piece of paper can mean the world, providing moments of incomparable happiness.

"The resistance has begun!"   The guards didn't come to our ward as often as before. We met for discussions in the isolation cells. They weren't used to isolate people anymore, only to intimidate new arrivals, so we used them for internal conversations. They lay at the end of the corridor, behind the baths and the toilets. From there we could hear whenever the first door to the corridor opened. By the time the second door opened, we'd be gone without a trace.

One day all the PKK women prisoners gathered there for a meeting. While a few kept watch outside, we discussed the courtroom events, about which almost everyone had an opinion. We assessed the current situation, examined our mistakes, our weaknesses, and our intergroup relations. A few friends were very self-critical. Most believed that we absolutely had to do something. The mood was good, and the give-and-take was friendly. Many women assumed we were in secret communication with the men and were getting information from them, so they took the meeting more seriously.

The meeting was winding down when a woman who'd been on watch burst in and shouted, "Friends! Fantastic news! They're chanting slogans!" Now we could hear it: "Down with colonialism!" We hugged each other in jubilation.

Everyone ran out into the yard. For the first time in three years, we all chanted "Down with colonialism!" A few prisoners from other groups complained, "Why didn't you tell us something was gonna happen today?" We hadn't known about it, but they didn't believe us. We chanted our slogans and hugged each other and wept for joy.

Fascist marches were still being sung in the next ward. From the window, I shouted at the top of my lungs,

The resistance has begun! At long last, stop singing those fascist marches! The enemy has been stomping on our dignity for years. If you have even a bit of revolutionary pride, if you still consider yourself human at all, you must join the resistance! Except for a couple of snitches, all the other prisoners are fighting. Join us—Mazlum's path is our path! The martyrs gave their lives to show us that what's happening today is possible. Out of respect for them, stop singing these marches. Don't be afraid—if we all act together, nothing bad will happen, and we'll win!

The women supported me by shouting slogans too, which made a great impression. Then very faintly, we heard a few small voices from that ward, "Down with colonialism!" Then the prisoners seemed to get into a fight. Small groups joined us in chanting and singing fight songs. Everyone was getting ready for a fight. Some ran back to the ward to put on their sturdy shoes.

A multitude of guards descended on us. At first we thought they'd come to beat us, but it turned out they were terrified, and they demanded that we return to our wards. My god, the world had turned upside down! The enemy was panicking! Here he thought he'd silenced us and stripped away our humanity, but now an overwhelming majority of us were rising up! How was it possible!? Oh, Esat should have been here now! Oh, Mazlum, Pir, Hayri, and the others should have lived to see this day! It was September, and their spirit of resistance lived.

It was as if we'd all met in a big square to celebrate a victory. "*Bijî PKK!*" we chanted. "Long live independence! Down with colonialism! Down with betrayal! Long live the honorable death from which new life grows! Down with torture! Down with the fascist administration! Mazlum is immortal! Kemal, Hayri, and Ferhat are immortal!" We chanted every slogan we could think of. Prisoners repeated slogans, and after some initial confusion, the chants moved through the prison in waves, reached the last ward, then turned around and came back, sometimes altered.

Some groups refused to participate, saying, "These are PKK slogans." The TKP considered us the most dangerous group after the enemy. Meanwhile the enemy would tell them that the PKK "are all terrorists, monsters—they'll be executed. You're different. Stay away from them." So the TKP prisoners normally kept their distance from us, responding to our proposals with "We won't do anything until we hear from our comrades."

"We started the resistance," we told them now, "and our people died, but you should participate anyway. You say you're revolutionaries—what are you waiting for? If we were in your place, we wouldn't care who started the action, we'd join."

But they were afraid of the enemy, considering him too powerful to challenge. Would they rather live in prison than resist? Well, some had been internalizing surrender for years and couldn't be freed in a moment. Prison brings to light everyone's naked reality. Nothing can remain hidden there.

None of this stopped us from trying to have a positive influence on the TKP-ers. Besides, we thought the resistance wave was going to sweep almost everyone up. If they didn't participate—well, you couldn't expect it from everyone.

Meanwhile the [PKK] women danced *halay* and sang revolutionary songs. The atmosphere was rapturous. We organized ward leaders to prevent extreme, excessive behavior and to make sure nobody inadvertently tipped the soldiers off. From now on, we, not the enemy, would choose the ward leaders. And we'd discuss binding decisions with the men friends to avoid mistakes.

The hunger strike of September 5, 1983   We decided to start a hunger strike right away. "It should be a death fast," I said, "not a hunger strike. The men will write a petition, and we'll sign it. I'll announce it in court." A hearing for the Elazığ group was imminent—I wanted to announce the action publicly there. I was really looking forward to watching the judges' fascist faces fall and seeing fear in their eyes.

We submitted a petition to the administration announcing an indefinite hunger strike and said we'd continue until the torture was suspended and all arbitrary rules and prohibitions were abolished. "Let's not use up all our energy at once," I said, "but plan and organize for the long term."

The enemy warned the TKP-ers, "The PKK started this action." They listened to him and wrote their own petition. They set a time limit for the hunger strike, and were moved to the lower cellblock at their request. The TKP and the DDKD ended their hunger strike after two or three days.

We were still dancing even on the fifth day of the hunger strike. Our enthusiasm held, and the mood stayed exuberant. Sugar water was distributed once a day. Small amounts of sugar had to be taken regularly.

On one of the following days, the door to our women's cell opened, and to our astonishment, Rıza, Muzaffer, Karasu, and a few other men friends came in. Cries of joy rang out. The sight of the men here, after so many years, unleashed intense feelings in us. The fact that we were doing a joint action gave the reunion special meaning. We all gathered around them, hugged them, and pressed their hands. It was amazing. We could touch them! For years we'd longed to hear a word from them—now, excited, we could all ask each other things!

They'd already described in court much of what they'd experienced in prison. They'd described the torture and other repression verbally or in writing. But they didn't know so much about our experiences, only what we'd been able to report in court on the rare occasions when the judge let us speak. The torture specific to women prisoners wasn't documented. During our trips to the courthouse and to the hospital, the enemy always tried to give the impression that we women had it better than the men. So our segregation within the prison had the effect of hiding our torture. Of course the men friends must have heard our voices sometimes. Actually, knowing the character of the enemy, they could have guessed what was happening to us. Still, Rıza asked, "Did they force you to sing marches?" Yes. He was so surprised, he could hardly believe it.

After a brief conversation, Rıza explained that to give uniformity to the action, a five-member committee had been formed. It would visit all the wards in the prison, one by one, even the smugglers' cells.

He told us:

In September, a group of our friends started a hunger strike, and later some TİKKO and Kawa members joined. They're chanting different slogans from ours. We are limiting our slogans to the main demands, ending torture and oppression, and also promoting our resistance. One ward will start chanting at a predetermined time, and the other wards will join in sequence. We have to do it in order.

The hunger strike has been going on for seven to ten days. We will do the death fast in groups. The first group is the one that has already started, the second and third are starting soon. Our demands are the following:

- An end to torture and all forms of repression; a lifting of prohibitions
- Abolition of military discipline
- Condemnation of those who tortured prisoners to death
- An end to repressive practices and prohibitions against visitors and lawyers
- Recognition of our elected representatives
- Delivery of materials necessary for a defense
- Publication of newspapers and books.

The committee was to negotiate on behalf of all the prisoners.

"They've installed a new captain," Rıza continued, "named Abdullah Karaman. He tries to seem moderate, but don't underestimate him."

Just at that moment, the captain strode into the ward. He behaved respectfully and seemed impressed by what he'd heard of Rıza's speech. Looking us over, he asked, "Which of you is Sakine Polat?" He'd surely been told what a "monster" I was, so he must have been curious. Of course he recognized me from photos, but he avoided eye contact. He looked to me like a devil with a friendly face. He stayed only a moment, then left.

I gave Rıza and the other men a brief rundown about the situation in the women's ward. "I'll change the hunger strike to a death fast," I said, and then the men departed.

Aysel, Fatma, and I decided to join the death fast. We wrote our own declaration, emphasizing our specific situation as women. After we handed it over, the administration announced that we would be moved to the lower ward.

The next morning I was taken to the courthouse, as we chanted slogans together. As I entered the courtroom, I saw all the male defendants sitting with their backs to the judge's bench, in protest. Wonderful! And now I could look at them all directly in the eyes. The men's tormented, bashful expressions had disappeared—all our eyes were laughing.

"Hello, how are you?" How I'd missed these simple words! All this was thanks to Mazlum, Pir, Hayri and the others.

The judges came in, surprised and indignant—a beautiful sight. "Who's in charge here?" one said. "What's going on in that prison? Get them out of here!"

"We've started a death fast!" I shouted.

A hunger strike. We're resisting, and we want our demands to be entered into the record. The court is responsible for everything that happens, and so we protest this court. It hasn't allowed us to speak here, and most of what is said hasn't been recorded. We've been tortured in front of the judges—they've even given orders for it. We'll continue our action until our demands are met.

Everyone talked at once.

The judges rose and left, not caring for what we were saying. After some points were recorded, we were returned to prison.

But we'd managed to make the death fast public! The prison authorities were now informed. The Elazığ group had resisted, even though Şahin and Yıldırım had promised we would all defect!

I was moved to the lower level, along with Aysel and Fatma. I'd just arrived in the ward when I heard breaking glass and screams, as well as muffled slogan chants. The PKK women in the upper level joined the chants. "Friends, what's going on?" I shouted. Then much to my satisfaction, the Elazığ group was brought into the ward next door to mine. They knocked on our shared wall and explained, "The soldiers attacked. Some of us are injured, including Meto, but overall things are good. We're participating in the resistance, but the other groups, not so much." They asked how we were doing. I told them about the women's ward. After less than five minutes, they were removed from that ward and taken elsewhere.

The hunger strike ended, after a week or ten days, and so we entered the death fast.

Every day a doctor was brought in to examine us, but we refused to be examined. He asked us questions, evidently to assess our mental state.

As the twentieth day approached, military marches and torture screams could hardly be heard anymore, except from new arrivals. The other prisoners continued the resistance with slogans—we met any attack from the enemy with an immediate and unified response.

At the ongoing court sessions, we said we would continue the death fast, and if our demands weren't met, more prisoners would join.

Phony imams   During the death fast, the friendly-faced-devil captain arranged for religious sermons, rather than military marches, to be broadcast over the loudspeakers. He thought prayers would undermine the death fast—a really interesting approach! An imam read Qur'anic verses and said over and over that it was a sin for people to punish themselves by not eating, since punishment is reserved exclusively for Allah. We didn't smash the loudspeaker, since we thought we might need it someday, so we put up with this noisy war of nerves.

Later, actual imams were brought into the wards, so that if we didn't listen to the sermons, this loathsome captain could publicly propagandize that we were infidels. Of course, he didn't give a damn if we listened or not—it was part of psychological warfare, to prevent more prisoners from joining our action. After all, many older prisoners were religious. The enemy wanted to drive a wedge between us, because if many prisoners participated in our action, it would gain legitimacy. Meanwhile even smugglers were joining our resistance.

One day the captain brought in a supposed imam, who it turned out was really a fascist torturer. "You've been duped," this man said. "You'll never achieve justice by starving yourselves. These traitors to the fatherland want to kill themselves to make Turkey look bad abroad."

The captain didn't care much for this approach. "Of course they have a goal, and they're even right in some ways," he said.

And to us: "We're not forcing you to do anything. Or do you think we are?"

With my stony gaze, I tried to make him feel like I saw through him. "What is torture?" I answered. "Yes, you use your batons, but torture doesn't consist only of beatings and electric shocks. What you're doing now is torture. Earlier you broadcast military marches over the loudspeakers, and now it's sermons. You bring in phony imams for psychological warfare. This guy doesn't even talk like an imam—he talks like all the other uniform-wearers. We gave you our demands in our declaration. Instead of fulfilling them, you bring in an imam. Every day a doctor comes, even though we've clearly stated we won't be examined. And by the way, we never got to see a doctor before. Many prisoners have been ill but got no treatment. And you didn't allow us to see our families for months—now you're letting them come here to try to persuade us to end our action. It's only to pressure us. And now you dare come in here and ask us if there's torture going on, saying that unsavory incidents were limited to the previous prison authorities? We don't want an imam! That'll only accelerate our deaths."

The captain said, "Well, that's what you think, but maybe the others think differently. You're trying to push them in a certain direction—"

Aysel broke in furiously. "What are you talking about? We're all participating in this action voluntarily!"

The enemy constantly made counterpropaganda [about us to other groups], telling them, "They're about to die—they want to die. They're just trying to promote the organization and send a message to the outside. That's no way to get your rights."

And he pressured the families outside.

You've got to tell your children to stop the death fast, otherwise they'll die. They're demanding more than we have the power to give—we can't do anything. No one's being tortured anymore. The prison chief has been replaced. What a shame that your children are being duped!

That's how they tried to sway the families. They even picked some of them up at home and drove them here to get them to try to talk us out of the death fast. Of course, the families were worried about us and wanted to see us, but they had to listen to this to get their visits approved.

Aysel's mother was one of the first to arrive. She wept and wailed and implored us to end the action—"You can't win this way!" Then she hugged me and whispered into my ear, "Don't worry, we're just saying these things so those dogs'll let us in here. We're behind you and are working to help outside." I was elated. "After we leave here, we'll go to the commander," she said. Obviously, the families had organized well. The prisoners' action not only expressed our joint strength but united the families outside.

Thereafter, on visiting days, we refused to go to the booths, except one group accepted a visit in order to exchange information with the outside. All day long the rest of us chanted slogans from the upper windows, so the families outside could hear.

The days dragged by. We wasted away, the enemy grew nervous. He didn't want to take any chances that we would die, so he sent us to the hospital.

I rode in the van with several men friends, who said they were fine and reported things they'd heard from new prisoners about events on the outside. "Armed groups have been formed," Selim Çurukkaya whispered.

> They're digging underground shelters for 20 to 30 people, and in some places small armed propaganda groups have carried out actions against agents [of the Turkish state] and collaborators. The people are delighted, and there'll probably be larger actions soon. The party is said to be planning to storm the prison and free us in an airplane.

As he spoke, the soldiers in the van were talking among themselves. In the past they'd paid close attention to whatever we said, but now they let us talk. Our resistance was having an effect!

At the hospital, we sat together in the waiting room for a while. The men wanted to know what had been done to us, and I told them what we'd been through. Fatma was silent. Her coldness was hard to take even in normal times, but now we were sharing our journey to death together. Everything about her was calculated and measured. What a strange person she was. I believe in recognizing life's beautiful sides. I wanted to die laughing and dancing. I think only those who know how to value life are ready for death. Otherwise, neither life nor death has any particular meaning. We needed to meet in the beauty of our spirits and beliefs and then we would be strong.

We women were taken to the top floor of the hospital, the men to a lower floor. As we parted, we wished each other success. "We'll keep going," I said, "till we hear otherwise from the committee."

We women were put in the birthing station. Almost every night there was a birth—the cries of newborns and their mothers woke us up at night. We were on a death fast, while these babies were starting new lives. Later, when they grew up, they could say, "I was born in a hospital where prisoners were on a death fast under armed guard."

Families arrived in the hospital. Once Fatma's, Aysel's, and my families were all together. While the soldiers were around, they sobbed and moaned, but then in whispers they told us how they were publicizing our cause outside. "We sent a delegation to Ankara and protested in front of the governor's office, and we've filed motions to pressure the administration."

That was nice to hear. But our relatives were also genuinely concerned about us. They did suffer, cry, and faint, and some turned prematurely gray. We told them what we'd been through and tried to make them understand what this resistance meant to us. All the crying at these encounters was wearisome for us, but we were patient. We warned them about the enemy's trickery and told them to unite. They understood that we preferred a dignified death to life on the enemy's terms and that we would not waver. The more they realized that the enemy wanted to use them against us, the more they respected our action, and they redoubled their efforts outside. So we turned the enemy's tactic against him.

Occasionally hospital staff, military officers, and prison administrators came to tell us we were ruining our health and should stop. Some doctors and nurses expressed concern for our weeping families and our ever-worsening condition, but most were fascist-minded creatures.

On the 27th day of the death fast, we learned that negotiations had taken place and that several more friends had been hospitalized. The men friends sent us the latest news in short messages hidden in newspapers.

That same day Aysel met with Selim, who told her that two friends from the committee had come and said the action was over. She came back and told us.

"What does that mean?" I said.

Friends from the committee came to the hospital without talking to us too? I don't believe it. What's happening with Selim? Who else was there? It could be another enemy trick. He could be trying to play you and him off against each other. You say Selim was so weak he could hardly speak, but if the action really was over, he'd be in better condition. No, I think we should continue the action until we're sure.

"We'll continue until the committee comes [to us]," I wrote to the men friends. The soldiers didn't deliver the written message but verbally conveyed that we were continuing the death fast. In the evening Selim was brought upstairs to our room. "Here's some milk and light food," he said. "Rıza and the others [on the committee] came to the hospital first, and now they're going to all the prison wards. They talked to us, and we've stopped. Why are you continuing? Don't you believe me?"

"It's not a matter of believing you," I said. "We're not in kindergarten. The enemy is always intriguing, and we've got to be careful. Why did the committee decide to end the death fast? Were our demands fulfilled?"

"Torture will end," Selim said. "Military discipline is abolished. They've acknowledged almost all the other demands. There are still a few points, like addressing the officers as 'commander,' but we'll eliminate that in practice."

"We women have never said 'commander,' and we never will," I said. "If military discipline has been abolished, then so must saying 'commander.' Hm, obviously the negotiations weren't conducted properly. You conceded too much to reach an agreement." And we women hadn't been consulted at all. I didn't trust Selim—he'd kept us from taking part in the July 14, [1982,] fast, and maybe therefore I had some unconscious reservations about him. But if we continued the action, we'd be overriding the party's decision.

So we women ended our death fast, depressed and unpersuaded. Why had we been presented with a fait accompli? We'd only been at the 27th day, so we weren't exactly at death's door. We decided that if the enemy tried to force us into anything, we'd resume it on our own.

Fortunately we didn't stay long in the hospital. We were soon transferred back to prison. Everyone hugged us happily. The brutal torture that had been going on for three years was indeed lifted—for the moment. Visiting time was extended from 2 minutes to 15 minutes. Prisoners no longer had to sing military marches. We could shop in the canteen with our own money. We were allowed to have "safe" books that weren't on the prison's banned list and were available on the market. We read and discussed the books we got, by Orhan H—— and others. We got daily newspapers and used the articles and analyses for our educational work. Even the textbooks of students who'd been arrested were of value to us. These changes brought a modicum of peace.

[This hunger strike ended on October 2, after 27 days. It was the largest collective action in Diyarbakir prison in this period.]

Uniforms   The new captain continued to seem moderate and friendly. The administration spoke to the prisoner representatives, the food was better and more plentiful. Overall, prison conditions improved. The prison administration tried to give the impression that it had wanted to make these improvements anyway and the death fast had nothing to do with them. Even while we were still in the hospital, it was already denying that the negotiations had led to the agreements, and as for [the rest of] our demands, well, they just couldn't meet them.

After the action was over, and the festive mood dissipated, problems arose or re-emerged among individual prisoners: tension, anger, selfishness, and individualism. Common torture and oppression weld people together but also damage them psychologically. Extreme pressure destroys a person inwardly, unless they consciously channel their hatred and anger toward the enemy. But handling that requires the proper analysis, as well as a solid grounding in the history and nature of class struggle. And we were still poorly organized.

After the death fast, we'd evaluated the current situation, and some friends expressed criticisms of others. But everyone had made some mistake or other in the past, and now prisoners easily turned on each other. For example, not everyone had participated in the death fast, and that led to distrust. Women sniped at each other. A prisoner who felt attacked would lash back in indignation. Some were afraid they'd be held accountable to the party outside once the connection was reestablished.

Those targeted had to be helped. I couldn't deal with Gönül's peculiarities all the time, so finally I put my foot down: "Gönül, decide: either you're one of us, or you leave." She was shocked, she cried, and she came to her senses.

And she finally came clean with me. "You know, I broke under interrogation," she told me. "A lot of people had already confessed, and I did too. Almost all the friends I'd worked with had been arrested. The enemy already knew everything. I confessed certain things about myself, about my relationship with Rıza. My relations with the friends in Urfa weren't very good, but that was my fault—I couldn't handle criticism and gossip. In prison, as a ward representative, I had constant contact with the administration. I didn't act decisively and consistently toward the enemy. When you women criticized me, I clammed up. I know you don't trust me, and it bothers me, and I also know I brought it on myself."

I liked what she'd said. "Okay, but be careful about falling back into your old ways. I was too hard on you sometimes, but we're in prison and constantly up against the enemy. Any negative behavior on our part immediately has an effect, both on the enemy and on the other prisoners. Just stay away from these guys finally, will you? And only talk to them when you absolutely have to. That's how we all do it. Set a limit."

Gönül took the criticism seriously. She got back on her feet, and overall seemed livelier, and her dealings with us all improved, which had a positive effect on our coexistence. We were friendlier to her and let her participate in discussions and decision-making.

Over time, the prison administration decided it couldn't accept the new situation. Abdullah Kahraman loathed making concessions, perceiving them as a sign of defeat. He downplayed the outcome of the death fast. When problems arose in the exercise yard, we were again forced to sing the national anthem once or twice a week. "Your representatives agreed to it," he said. "If you don't stick to it, we'll take back the other promises. If you refuse to march in a row, we won't let you into the yard. Same goes for visits."

What! Military discipline was supposed to be repealed, and now the enemy tightening the reins again. He also referred to the slogan chanting during the death fast as a criminal offense and brought charges against us for doing it. He brought more charges against us for making statements in court.

Yes, tension had diminished for a while, but now it came roaring back. The enemy didn't implement all our demands. He withdrew many of the rights we'd fought for or never put them into practice at all. He censored the newspapers—he cut out the most important articles before we got them. Books we ordered arrived after months of waiting because they were supposedly being "examined." He rejected requests made by the prisoners' representatives. He wanted to keep us from knowing that our resistance could ever succeed, and to keep us in constant fear.

Uncertainty was brewing. Communication between the wards remained difficult, but some messages from the men reached us, verbal and written, saying that the enemy now insisted on them singing the national anthem once a week, addressing the captain as "commander," and counting off. What did we think about it? they asked. "If you don't go along with it, then we won't either," the men wrote.

But another message said they'd decided: "We decided to stick to the agreement for a while, to see what the administration would do." That bothered me. So far, the enemy had failed to force us [women] to address him as "commander." For a time, our representative had said "commander" during roll call, when she called out her number, but we'd stopped that too. We'd sidestepped a lot of rules or just ignored them. For us to start following that rule now, when we hadn't before, would be a big setback, and it would mean we were submitting to military discipline.

I wrote back, "We won't abide by your decision. It puts the whole resistance in a bad light." The men criticized that but let us decide for ourselves. We communicated our decision to the representatives, to the other prisoners, and to the families, who made a joint petition to the military commander. We informed the lawyers, but they were even more useless than our families—they did nothing.

The prison authorities issued a new order: "Every prisoner is a soldier and is to be treated like a soldier." It went on and on.

And then finally a rumor started that we were to get prison uniforms.

Uniforms! We couldn't imagine it—we thought of the striped convict garb in American films. Were they going to make us wear standardized blouses and skirts or shorts? We laughed about it, but seriously, what did it signal about the prison?

The men friends warned all wards: "The purpose of the uniforms is to create a unitary human type. They are an attack on the resistance. We will refuse to wear them."

We took to wearing several layers of underwear under our normal clothes, in case the enemy tried to take them away. The idea of being stripped made us cringe. The soldiers would certainly attack if they set eyes on naked or half-naked women. It would be ugly. But we were determined to refuse the uniforms. Nor would we take a step backwards or give up improvements we'd gained in the death fast.

Then we heard that some of the men had been isolated for defying or insulting the soldiers. When we saw them in the courtroom or the infirmary, they looked pale because they were being denied time in the exercise yard. Diseases were spreading.

None of the TKP women prisoners were forced to comply with the new rules, due to their conciliatory attitude toward the enemy. Once when Abdullah Kahraman was talking to a few TKP women in our presence, he pointed to some of our 13- to 15-year-olds and said openly, "These PKK crazies are a lot scarier than other groups' cadres. I'm not

6 Four prisoners at Diyarbakir, undated. *Standing, left to right:* unidentified, Cansız, Ali Asker Özdoğan; *at front:* Fethi Yıldız.

scared of you, but these crazy PKK kids go around saying, 'Long live communism, long live Kurdistan.' They're terrifying." We chuckled—he was right, maybe for the first and only time ever.

The TKP women said they felt sorry for our young women—after all, the PKK had ruined their lives! They hadn't even had childhoods! So in their view, it wasn't the enemy who was to blame—it was us, our party! We were even responsible for the military coup and the torture! Above all, they hated us for wrecking their lives—they'd settled so nicely into their political clubs, publishing their magazines about revolutionary lifestyles.

But then, such people should never have been jailed in the first place. Their miserable approach to revolution hardly qualified them for imprisonment at all. They really had no business being here. We were ready to take on the heavy burdens of making the revolution, but they … And sure enough most of the women from other political groups were soon released. Now they would go around trying to capitalize on having been political prisoners. Oh, the thought was unbearable.

The enemy was really mainly concerned with us, the PKK prisoners. Now we were alone in prison, just us. Our relationships became more intense. If the enemy wanted to make our lives hell and go back to the previous regimen, well, we would defend ourselves at all costs. Together, armed with this knowledge, we prepared ourselves.

The uprising of January 1, 1984 The enemy launched a new offensive more brutal than ever before. Torture and military discipline resumed. On the way to court, prisoners were beaten on any pretext. Anyone who spoke out in the courtroom was confined to isolation afterward. The whole prison went on a five-day warning hunger strike. The enemy deployed special units.

Opposite us the upper ward was a large torture chamber that we called the movie theater. The door slot was directly across from ours, so we could see what was going on in there, or at least the upper half of people's bodies. The room was unfurnished, with no beds or anything.

Prisoners were brought to the movie theater in groups, and the enemy used every conceivable means of torture on them. He unleashed dogs on them, gave them electric shocks, inflicted the falanga, and stripped them naked. The screams and moans were unbearable, echoing in our ears. Sometimes it's easier to have the enemy attack you than to listen to your comrades being tortured, so we chanted over and over, "Bastards, why don't you come for us?" Our chants had no effect.

And we also heard the prisoners resist too: "No, I'm not saying that," or "No, I won't wear the uniform." No, no, no ... We rejoiced at every *no*. "Did you hear?" we would shout. "He said no!" The agonized screams that followed tore at our hearts.

We'd lived under torture for years, but now we couldn't stand it anymore. How did we ever endure it in the first place? Had our reflexes been dead, our hearts petrified, our vocal cords ruined? But now we couldn't keep silent. The spell was broken, the shadows ripped away.

Clearly we were not going to accept the resumption of torture. We'd previously discussed what to do. On January 1, 1984, our uprising began. We built barricades, placing iron beds and tables at the doors. The steel lockers were as tall as the doors, and the inner and outer doors were separated by only a short distance. The soldiers were afraid to open the outer door. Looking in through the slot, they just saw a steel locker.

[Unlike the 1983 death fast, leadership cadre did not organize this action. The morale, experience, and confidence gained by the September 1983 resistance enabled broad participation.]

Knowing they'd throw smoke bombs in through the door slots, we taught all the prisoners how to cover their mouth and nose with a damp cloth. We banged plates against the iron window frames and against the doors, making a racket. We chanted slogans, and sang revolutionary songs, and recited poetry. That was how we protested torture—we didn't have any other way.

The barricades reminded me of what I'd read about the Paris Commune. The people and resistance units had built barricades on the streets and fought behind them. We knew about barricades from novels and movies. Now we were constructing them ourselves, under very different conditions. Our only weapons were our beliefs, our will, and our naked bodies. At the moment, only our voices were fighting.

The enemy could still break open the door, tear down walls, or come in through the windows—but we didn't care. The important thing was to make it as hard as we could for him. Later we found out that barricades had been erected in many other wards as well.

But prisoners were still dragged to the movie theater. Those who refused to wear uniforms were stripped naked and tortured. Those who capitulated and accepted the rules were housed in a ward together.

We tried to communicate with the more distant wards by screaming through the windows and then trying to interpret the fragments that reached us. We heard that the resistance was being directed from 25th ward. The men in the isolation cells couldn't communicate with all the wards, the 25th handled the coordination. Mehmet Şener, who was in the 25th, issued instructions and forwarded news to the 35th [where PKK leadership cadre were housed].

We heard that prisoners from the 27th had set a fire and been hospitalized. Remzi Aytürk and Yilmaz Demir died. Kurdo was wounded and taken to the hospital. Now we realized what the black smoke had meant, rising from the rear wards to the sky. "Let's set a fire too!" a friend said, but we stopped her. At such moments, when your mind is on fire, it's very hard to judge what's right, hard not to behave like madmen.

Finally, we said, "Let's set a fire to split the enemy forces and siphon some of them toward us. We can draw off at least 50 soldiers." We piled up mattresses and old clothes and set them on fire. The ward filled with black smoke. We lit the curtains in front of the windows, so the smoke would attract the attention of the soldiers who we knew were housed opposite the movie theater, even if we couldn't see them.

We piled wood from benches and boxes onto the fire. Should I do a self-immolation too? I wondered. Yes, why not? But our fire wasn't big enough. You needed turpentine or something else highly flammable. I'd have no chance of success with this fire. And the friends around me would've pulled me out of it.

Still, I told Aysel I thought it was a very attractive idea.

She looked at me in horror. "What, that's crazy—you're not really thinking about it?"

"No, but the idea is very appealing. It'd have a big effect. Dammit! Nothing I've done so far has succeeded!" Dying was supposed to be so easy, but here even that seemed impossible. I sighed. Finding the right place and time for death is an art.

We tried to generate as much smoke as possible, but the fire burned for so long that some of us fainted due to lack of oxygen. The soldiers didn't show up, and we concluded the enemy was deliberately avoiding us. We stopped shouting. We'd been exhausted and sleepless for days. Anyone looking through the door slot would think we were all unconscious or dead. The enemy, for his part, seemed indifferent. He was so busy with the men that they didn't notice either our fire or our silence.

When the soldiers finally noticed the smoke, they streamed water into the cell through the door slot with a high-pressure hose. Of course they hit us too. The cell filled with water. We threw plates and sharp objects back at them. Ali Osman showed his face—we were glad he witnessed this uprising. "Ali Osman! Fascist! Murderer!" we shouted. "Evil torturer, have you come back to kill more people? This time it's your turn!" The soldiers shouted back to us, "Ali Osman is the greatest!" Ali Osman himself just said, "Keep it up!"

That evening the captain, along with several officers, soldiers and a policewoman, came to our door. "Tear down the barricade," they said. "We want to talk. There won't be an attack." We immediately started up a slogan chant. They left and came back later. "The female inmates won't get uniforms," they said. "So open up. You'll get food." We decided to open the door. Of course, they searched the cell.

The next day we found out that Necmettin Büyükkaya had died. His wife Cemile had previously been released. In all, there were three casualties. That was why we hadn't been attacked.

At one point Gönül was looking out through the door when she said, "Oh, I can see Karasu, Rıza, Yilmaz—they're wearing them!"

"How dare you!" I said, "You don't utter the names of our friends! You're just trying to spread your pessimism everywhere!" I said a lot more too. I wanted to smack her on the mouth.

Gönül was shocked and cried, "Take a look yourself—why should I lie?" Everyone crowded around the door. They looked in silence— maybe they were afraid of my reaction. None of us could believe our eyes. The men prisoners were wearing uniforms!

The enemy said everyone had accepted the uniforms, even the 35th ward men, but we didn't believe him. As we found out later, the prisoners in the movie theater had been tortured until they passed out, and then the enemy put uniforms on them. That was what we saw. After they revived, they took them off.

On January 18, we heard a strong distant voice announce: "We've entered the death fast."

"Okay, that's what we've been waiting to hear!" I said. "Women, did you hear? We're doing a death fast!" I shouted out the window, "All right, we'll start too." Aysel insisted on participating, and so did Gönül and Fatma. Just remembering the brutal old days stirred incredible anger. There would be no return! We wrote a petition and started the action.

After we began the death fast, torture diminished. Sometimes we heard military marches, which was troubling—had some given up the resistance? We didn't want to believe it. Perhaps some whose resistance had been broken had been collected into one ward.

There was something we couldn't imagine and didn't want to imagine.

One day we heard noise coming from the ward next door. We pounded on the wall, and from the other side we heard a muffled, "I'm Mehdi Zana. How are you? Who are you?" We shouted our names and said we were on the death fast and were fine. He and several others had been transferred here after a trial.

During the silence of the night, he shouted to his friends in the 35th ward, starting a lively exchange of information. Shouts in Zazaki, Kurmançi, Turkish, and even English ripped through the air. It was exhilarating! The enemy set up loudspeakers in the yards and made noise on the rooftops to prevent communication between the wards, but it didn't work. We in the women's ward joined in—Kezban had a very strong voice.

On the other side of the wall, Mehdi Zana sang Kurdish songs. I always liked Kurdish music, especially the song "Xezal," as sung by Şivan. We asked our "Xalo" to sing it to us. His voice was very nice and easy to listen to. It expressed all the anguish and longing that had built up in us.

After a while Aysel and Gönül were taken to the hospital for circulatory problems. Later Fatma and I were also brought there. She was put in an adjoining room. I saw some men friends who had been exhausted from the torture even before they stopped eating, so the absence of food had weakened them quickly. One was lying on a stretcher.

They took me on a stretcher upstairs to the room I knew from the last death fast. Gönül and Aysel were there and were glad to see me. Fatma was brought in. I asked her where she'd been, and she flew into a rage. "Did they offer you medical treatment?" I persisted. She got even angrier.

Every day the doctors asked us if we consented to medical treatment, and every day we said no. Sometimes they whispered to us, threatened us, scolded us, or tried to provoke us. Sometimes they singled out one person and explained that the other death fasters had just consented to undergo medical treatment. A few actually fell for it.

Hard times are best for judging people correctly, as they're exposed, naked. On a death fast, your cells are dying every minute, causing you unbearable pain. If you keep your spiritual strength, your humor, and your will power in such conditions, you will intimidate the enemy and fill him with fear. If not, your fear of death will eventually lead you to betray. You hover between life and death. Your weakness is reflected in your eyes. Your face gets ugly, as if it's soaked up all the fear and hopelessness like a sponge. You're nervous and frightened, and you hide your crying under the blankets. You get even more frightened and can't speak anymore.

The doctors came to us at least three times a day. They worried most about Aysel. When they arrived, they went to her bed first. One day Aysel was not doing well, and we let them take her blood pressure.

"Stop smoking," I told her. "You're speeding up your own death. Don't do it." Her indifference irritated me. She was always suffering and so pessimistic. Because of her tuberculosis, we'd requested extra cups for her, but they were forbidden. I warned others against using the same cup as Aysel, and she got annoyed. "We're all going to die," she said, "yet you're still on my back!" I said, "Even if I die, I don't want to get infected beforehand." I didn't mean to annoy her, but her indifference really bothered me. Why make it easier for death? Death should be afraid of us, not the other way around.

More prisoners were being hospitalized every day, the soldiers told us. Comrade Karasu was here. We weren't allowed to send messages, but he sent us a newspaper. It did us good just to be in the same place with him and other men friends, even if it was the hospital.

It would have been good to hear from Karasu, as a survivor of the first great death fast. I wished he weren't here this time. He'd started five days before we did, while in isolation. The men friends had been subjected to much stronger attacks than we women were, and Karasu had already been through an extraordinary time. He and the others just had to survive this time. If someone had to die, it should be me. "Dear God, please let me die first," I prayed. The very thought of others dying was unbearable.

"I want to die first," I told Aysel. She answered, "No, I'm first." It became a kind of joke. "I'm closer to death," she sighed deeply. It was true—she was getting weaker by the day. Sometimes she lay immobile for hours, like a corpse. It broke my heart, and I'd whisper her name until she showed some reaction.

In death fasting, you can't let yourself be defeated by the dying body cells, or the terrible halitosis, or the ubiquitous pain. The battle you're waging is like none other in the world. It's a war against your own body. Every organ represents a war front, every bodily cell tries like a monster to occupy your heart and your brain. Your bones are like tanks. The side you're currently lying on rebels against you. Every time you turn over, you lose more energy. Every fit of anger means a loss of power, and every glance burns your eyes. You're afraid to look at your comrades or at yourself. The bones in your hands protrude, your skin is dull, your fingernails turn blue. No, you mustn't think about it—it would become a nightmare.

When your organs lose their functioning, you experience shock and dizziness. This creates new fears. Terrors dart through your tortured brain. If you give in to them, you'll expose your fears to the enemy, and your defeat will begin.

Gönül gradually declined. Her eyes widened, and she pulled the covers over her head, moaning in agony. The hospital's staff officer came in with the doctors, who asked her questions. She responded with a moan. "If you want, we can treat you," the officer said, sensing an opportunity. "If you want to go on, then do so. Or are you scared of something?" He gave me a sidelong glance. Maybe because my eye sockets were enormous, he averted his eyes. I smiled at him as if to say, *Forget it, you won't succeed.*

Fatma lay on her stomach listlessly. I could never tell how close she was to death. She rarely spoke, and it was hard to guess her thoughts. Once when a doctor asked her a question, she paused for a long time before answering. The doctor said, "People usually respond in seconds. Her taking so long to answer suggests she's a psychiatric case." Of course, this doctor was an enemy, but we found it strange. Even in a silent person, some reflexes can't be suppressed. Fatma's extreme lack of interest in everything around her was dangerous. Why did she even participate in the death fast? What was her goal? Who were we to her? Who did she love or trust? I had no idea. People are usually friends to friends and enemies to enemies, but people who are neither a friend nor an enemy—no definition exists for them. I decided that whenever she was released, I'd suggest to whoever came for her that they have her examined at a psychiatric hospital, perhaps in the Soviet Union—they were supposed to be experts in this field.

Our families visited almost every day, another front in this war. Mostly they were helpless, watching their children get weaker every day, and they were ashamed that they weren't strong enough to withstand the enemy's pressure. In movies, I'd seen people's hair turn gray suddenly, in the wake of a tragic incident. I thought that was phony, but it was happening now in our own movie where everyone played themselves. Actually, a good director could have made a masterpiece out of it.

From the media we knew about Bobby Sands in Ireland—IRA prisoners had done their hunger strike at about the same time as the 1981 death fast in Diyarbakir. The Iron Lady didn't give in, and so about ten revolutionaries lost their lives, starting with Bobby Sands himself. He had told his mother, "I refuse medical intervention, but if I pass out, you have to do it for me." His brave mother didn't allow the doctors to save her son's life. She did right by him, keeping to his wishes. This story touched us deeply, and we included him at a memorial service for our martyrs.

But our families—well, they just didn't want us to die, and the pain was grinding them down. In their helplessness, they cried, tore their hair out, and said they wanted to kill themselves. Instead of demanding justice from the enemy and venting their anger at him, they tried to persuade us to stop the action. They cried so intensely, they didn't hear what we said. By disregarding our will, they made it harder for us. They wore us down. When the enemy told them to go to the hospital to pick up our bodies, some families even brought coffins.

Only with great difficulty could we get them to redirect their anger at the enemy. "Go and attack the prison headquarters or the military commander! Call a demonstration, go to Ankara. Maybe you'll be able to prevent our deaths that way, but you won't do it by crying!" Finally they listened. Families attacked the prison with stones and even a staff officer during a conversation, saying, "They're killing our kids!" A delegation of them drove to Ankara.

The enemy didn't yield. Twelve from the first group were near death. I could still read the newspapers, although sometimes the words blurred. Gönül's bed was next to mine on one side, Aysel's was on the other, and Fatma's was opposite. Aysel was spitting up blood, and Gönül and Fatma couldn't stand up anymore. Aysel and Gönül lay in bed as if they were dead, although the occasional eyeblink or soft moan told me they were still alive. If a long time passed with no sign of life, I spoke their names, and they always responded. Sometimes Aysel answered with an

irritated "What?" but then, she did that in normal life too. Except once
she didn't answer at all. Terrified, I dragged myself over to her. She was
alive.

My eyes wandered among the beds. I prayed to be the first to die, not
because I believed in any religion but as I'd prayed when I was a kid in
dangerous situations.

One day my father said,

> I can't bear the death of my daughter and my son. I want to die before
> them. My children have done nothing wrong, they've committed no
> crime. They've fought for humanity, and for their own honorable cause. I
> can't say anything against that. But they haven't thought about us. I can't
> stand the pain, so I'm going to hang myself.

The family screeched in chorus. And some nurses, soldiers, and doctors
wept, unable to restrain their tears.

Karasu and the other friends were deteriorating too. Karasu was
very weak. Orhan Keskin and Cemal Arat were taken to intensive care.
Orhan's parents didn't know about it and searched frantically for their
son. His mother was so desperate that she came over to me, covered my
feet with her hands, kissed my feet and hands, and begged me to tell her
where he was. "You know where he is! Why won't anyone tell me?" It
was heartbreaking. I didn't have the strength to stop her from kissing
my feet and hands. "Don't worry, he's fine," I could only say. Finally she
left the room. I had no idea what was going on. I didn't find out until
several months later that both Orhan and Cemal had died.

My mother was the same. "Meto is dead, Karasu is dead. It's enough!
The men say, 'When Sakine gives the word, everyone will end it.' So say
something, stop all this, I beg you!" she pleaded.

Metin and Karasu were dead? What was my mother talking about?
She almost killed me with those words and didn't even notice. Of course,
she was only trying to get me to stop the action, but she had no idea of
the impact. I signaled Aysel's mother to come over and asked her about
Meto and Karasu. "No, nothing like that happened. I've just been there,
they're weak but still alive," she said calmly.

A few days later Metin came to me. "Talks are going on this morning,"
he said. "There are representatives from the command and from the
prison. They've accepted most of our demands, but they won't budge
on the uniforms."

"What kind of uniforms?" I asked, feeling as if I'd fallen into a hole, an emptiness, a nightmare. What was he saying? Had the prisoners accepted wearing uniforms, or was that being negotiated? I remembered the time Gönül had said the 35th ward men were wearing uniforms. But Metin hadn't said that. I couldn't imagine it, but worries plagued me—did they arise from my subconscious?

Metin stayed only briefly. "Rıza and the others are waiting for me. We're going to the prison to discuss the results. Make a list of your needs [for the families]. We'll let you know later."

I said, "One of us [women] should be present at these talks. But we're never on the committee, and we never have a chance to argue with them. The men don't do anything about it."

Metin left. The families were informed and showed up in force. That day we received no further message, nor the following day. Apparently the death fast wasn't over yet. We were glad we hadn't handed over our needs list to our families.

We heard Karasu was even worse, while Hamili could barely see or hear. Hamili's family visited me. My God! Even on the first visit, they begged me, "Our son is dying! Aren't you afraid of Allah?" Relatives of other friends said the same thing, making me feel guilty. "You and Karasu have got to do something! Karasu is nearing the end, his condition is serious. Just a word from you would make it all finally stop. Please, don't let them die!" That's all. It was the worst kind of pressure imaginable.

"Call the officer," I said. He came. "I want to talk to Karasu," I told him.

The agreement should have been reached the previous day, which would have led to the end of the death fast. But the negotiations had apparently stalled. Were these bastards intriguing again?

Aysel's mother and my mother blamed Mehmet Şener. "He's the one who won't allow it. He spoke against it, over in the prison—the staff officer told us so. What does he want from our children?" I was annoyed: "The enemy keeps telling you things to fool you, and you believe them. The enemy apparently agreed to one thing and said something else in prison."

When I called for Karasu, the families' hopes rose. The weeping quieted. Everyone waited anxiously.

Karasu was brought on a stretcher and set in front of my bed. An excited murmur rose. Aysel and Gönül and Fatma pulled themselves up from their death positions and looked over. I half sat up and saw Karasu's tiny body on the stretcher. If he hadn't been wearing several sweaters, he'd have looked even smaller. Only part of his face was left. His lips were white and dry. I felt tears rise, but my eyes stayed dry, and I composed myself. It was enough for the relatives to cry. Not me too. No, impossible—the enemy was everywhere.

I asked Karasu how he was doing, and he had trouble answering. Had he heard me? After a while, he said, "We're fine, all the men are fine."

He closed his eyes. He looked like a sick person coming out of anesthesia. The relatives stood in a circle around him. Then Karasu said, "The enemy didn't keep his word. The friends couldn't visit all the wards. In the first ward they named the demands that had been met. Then the captain, that filthy fascist, claimed he'd never agreed to these demands. But I was there when he agreed to them! So the negotiations came to an end. The friends went back—the trip had been so burdensome for them, but it was for nothing—the enemy played a double game.

"Back in the 1981 death fast, the staff officer gave his 'military word of honor.' What honor? Nothing changed. Ali Erek died. They promised on July 14, but our precious friends died. They didn't stick to it—they have no political ethics.

"Now they're waiting for us to die. Don't be angry at us, but go after these people. Their word of honor isn't enough. We're determined. Even if dozens of us die, we want to succeed this time."

"So they're deliberately delaying a decision," I said. "This absolutely must not end the way it did in September. The main demands aren't up for discussion, although some points need to be clarified. We're determined too. Metin came here, but we haven't heard anything since. We want to be informed and clear and to know how you were doing. That's why I asked for this meeting. I won't strain you any further."

He was carried away. The families had expected something different. The fact that we'd mutually affirmed our determination destroyed their last hope. Karasu wasn't even out of the room before they burst into lamentations. The staff finally escorted the women, weeping on their knees, out of the room.

We dictated our last wills to our relatives. To my mother I said, "I want to be buried in Dersim, on the hill in the Mamik cemetery next to Aydın Gül, you know, with the white marble that you can see from everywhere."

I really wanted to be buried next to Mazlum, but had his body even been released?

My mother sobbed so much, she didn't even hear me. "Oh, just don't," I said. "Just don't. We're fighting for an honorable cause, and we're ready to pay the price. One day Kurdistan will be independent—that's what we're fighting for. You've got to accept it. This is a fight where death is important too. Look what worthless lives some people lead, and then they die ugly deaths. You can't want that. Tell the friends [outside] we trust them. They'll avenge us and carry on the struggle."

"Don't talk like that!" my mother shrieked wretchedly.

I don't know how many days passed. The relatives were in an uproar. My mother said, "Some of you obviously don't want a solution. This Şener—it's probably his fault. And his mother, Sahila, is insane, she messes up everything outside too." Aysel's mother agreed.

Exasperated, I explained once again: "The enemy is playing with you, and you still believe him. You know the decision doesn't lie with the friends in prison but here with Karasu and the others."

Our families left. "What's going on over in the prison?" I asked. "Something's up. What's Şener doing? Isn't he going along with what was decided in the hospital? Did they set up their own committee? No, I think the enemy's waiting for us to die. Karasu and the others aren't doing well. The enemy will give in after they die. He'd have given in already, but he's trying to delay further. We should tell our friends what we think about it. If only I'd been able to talk to Karasu about it, but that was impossible with the families around."

Aysel agreed, but Fatma said, "Don't speak on our behalf. I'll continue the action, or should we believe what the families tell us?"

Again, a strange reaction from her. I hadn't said we should stop the action or make a decision by ourselves. "Don't point at me," I said. "The enemy seems to have a specific goal, and it wouldn't be wrong to talk about it with the men."

I was determined to share my opinion with the men. My gut told me that I had to act. But it wouldn't be good to strain Karasu again considering his health. I told a soldier I wanted to talk to Hamili. I could speak Zazaki with him, so the soldier couldn't understand us.

Hamili was brought in on a stretcher. I told him, "The enemy's attitude makes me suspicious. Our families say the friends in the prison are preventing an agreement. Why are decisions being made in the prison? The decisions have to be made in the hospital. I'm worried about Karasu. I think we should try to bring the action to a close here in the hospital. The enemy should talk only to us. Do you understand?"

He agreed. "I was present at the conversation," he said. "We discussed it too. The TİKKO prisoners disagreed."

More days passed. The death fast had now gone on for 50 days. For Karasu it was the 55th. He was on the brink of death.

The room was quiet that day. I squinted at some words I'd written on the wall, but I couldn't make them out anymore, not from a distance. The newspapers were brought in. Suddenly, as I worked on the crossword puzzle, I felt sick. Foul-smelling blood gushed from my mouth. I laid my head on the pillow. After a while, I tried to pull myself together. I had to stay awake. Every time I looked at the newspaper, I felt sick again. I tossed it away and stuffed the pillow under my back. It was as if I were waiting for something.

Night fell. I gazed out the window into the darkness, at places illuminated by streetlamps. I didn't like darkness here—these cursed nights just wouldn't pass. Outside, I'd loved to go outdoors at night. How delightful to walk along the sea in Nergis in Izmir and feel the cool water. In Elazığ, Meral and I used to climb the path to Esentepe, then sometimes run back down. I loved walking in the moonlight. The moon filled my heart and enveloped me in brightness. In my grandmother's village, when we slept on the roof in the summer, I used to gaze at the moon for hours while listening to her prayers and incantations.

Was I losing my vision, or were the lights being dimmed? The silence and the air in the room oppressed me. The walls were painted half gray and half white. I felt for my pulse on my left wrist and couldn't find it. Were my veins dissolving? Then came a light throb from the depths.

At that moment, I heard voices outside the door. The watchman came in, and two hospital beds were placed across from mine. Karasu lay on one, Hamili on the other.

"Sakine, it's us," Hamili said. "I'm Hamili. Karasu is next to me. Do you recognize us?"

"Of course I recognize you. My eyes are fine. I even read newspapers."

"We've just come from the prison. The action is over, an agreement has been reached, it's good. But the ride really weakened Karasu, and he needs immediate treatment, so we can't stay here long now. We'll talk later."

"Have all demands been met?" I asked.

"Yes, of course."

"Has anyone died?"

"No," said Hamili.

"Tell the truth!"

"I'm telling the truth."

I was glad but unsure whether to believe him.

"Take care of yourself. The doctors will take care of us all now. Send greetings."

The doctors and nurses came in immediately and started treatment. A sleepy nurse pushed a needle into my thigh as if I were a regular patient. I'd never felt such pain—it felt like she shattered the bone. I screamed, and she jumped back in shock. "Damned woman," I said softly.

I felt better quickly. Even before the fluid finished running through the drip, I was sitting up. By morning I was on my feet. Slowly the others revived too. We hugged and congratulated each other on the outcome. At some point our families came and crowded into the room. They couldn't believe how much our condition had improved in one day. The mood was joyous. I put on some clothes. The smell of death still wafted around me.

Treatment continued for a few days. We were initially fed on a drip and later on light food, and our bodies slowly revived. We still couldn't walk or talk normally, and our metabolism was still confused. The doctors said we'd turned science upside down. "That's the spirit of the PKK!" we said. "It turns everything upside down."

Not until we were back in prison did I learn that Cemal Arat and Orhan Keskin had died. In all, there had been five deaths. Two had burned themselves, one had died under torture, and two had died on the death fast. In the van we got another shock: the men were wearing uniforms! At first I thought they were defectors, but then I realized they'd all participated in the death fast. Maybe they didn't have their own clothes anymore? I wondered. In January, they'd been forcibly dressed in uniforms. Maybe they'd even been hospitalized. But to my surprise, the friends said, "You didn't know?" They'd been wearing prison uniforms since January, the day the death fast began. After that the attacks stopped. The prison uniforms and the end of the torture were negotiated, but they rejected these demands. The others are all met.

Prison uniforms? I would never have expected the friends to accept these clothes during the action. When Meto visited me, he hadn't been wearing a uniform. Or was I mistaken? Did the right to wear civilian clothes apply only during the death fast? My eyes met Gönül's—she looked at me as if to say, *I told you so, but you didn't believe me and even insulted me.*

Together yet separated   Why did our actions always end in such lame agreements? It took me years to understand how this particular one came about. Meanwhile I was given this explanation:

> The enemy was using the uniforms as a red herring, to prevent a solution, and [by agreeing,] we took it out of his hands. The other issues were more important, and we insisted on them. We'll take off the uniforms when the conditions are right.

I just couldn't understand it. "They're wearing the uniforms just as a tactic," I repeated, trying to convince myself but not succeeding. I took care not to express my doubts openly and waited eagerly for the moment when the men would set the uniforms aside.

It took two to three months for our health to return to normal. Karasu and several others remained in the hospital for a long time, and many of the men suffered long-term health damage.

We women got news only in bits and pieces. We were staying in the same prison as the men, and yet somehow we were always on the outside looking in. We wanted to act in the interests of all the prisoners, and we needed to be informed so we could do things in the right place and at the right time, but we somehow couldn't break through the segregation and participate in vital decision-making. Everyone else considered it normal for women prisoners to be peripheral, but whatever we lacked in numbers, we had plenty to say about decisions important to us. As it was, informing us was left to chance. We initiated almost every attempt at communication; the men didn't reciprocate. To them, we were out of sight and out of mind. They approached us emotionally, felt sorry for us, and thought we didn't belong in prison. Still, we gave each other courage and hope.

We were eager to discuss with the men what we should all do next, and how to continue organizing, and our relations with other groups. We requested permission to meet at least with the men we were related to, family members of first and second degree, saying we were concerned for their health. The men made the same request. We were usually denied, [but finally the administration allowed us to come together with the men on a visiting day]. We hadn't seen each other for a while, and everyone was looking forward to it.

Almost all of us had real or presumed relatives in the prison, so most of us participated in the meeting. Rıza, Hamili, Selim, and Meto were there. The soldiers and officers monitored us closely to make sure we didn't exchange any messages. They would've been stupid not to pay attention.

We had only a little time, but I was so excited as we hugged each other. I hardly knew what was most urgent. I spoke frankly to Rıza, telling him what I thought of Gönül—after all, it wasn't just a personal problem—the party had to know about it. I asked him to talk to her and be positive. And we talked about Cahide, who'd participated in the last ten days of the death fast.

Then I brought up the subject of uniforms, telling Rıza how we'd found out about it and what I thought of it. "The whole action has to be evaluated in detail," he said.

> Of course, mistakes were made, but it was the consensus, not the view of just one or two people. Yes, some things remain to be clarified. If we have a chance, we'll send you some texts, and you can share your thoughts in writing too.

He didn't get any more specific. He just didn't understand my frustration. I'd been so eager for this meeting, to catch up on things, but everything he said was vague.

The men told me they maintained written exchanges with the other groups, and that their future relations would depend on whether these groups did self-criticism, challenging their own past behavior.

Hamili came to the meeting wearing an undershirt—he didn't want to put on the prison clothes, knowing how much it would bother me. Still, it clouded the joy of our reunion, and I could hardly speak to him. Something always went wrong—this time it was the men's clothes. In the past, just a look or a single word had been so important, since that was all we had. Now anything associated with the enemy was unbearable. The white undershirt and the missing prison jacket still created a distance between us. It was all probably even worse for the men.

Nor was my encounter with Meto a pure joy. The betrayals in the Elazığ group were like a black spot that tainted everyone in it. The enemy used any means to destroy every member of the group psychologically, subjecting them to the severest tortures and the most manipulative psychological warfare, leading to the most disgusting betrayals. In 1982, the peak of the enemy's brutality, they were tortured into signing statements. Some chose betrayal, some gave up their beliefs, and some managed to hold on and endure the phase.

Metin hadn't forgotten how mercilessly I'd cursed him out. He was still uncomfortable about it, since normally I was warm to him, and he'd probably found my reaction overly harsh. But that time when I saw my beloved comrade and brother Metin in among traitors, my heart had almost stopped. At this brief meeting, we could barely speak, although we understood each other without words. I talked more with Hamili and others, and when I realized that, I was sorry. Was it always the case with siblings in the struggle that they were so close yet so far apart? Was that a natural contradiction?

In general, the incomparable resistance of Mazlum, Ferhat, Pir, Hayri, and the others transformed the prisoners' attitude. Their message of resistance was clear, and the important thing was to continue resisting in an organized way. Karasu played an important ideological role—he'd been there from the beginning and was widely trusted as the leader of the resistance and the presumed representative of the organization. We felt the same bond with him that we'd felt with Mazlum, Hayri, and Pir. On the other hand, we as prisoners needed to be reorganized, and that work couldn't be done by ideology alone. First we had to make a correct analysis of the events of the last three to four years.

A spirit of resistance had emerged in 1982, and in September [1983] we prisoners were prepared to rise up again, but in January, before we could organize ourselves, the enemy had made a wholesale effort to obliterate our resistance altogether, with more brutality than all the recent torture methods combined. He wanted to force us to surrender and then physically annihilate us. Of course, it wasn't just about the uniforms—that was just a pretext to break our will, before we had a chance to regroup and organize.

Many questions persisted about why despite the deaths we had accepted the uniforms, but we didn't have the chance to discuss it thoroughly enough. In fact, there was silence on this topic. Nevertheless,

I wrote a report about the course of events since 1981. I talked about our numbers, the persisting problems, and the situation of individual friends, especially Gönül and Cahide. It was still difficult to exchange written messages reliably—it still depended on chance, and I was always looking for good opportunities.

Our trial came to an end. In absentia I was sentenced to 24 years imprisonment. My sentencing read: "A penalty reduction is excluded because the defendant did nothing that could point to a good behavior and persistently defended the terrorist organization." In fact, I was charged all over again just for making a political defense. Hamili was sentenced to death. Metin got 18 years. Those who had already served out their time were released. The traitors, for their part, were sentenced to small penalties and released en masse.

August 15, 1984: a day to celebrate   It had been four years since the military coup. The fascist generals had run things for three years, then in 1983 they installed the allegedly democratic [Turgut] Özal government as the junta's civilian face. Turkey's leftist groups had been severely damaged, and many leading cadres were imprisoned or executed. The enemy said, "You have to crush the snake's head while it's still small." Esat had crushed the resistance at Mamak before coming to Diyarbakir to do the same. The arrests and betrayals had hurt the party badly, but our snake was much larger than he assumed, and its head remained intact and wouldn't be crushed so easily. After our 1982 action, Esat had fled without achieving the desired result.

Immediately after the arrests in Elazığ, the chairman had taken precautions: very deliberately and methodically, our party had withdrawn its cadres from Turkish soil. The horrific conditions both inside and outside the prisons damaged us and terrified people, but the move abroad [to the Beka'a Valley of Lebanon and the mountains of northern Iraq] offered a glimmer of hope. So did our prison resistance and our courtroom speeches, which sent the message, "Our struggle isn't over. Our party and our chairman are preparing abroad to continue the struggle in Kurdistan."

During the September 1983 resistance, we learned that armed propaganda units had filtered back into Turkey. In the first years of the struggle we had already speculated about where the armed struggle should begin. Perhaps in the area between Hakkari, Van, and Çatak, bordering Iran and Iraq, so the struggle could affect three parts of Kurdistan? I didn't know the geography, but the discussion was exciting. It was like the times when the revolution in Iran took the shah down. For us, all parts of Kurdistan were equally important. The party's draft program addressed the special conditions for organized revolutionary struggle in all parts. Where similar conditions prevailed, a common struggle would arise.

Mehmet Karasungur had once asked us if we would be prepared to go to Iranian Kurdistan to fight as volunteers. At this time, armed groups were fighting in Baluchistan and Azerbaijan, and there was also the People's Mujahedeen. Developments in one part of Kurdistan directly affected the others. What a tragedy that Karasungur later died in the Qandil Mountains from a traitor's bullet.

As a result of the January 1984 death fast, we were allowed to have TVs—a demand that was fulfilled—and we bought them with our own money. So it was that on August 15, we heard over the evening news, "A group of terrorists, including women, have occupied the rural towns of Eruh and Şemdinli. They bombarded government facilities with rocket launchers and automatic weapons, then fled in vehicles." Raucous cheering broke out, and everyone leaped to their feet to dance. We could hear the same jubilation in the neighboring wards—the whole prison seemed to be dancing, whistling, sobbing for joy. My god, that we could be experiencing this! It was just too beautiful. "The armed struggle has begun!" we exulted. "The friends said they were preparing for an action in the countryside, and now there's a guerrilla force, and it will grow." Kurdistan would become Vietnam!

It was impossible to silence the friends, but we wanted to know more and tried to focus on the TV broadcast. It showed adults and children hiding in bathrooms. A terrified officer said, "I saw it with my own eyes—a woman terrorist fired an automatic weapon with one hand while driving a vehicle with the other." The information that the group took some teenagers with them brought us special joy—if the armed struggle spread, all the young people would join, since they had only two choices: prison and unbearable torture, or the mountains. Of course they would choose the mountains.

So joyous was the mood that I might have died from it—but neither death nor torture could have anything on us anymore. If only Mazlum, Hayri, Pir, and the others could have seen this day! I thought. If only

SARA

Hayri could have heard these cries of joy! The only blot on our happiness was his and the other martyrs' absence. Without them there could be no true joy or life. There were always feelings of betrayal and guilt, and life was not life without them.

The armed struggle had begun! How would it go? More soldiers would be stationed in the area, and the enemy would intensify his repression and torture in the villages. During the Vietnam War, the United States had created "strategic hamlets." Maybe the enemy would try that in Kurdistan. Maybe he'd bomb the villages, bomb civilians. Many scenes of terror ran through my mind. Or maybe the opposite would happen. The brutal repression could cause people to join the struggle en masse. The people were patriotic, and the armed actions could accelerate [revolutionary] developments.

In Vietnam and Angola, armed propaganda units had been founded first. In Guinea, the struggle had begun in the cities. The enemy had reacted by massacring unprotected people, so the tactic was changed. Only after propaganda units worked actively in rural areas did armed units gain control. Probably it would go something like that with us. Conditions in Kurdistan were of course different, but the people had suffered for years under the enemy's brutality. Their paralyzing fear must, at long last, be broken. News of our armed actions spread throughout Kurdistan like wildfire. The military junta had said it destroyed all revolutionary efforts, but the people would see that that wasn't true, rekindling hope for a revolution.

In prison, these events gave us strength and hope—and not just us but prisoners from other political organizations too. Some accused us, once again, of reckless adventurism—we'd heard that a lot when we first got to prison, especially from Kurdish leftists. They said it was madness to wage an armed struggle against the junta, which would then take revenge on the civilian population. But they feared the enemy more than they cared for the people. They thought of the enemy as an invincible, all-powerful force. When things got hot, instead of fighting him, they preferred to take a break. When the enemy proclaimed that he had annihilated all revolutionary thoughts, they believed him. Ultimately they just didn't believe in the revolution.

The great prison resistance actions had always sent the enemy into a panic. Now with the armed actions in Eruh and Şemdinli, surely he'd panic—they'd been totally unexpected. He might take us hostage

209

and then exact revenge on us. Would he dare execute prisoners? we wondered. "We have to be ready for anything," we said, and were full of ideas. "When the enemy lines us up against the wall to shoot us, we'll all shout, 'Long live the resistance in Eruh and Şemdinli!'" "We could make the gallows tip over!" We had a lively discussion about which type of death was preferable: "I'd rather be shot than hanged." "Will they blindfold us first?" We mocked death. And we all agreed that if it meant the armed struggle had finally begun, we would accept it.

But we were off the mark. [Unknown to us,] during the interrogation period, the torture police had said,

> It's dangerous to execute PKKs. If you execute others, their groups will go quiet, but if you execute a PKK member, the Kurds go out and riot. They become a plague. They've threatened to kill a thousand of us for one of them.

That appeared in the press, which we didn't see, but we prisoners took it further. "If the enemy executes even one of us," we said, "it'll cost him dearly. The party will tear down the whole world. The world public would cry out." Soon the developments outside had an affect on the courts.

At the first court hearing after August 15, the sentences for the Mardin group were to be announced. Many expected to be released, mostly sympathizers and regular patriots but we warned them, "Forget it." The enemy might not use force in prison anymore, but in court it was different. We were right. The whole group was sentenced to the harshest penalties to date: a minimum 24 years in prison, the maximum death. Half the group got one or the other.

After the sentences were handed down, we shook the courtroom with shouts of "Long live the PKK! Long live Apo! Long live the resistance in Eruh and Şemdinli! Down with colonialism!" Normally, only those sentenced to life imprisonment or death chanted such slogans, but the Mardin group was furious, and almost everyone joined in. That too was considered a crime, so new criminal charges were filed right away. The judges decided to identify the offenders and initiate preliminary proceedings—that was utterly normal by now. The military tribunal initiated new proceedings at the slightest sign of rioting.

New arrestees showed up in our ward, mainly students and patriots from rural areas who'd been charged with supporting the PKK. We queried them about the latest events outside, but they couldn't tell us much more than we already knew from the media.

But then Mevlüde [Acar], code name Besê, arrived. We'd heard about her arrest, and then she'd been interrogated in Mardin and Diyarbakir for months. When she didn't turn up in prison, we feared she'd been tortured to death. One TKP woman, Emine Isfendiyaroğlu, said, "Our party rejects the PKK and propagandizes against it. I never thought twice about that. But frankly, my opinion of the PKK changed after I saw how this woman behaved under torture. I was ashamed. She impressed us all."

Mevlüde (who had also used the code name Cihan for a while) came from Sivas and had Turkish roots. She had joined the party at the Teachers School in Mardin. [After the 1980 coup] she'd been in a group that went abroad. So she could provide us with plenty of information on almost anything. The gods could hardly have sent us anyone better!

Mevlüde was a short woman with wonderful long hair. How did she care for it in the mountains? we asked her. Her thick eyebrows made her look very natural. But she was physically awkward: when her tea spilled, she just wiped her glass with her hand. But she was incredibly intelligent, her mind working like a computer. We got her to report on everything that had taken place outside: the first [party] conference [July 15–21, 1981, in the Beka'a Valley], the second [party] congress [August 20–25, 1982, in Syria], the [military] training at the Helve Camp in the Beka'a], the 1982 Israel–Palestine war, the fighting in Lebanon, education and life in general. ... We asked her about all the friends, starting with the chairman.

We discussed and evaluated everything Mevlüde told us. Finally, we had specific information about developments outside! And we could use it for our defenses too. We asked her to write down everything she knew: about the revolutionary violence in Kurdistan, about the organization, the tasks of cadres, alliances, and unified resistance to fascism. She was a mother lode of information.

Her knowledge was of such immeasurable value that we tolerated her sometimes obnoxious behavior. She tended to squabble and interfere in everything. When bickering erupted, and women got angry at her, I tried to calm the waters by emphasizing Mevlüde's positive qualities. But Mevlüde herself never shied from conflict. Replying to the general criticism of her, she said, "In the past I was worse—sometimes I couldn't adapt at all. That's why the friends sent me home. But I'm beginning to change myself and my behavior here."

7 Ten prisoners at Diyarbakir, undated. *Back row, left to right:* unidentified, Cuma Kuyukan, Emine Turgut, Mahmut Barık. *Middle row:* Cahide Şener, Irfan Güler, Cansız, Mustafa Karasu, Besê (Mevlüde). *Front:* Celal Baymış.

Mevlüde had had a chance to do the kind of military and political party work that we all longed to do, but she hadn't been able to cooperate with the comrades. We couldn't quite figure out how, but she was sent home to Sivas in the company of two militias. But before she reached her home village, her relatives turned her in, her own father, or that's what she claimed. So cruel was he, so great his fear of the state, that he sent her to jail, to the torturers. She had gone to the mountains to become a revolutionary, which wasn't right with him, and then she'd given up the revolutionary life and returned home, which wasn't right with him either. His reactionary concept of honor clashed with his fears. Later we heard that he couldn't deal with the pain of having turned her in and died. But even if Mevlüde hadn't been arrested, she could hardly have returned to normal family life. The daughter who wanted her family didn't exist anymore either. Anyone touched by the PKK was no longer the same person.

Mevlüde brings news All our thinking, dreaming, and discussing gave rise to energy and creativity, so we decided to publish a newspaper, Cirûsk [Spark]. The logo showed a mountain, a weapon, and a book. On the masthead was the motto, "Surrender leads to betrayal, resistance to victory." The newspaper consisted of four pages, each with three columns. As usual in prison, the font had to be very small. We'd developed the ability to cram a lot of text onto tiny scraps of paper. Gönül was especially good at it. Her self-confidence grew when we asked her to write for it.

In the lead article, the news section, and the commentaries, we covered the latest developments on the war front, the international situation, our interpretation of the news from TV, newspapers, or radio, and news from new prisoners or families. In the education section, we discussed the party, the guerrillas, class struggle, people's war, socialism, and imperialism. A column was reserved for worldwide revolutions and liberation struggles. Other contents included the work of our party abroad, the speeches of the chairman, and the function of the armed propaganda units. The page for art, literature, and culture featured poems, memoirs, book reviews, and the like. The only artwork in the paper was a sketch of the chairman with a full beard.

The newspaper appeared every two weeks. It was exhausting to write and edit the texts secretly at night, but also a lot of fun. Most prisoners didn't know who wrote them, or when and where. We worked conspiratorially, since unannounced cell searches were common. The newspaper served as educational material and at the same time consolidated our relations with each other. We often discussed betrayal and the enemy's policy of dehumanization.

We sent Mevlüde's reports to the 35th ward, and they also appeared in *Hawar*. It was nice to busy ourselves with such things in prison. The newspaper was distributed to all wards, and everyone was reading it, so we tried to improve the quality. Other wards submitted texts for publication. We received critiques and suggestions.

The Law of Repentance Traitors were housed in the ward next to ours. After the death fast ended, we took to pounding on the wall at certain times every day and night to disturb them. We used plates and benches. We could hardly stand the noise ourselves. We gave the administration an ultimatum: "If the traitors aren't transferred, we'll drive them insane." In the end, they were transferred. Some men friends, as well as prisoners of Kurdish and Turkish leftist groups, came into their ward.

We exchanged messages with them. The windows overlooking the yard had been welded shut to prevent message exchanges, but if there were no soldiers in the yard, we could toss our messages to the men. Sometimes we used the door slots when the corridor was being cleaned.

The betrayals reached new dimensions. Following in the footsteps of Şahin, Yıldırım, and the others, Ali Ozansoy was the new star in the drama of betrayal in Diyarbakir. He was the vanguard! Special TV programs showed the defectors: he recalled his time in the mountains. The enemy used him to discredit the actions of August 15. His betrayal had a devastating impact. Hundreds of patriots were arrested, and torture in the villages intensified. The people suffered greatly from the brutal repression. The enemy used all imaginable methods to reverse the events.

New additions to the prison were built, to house the growing number of prisoners. The men confirmed it. Around this time Sabri Ok and other guerrillas in the mountains were captured. They'd been on the front lines in Kurdistan and had participated in the fighting there. In prison they told us how the actions of August 15 had affected the people. Masses of young women and men had wanted to join the guerrillas, but the party wasn't ready for them. Many were sent back, told to wait until conditions for their admission were in place. For now Sabri didn't go to the 35th ward but stayed with his group first, as he was needed there.

Meanwhile the party made new preparations. It founded the HRK [Hêzen Rizgariye Kurdîstan, Kurdistan Liberation Units, the PKK's armed wing]. The guerrillas got their own uniforms and an official emblem. The prison would soon teem with HRK-ers.

HRK! Everyone was thrilled by this news. The actions in Eruh and Şemdinli had stirred great hopes for an armed popular uprising in Kurdistan. Armed propaganda units were the first step in forming an army. We discussed the various stages of the people's war, the characteristics of each stage, and how theory played out in our reality. We exaggerated because we were guided by emotions. We wanted to skip the stage of strategic balance and go straight to strategic attack, referring to what we knew about the revolutions in Guinea, Angola, Vietnam, and Cuba. "Guerrilla warfare is the most important thing in the people's war. There are various forms of insurgency, and when a rebellion breaks out in one place, it spreads quickly. But it never develops evenly."

We couldn't agree on what stage we were in at the moment. When Mevlüde mentioned the stage of strategic defense, a storm of indignation broke out. With all these groundbreaking events, surely we had to be past this stage. In our dream world we moved much faster. But as we talked, we saw our mistake. In many areas, armed propaganda units hadn't even emerged yet, and the guerrillas had to be expanded.

We published the newspaper, organized continuing education, worked out regularly, and led a community life. We'd defended ourselves politically in court and were sentenced to long terms. An atmosphere emerged that appealed to newcomers. The enemy accepted the PKK prisoners as contact persons. The PKK was his primary target of attack and at the same time carried the most weight in negotiations. Dozens of PKK prisoners lost their lives in the resistance. And outside, they waged an armed struggle.

The enemy launched a new offensive under the Law of Repentance. Under this legal framework [of the Turkish Penal Code], guerrillas who capitulated [and gave information] were promised reduced sentences. Prisoners who showed remorse would be amnestied, even if they'd committed murder. Repenters were even offered facial surgery—it was all an attempt to make betrayal more appealing. It was offered to smugglers, robbers, killer gangs, and perpetrators of blood feuds, but it was mainly aimed at the PKK and the Kurdish people. For days, TV news reported on former fighters who surrendered or became traitors in captivity, and newspapers announced them in bold headlines.

We studied the enemy's new tactic. Previously, he had used torture to try to coerce prisoners to repent. This wasn't torture anymore, but it created an atmosphere that was even worse. Now he used laws, promises, and threats. What he hadn't achieved through torture, he wanted to achieve through the Law of Repentance. Prisoners wrote articles about it, which were published in our prison newspaper, *Hawar*, and as brochures.

In 1985 a Rizgarî member was transferred to us, Leyla Akbas. Unknown to us at the time, she was benefiting from the Repentance Law. But as we were ignorant of that fact, we talked freely with her. We helped her contact her comrades in the judicial proceedings. Leyla was surprised by our liveliness and tried to participate in our community life. She often exclaimed, "Even after all these years of torture, you're alive and well. And you've created a working political atmosphere here. It was so oppressive in Adana and Mersin—so glad I came here!"

She repeatedly left the cell, supposedly for doctor visits or court hearings. Leaving the ward was a sensitive issue—there were only certain times for such trips. Leyla changed clothes for these trips and put on makeup. On her return, she had black rims under her eyes. When we asked how her lawsuit was going, she responded evasively, and if we looked at her with suspicion, she reacted aggressively. We took to monitoring her letters, from which we found out that she was planning to provoke an incident to change wards. So we warned the friends in the next-door ward, "You have to warn people. Leyla has contact with the administration, she works with the enemy."

Once upon a time I'd told Leyla: "If any woman from this ward ever becomes a traitor, we'll kill her." Now she was scared.

We'd probably given Leyla more respect and attention than she'd ever received in her life. Yet she had told the enemy everything that happened in prison, in secret sessions with the prison authorities. She arrived after our comrades had already sacrificed their lives in the resistance— and she had betrayed without the enemy even slapping her face. She'd reported on each and every one of our movements. The enemy already knew almost everything about Rizgarî—he was interested in the PKK, in us. She became the star of the Law of Repentance. If Esat Oktay had been here, he'd have howled in triumph, maybe over the loudspeaker. For the first time, there was a snitch in the women's ward! At least she wasn't PKK.

Fury raged in me that a woman could sink so low. Betrayal and spying were serious offenses. Beyond that, to save her own little life, she'd betrayed women who'd withstood torture for years! No, this was unacceptable. No way would we Apoçu women let her get away with it. That would have betrayed the spirit of resistance that our martyrs had created at the price of their own lives.

Our anger had nothing to do with her being in another political tendency. We'd shared things with dozens of women from other groups, and despite political differences, we'd resisted the enemy together, even if [behind our backs] they denigrated us as murderers or adventurers or nationalists. But if someone was secretly benefiting from the Repentance Law, all the prisoners had to know about it, so they could defend themselves. We had to warn the other prisoners about her. So we four [Gönül, Mevlüde, Cahide, and author] decided to make a symbolic punishment, to denounce the administration's use of the Repentance

Law but also to publicize that Leyla was letting the enemy use her and accusing others to get herself off the hook.

"Leave her to me," I said to the others. I wanted to beat her as a traitor, to break her nose with my fist. The Law of Repentance, after all, provided for facial surgery. In the future whenever she looked in the mirror, she would remember what the PKK women had done to her.

Early in the morning she was supposed to go to the back cell to get dressed and get ready for breakfast. We would interrogate her there. But that morning she sensed something and glanced around nervously. The women friends had shut the door behind her. Leyla panicked, ran to the door, and pounded, screaming for help. I ran in, grabbed her from behind, and yanked her back. She was strong and resisted. When she screamed, I held her mouth shut. She bit my arm, and I hit her with my other fist. "What's your hurry? Here's something for you," I said, crushing her nose with my fist. "You repulsive woman. Your nose was ugly anyway, you can have surgery later."

When the other women friends heard the commotion, they ran into the back cell. Fatma rushed in. "I just woke up—what's going on?" She'd opposed this action—whenever risk was involved in something, she always held back—and now she tried to stop me.

I snarled at her, "Get out of my way! We have a traitor, and you're trying to restrain me?" At that moment, I was angrier with her than with Leyla.

"Why did you betray us?" I demanded of Leyla. "How long have you been giving the enemy information?"

"I'm not accountable to you!" she shouted.

"Oh, yes you are, you rat! For years the enemy tried to turn us into snitches but never succeeded. Now you pass information to him—just to get yourself out of here! You weren't even tortured! Why did you do it?"

She didn't answer, just huddled on the floor like a pile of shit. Everyone spat on her. How could anyone sink so low? We named some dates and asked her why she'd gone to the administration or to the court on those days and what she'd said there. She kept silent.

We pelted her with questions and accusations. "You pretended to be a classical revolutionary, but you put on makeup to go to the court. You're a whore!" And: "You've informed the enemy about our plans. You even gave him messages from your comrades. You, the great revolutionist of Rizgarî! You're just a double-dealing traitor!"

Zübeyde took a short hose from the tap, wanting to whip Leyla with it, but I stopped her. "We could kill her if we wanted to, but she's not worth it. She's as good as dead anyway. Life has no meaning for a woman who's given up her humanity."

Later, during the roll call, a prisoner was missing. "Where is she?" the officer asked.

"Leyla Akbas is in the back cell," I answered. "You can go pick up your colleague there. We beat her up and threw her out."

Surprised, the officer had Leyla brought in. Her nose was swollen, and the skin under her eyes was blue. "Go on, get some plastic surgery," I spat. The officer gave me a sharp, disbelieving look.

Although it was Sunday, Cahit Aydoğan himself appeared, the notorious fascist prosecutor at the military court. He hadn't come here while we were being tortured or when prisoners had died. In the courtroom he'd cut us off when we tried to speak. But now that we'd beaten up a traitor, he showed up on a Sunday to take our statements and punish us for slapping Leyla a few times!

Gönül, Mevlüde, Cahide, and I claimed responsibility. I took responsibility for actually beating Leyla while the others made clear that we were protesting the Law of Repentance. We took turns making our planned statements.

I said, glaring at Cahit Aydoğan,

The Law of Repentance encourages prisoners to lie and to accuse others. This woman would do anything to be released from prison. We were convicted based on the statements of the traitor Şahin, and now based on Leyla's statements, the administration will try to attach new crimes to us. I protest this practice. It's well known who tortures and oppresses whom here, dozens of our friends have died, and more dozens have long-term injuries or illnesses. Why do you ignore those prisoners? Why not pay attention to them? Since when is Sunday a business day? I'm done.

I finished, and stalked out of the room.

The enemy was determined to make us pay for our attitude. Leyla was officially said to be ill for the next 12 days: her medical record would be used as evidence for a new indictment against us.

The media reported that we'd beaten Leyla Akbas. Some prisoners congratulated us on our action. For the first time a defector had been punished in prison, and the responsibility for it had openly been taken.

Initially the male Rizgarî prisoners stood behind their alleged comrade and demanded that the PKK men criticize us. They did criticize us at first, claiming Leyla wasn't worth it. But when it came out that she'd been working for the enemy, they fell silent.

Some were alienated that women had beaten a woman. They overlooked the fact that this woman had betrayed her fellow women in an ugly way. For us to spare her just because she was a woman would've been not only feudal but a crime. She wasn't poor, helpless, or weak. Some were surprised even that there had been a traitor among the women prisoners.

These negative reactions bothered us. We didn't expect praise or congratulations, but at least we wanted our action understood as a human duty in response to betrayal. I became the target of attacks. The price of blowing the whistle on traitors was high, but at least it had foiled the enemy's plans.

"Colonial courts can't judge us!" The first days of my new trial went well, since there was no concrete evidence, and it was hard to convict someone for a mere slap. I told the court that the attacks on women prisoners were intended to create more snitches like Leyla. In the end, I was convicted of assault and sentenced to three years and a few months in prison. Then again, the very fact that I had mounted a [political] defense was considered a criminal offense. These trials would go on for two years, since every defense gave rise to another trial.

Meanwhile the court annulled the verdicts of some of the prisoners of the Elazığ group because it found their membership in a terrorist organization to be unproven. Considering the years they'd already served, they had to be released. Hamili's death sentence was commuted to life imprisonment. The military court refused to alter my own verdict. Normally, the court followed the decisions of the higher authorities, but not in my case. "I don't acknowledge any decision," I said, "whether it's to my advantage or not. I've already stated in my defense that colonial courts can't judge us."

One trial followed another. The enemy was stubborn. The trials were like torture. They didn't let me finish talking, but every word I said became the subject of another trial. At a hearing on September 12, I protested the fascist military junta. It was the last time I appeared in court. From then on, I would learn about the proceedings only from official documents and newspapers. I would be sentenced, and charges would be brought against me, but I never saw the faces of the fascist judges again.

Assessing our resistance   After the January 1984 uprising, we evaluated the events of the previous four years, in discussions and in writing. We analyzed our actions, the circumstances under which we'd undertaken them, and the revolutionary qualities of the comrades who'd played leading roles.

The 1982 resistance had been a direct clash between the enemy and the PKK, extending even beyond prison walls. The enemy had wanted to vanquish the PKK by eliminating its leading cadres and thereby snuff out the people's newly awakened revolutionary hopes. By dealing a deadly blow on the prison front, the enemy thought he could also attack the party work outside. Despite his technical superiority, he had failed, and the PKK prevailed.

At a time when the enemy claimed to have shattered all revolutionary aspirations in prisons, Mazlum, Hayri, Pir, and the others demonstrated the PKK's spirit of resistance as well as its attachment to Chairman Apo. Aware of the historical responsibility of prisoners to resist, they accepted a leading role and fulfilled their duty to protect the party. Losing them was painful, as revolutionaries like them were rare. We felt guilty about them and all wished we'd died in their stead, but we could do them justice only by continuing their struggle.

The best response to their deaths was August 15 [the start of armed propaganda], because their spirit lived on in the PKK's conflict. In the September uprising, we prisoners awoke to new life, but afterward their outlook contracted, and we lost foresight and vision. Before we could pull ourselves out of this phase of weakness, the enemy attacked again in January 1984. Meanwhile outside, the military junta pursued its plan of providing a veneer of democratization.

The prisons in Kurdistan and Turkey were a pillar of the enemy's political plan to extinguish Kurdish identity, finally fulfilling the policy that had been in place since the Republic's founding. Prisons were like experimental laboratories where the enemy studied peoples, nations, personalities, organizations, and genders. He conducted experiments on every aspect of the human psyche and body, as well as organizations and means of fighting, using all available technology and science.

The prisoners were like chemical elements in this lab: they could decide if they wanted to be mercury, iron, or something else. Your situation depended on which elements you allied with and which you separated from. The impulse to bow to the enemy's superior power led to betrayal. Or you could interrupt the experiments and undermine the enemy's methods by blowing yourself up, as the friends did in 1982.

The enemy believed he so thoroughly controlled his prison lab that prisoners lacked the option to kill themselves. "Only I have the right to your life and death," he pronounced. But Mazlum, in his empty cell, was like a chemical compound in a beaker. He had needed only a match and a necktie to extinguish the darkness, the fear, the surrender, the monster of betrayal. The secret is to embrace life with love and tenderness. Only then can one act with self-determination, express responsibility and deep conviction, and live the future in the present. Nobody had expected anything like his action, and everyone was profoundly shocked.

The Night of the Four, an action that also required great courage and deep conviction, had special meaning as well. To join Mazlum's action, they had had to choose the right time and place, and the leader of the Four did so. The fire, the cries of victory, the flaming flesh, and the blood had terrified the enemy. One soldier, a torturer, remarked in awe that the Four were "still chanting slogans as they burned brightly. What kind of conviction is that?" It was the PKK! The conviction of the Four was the conviction of the PKK. If the soldier was deeply impressed, the prisoners were far more so. How many times did this fire burn in my heart, make it bleed, break me to the marrow of my bones? Feeling the magnitude of this action was enough to keep a person alive. If we were still alive, it was only because that fire inflamed our hearts, and because that pain remained.

So 1982 had been a turning point for us. Then came the death fast—we never tired of telling each other about it. The more details we learned, the more we understood how incomparably great an act of resistance it had been. Every dying cell had been a blow to the enemy. With the foul smell of our hunger, we condemned the rotten acts of the traitors. How could anyone carry on a death fast for 60 days? Medicine has no answer, it just can't be explained. Our whole life revolved around these instances of resistance, where past and future came together.

These actions shook everyone up, and impressed everyone, but they didn't affect all the prisoners the same way. The sensations weren't equally deep. Some felt defeated despite resisting. Some had been broken not only physically but mentally, in their will and their convictions. Some surrendered without resisting, while others let themselves be dragged along. The enemy had tried to dehumanize the prisoners with torture, oppression, threats, and promises, and many felt surrender and defeat. How much he damaged individuals' personalities depended on the strength of their beliefs and their will.

For many, everything that made us up was expressed in the resistance. Our circumstances left us no choice but to resist. Without it, we couldn't even breathe. Resistance was our whole life. Before 1984, the enemy had tried to force us to wear prison clothing or to pray before eating or to say, "I'm a Turk." But the spirit of resistance of 1982 had taken root, and now we were about changing the mood of capitulation and recreating the conditions for an organized resistance.

Thus the broad participation in the September death fast was inevitable, as the conditions for an uprising had matured. But before we could catch our breath, the January attacks came: they were extensive and aimed at coercing betrayal. After the end of the hunger strikes, the enemy targeted our internal problems, hoping to benefit from them.

Up to this point, apart from the resistance actions of 1982, the party had considered our struggle in prison to be a phase of defeat and surrender. The armed struggle outside, culminating in August 15, seemed the only guarantee of positive events. But in 1985, we received a party report that expressly emphasized the importance of prison resistance for the national liberation struggle. It did us good. We continued our self-critical treatment of the past few years in order to work through our mistakes. But it remained superficial, and we failed to get to the root of our organizational weaknesses.

Fuat Çavgun's action   The men friends were facing internal discontent. Factions were formed, pressuring the party's prison leadership. We women were briefed only in general terms because we weren't considered part of the situation.

But one day the men friends wrote:

> Lately we've had to deal with internal issues. Some time ago we sent you a text written by Fuat Çavgun and others that criticized the leadership. We took this criticism seriously and agreed to address it. But some tried to exploit the dissatisfaction with the leadership that existed at the base. Especially those who had various problems were stirred up against the leadership. These

conflicts weren't solved. In addition, the administration didn't implement some of the promises it had made. So some problems await a solution, and we've not been able to clarify them. But we weren't delaying deliberately.

Finally Fuat wrote a statement dissolving the leadership. He wrote, "I dissolve the leadership because it's not doing its job. We'll do it." He insisted that his message be forwarded to everyone. Some are now under his influence. We wrote to him and asked him to discuss the problems with us. If the leadership is to be changed, it must be done jointly. He didn't respond, but instead, he declared himself an organization and published newsletters in the name of the party. What do you think about this situation? We look forward to your evaluations and suggestions.

We were surprised. This was serious. I jotted down my thoughts:

The text [by Fuat] is cleverly written, it has a political appearance and also contains some valid points ... But ultimately it is a coup against the organization. Treachery in various forms has long existed in prison, but this is something new. I suggest punishing Fuat Çavgun. Offenses against the party in prison should no longer go unpunished. If Şahin had been punished, the betrayals wouldn't have been so widespread and wouldn't have done so much damage.

The men found my proposal too radical. I couldn't understand why. "Punishment inside prison is out of the question," they wrote back. "It would have negative consequences." That meant we had to bow to circumstances. In my opinion, betrayal must not go unpunished anywhere.

Meanwhile Fuat and his associates didn't respond to their invitation to dialogue. This made it clear how serious the situation was. To be separated from one's own comrades in prison means ultimately to go over to the enemy, or that's how I've always seen it.

Fuat had suffered brain damage and paralysis as a result of the July 14 death fast. I had respect for him, as well as for all friends who were injured under torture or in resistance or who suffered permanent health problems.

But Fuat was also the brother of Halil Çavgun. "If they had a spark of respect for this valorous man, they would've behaved differently," I said. Fuat had betrayed Halil. He couldn't accept his new physical limitations. Instead of avenging himself on the enemy, he attacked us, the party. The enemy deliberately targeted family members of valuable comrades to try to use them for his own ends.

The incident affected me deeply. How could a person change so much? How did a person become a traitor, a defector?

Around this time the prisoners from the ward next door were transferred, which broke off our contact with the men again. For weeks we looked for a chance to send them messages. Leyla Akbas had exposed our means of communication—even the method of throwing bread balls from the roof to the next ward wasn't safe anymore. When our messages didn't stay on the roof, they fell into the hands of the soldiers. So no important messages could be passed on this way.

Suphi's action Suphi Çevirici and his group were brought to the ward next door, along with defectors after their arrest. After figuring out how to exchange messages, he wrote us a letter.

He had parted ways with the friends. He was angry and had split off— and left behind everything he had learned during training abroad, in the mountains. Finally he was reported and arrested. Under interrogation he made some statements, but he didn't betray anyone. Now in prison he wanted to find his way back to the party. He was ready to return. The men friends said, "He can make amends by asking the party's forgiveness and admitting that he was obligated to them." Suphi agreed and started writing his defense, denouncing the enemy and confessing his own weaknesses and mistakes.

Meanwhile the enemy wanted to coerce Suphi into betraying the guerrillas in the mountains. They were going to fly him there by helicopter. If the enemy became aware of his new rapprochement with the party, they might murder him.

We asked him about the party work abroad that he'd seen. He told us about problems in forming coalitions, about areas where official representation had been established, internal issues, and tendencies that deviated from the party line. He fed our hunger for information, and it was splendid—the events outside were much better and more comprehensive than we'd assumed. He wrote it all down and it was published in *Hawar*.

Since he was very diligent and knew what interested us, he sent us one message after another. Our exchange of information was secret, but at one point the defectors around him found out about it. Suphi threatened them, "If you say anything to the administration, I'll kill you." He understood what was going on with them.

One day while he was in the bathroom reading one of our messages, soldiers attacked him. He couldn't destroy the letter completely in time, so scraps of it fell into the soldiers' hands. He was transferred to a ward with mostly newly arrived prisoners, where he continued to write his defense.

The enemy intentionally delayed his trial. He finished his 50-page defense. "I didn't do justice to the party by my behavior," he wrote. "My weaknesses and my anger led me to make serious mistakes, but I didn't capitulate, and I committed no betrayal."

[In the spring of 1986] Suphi hanged himself in the ward's toilet area to protest the delay in his trial. I wished he had been able to express his anger and stayed alive. He was so capable. He left behind his writings, his pain, and his struggle. The party acknowledged that he had fallen in battle. At one of my hearings, I said,

> Comrade Suphi Çevirici was tortured for months in police interrogation, in collaboration with the court. So the police, the court, and the administration coerced him into betrayal. He deliberately hasn't been brought before the court because he would have made this procedure public. The court is directly responsible for his death, and I protest. Suphi Çevirici has fallen in our struggle, and we will continue it.

For once the judges listened to me without removing me from the courtroom.

Hamili and me! The judge ordered the prison administration to release the prisoners who had done their time and weren't subject to any other proceedings. They included [my brother] Metin and several others from the Elazığ group. Their files went back and forth between the court of appeal and the military tribunal.

But then another proceeding began against Metin, and his release was put on hold. During the September resistance he had been attacked in a visiting booth, and the glass pane had been broken. The judges were also upset about the death fast and about the way we had protested in court by turning our backs on them. That day some of the men friends had been attacked in the prison, and Metin, Mustafa, and Abdullah Bucak were severely injured. They were put under interrogation in this condition but refused to testify. They were then transferred to the second ward, housing the Bucaks and Süleyman, another form of torture. They protested and were finally relocated. That's what Metin's new proceeding was about. Unable to find any reason to detain them, the enemy charged them with breaking the glass and "resisting the military."

But his release was suspended. Earlier, Metin had written to me that his release was very likely. He told me how important our comradely relationship was to him and said he'd stay committed to the fight and vindicate us. He praised me for my attitude in prison.

In his letter Metin talked to me about Hamili. He said it was good that I behaved so naturally and informally toward him, but Hamili thought about me in ways I didn't notice, and he advised me to pay careful attention to my behavior.

What did that mean? What was I to pay attention to? I didn't understand it at all. Hamili and I saw each other only once a month for five or ten minutes. I didn't treat him differently than Metin.

I always greeted Hamili and told him I missed him—was that what Metin meant? But we all did that. My family and friends liked Hamili, and I'd talked about him for years. I missed all the friends in the 35th ward, but Hamili was closest to me. We'd gone through a lot together. Did I treat him differently than the others? Was that what Metin was trying to warn me about?

I handed Metin's letter to Cahide, saying, "Please read it. I don't understand this one part." Cahide read it and grinned impishly. "He's saying Hamili's interested in you. What's not to understand?"

Her words hit me like a slap. "What's that supposed to mean?"

Cahide murmured, "I don't know, it's just in there." My annoyance must have frightened her.

I didn't know what to think, then I got a little crazy. It shook me up. It seemed like a sin, a crime. I could have screamed in panic. Anyone watching me would've thought I'd got a death notice. Fortunately, there were only four of us in the ward, and the others were preoccupied.

I thought about my behavior toward Hamili. I hadn't said or done anything misleading. Or had he misinterpreted my relaxed, natural way of being with him? But no, I just couldn't imagine that he was interested in me that way. Metin's warning to watch my behavior didn't make sense, since my feelings for Hamili were no different from my feelings for Metin himself. My behavior toward both was straightforward, sisterly, and cooperative. My relations with them were beautiful. I wouldn't have given them up for anything.

Not that I was interested in being a nun. Nuns had always seemed so artificial, attempting to mask the naturalness of women. In movies they were cold as ice, with impassive faces. Nor were they good angels. I didn't even like their humanism. Only their church services, their fervent prayers together, appealed to me. I found this side of Christianity attractive, maybe it was because I could empathize with the pain of Jesus at the Crucifixion. Still, a nun's life wasn't what I wanted.

I'd already lived with a man, in a relationship that sprang from difficult circumstances, tradition, my own weakness and helplessness, my lack of revolutionary experience, and my dreams of freedom. Probably no one ever paid such a high price for a marriage that lasted only a few months. I was open-minded toward men. If a man had been around who I could love, and circumstances had been right, I would've loved him. I loved most of my comrades without limits—I enclosed them all in my heart.

Then why did Metin's one-sentence warning so confuse me? Love wasn't a shame or a sin, but somehow it felt that way. My comradely, sisterly feelings for Hamili had settled in my consciousness years ago. He'd been one of my earliest comrades. We had gone through school together, then served on a district committee together. We were arrested together and sentenced at the same trial. We had defended ourselves together. We had watched as some of our former companions committed treason: Şahin, Ali Gündüz, and others. For me, Hamili was inseparable from both the martyrs and the living resisters.

Yet on the outside, our contact had been relatively limited—I talked more to the other friends I worked with. Hamili wasn't very talkative anyway. He rarely addressed me and always kept a distance. When I ran away from home, he looked for me on the banks of the Munzer, or so someone later told me. The day he got engaged to Ayten, I happened to be in Dersim and went to the party—and didn't notice his sadness. After his wedding, I visited him with Ali Gündüz—and didn't notice his embarrassment. Once our eyes met when we were having breakfast together in someone's home. He looked sad, which again didn't register. Actually, I overlooked many indications of Hamili's love, as I would later find out.

So often I behaved recklessly, acting from impatience rather than logic, without considering the consequences, forging ahead blindly.

I wrote to Karasu in the 35th ward and told him Hamili had hinted certain things to my brother Metin, and I criticized Hamili for it. We were revolutionaries, I wrote, and it wasn't right. It was a shame that our close comradely relations had contributed to it, I said. Instead of talking to Metin about my behavior, I said, Hamili should have talked to me directly. Besides we were in prison, a site of endless suffering and shared pain. Allowing such feelings meant ignoring the severity of our situation. That's what bothered me the most, underlying the shame, embarrassment, and restlessness I felt.

Karasu wrote back, telling me he didn't understand my letter, so he'd given it to Hamili. "Don't take such things seriously," he advised. Attached to his letter was a message from Hamili, who called me his "sister in this world and in the hereafter" and explained that my reaction had saddened him. Metin had got something wrong. I was glad to hear it and had to laugh at myself. At the same time I was annoyed that I'd written so hastily to Karasu. I should have checked with Metin first. *Well*, I said to myself, *the important thing is that it's not what I thought. My mistake wasn't so important. I can explain everything to Hamili if I have a chance.*

8 Cansız with Mustafa Karasu and Hamili Yıldırım, at Diyarbakir, undated.

Then sometime later, when we went to the courthouse for a hearing, Hamili didn't greet me in the outer corridor. His face was sullen, and he even turned his back to me. This went on all day. As we sat in the courtroom, I turned and looked back at him. I asked the men closest to me, "What's up with him? Did something happen?" They said no. He got up from his seat saying he was sick, which wasn't believable.

Once a month, the families could meet with the prisoners for ten minutes. We always looked forward to getting news from the outside and from the other prison wards. The visiting time was short, and everything had to be said quickly. The room was crowded with people. Metin had finally been released.

I met with Hamili, as he was supposedly the son of my maternal uncle. In the past I would hug him, grab his hand, and barrage him with questions. Now we sat in an awkward silence.

Finally, I said, "I made a mess the other day, unnecessarily. I misunderstood Metin's message. I'm so sorry." Then I went on. "Your family once mentioned something to me. Maybe our meetings were misinterpreted and talked about. In any case, I hope there's nothing to it."

Hamili sat in silence for a while and then said, "It's true."

"What's true?"

"I've been interested in you since 1975," he said.

"What! That can't be!" I gasped in amazement, squeezing his hand. "I've always loved you like a brother."

Silence again. Then at the first warning whistle, before he was even required to leave, he rose and left without saying goodbye.

Süleyman looked over at me questioningly. Even the soldiers looked surprised. Usually they had a hard time dragging us out of the room. We always tried to extend visiting time by a few minutes and would keep on talking while standing, regardless of the whistles.

I said to Süleyman, "Take care of Hamili," and went back to my ward sadly.

What kind of person was Hamili? In his last letter, I'd been his sister. Now all of a sudden, I was his years-long what-do-I-know! Or had I misunderstood?

Sometime after that meeting, I got a message from Karasu, who talked about general events and a recent decree by the enemy. He said they'd soon make the decision to refuse the uniforms. I was glad—we'd been talking about eliminating those eyesores since 1985. But there had been different proposals, and internal conflicts, and it had all dragged on. The Leyla Akbas affair had lasted two years, and then the enemy used it as a pretext to threaten a crackdown. As if a threat of punishment could induce us to retreat.

Then Karasu brought up Hamili, calling him a good and sincere friend whose defiant personality was well known to me.

Hamili is sensitive. He sometimes misunderstands even the slightest criticism. He takes things to heart. Even revolutionaries feel love and mutual interest, which shouldn't be denied. You should consider his sensitivity in making your decision. You know what you're doing. We won't tell you what to do.

Ah, so they expected me to sacrifice myself. It was absurd.

Another message came from Hamili, a long one, written in an elaborate, ornate handwriting that was as strange as he was. It made me laugh out loud. I hoped nobody could hear me. *Ornate font! Ornate lie! Ornate star! Ornate love!* I didn't want to use that last word but did anyway. Love is beautiful and simple without ornaments.

"Seko," Hamili began. He'd always called me Seko. So had my mother, when she was angry with me. And Meral had picked it up from Hamili, calling me Seko at least in written messages.

It all started in 1975, he wrote. He described his reaction to my flight from home and then to his engagement. He had written his previous message only because he was afraid of my reaction.

His letter struck a nerve. Oh dear. When I finished reading it, I wept. How had I failed to notice his feelings for me? Why hadn't he declared them? In his place, I would have. I sensed that his feelings were deep and sincere, and I loved and respected him for it, wondering, *Is that love?*

I ruminated for a week, then got sick and stayed in bed. For years I had suffered torment in prison, but it had never kept me in bed. Only Hamili succeeded in doing that.

Either I was too callous or I was too emotional. The constant confrontations with the enemy, all the hatred and anger, had turned my heart to stone. I carried the pain of many years in my heart and forgot nothing. But with my comrades, I was different, as everyone who knew me was aware. Hamili knew me very well. They all had my passionate love. Love means feeling what the other feels. Maybe my heart wasn't big enough to feel everything, but I felt my comrades' feelings in the marrow of my bones.

I wrote a long letter to Karasu, explaining "I love you all" and that Hamili and I had been respectfully close for years. I was worried that he would tell the friends I returned his feelings. That's normal for men, I thought—they think up scenarios and tell them to their friends as if they were true. The fact that Hamili had told Metin about his feelings, and that even Karasu knew about it, raised this possibility. No, the friends had to know the truth. Illusions and scenarios had no place here. No one should attribute to me things that weren't true, even out of love. I was sensitive on this point, so I wrote in great detail.

Meanwhile my correspondence with the 35th ward continued. We wrote commentaries on a new decree that provided a legal framework for methods the enemy had already been using. Repression and torture were now official policy. The decree provided for everything—uniforms, internal order, attorney talks. Mostly it was a list of prohibitions, applicable to all prisons in Turkey and Kurdistan. We thought of doing simultaneous actions in different places. We tried to smuggle messages with our thoughts to friends in other prisons via relatives. It took us a lot of time to come to a decision, as each group in each prison had to discuss this issue first.

I got a message, signed "M. Şener," that attempted to persuade me that Hamili's love was authentic. Şener described Hamili's feelings for me, although he rather overdid it. Astonishingly, Hamili even referred to the clothes I'd worn when I came home from Germany, the black bell-bottoms and the blond wig! It made me uneasy—why was Hamili talking to others about that? He didn't say anything about his love directly to me, but he was telling everyone else. How strange that he resorted to intermediaries, who wrote as if they were trying to coax a spoiled child.

No, I have to think for myself, I told myself. We were still in prison, where the enemy would undoubtedly use a relationship or marriage against us. We had to be careful. Cahide and Süleyman had got engaged before they were arrested, during the fighting in Siverek. The enemy had found out during interrogation. Since they didn't have the same surname, their families couldn't visit both of them in prison. They talked about getting married, and the 35th gave its approval, but I argued against it. Lately, I pointed out, newspapers had been reporting on prison marriages. "The enemy would run headlines: 'Wedding in Diyarbakir Prison' or 'PKK-ers Marry in Jail.' He's just waiting for such an opportunity." I persuaded Cahide to give it up. The suggestion hadn't really been hers—rather, the men had raised it and got everything ready, even designating Mehdi Zana as best man. But such a discussion among friends seemed questionable to me.

On the other hand, Hamili was suffering, which disconcerted me, and I felt sorry for him. In prison, death is never far away, but to firmly reject the love and affection of a friend—that struck my conscience. I already loved Hamili—what would it mean to add another dimension? Should I accept it? But if I were motivated by compassion, then wouldn't I just be bowing to the will of another? Making a sacrifice? I had already done "sacrifice," and it had preoccupied me for a long time. You have to strike a balance between your willingness to sacrifice everything for the revolution and your ability to choose the right place and time.

Love can't develop from one-sided desire. What is love anyway? In general, it's connected with the effort you put into a person. I had put a lot of effort into Hamili, going back when he married Ayten, and I valued my memories of his love and affection. He would always be part of the love I carried inside me, love that was so beautiful that its naturalness, warmth, and charm were sufficient. Could it be individualized to one person? But I couldn't belong only to one person! And just as little could

9 Cansız with Hamili Yıldırım, at Diyarbakir, c.1986.

one person belong only to me! I was Seko to all of them. I saw Hamili in all the friends, and in all the friends I saw Hamili.

I wrote to him, "My love for you is deep, but it is nothing new, although I must admit that my petrified heart has softened. I'm touched that you carried these feelings for a long time without letting anyone know. That's probably love." With difficulty, I wrote to Karasu that I'd made a decision, but no one must know about it. There would be no official engagement. Hamili and I would continue to write.

Internal problems Living together in a confined space had the advantage that no activity remained hidden. Everything happened out in the open. But the wards were separated from each other, so they underwent different developments, and mistakes and offenses that happened in one ward weren't known to the others.

For years now, in the men's wards, conflicts between the cadres and the base had been simmering at a low boil, with lots of accusations and counter-accusations and no overall solution in sight. No sooner was one issue resolved than another one sprang up. The party inside prison was still structured as it had been when we were outside, when our movement had consisted of only a small group. The most important decisions were made together, but much information was shared only within a narrow circle.

We women still felt cut off from the men. We found out only very late about many problems and weren't involved in resolving them. I didn't know the men well enough to understand the specific roles they played—I saw them only in court and during resistance actions. The reports I read discussed only the overall problems, not their causes. And the men told me about events only sketchily, since they didn't want to influence me negatively, or maybe they just thought I didn't need to know certain things because they didn't affect me. I asked questions about things that didn't make sense and offered suggestions. One of the most important topics we all talked about was taking action against the general decree. I was constantly reformulating my thoughts and passing them on.

The ongoing give-and-take was important to me. I communicated much more actively with them, sharing everything I knew. We women had fewer serious conflicts than the men did. Individualism and selfish behavior were always just below the surface, but it was mostly in our day-to-day routines that we irritated each other. Cahide's behavior was a problem for a while, but after her suicide attempt, she got more involved in our common life. Gönül's mood swings had been annoying, but we didn't let her decline any further. Later, after she was released, I had written a brief report to the party outside, suggesting they keep an eye on her and not give her any tasks that involved responsibility.

One source of uneasiness involved [Mehmet] Şener. I didn't know much about him—who he was, or what role he played. He was a leading cadre, influencing decisions and pushing himself into the foreground, but his name came up in correspondence—some said he lacked integrity.

He was criticized for his behavior during the January uprising. One message said:

> [Şener had] influenced the decision on uniforms, although it was ultimately a joint decision, but it was sometimes even portrayed as if Şener had made that decision alone. Şener denied it, saying most of the prisoners were already wearing uniforms. We wanted to eliminate it as an issue and after a long discussion decided to accept uniforms temporarily, then later refuse them in an organized manner … As a leading cadre, he should have behaved differently … We had agreed not to accept the rules, period. So his behavior could be considered surrender and even betrayal. Ultimately, it was rated as weakness. Şener was stripped of all duties for two years.

According to another message, "At a meeting between Şener and Saliha, a message fell into the hands of the enemy." Who was Saliha? I asked the friends. "Saliha is blind and is Şener's mother," they explained. "The families have complained about her a lot. She's very talkative."

"How could it happen that a message was found on them?" I asked. "They have to be called to account." The message "fell out of her hand when she was handing it to Şener," the friends told me, "and a soldier saw it. Şener bent to pick it up, but soldiers stepped in and grabbed it, and there was a scuffle."

Outside, a families' movement had been established, in which Şener's sisters participated. It was alarming that, despite the rumors about Saliha, she was still being used as a courier to smuggle important messages. I sent a message to the friends in Mardin: "Saliha shouldn't be given important messages. Ordinary messages are still okay. Make sure she doesn't notice, so she won't be adversely affected."

[A further message said:]

In another incident [during the death fast], Şener and Necmettin Büyükkaya were taken to the hamam and tortured there. Necmettin died. Şener was tortured until he finally swore the oath and sang the national anthem. He says he was unconscious.

The more we learned, the more I realized how far away we women were from these complex problems. We would have been much concerned, but we had a lot of faith in the men friends. "The men know what they're doing," we told each other. So we held back and didn't insist on giving them our criticisms and suggestions.

I found out that Hamili was having problems with the organization too. I'd always assumed he had a leadership role, but he was actually staying out of leadership deliberately, as he had done in Elazığ. Back then he and I had had heated discussions about it. It was important to take responsibility, I insisted, especially in difficult times. There were so many problems, and nothing could be achieved with antagonisms. Once I accused him of being risk-averse. But especially in prison, where the enemy tried to control everything, leadership was crucially important. In difficult times, we needed everyone capable to represent the party and fulfill the tasks of a cadre.

Why was Hamili still not in the leadership? I wondered. Did he feel slighted? Was it calculation? Often he tended to both. One day, as we waited for a hearing to begin, I asked him directly.

"Who says that?" he said. "It's not true." Then, temples pulsing, he added, "As I said after the police interrogation, I didn't want to take on any more tasks. We made a lot of mistakes, we got arrested, we didn't live up to our responsibilities, and then we didn't resist enough. Since then I haven't wanted to take on a leadership role. It's a long-ago decision that has nothing to do with current events."

"I don't believe you, Hamili," I replied. It was the first time I'd criticized him so directly and severely.

His eyes darkened. "Who told you something? What do you want to hear from me?" From his tone, I realized he didn't want to speak frankly about it. Why? What was he afraid of? I knew him pretty well and didn't want him to do anything wrong. Why did our party have so many problems in prison, when we had so many cadres here? I was worried—

I'd recently heard about a possible split among the cadres. There was still so much I didn't know. And this was also about our relationship—above all, we had to be straight with each other.

But ultimately the internal organizational problems were the worst. It annoyed me that I got so little information. Why didn't anybody tell me anything? Were they trying to spare me? In a message to Karasu, I criticized this and said I wanted to know everything important, including about Hamili's situation. It wasn't just about the relationship, I said, but much more about the interests of the party. I also expressed surprise that such things were kept secret from me.

We women had great respect for the resilience of the men friends, and great confidence in them. They represented the party, and sometimes it was enough for us to see them from a distance and to know that they lived and that they defied the enemy. This feeling outweighed all our conflicts and contradictions. When something openly violated our ideals and principles, we stood up to it, but what went on behind closed

10 Twelve prisoners at Diyarbakir, undated. *Standing, left to right*: unidentified, unidentified, unidentified, unidentified, Cahide Şener, unidentified, unidentified. *At front*: Emine Turgut, unidentified, Faruk Altun, Cansız, Mehmet Şener, Mevlüde (Besê).

doors was beyond our imagining. But the more I learned about the internal problems, the greater my disagreements became on the mental and emotional level.

Treachery, defectors, spies—we knew about them. Some prisoners, in one way or another, had originally been impressed by the PKK's struggle, then lost their courage when facing the enemy. Others found themselves unable to break with their families and abandon traditional thinking. Or they didn't know the ideology of the party or the enemy and knew nothing about politics. At least we understood this kind of behavior. But other behavior wasn't so easy to understand. What did it mean to work against the party in prison? What form did such an opposition take? It wasn't always possible to explain everything in terms of good or bad intentions.

Preparing for the great escape At one meeting, Hamili told me that preparations were under way for a major escape. A tunnel was being constructed. Leading cadres, more than 40 people, were to escape. "And we'll take one or two from TİKKO," he said.

In the prevailing organizational confusion, the tunnel construction was a ray of light. The escape of 40 cadres would be tremendous. The men friends asked us to get plaster from outside. Cahide, who had graduated from the Girls' Trade School, knew about pottery. She told the administration she needed plaster, paint, and such to make gift items and sell them outside. After some effort, she finally got the permit. In order not to attract attention, we shaped some figurines and gave them to the guards. We used white bread to save plaster. We painted over it, so it didn't show. The rest of the plaster was taken to the 35th ward for the tunnel cover. It was exciting, and we were happy to be able to contribute at least a small part.

But the longer the work dragged on, the more the existing problems became a plague.

We developed a plan for action against the decree, but it fell into the hands of the administration. They discovered an area where mainly prisoners from other groups stayed. We started a hunger strike. Then two days later the administration agreed to abolish the uniform requirement, although "if someone voluntarily wishes to wear prison clothes, nobody may interfere."

That's how easily the uniforms were abolished! We interpreted this development positively. The action plan the enemy had found was very comprehensive. "The enemy didn't want to risk the action spreading to other prisons, so he preferred to give in quietly," we told each other. In the uprising against the uniforms, five friends had died. Now the enemy capitulated after just two days of a hunger strike! We tried to fathom his motives. Of course, it wasn't right to constantly risk high losses in order to achieve something. After the unsatisfactory outcome of the previous death fast, our situation wasn't all that brilliant. After much discussion, we came to the conclusion that the enemy was aware of our internal problems and wanted to prevent the imperative of resisting him from reuniting us. In his view, it was better to keep us stewing in a pot where our internal conflicts worsened.

In court, we decided to make our statements and defend ourselves in Kurdish. Use of the Kurdish language had been one of our demands, since many families couldn't speak Turkish. In the time of torture, when it was banned, we could hardly talk without it, and a visit without a conversation was hard to endure. Now the ban was temporarily lifted. Most of the main trials were over, and the others were nearing an end, but there were still hearings on other charges, where Kurdish could now be spoken. Mehdi Zana made a statement in Kurdish. Interestingly, the media portrayed it as if it had been the first time, and newspaper headlines put him in the foreground.

The day Agit died On March 28, 1986, we heard over the TV evening news that Comrade Agit had been killed. A close-up on the screen showed him lying in the snow of the Gabar Mountains, looking as if he were asleep, wearing a kefiye. A hush came over us. Some wept. Many of the young friends knew him from Batman, where he had urged them to join the fight. We didn't want to believe it. What had happened? At Newroz the initiative should have been ours. Had he been betrayed? "There must have been an internal betrayal," many friends said, "otherwise Agit would never have died." That night I couldn't fall asleep. Once everyone else was finally sleeping, I pulled the cover over my head and cried my heart out.

We had lost a valuable guerrilla commander—Agit had helped build the guerrilla force after the betrayal of 1985 [by the KDP]. Except for Mehmet Karasungur, he was the first leading commander to be killed in the mountains. The next day we held a memorial service for him. We hadn't known him well, so we couldn't say much about him. Later the men sent us texts about events he had decisively affected. They detailed his military prowess in August 15 and filled us in about the structure of the HRK. When the AGRK was founded at the third party congress [in October 1986], it was dedicated to his memory.

For a few days in 1987, the news reported on several armed counterinsurgency actions, attacking Kurdish villages, killing women and children. Meanwhile the state was running a full-bore propaganda campaign against us, trying incite the people against us and undermine our armed operations.

And what was the party doing to counter the propaganda? we wondered. Did it offer any explanation? We didn't get much information, just noticed that something was missing.

Around this time, several delegations of journalists, from domestic and foreign media, visited the prison to ask what we thought of the raids on Kurdish villages. The state was trying to prove we weren't being tortured.

We protested the attacks in court, saying they had been carried out by counterinsurgency forces. The defectors said it was the PKK, and some new arrestees claimed, "It was us." Some pointed out that civilian casualties were normal in a war. What a mess. But in our defense speeches, we called the enemy out for his intrigues: "The counterinsurgency is trying to discredit our party and the national liberation struggle, by carrying out provocative actions wearing guerrilla clothing. The counterinsurgency and the village guard system must be removed." Of course, the press didn't publish the substance of our speeches, just picked out snippets here and there and published them out of context, to make headlines that served the counterpropaganda. Another aim was to stir up strife in the prisons and give the impression that PKK prisoners disapproved of the PKK outside and the guerrillas.

Failures and missteps   The tunnel was finished, we heard. [The escape was to happen that night.] Nobody in the women's ward was in on it. That night I couldn't sleep, alert for any sound. As the hours dragged by, I daydreamed. Would more than 40 cadres really manage to break out and join the guerrillas? That would change everything! The party and the people would be jubilant, and the enemy would go nuts. Our experienced cadres would infuse the party outside with fresh energy. Superb! Were the friends in the mountains ready for the friends from prison? How long would the men need to get there? What if something went wrong? But no, the escape had been thoroughly prepared. The tunnel led to a house, and the friends would exit the tunnel only once they were in the house.

I remembered Mazlum's escape attempt. He'd hidden in that dumpster for hours, and he would have succeeded if the friends had arrived just ten minutes earlier. They could easily have knocked off the two soldiers.

I thought of my own attempt, back in Malatya. What a beautiful night! I'd been overjoyed, as if I'd done some important action. I'd actually succeeded in getting physically outside. I'd told myself, *Now I've done the hardest part, I'm home free.* I thought I'd really escaped. I imagined telling the friends about my successful escape. It was like a movie: August 20, 1980, the only beautiful night in Malatya! But no, I just made it to that point and didn't know what to do next. I hadn't done enough planning, and I didn't know the area, so my success was short-lived. If I could have walked directly into a forest, I would've made it. In the mountains you can always hide, they provide protection.

It was probably worse to be captured outside than to have not tried at all. If you're too weak or clumsy, faint-hearted, or otherwise unable to even try something, that's understandable. But to succeed at the hardest part, and still have enough strength to keep going, yet ultimately fail because you didn't think far enough ahead or because you are overconfident and drunk with success ... Did I enjoy taking risks? Being a victim? Making sacrifices? I had to think more about the concept of sacrifice. It had all started when I got angry. Conventional wisdom has it, "Those who stand up in anger, sit back down damaged." But of course that was no justification.

[When I woke up the next morning,] things were normal, nothing unusual. Either the escape hadn't taken place, or it hadn't been noticed yet. I expected all the wards to be searched for more tunnels, and the panicked enemy would count all the prisoners. But nothing was out of the ordinary.

After a while, as a test, I sent a message to the 35th ward asking for an address that I supposedly needed. When an answer arrived, I knew the friends were still there. What had happened? I waited anxiously. Then at some point in the night I heard sounds, people running around. That had to be it—they'd done it! I pressed my ear to the door. "The friends must be gone," I whispered to Cahide, who knew about the plan but not the timing. She got excited too.

Later we learned what happened. The tunnel turned out to be a few meters short—it didn't reach the house! And at a point underneath the road, while the friends were inside, it had collapsed! Fortunately, a truck was parked above, near the collapse point. What to do? Some thought they should climb out anyway, but the opening was just across from the military post. The soldiers on duty would notice even a small movement, so it couldn't possibly succeed. They'd turned around and come back. The escape failed. Even before I knew the details, the failure made me sad and angry. Tunneling is a sensitive matter and can be exposed by even a slight moment of carelessness. Many people had been privy to the plan. Or a betrayal could have ruined it in one fell swoop. All kinds of thoughts teemed through my mind.

Before the escape attempt, Hamili and I had written goodbye letters. I told him I believed he and the others could contribute a lot to the fight outside, and I asked him to give up his stubbornness and participate actively.

> I want to see you a great commander, a general in our war. Maybe we won't meet again, anything is possible in combat, but I'm hoping to see you again, and I believe we will see each other in the mountains.

His beautiful response: "I'll become a general, and when you come to the mountains, I'll welcome you with cannon fire."

But he didn't leave—nobody left. This grim fact plagued me. The next period of time would be crucial. Would someone betray the escape plan? Would the tunnel be discovered during some routine search? Would the collapse be discovered? The men didn't seem nervous, saying, "There's only a little bit left, then we'll try again." But then another problem arose: water was apparently leaking into the tunnel, from some underground pipe. It made the digging harder. The men said they wanted to keep working and bring the water out of the tunnel in canisters. I was very tense—it was worse to observe from a distance than to be there.

As far as we could tell, the common cause of tunneling had pushed the internal conflicts into the background. The men had decided beforehand who should go, including many who'd been targets of criticism. Other names were discussed, but as always, the men shared little information with us, while we shared our views at every opportunity.

The play of love and politics Love is not a quiet feeling. It's an active attitude. It creates values. It is to be judged by how it aligns people with their ideals and empowers them.

As a young girl and later as a woman, I didn't dream of being with a man who belonged only to me, or living in a little house with my own little family. My rejection of marriage and my escape from my parents' home had been an important step in my revolutionary aspirations, but I was still inexperienced and unprofessional, not yet strong enough for much else.

I was forced to tie myself to a man [Baki] as an interim solution, then had to try to function politically in a relationship that lacked foundation. Baki was a good revolutionary, but I wasn't really interested in love or marriage. All my thoughts had been on escaping, not on where to go or what I was looking for. I made no advance arrangements, just bolted away recklessly.

Baki and I had clashed over our ideological and organizational differences. If we had resolved those problems, could our relationship have lasted? It's doubtful. My relationship with him was loveless. Even if he had joined the PKK, no love relationship would have been possible. We would've had a traditional marriage with slightly different standards. If I hadn't ended it, I'd still be there, living a traditional life. But a romantic relationship requires an equal and free foundation.

Breaking away from this ownership-based bondage had been a revolutionary action, but I did it in a disorganized and haphazard fashion. As a person I had been weak, as a revolutionary I was still in my infancy, and as a woman I was still influenced by traditional values. I hadn't yet found my true self. I had not yet internalized standards of freedom and revolution, so I was weak and vulnerable. I acquired certain abilities, and some of them contributed to a way of life. But I was far below the level required for ideological, political, and organizational struggle. If you don't focus your life energy, your fighting spirit, on your political goals, you will lose yourself in emotions and look at the world one-dimensionally. In the merciless arena of politics, your energy will fizzle. If you don't have a stable organizational foundation, you will end up leaving the political sphere behind.

But my persistence in revolutionary ideals had benefited me as a woman. My ideas about love developed along with my quest for liberation. A revolutionary life brings a corresponding ideology, organization, and form of struggle. In the absence of this foundation, I couldn't have a love relationship.

I wasn't a good actress in the play of love and politics. [In Elazığ] I managed more or less to defy the enemy's attacks and land on my feet. But I didn't handle internal party affairs with the same intensity as I fought the external enemy, and I didn't take any protective measures, so the unexpected consequence hit me hard. [In prison] I entered a theater of war in which politics and emotions both played a role.

And now here I was in prison, once again afflicted by the interplay of politics and passion. And again it became a scourge for me, and I thought I had to sacrifice love for politics, so I did. Yes, sacrifice—this dangerous term shouldn't exist either in politics or in love. It means something is taken from you. It means driving love to its death. Only when you have the strength to allow something new to emerge can you truly speak of love. You must expand and enlarge what you have created, but never sacrifice yourself to it. On the political stage, you have to be creative and constructive. The same goes for love, which must not tie you down.

I'd once trusted Hamili fully and seen only positive things in him, but now as our arguments waxed and waned, I got to know his other side. Not that we clashed openly. Back in Elazığ, it troubled me that he had stayed out of the leadership, avoided responsibility, and acted on his own, even in prison. But we had serious problems now, and he was needed. If I criticized others, I had to criticize Hamili, but he was sensitive to criticism, quick to take offense or light up in anger. Karasu, who valued his opinion, refrained from criticizing him.

It wasn't just Hamili's avoidance of party responsibility that bothered me. It was also his handling of our relationship. On both points, my eyes were now open. How could I have overlooked his idiosyncrasies before? He thought of me as a flower blooming by a remote mountain rock—one he had picked, for himself alone, so he could have access to me anytime. Selfishly and individualistically, he thought he had a right to me. If such possessiveness flows into love and occupies the space formerly occupied by comradeship, then you have an ugly mess, which I did.

Hamili was a valuable comrade. As a revolutionary, he had worked with a lot of women, and that had improved his attitude toward women generally. When men work with women, I've found, it often has the positive effect of breaking up their old-fashioned thought patterns.

Women had played a role in Hamili's revolutionary life. The educational work had created a set of standards for mutual interaction that simplified comradeship in all areas. Hamili lived with a woman who was a member of the movement. In prison, he participated in the resistance alongside women.

Ours wasn't an ordinary, egotistical relationship that had come about because of circumstances in prison. We had known each other for a long time, been through a lot, and given each other strength. Our relationship was cordial and close, but it was not private, special, or exclusive—anyway, that was how I saw it. And it was loving, in the sense that I loved his spirit of resistance, his revolutionary determination to fight despite everything. I loved our bond, with its stable foundation, felt connected to it, and jealously wanted to preserve it. The new form of relationship would have to build on that foundation.

And yet his image of women followed a certain logic. He admired women who fought with revolutionary determination, but he really couldn't understand them. His image of women was unclear and erratic. Theoretically he advocated equal rights and freedom, and superficially, his behavior was consistent with this attitude. In practice, however, the corresponding revolutionary commitment was missing. His thinking followed the logic, *What's beautiful is what's mine.* Ultimately his interest in women was narrow-minded and selfish.

If his love was sincere, why had he mystified and concealed it for so many years? Initially, it impressed me—I thought it showed willpower and a refusal to burden our comradely relationship. After all, it is natural and even beautiful to be attracted to someone. But to expect the other person to have the same feelings, and even to pressure them, is primitive and anti-democratic. Such behavior is incompatible with revolutionary claims. Hamili had initially respected my will, but only as I gradually registered his true values did I realize that his claims were possessive and contradicted my nature. Now, rather than patiently and respectfully expressing his interest in me over the years, acknowledging my will, taking into account our principles and struggles, and waiting for feelings to develop in me, he appointed intermediaries to urge me to consent immediately.

And he did pressure me. He thought this relationship must come about, otherwise he'd be offended, irritated, hurt—he'd behave worse than before. Karasu and Şener said he was a good person but they were worried about him, and of course they influenced me, as I was worried about him too. But that's no excuse. In love there can be no pressure. No one in a pressuring mental state can make a strong, passionate declaration of love.

In this mess I felt cornered and made my decision, and maybe it was the first time I deliberately made a mistake. I sacrificed myself—that word again—to a comradely relationship of love, connectedness, and trust. We gave each other our word, although not in a binding way—we were free to change it, so we would have to behave respectfully, openly, and flexibly.

I should have stuck to my first inclination. Hamili would have been hurt and angry, but we could have talked it through in peace, without fixating on yes or no. Or we could have taken our time and come to a joint decision. The final answer, yes or no, would have had no major impact on our comradely relationship, because the main problem was the internal party conflicts. But we could have looked for a solution together and even grown closer.

Instead I acted like a person who willingly sacrifices, who makes herself accessible and emotionally open. Love shouldn't be offered so easily, otherwise it will be used up quickly. And why did I always have to be the one to sacrifice? That willingness had been the starting point for my biggest mistakes. You can't promise you will love someone. We hadn't been promised to each other in the cradle or been married before an imam or civil authority. We were revolutionaries who weren't subject to traditional constraints. But love doesn't develop from a promise, love is the promise, the most beautiful decision.

Hamili, for his part, believed that after ten years, he had won me. But what is winning a person? It definitely doesn't mean winning the rights to them, or harming or degrading them. Possessiveness in a romantic relationship destroys love. Hamili tried to force his beloved into the narrow framework of his primitive and selfish desires.

When I finally recognized his feudal, petit-bourgeois possessiveness—which existed along with his fighting spirit and his other positive qualities—I panicked. A romantic relationship could not be claimed as a special privilege. Having a relationship with him didn't mean I belonged to him, as he wanted. His notions of love relations weren't all that different from traditional male-feudal ones—in fact, they overshadowed his revolutionary attitude. But his personality was his life reality, and he couldn't behave any differently, even within the party.

The same personality prevented him from taking on responsibilities in the organization and working cooperatively. It was why he was always clashing with the cadres.

Both his love and his anger were like mines that could explode anytime, anywhere. I didn't have the skills to defuse them. Again and again, I triggered explosions, and every time I lost a piece of myself.

Love requires awareness, mutual understanding, deep sensitivity, consciousness, and knowledgeable and sensitive behavior. Love is the life force, it makes you happy and gives you strength, it completes you, it seeks mutual understanding, and spurs creative energy. But with Hamili, love made us bad-tempered and prickly rather than mature and patient. We proved to be unsteady and thin-skinned. I created problems out of many small things. I made every minor deficiency in his character into an issue of his whole personality. I told him a few times that we should end our relationship, and he threatened to commit suicide. Built on such a weak foundation, every mistake, every inconsistency, and every mishap contributed to the destruction of our relationship.

Moving around the prison After the February hunger strike, the prison's military administration was replaced by a civilian one. There were now civilian guards and two or three civilian directors. Most of the new guards were personnel from other prisons. Mehmet, who had been an administrator in the Malatya prison during my time there, was now a deputy director at Diyarbakir.

[From now on, the women prisoners would be allowed to move around the exercise yards with the men.] On the first day, our door was opened late. When we asked why, the new director complained that one of the new guards had thrown his cap to the ground in front of him. He said, "You call me a fascist director, and he calls me a friend of the prisoners." It turned out the guard was upset that women prisoners were allowed into the yards with men. "My director, I can't work in a place where men and women use the yard together. I resign!" And he threw down his cap. The director sighed to us: "I'm sitting between two stools—what should I do?"

The first time I visited the yard of the 35th ward, the party headquarters, everything there spoke to me of Mazlum, Hayri, Pir, and the others.

In the women's ward, the number 35 had taken on a special meaning. Whenever we happened to see it on a piece of plastic, in a newspaper, or on a water canister, it was as if we'd chanced upon a sacred relic.

We handed it around to each other, touched it reverently, kissed it. Whenever anyone mentioned the 35th ward, we perked up our ears. The number 35 meant pain, joy, and hope. The 35th ward was a holy place, the Kaaba of the dungeon. In fact, in our writings, we used the term *Kaaba* to refer to it.

Across the corridor was the 36th ward, where Karasu [and Hamili] stayed. The leadership cadres always stayed in these two wards, but our martyrs had been in the 35th, so it had symbolic meaning. I visited there first, in the exercise yard, and met many friends for the first time—I'd seen some briefly in court, but most I didn't know. I hugged them all.

I didn't know which of them belonged to us [PKK], but it didn't matter. I loved the people from the other groups, saw them as companions in prison, comrades who had survived the horrors of torture. I valued them, and they me. There were only four women among the 1,000-plus prisoners, so we were their sisters, their roses, their mothers. Even the oldest prisoner called me *abla* ["older sister," Turkish]. They were so affectionate that it brought me to tears.

11 Seven prisoners at Diyarbakir, undated. *Standing, left to right:* Hasan Atmaca, Faruk Altun, Samil Batmaz. *Sitting:* Sinan Caynak, Cansız, Mehmet Şener, Fuat Kav.

I asked them for their names and what they'd been convicted of, in which trial. I didn't really know much about the men's trials or their sentences. I asked more out of politeness than anything else. There were more important things in life than laws, courts, trials, and punishments. What interested me were the trial dates and the declarations that prisoners made during their defenses.

The main trials and several others were over, so the ones who had been sentenced could be transferred to another prison at any time.

After years of isolation, I was starved for information about the most important events, the cadres, the candidates, the problem cases, and even the smugglers. Karasu caught me up. "Talk to the cadres," he advised.

> Discuss with them. Fuat Kav and Hasan A[tmaca] have been through it all. Can, Muzaffer [Ayata] and Rıza Yilmaz Uzun have been transferred. Samil and Sait Uclu can give you important insights. Now that you can move around the prison, you should talk to everyone. The men are glad for it, and you can talk freely to them.
>
> Our reality is not as it appears from a distance. Talk to the friends and form your own view. You're an honorary member of the leadership anyway. Up to now, we could hardly even exchange messages, otherwise you could have contributed more. Now you can participate better, especially in decision-making. You won't be able to attend meetings in person, but you'll be asked for your opinion before and after and can make suggestions and influence decisions that way. Maybe in the future there'll be a way for you to attend meetings. Sometimes we can hold inconspicuous short meetings in a corner of the yard. We have representatives in every ward, every block. Visit everyone and get their opinions, especially in places where we can't go. If you can visit everyone and gather information, we can stop written messages altogether.

Karasu is banished   One night in early March, we learned that a large group of prisoners, including Karasu, were to be transferred elsewhere. We considered these transfers to be banishments. "It's a new strategy to reduce the number of cadres at Diyarbakir," someone said.

> Back in 1980, the enemy wanted to concentrate us all here. But the local people got so patriotic, they now react immediately to every development in prison. And the families act as a united force. So the enemy wants to break that up by spreading us around again.

Our slogan chants were so deafening, they shook the walls. Some wanted to start a riot, but others objected, saying, "We can't do anything because there's a court order and legal requirements."

Karasu and the others went from ward to ward to say goodbye, and we welcomed them with slogans. It was "a real ceremony," said one friend. Karasu told me, "Yesterday we had a meeting in 35th and chose the new leadership. You'll participate as much as circumstances allow."

The next morning we met in the corridor with all those who were to be transferred. I had initially thought we should protest the banishments, but Karasu persuaded me otherwise. We'll make every place into Diyarbakir, he assured me. That was the main slogan that day: "Every place will become Diyarbakir."

Karasu was part of the legacy our martyrs had left for us. To express our attachment to him, we stayed with the banished ones until the processing was finished. When they left in a transport vehicle, we chanted slogans until the engine noise faded away.

"An honorary member of the leadership" The party leaders in the prison were now Hasan A[tmaca], Fuat Kav, Sinan Canyak, Faruk, [Mehmet] Şener, and myself. On important occasions we met in the exercise yard and discussed in pairs, or in threes, sometimes in fives. That was fine, but we couldn't hold extensive discussions in this way.

The old leadership around Karasu had been criticized for its conduct during the [January uprising], when Şener had been stripped of all responsibilities. Şener was the one who had interfered in the leadership's work, but Karasu and the others were criticized for it. Şener had emerged stronger and worked with others to install an alternative leadership, which included him. It was a chaotic time. The more I found out about it, the messier it seemed. Even in government, problems weren't taken to such extremes: coalitions, commissions of inquiry, petitions! I couldn't understand how this disarray had come about.

The old leadership had failed to identify problems and work through them. As a result, problems had accumulated. General rank-and-file problems mingled with the leadership cadres' problems. I had known a little about the latter, just the broad outlines and certain consequences, but the causes weren't addressed. The leadership's approach had been liberal, bureaucratic, narrow-minded, and centralistic. Meanwhile the rank-and-file didn't participate in decision-making, so they grew passive: *Let the leadership arrange everything, it always does anyway.*

But our new leadership, starting after Newroz, would discuss issues more openly. We would deal with the mistakes and weaknesses of recent years. As a first step, the cadres would have to do self-criticism. We'd lay all the suspicions, allegations, and accusations out on the table so the prisoners could work together to resolve them.

So we circulated a draft explaining that the cadres were to write self-criticisms. They were to answer questions about their attitude toward party ideology and politics, then hand them in to the 35th ward. All the other cadres would read them and even be required to express their opinions of them.

Şener gave me his report to read before he turned it in. He didn't know me well, but he probably realized I was fairly candid and straight-forward in defining and discussing problems and pointing out contradictions.

After I read it, he asked for my opinion. I said nothing. It didn't strike me as spectacular, but then, I didn't know all that had gone on here for the past few years. So I decided I'd better read all the reports before forming an opinion. But one point in his report bothered me, concerning the January 1984 resistance. I had felt the same discomfort back then, when the friends had written to me that Şener had lost consciousness under torture. Had he really? I couldn't get the question out of my mind, and it bothered me. Şener's behavior had finally been rated as a weakness in the face of the general surrender. There was no other clue, and I couldn't ask him to his face, so I suppressed my doubts, even if it still rankled.

He kept asking what I thought of his report, but I just said, "I read it, and the friends will talk about it." Maybe it was obvious that I had reservations. I'm bad at hiding my feelings. My expression, my eyes, my voice—they're an open book. So people would often ask me, "What's wrong?" Or when I was talking to someone, they would suddenly confide in me, because I sensed something was going on in them.

Şener once said to me, "No one can hide anything from you. You're like a holy place or a Christian confessional. Do you realize that?"

"That's probably because I'm transparent myself," I said. "I'm not hiding anything."

The cadres in the 35th read the reports and evaluated them, then forwarded their critiques to those who had written them. Some other wards also read the reports and sent their evaluations to the center. When Şener's report was read, many friends, especially Gezgör, tore into it, attacking his behavior in January 1984 and criticizing him harshly. But Hasan A. and others reaffirmed the previous leadership's assessment that accepting uniforms had been a collective decision and not Şener's only. Some demanded that Şener rewrite his report, but he just added a few points verbally, and finally his self-criticism was accepted.

Everything was transcribed. We wanted to send the transcript to the party, along with the reports, so they could get an overview of the events here and our discussion of them.

Hamili's self-criticism report was also problematic. It was very long and bore the strange title, "Documentation of My 14 Revolutionary Years." The cadres rejected it on the basis that it wasn't self-critical enough and blamed others too much. They demanded that he rewrite it. Hamili refused to rewrite it, considering it a punishment. "This decision is not correct, it has been manipulated," he said.

Hamili's refusal might have been justified, and I tried to understand his anger, but my arguments with him intensified during this period. He complained incessantly and talked trash about some party members all over the prison. It was alarming. And his criticism wasn't constructive, it was full of vague and destructive insinuations. He rejected all criticism of himself, claiming people were out to get him. If you asked him why he didn't try to change things, he'd blow up. He had always claimed to be autonomous—he never wanted to be in the leadership. Now he was on a collision course with everyone, especially the organization.

Even though his criticisms often had a kernel of truth, his abrupt handling of them only created confusion. I don't know what motivated him to do all this. Was it careerism? Or jealousy? I had to consider all the possibilities. His rejection of all criticisms of himself became a major problem. Everyone was annoyed. What were the facts? I wondered. Was he twisting things? Was he trying to distract us? All kinds of thoughts came to my mind.

Hamili and Şener knew each other well—in the past they'd been close, confiding in each other and sharing their sorrows. They knew each other's weaknesses. They had a buddy relationship in addition to a political relationship. Now Hamili slammed Şener harshly, saying, "This son of a b___ would do anything for his personal interests." His

12 Large group of prisoners at Diyarbakir, undated. *Back row, left to right*: Mustafa Okçu, Hıdır Kırmızıçiçek, unidentified, Mehmet Şener, Mahmut Tanrıkulu, unidentified, Sait Triple, Cahide Şener, Faruk Altun. *Middle row*: Şükrü Bilici, M. Ali Artuk, unidentified, unidentified, Cansız, unidentified, Fuat Kav, unidentified. *Front row*: unidentified, unidentified, unidentified, Ferit Aydın, Mustafa Çelik, unidentified, unidentified.

criticism was out of bounds, not referring to any specific points. But he also praised and supported Şener's leadership work, saying, "Nobody but Şener can do that." I found this inconsistency very strange.

Şener, for his part, chose his words carefully. Whether it was about general issues or individual problems, he always phrased things precisely. Whenever he talked to Hamili, he always opened diplomatically, by saying, "Don't get me wrong" or "I don't want to bring you down." *Are they acting something out?* I sometimes wondered.

I couldn't figure out what their relationship was anymore and what role it played in the current situation. But they both carefully tiptoed around subjects that they knew were sensitive for me. That they shared this strange and unusual behavior made me uneasy.

The other leadership cadres, especially Şener, noticed my discomfort with Hamili. "Don't make any decisions right away." But Şener's own behavior aggravated the general conflict with Hamili. As a leadership member, it wasn't appropriate for him to write to Hamili directly, but he did anyway. I was Hamili's contact in the leadership, and I was responsible for forwarding messages between him and others, which involved me in all discussions. But whenever I delivered messages to Hamili, he tore them up and threw the confetti at my feet. Was he aware of how provocative he was being? Far from clarifying problems, he overreacted, showing no regard for the organization, so I had to explain to him how our party worked. He said, "Ah, they've already influenced you."

"Leadership work is group work" Since August 15, [1984,] most of the arrests had been made in the mountains. People from the guerrilla forces, the militias, and the general population arrived in the prison. By 1988, the prison was like a miniature model of Kurdistan—and almost half of our prisoners were from civilians.

The media continued to issue false reports about the guerrillas, making special broadcasts for months about raids on villages. The guerrillas were portrayed as "murderers of children and women." The Law of Repentance expired in 1987, but it was renewed. The guerrillas were constantly called upon to surrender. The media spared individual guerrilla commanders and indirectly invited them to ally with the enemy. It was trying to convey the impression that the party could split at any time. Under the headline "Split in the PKK," the press published photos of defectors, tagged as "right wing," "legendary commander," "multiple murderer," or "militant's terrible confession." These methods of counterattack were pretty easy to see through. But the enemy's most important technique was to distort our ideology and dilute the party line, stripping progressive developments of their importance.

Inside prison, after the self-criticism phase, the organization introduced a subdivision into cadres and committees. The most important criterion was how much a person had participated in the resistance; their ideological and political level and way of life were also considered important. I suggested Samil and other friends for the central committee. My suggestions mostly coincided with those of Fuat [Kav] and Sait [Uclu].

In 1988 [the PKK monthly] Serxwebûn [Independence] magazine reached us for the first time [since its founding in 1982], along with Berxwedan [Resistance], money, and tools. So now we could follow the party work outside, receive analysis and instructions, and relay our own reports to them. Most of the magazine's articles were in Kurdish. We created an educational program for new arrivals.

Şener was in top form, writing many pieces—doing most of our writing, in fact. In 1987 our newspaper *Hawar* had extensively discussed the changes in the Soviet Union and the problems of the socialist system. One issue had offered varying opinions about the glasnost and perestroika initiated by Gorbachev. Proponents and opponents attacked each other. I later learned that Şener had written most of these contributions—they were published under different bylines to spur discussion. But nobody knew the party's attitude, so it made no sense for individuals to insist on their views, and the debate ended. Finally an article by the chairman was published in the journal *Kurtuluş* under the pseudonym Ali Firat, which was decisive for us.

I liked Şener's agitational writing style. We wrote texts for leaflets and sent them outside, mostly starting with "To Kurdish youth," to expand our range of work.

Around this time Sinan Caynak and Hasan Atmaca were released from prison. Hüsnü Altun and Sait Uclu replaced them in the leadership. Şener knew Hüsnü, but I didn't. "It's good that he's from the guerrillas—it creates a balance," Şener said.

Hasan had been the secretary, and before he left, he delegated that responsibility to Şener. But after he was gone, Şener said, "Someone else should do it. I don't want it. Fuat could do it, or you could. I can contribute better in other ways. Besides, I'm already overloaded."

Fuat absolutely refused to succeed Hasan, saying he'd rather not be in the leadership at all. Was it due to his modesty or the seriousness of the task? The secretary job wasn't easy. Leadership work was very difficult. The leadership bore overall responsibility for the work in prison. It involved taking risks, yet it was much speculated about. Past conflicts and resentments were still very much felt.

"I'd have difficulties as secretary," Şener said. "I'm already so controversial, there would be misunderstandings. The base might become irate. After all, I once stuck my neck out very far to protect the organization," by which he meant consenting to the uniform. Although it had been a joint decision at the time, Şener had been held responsible. There had been serious charges against him, and the organization had sanctioned him.

"You act like it's an individual problem," I said. "Leadership is group work. We all work together."

He referred to Hamili. "Look, I'm already in his crosshairs, and if I'm secretary, he'll attack me even more."

"We all defend ourselves against attacks," I countered. "Don't run from responsibility." Leadership didn't scare me, or maybe I just didn't know enough about it. What did frighten me was the crazy way the friends sometimes dealt with each other. In addition, I felt responsible because many valuable cadres had been transferred. There were many new prisoners, and I didn't know all the cadres. Politically and organizationally, we were blinkered, seeing only the problems prevailing in prison. Our contact with the outside world was limited to the families' movement.

The other friends favored Şener becoming secretary, but I was the most zealous in trying to persuade him. I knew his skills. He was talented and influential. Assuming the responsibility of secretary would be like a test. If there really was something to complain about in Şener, it would become obvious. Otherwise, his skills would benefit the organization.

He said, "I'd rather not, I can contribute better without being secretary."

"You must not shirk responsibility!" I said. Clearly, he would have influence whether he was secretary or not, but as a top leader, he would

13 Cansız with Mehmet Şener, at Diyarbakir (detail of Figure 12), undated.

also have to behave more prudently. His successes and mistakes would all be obvious and open to judgment.

[In the end, Şener became secretary.] It became his task to poll the others when a question was introduced. But sometimes he jumped into the discussion and made a proposal right away. He took a dominant role in discussions, and our meetings were often riven by conflict and polemics.

Fuat, Şener, and I were in charge of communication with the outside. We organized and inspected all correspondence. I was in charge of communication between the wards. I moved around the prison visiting the exercise yards. I talked to everyone for at least a few minutes, greeting each person and asking how they were doing. In some wards I stayed as long as half a day.

There were many PKK prisoners, and many wanted to talk to me, especially those who had known me from before prison. But I couldn't talk to everyone. Some criticized me for that, and I felt bad that I couldn't fulfill this need, but the prison had more than 20 wards full of PKK prisoners. As a member of the leadership, I had to stay in touch with the ward representatives, which presupposed an organizational hierarchy. It was quite bureaucratic. I had just enough time with each to summarize the issues, provide general information, and talk to a few friends. I was constantly on the move. I didn't rest for more than five minutes at a time, and I still didn't have enough time. I sent Şener the information I'd assembled, and we talked about the work under way.

Sometimes we went to other wards together. On public holidays we visited the other groups and even the smugglers. The leading cadres of TİKKO were on the 35th ward. Overall, we had good relations with them. There was no more exclusionary, accusatory, exaggerated, or sectarian behavior. Some of them were also participating in the tunnel escape.

Breakup with Hamili Just before Hasan Atmaca left, I had told him, "I'm going to end my relationship with Hamili. I can't stand it. Please pass that along to the party outside. If the relationship has become known out there, just tell them it's not true." Hasan's release had come unexpectedly, so we couldn't talk in detail. He just said, "Okay." He knew about our arguments. Even if we had wanted a private affair, we couldn't have had one in this hothouse atmosphere.

Şener took more interest in it than anyone. He was engaged to a woman named Elif, a party member, so his interest didn't seem strange. I confided in him, really told him everything, because I didn't consider it an individual problem and was looking for a solution. Because Hamili was selfish, individualistic, and possessive, the core of the relationship had a negative impact on those around us.

Had the relationship not existed, my bond with Hamili would have been stronger, and I could have helped him more. Back in Elazığ, I had treated him firmly and had a positive influence on him. He knew he was important to me and understood that I was concerned about the party, so he had taken my criticism seriously. But now he dismissed my criticisms, saying I was being influenced by others who wanted to hurt our relationship. He always found new excuses and was increasingly irritable. I could barely talk to him.

Şener told me, "People are scared of you, you know. You're merciless." But this relationship was weakening me and draining my energy. It harmed both of us more than it helped us. It was all wrong for him and for me, and I wanted to extricate us both from this situation.

I dreaded Hamili's reaction, but the longer I waited to break it off, the more our comradely relationship deteriorated. Finally one day in the exercise yard, I said to him, "Let's end the relationship. It's just hurting us. We used to love each other so much more."

"Then I'll kill myself."

Hamili's reaction was so frightening, so intense, I backtracked right away. I wanted an immediate breakup, but he closed his mind to it. I had to help him see that this relationship didn't make sense, but he refused to discuss it or even try to understand how it was with me. And I admit I failed to display the patience and maturity necessary to help him understand.

I've always been Apoçu!   European governments began attacking our movement in Europe. Dozens of cadres were arrested, as part of a plan directed against our work and our chairman. Abbas [Duran Kalkan], Fuat [Ali Haydar Kaytan], Meral [Kidir], and others were arrested one after another. It was no coincidence—we suspected a connection with other provocations. I was told the party archives were confiscated too. "How is this possible? Why didn't they take any precautions?" we asked ourselves.

Around this time, we learned that [attorney] Hüseyin Yıldırım had left the PKK and taken our files. Now he was propagandizing against the party, attacking the chairman, and announcing that he wanted to refound the PKK as a democratic party! We were riveted on this development, at the expense of everything else.

I had had suspicions about him back in 1979 and officially communicated my opinion to the party while I was at Malatya, so this latest move wasn't surprising. He had been just an ordinary lawyer when the prosecutor's office of the military tribunal allegedly gave him the secret files of some major spies. He must have been in contact with Cahit Aydoğan during this time. Both later came to Diyarbakir.

[Then in November 1981] Hüseyin Yıldırım was arrested, deliberately, to dispel our suspicions about him, while Cahit Aydoğan became a prosecutor in our trial. Hüseyin told me he was willing to sacrifice himself so that Mazlum and I could continue fighting outside. "You and Mazlum are needed out there. Just renounce making a political defense, and they'll release you." He'd even tried to use our families against us. I'd never trusted him, and he knew it.

Upon his release, Hüseyin Yıldırım got a lot of attention, like any former prisoner. He went to Europe, where he presented himself as a survivor of the Diyarbakir dungeon and pretended to be loyal to Mazlum and the other martyrs. He called himself a representative of the Left and accused the chairman of being right wing. But anyone who knew him knew he was just a puppet. For hypocrisy and mendacity, he was unbeatable, just repugnant. His provocative statements were quoted in the newspapers.

Curiously, several of my visitors spoke positively of Hüseyin Yıldırım. Uncle Haydar Akyar didn't stop praising him. Finally, I said,

So you think I should apologize to Hüseyin Yıldırım? But I've always had a bad feeling about him. I've told the friends what I thought of him, and if I had a chance, I would've warned the party about him when he went to Europe. Now you're telling me about his activities and that he's a leader. If he does a good job, I'm willing to apologize self-critically, no problem. But he knows what I think of him.

Was this adulation part of the plan to split the party? Were we to be given the impression that Hüseyin Yıldırım was loyal to his former inmates and did good work in Europe?

Hüseyin Yıldırım was reported to have ties with [Öcalan's ex-wife,] Kesire Yıldırım. [In 1987 Öcalan and Kesire had divorced, and Kesire fled to Sweden and joined a PKK opposite.] When we learned of Kesire's escape, we suggested the party punish her. Şener wrote the proposal—he was good at that. It was a radical suggestion, but I had reservations: "The enemy will use it against us. After all, she was married to the chairman. The papers will write that he killed his own wife."

Şener replied, "I always thought you were a radical leftist. What happened?"

"What am I then, a right-winger?" I asked.

"No, you've always been Apoçu," he answered.

It made me happy and proud. I was an Apo devotee!

We would write to Hüseyin Yıldırım too. "You write to him, you know him," said Şener.

"No, you can write better," I said. "We should focus on how he's trying to present himself as a democrat who wants to save the PKK from a dictator. What is leadership for us? The chairman and the party are one—we have to emphasize that."

In 1988 Hüseyin Yıldırım visited the Party Academy [in the Beka'a Valley] with [journalist] Mehmet Ali Birand and pretended respect for the chairman. A newspaper photo shows him in a humble pose. Supposedly he wanted democratization to replace the revolutionary struggle. But he was just a stupid pawn on the large chessboard of politics.

Now we learned he had written a letter to Karasu and was appealing to the prisoners to save the PKK. From whom? Why, from the chairman! That told us everything we needed to know. Anyone who attacked the chairman also attacked the party and the revolution. There was nothing more to discuss. We regarded this move as "an organized provocation against the party, the chairman, and our struggle." It was clear that he just wanted to sow confusion in prison.

Opening a letter Around this time, we got a letter saying a package was to be sent to us. It arrived, containing a letter addressed to Hamili. I had mentioned it to him in advance. Now he said, "No, the package is for me, I asked for some things from home, from my family. The message is personal for me, it's a private letter. I've asked the daughter of my uncle's father some questions, and I'm waiting for the answer."

I saw through it. "Don't do this again. You know how the organization works. Your name was just used as the addressee. As a party member, you have no private matters. Turn the letter over to the leadership. If it's intended for you, you'll get it back."

He answered, "No, it's my letter, and I wouldn't give it to Allah Himself."

When I told the rest of the leadership about his attitude, they got upset. Şener said, "Or could it be something else? Maybe Hüseyin Yıldırım sent Hamili a letter. That would explain his behavior." Şener masterfully exploited every weakness and dissatisfaction in the leadership as well as the other cadres' anger.

That suggestion seemed to me too harsh. Even if Hüseyin Yıldırım had sent Hamili a letter, it wouldn't mean Hamili was untrustworthy. "No," I said, "I know Hamili. He's seething because his self-criticism report was rejected for the second time. His party membership is up for discussion, and he's been stripped of his duties. And he and I are having problems in our relationship—that's why he mentioned his cousin." He'd once told me his family wanted to engage her to him— he'd mentioned her now to make me jealous.

Now he set conditions on opening the letter: "I'll open it in the presence of a friend and read the salutation. If it's not intended for me, I'll hand it unread over to the leadership."

Our protocol had it that the letter had to be forwarded to headquarters first. If that wasn't possible, then another friend could open the letter and read it. Hamili was deliberately breaking the rules, violating party discipline. We had no idea how to deal with his stubbornness rationally, patiently, or politically. And why this exaggerated anger?

"Oh, let's stop it!" I snapped. "Let Hamili do what he wants, and we'll deal with it. If both sides go on being stubborn, nothing good can come of it." Fuat Kav agreed—it wasn't right to get bogged down on this point. The danger of both sides digging their heels in ... my god, what problems we had to deal with! We'd never move forward with such pettiness.

Hamili opened the letter and saw that it wasn't intended for him. He handed it to us. Once again, he had created a situation about himself. In his view, everyone was against him. He took every criticism personally. When he was asked why he had taken the leadership's decision personally, he said he had nothing against Şener, but both sides had acted provocatively. Someone suggested sanctioning him for the rule violation and having him write a self-criticism.

Literary writing   Sometime earlier I had written a detailed report, a comprehensive 500-page history of events in the women's ward, from the beginning to 1986. The men had read it together, in a large group. Some said, "You wrote a novel. It should be published someday." It was to be smuggled outside, but it fell into the enemy's hands on the way out.

Now some of the prisoners were writing novels. Since my long report on the women's ward had been described as "novelistic," I was thought to understand literature, so I was often asked for my opinion on prisoners' novels.

Once Şener asked me to read a part of a novel he was writing, about various aspects of prison life. I was struck by how his portrayals of women, love, and passion corresponded to petit-bourgeois thinking, or to those of writers in other countries. "He describes his own dreams and standards," I thought. It was about his own reality. It met with little interest from others, and he probably dropped it.

Many prisoners also wrote poems. We had to read them critically too, even if we didn't understand much about poetry. A sloganeering style had developed that had little to do with poetry. Poetry involves capturing details and navigating the labyrinths of life. Poetry is passion, emotional intensity, flowing liveliness. It reflects inner desires, mysteries, dreams, and fictions. Writing poetry is an art! So I liked poems, but I wasn't critical. Usually we evaluated poems by our first impression. We didn't spend much time with them but sent them to the outside.

Şener's poems were different. One day Hamili came into the exercise yard. Şener had written a long poem and dedicated it to me. [Şener was nearby,] and I read it aloud to both of them. It was about Mazlum, our cries, tears, and defeats … I wasn't capable of criticizing it, I was too touched. Hamili said he liked it too.

I really didn't understand it completely. One of Şener's lines read, "You're my sister, my mother, my beloved." It aroused no special associations in me. My whitened hair upset him, he wrote in another passage, saying he kept a single hair to give himself strength. No special meanings came into my mind.

I openly told all my men friends that I loved them. I kissed their eyes, I clutched their hands, I touched them. Verses were unnecessary!

Many even worshipped me, but none of them expressed their love as demonstratively as I did to them. Still, if anyone had a special interest in me, it quickly became apparent. When someone approached me clumsily and impulsively, I understood, and I also noticed when they subtly hinted at something secret. I really wasn't so obtuse that I didn't notice. But I didn't respond to their expressions of affection and never attributed any underlying purpose to them. Such suspicions were ugly to me. There could be real love, honest admiration and genuine interest—people have beautiful sides as well as weak and ugly ones. But not every feeling of interest or admiration, not every impulse, has to be acted on.

What was I supposed to do with my hair? Why did he write "sister, mother, beloved"? The longer I thought about it, the more incredible it all seemed. Had things gone this far?

After his first positive reaction [to Şener's poem], Hamili's expression changed. Why? I reread the poem. No, I couldn't find anything in it. But Hamili saw it differently. He knew Şener, and in his selfish, possessive way, he perceived only that Şener was poaching on his turf. Instead of living up to his responsibility as a party member, putting Şener in his place, and explaining to me what he was doing, he saw only that Şener had attacked his "honor"—

14 Cansız with Fuat Kav, at Diyarbakir, undated.

SARA

And then at that moment, he surrendered. He uttered a single sentence: "I end this relationship." As if to punish me, he used only this word "end." And so tragicomically, he revealed the hollowness of his "love" after all. Real love couldn't and shouldn't end like that. And then he left, handing me over to Şener.

I sat motionless for several minutes. Şener said, "I'll talk to him."

"No!" I said. "No one's going to say another word on the subject. This is not a game. I just want you both to be respectful to each other."

I retreated to the edge of the yard, where Fuat Kav asked me to walk back and forth along the wall with him. "What's wrong?" he said. "You look depressed."

"It's nothing," I said. "Oh, I feel like I've just relieved myself of a great burden."

Yes, it really had been a burden, one that in the name of love had constantly depressed me. The love of a man! It had been like a nightmare, like a dagger in my back! I'd tried to solve the problem amicably and with mutual respect, but he hadn't responded. Now he had ended our relationship his way, with the hurt vanity of a traditional man. Although I was oppressed by this fact, I felt like I'd been released from a vise grip. We had been quarreling almost every day.

"I didn't like it from the start," Fuat admitted. "I thought so even at the meeting with Karasu, but I didn't say anything because I didn't want to hurt you. Well, now it's over. But is this guy crazy? Why did he tell you that in front of Şener? He could have talked to you alone."

Later, I took my journal out and let Fuat read an older entry: "Perhaps for the first time in my life, I've deliberately made a mistake, in the name of sacrifice ... Now I see what it leads to and how it's damaged my revolutionary dignity. It hurts a lot." Then I took my journal back. "That's enough, don't read anymore."

"Why didn't you talk about it?" Fuat asked.

"I talked about it all the time!" I answered.

The next day I heard that Hamili wasn't feeling well. I didn't ask what was wrong. It was clear he wanted to emotionally blackmail me.

Fuat said, "He wrote a message and gave it to Ali, as his last will. Then he did something to hurt himself." But the friends had intervened. Fuat went to Hamili in the 36th ward and talked to him for a long time. Hamili told him he did it because the relationship had ended.

263

My spirits plunged even lower. How sad that he had got himself into this situation.

As word got around, the prisoners reacted in various ways. Some cadres thought Hamili should be stripped of his cadre status, but others found that punishment too extreme. Samil, careful not to prejudge, was worried about Hamili and criticized me. Early in our relationship, when Hamili and I were only able to write to each other, Samil had said he was happy for our happiness and wished us all the best. We didn't become happy though. I had truly behaved immaturely.

My relationship problems were discussed in strange places. Excessive openness and extreme secrecy ultimately amounted to the same thing—neither really solves a problem. Sait said, "Don't do things like that so openly." I burst out,

> I know him! He decided to end it out of rage, then tried to grab attention by harming himself. He makes threats so no one will hurt him—he's been criticized a lot recently and there have been sanctions against him. He acts so unreasonably. He ignores how useful it all is to the enemy, and how the other men react. He's way out of bounds, in my opinion. Fuat should talk to him—he can be neutral. I'd just inflame his reaction.

Yet I did feel guilty about what had happened. How should I have behaved? What had I overlooked? What did I need to pay attention to in relationships? The difference was this: Hamili hadn't been communicative from the start. He'd avoided discussions about our relationship. He also kept a low profile organizationally, but I was always extremely open on every aspect of it.

Then recently, after we failed to find an amicable solution, I had provoked Hamili into ending the relationship. Getting others to solve a problem is not strong behavior. I lost all moderation. I damaged my own reputation. I should have seen my own mistakes. I admitted my weak points, my lack of emotional moderation. I had criticized Hamili, but I'd behaved badly myself.

Had it just been a fight between Hamili and me? No! There was a ground for conflict, but how had we positioned ourselves on our respective fronts? What role did personalities play in the game of love and passion?

How do love and struggle fit together? How are feelings to be handled?

Tunnel plans   Gezgör insisted on draining the tunnel. He had rheumatism that threatened his heart, yet he worked past exhaustion. The enemy was always dredging somewhere and dug deep ditches around the prison. The prosecutor in charge of the prison said, "We know there's a tunnel, but we can't find it." Many other prisons had seen escape attempts.

Allegedly, since 1981, [the party] had been planning to free prisoners from the Diyarbakir dungeon, perhaps even with an airplane. Rumors had been on everyone's lips. The plane idea didn't seem particularly realistic, but we believed the party would come up with something.

Every time I went to the third ward's exercise yard, Filo came over to me with a notebook and whispered, "Let's talk a little, if you're free." The other friends watched us, some smiling under their mustaches. What escape plan had he devised now? His inventiveness was fantastic, but unfortunately all his ideas were highly unrealistic. He envisioned running a cable car from the prison's top floor (it had three) to a house opposite. He showed me a map he'd drawn. He mounted the rope on a spool so the escape could be quick, during the brief time when the guard changed. Everyone would be out in minutes. He told me about it in all earnestness. I admired his zeal, but as soon as I mentioned any obstacle, his face clouded, and he went off to work out a new plan. Filo's escape plans became the butt of jokes among the prisoners.

Prisoners always think about escaping, they dream about it. I was passionate about it. I never expected a normal release, since the enemy always came up with new charges against me. How many times did I imagine climbing over these walls! Back in Malatya, after my failed attempt, I'd vowed to try again. I'd even told the prosecutor, "I'll try again, the first chance I get. I'm a revolutionary, so it would be unnatural not to think of escape." The prosecutor had shaken his head in amazement at my frankness, but he could understand my flight fantasies.

I wanted to join the group of prisoners scheduled for the tunnel escape, but they'd turned me down because it would be too hard to escape from the women's ward. This was back before I could move around the wards. Then I suggested a plan to have me hospitalized so that I could escape from the hospital. The plan was low risk and just required luck. Hasan Atmaca, Sinan Caynak, and Hasan Güllü, now on the outside after their release, were in charge of making preparations for the tunnel escape and now also for my escape.

Şener said, "To be honest, I don't want it to work. No one, not even God, will hear my curses, and maybe it's selfish, but I hope it doesn't work."

"You're supposed to wish the person success before an action!" I retorted. "I've never heard anyone wish for failure."

I made it to the hospital, but the friends who were supposed to pick me up there didn't show up, and I was returned to prison. Since I hadn't placed a lot of hopes on this plan, I was able to deal with the failure. Still, it was depressing that something always, always went wrong. Over the years, I'd made so many plans, all in vain. But giving up was out of the question. *I've got to get out of this dungeon!* kept running through my head.

When I got back from the hospital, Şener said, "I thought you weren't coming back. Maybe you'll be angry, but I wasn't feeling that well and didn't go into the yard. When you're not here, I never go to the yard." I was amazed. Did I actually mean that much in his life?

"Oh well, maybe I should be glad. But you know, something always goes wrong. Why didn't the friends show up at the hospital? They'd said I could go there anytime, that they'd know about it and would come and get me. But I don't think they meant it. We're not in our father's house here, able to leave at will. They don't seem to understand that."

Then I said the tunnel escape shouldn't be delayed any longer, that delay would be too dangerous. Now that I could move around the wards, the escape group accepted my proposal to join them. There was general approval.

Here was the specific plan: I would go to the 35th ward. Meanwhile someone from there would go to the third ward, and someone from the third ward would go to the women's ward, someone slender enough to slip through the door. During roll call, this friend would stay in bed. The women would say I was ill. The guards would glance at the bed from the door and see a body under the blanket. Since we were only very few women, this camouflage would be enough. If we hadn't managed to escape by then, I would stay hiding in the 35th ward. We talked the plan through—on paper, it was perfect. What a shame that many of the friends who were supposed to escape this way had been transferred to other prisons.

Hamili was still sanctioned, and the question arose as to whether he still belonged to the escape group. Did Hamili "deserve" it? some asked. I didn't want to discuss it. "Removing Hamili from the group would have negative consequences, and the sanction is no obstacle," I said.

"Hamili himself has said he won't come along," Şener told me. "Your breakup bothers him."

Love is always misunderstood   I felt guilty about Hamili. It hurt to know he was suffering. Inflicting pain on another person was awful, and it wasn't the first time in my life I'd done it. I didn't want to do it, so why did it keep happening? Was it because I initially sacrificed myself to the wishes of another? Or was I using love as a means to an end? No! Love is not a means, love is direct action, it is life itself.

Love is always misunderstood. You can't force or negotiate it. You don't play with it. Love can't be concealed, but it shouldn't be shared carelessly. It was wonderful to be loved, but Şener had hit one of my weak points when he spoke of my revolutionary personality and called me Apoçu. My emotionality, my search for love, and my femininity lacked a solid revolutionary foundation. I finally had to be clear about where love began and ended.

"Everyone is impressed by your revolutionary personality," Şener told me. "You're very natural. You're like the colors created by arbitrary brushstrokes on a canvas. Not everyone can understand what these brushstrokes mean. They're impressive, but not everyone understands their meaning."

"You speak so philosophically and romantically," I said.

After we talked awhile longer, he said, "If I weren't engaged, I'd fall in love with you."

"That's enough," I said seriously. "It's good that we can talk about anything, but that doesn't mean you have to say everything that enters your mind."

"You can't impose an embargo on love," he said. "Feelings can arise unwanted."

I was silent. Where did Şener get off talking to me like that? This was wrong. He had a fiancée, Mediha, whom I'd met in 1978 in Elazığ. He wore a ring on his finger. He'd told me about her and said they exchanged letters. The reason I'd talked to him about my conflict with Hamili was that he had that relationship and I might find a solution.

"Why are you crying?" Şener asked. "Have I hurt you?"

I struggled to compose myself. "You love one of my comrades," I said. "You're engaged to her, and you should treat her respectfully. Your words are touching, but I have to be frank."

I left the exercise yard early and went back alone to the women's ward. I told Cahide I wasn't feeling well.

Was it possible to love several people at the same time? It seemed neither ethical nor rationally comprehensible.

I was free of my chaotic relationship with Hamili, but now he was hostile to me. We had quarreled constantly for a year, and now we didn't even talk to each other. I wanted to resume our comradely relations, but he didn't, so maybe it was better to avoid an encounter.

Rather than discussing this subject with Şener face to face. I wrote to him. My warm relations with my friends were not an invitation to get close to me, I explained. I'd be more careful in the future so I wouldn't be misunderstood. I told him his words had shocked me because he was engaged to Mediha, and he had to be respectful to her. I criticized his view of love. The next day I gave him the letter. After reading it, he wanted to talk to me, but I avoided him by striking up a conversation with other friends.

Seeing that I was avoiding him, Şener wrote to me, saying I'd overreacted. He did respect Mediha, thoroughly, he said, but love was more than bowing to the rules of society and being tied to a person even when circumstances change. Being attracted to another person is neither fraud nor deception. "I'm honest with Mediha and have nothing to apologize for," he wrote. He found my attitude narrow-minded and conservative.

He and I still cooperated, but this altercation created distance between us. I wasn't as informal as I'd been and didn't raise the subject.

Şener, for his part, behaved himself. At first he had been much more careless, chaotic, and reserved. Now people noticed the change. I have to say, the friends' personal habits sometimes repelled me. From a distance, things might seem fine, but from close up, it could be a bit strange. I often criticized their everyday routines. Şener took my criticism seriously and changed noticeably. The men friends told me, "Since you came to us, everyone has changed. Everyone is paying attention to their personal hygiene, the volume of their voices, and their behavior. Şener was the messiest of all, and now even he's changed."

The enemy was impressed by my dealings with the men friends. One women guard said, "In the past, the men guards ignored us, but now they have manners and stand up when we enter the room. Even the director offers us a chair." Our manners had had a positive influence on the enemy!

The enemy is as afraid as we are   After Karasu and the others were transferred [to Ceyhan], we had criticized ourselves for tacitly accepting his banishment. Presumably, the enemy would now proceed to transfer prisoners one by one or in groups. "We have to rethink our attitude," we said. After a long discussion, we decided, "From now on, we won't allow ourselves to be banished. We'll resist, without provoking a rebellion." Nobody could have imagined that the next transfer would involve just us women.

In the first week of May, the administration announced: "The four women should pack their things. They are being transferred." Banished! The news spread like wildfire. Immediately we set up a barricade and chanted slogans that the entire prison shared. Prisoners chanted the names of those to be banished. The administration tried to placate us: "It's an order from above, we can't do anything about it. There's a court order. It'll be better for you because you'll be in a civilian prison. It's even here in the city. You'll stay in Diyarbakir."

"No, our litigation is still ongoing, and we want to be in the same trial as the men. This decision is arbitrary. Why is this happening now? We don't accept it," we said. The decision had no legal basis. We held firmly to this point.

The administration knew I moved around the exercise yards, serving the organization. But a direct ban on moving around the ward would've led to angry reactions. By transferring us to another prison, they wanted to solve the problem once and for all.

"You've started a riot in the entire prison," said the prosecutor. "Look how fast the news got around! Obviously you're running this prison." The situation gave him a headache.

The male prisoners responded spontaneously and emotionally. "We don't trust you," many of them told the administration. "How do we know where you're going to take them? No, they will not leave this prison."

When we women went into the yards, the men shouted from the windows that they'd stand by us to the end. "You can carry our corpses out, but not our sisters!"

Hüseyin Eroglu, a friend in the third ward, climbed out onto the windowsill and told me, "One fascist threw his cap on the ground and resigned," he said.

> Everyone knows you go to the yards and have great influence. Nothing like that happens in any other prison. We won't let them take you to some other place. I've got a razor blade, and we told the guy frankly there'd be suicide actions if you got banished, which scared them.

Another reason for the banishment was that the enemy wanted to house defectors in our wing. It was an enclosed area with its own visiting rooms, yards, and baths. It even had its own access to the outside. Prisoners here could come and go without the others knowing. They could be taken outside unobserved. They could even have contact with the administration unknown to the rest. This plan, along with my position in prison, was reason enough for the enemy to banish us. He just hadn't counted on getting resistance from the prisoners. "We've made a mess," the directors said.

We always had to consider the possibility of a deliberate provocation. The atmosphere was tense. Both the enemy and we were scared.

I can't remember how many days the resistance lasted, but there were negotiations, and the enemy relented. After only a week the director and the prosecutor came to tell us we wouldn't be transferred after all, and they brought Şener as a prisoner representative. We dismantled the barricade and ended our action. I was able to go back to the exercise yards as before. Still, we had to be prepared for another attack.

Visiting Mazlum's cell   On Mother's Day, for the first time, the families were allowed to come in and visit the yards and the lower corridor. They wanted to see the cells of Mazlum, Pir, Hayri and the others. I went ahead of them. It was forbidden for us to visit the wards on the day of the visit, but the guards let me. For the first time I saw the cell where Mazlum had carried out his action. This cell was different from the others because the men didn't use it. It still belonged to Mazlum.

I begged to be left alone in the toilet area where Mazlum had hanged himself. I leaned against the wall and wept bitterly. He had tied his tie to a pipe. I kissed the wall he had touched, as if he were there now. The room was like a monument to his incomparable greatness. His act had been full of life. In this prison, I had seen the martyred friends alive only

15 Cansız with Zeynep (mother) and Cahide Şener, at Amasya, Mother's Day 1989.

in court, once or twice. The men had arrived holding their heads high, their eyes bright. I slowed my pace and didn't care about the soldier who barked at me to hurry. That was all. But we always had them in our minds. They were always and everywhere present. Their idealism filled our hearts.

Without thinking, I pounded the wall with my fist. Suddenly Şener was behind me, saying, "No! Don't touch that wall! That's where the tunnel is."

"The tunnel's here? Really?" What a coincidence! I looked closely. Exactly where Mazlum's head and heart had come together was the door to our escape. The camouflage was perfect: a compressed-wood panel covered with lime and gypsum. From here the tunnel descended five or six meters, then veered to one side.

I left the cell, and the families arrived, entering one by one.

Love is part of struggle　For me, love was part of life, part of struggle—there could be no "private life" outside my revolutionary life. I had resisted love when I didn't see any point in it. I wanted to love within the struggle. I wanted to love as I fought.

Şener's younger sister, Fatma, and his mother, Saliha, visited. Şener had an animated conversation with Fatma, then called me over to her. She was upset and wanted to talk to me.

"What's happened?" Fatma asked me. Şener had turned his engagement ring over to her, she said, and told her he was ending his relationship with Elif [Mediha]. "They've been engaged for years. What's happened?" she repeated in surprise.

I felt uneasy. Why had Şener done this? Fatma might misunderstand. "I don't know," I said. "It's not right for him to burden you."

Afterward I confronted him. "Everyone will ask why you suddenly aren't wearing the ring. Not only your family but all the friends. Maybe it has no special meaning, but you always wore it up to now. Why did you give it away?"

First he said he'd heard some rumors about Mediha. Hüsnü Altun had said she'd had relationships with various men in the party. But Şener didn't accuse her.

I know her, she's broken with traditional standards in relationships, and I don't blame her, I trust her judgment.

No, it's about you. You're sacred to me. It would be dishonest for me to conceal my feelings for you, and so it would be wrong to continue to wear the ring. I love you as an Apoçu. You've changed my life. You've even changed my view of death. I was afraid of death, and of life a bit too. Now I am at peace with death, or it's become a matter of indifference to me. And in my life now, I have standards. But no matter what I do, I see you everywhere.

He said he wanted to speak candidly. Our conversation lasted hours. I cried. The other men noticed my condition, and I wanted to leave, but I stayed anyway, lest the enemy notice something too. Finally, I went to the men's bathroom toilet and washed my face and hands. The men were surprised by my red eyes, but didn't dare to ask me anything. And I couldn't have answered them.

Şener didn't let up. He argued scientifically, sociologically, psychologically. He knew I was attracted to his ability to impress people. He knew how attentive I was to our internal problems and how much I was trying to find solutions. He knew what I wanted and expected. He knew I had argued with Hamili because he was a resistance fighter who didn't use his abilities for the organization and that in the end that had destroyed our relationship.

16 Cansız with Mehmet Şener, at Diyarbakir (detail of Figure 10), undated.

Hamili used to complain, "Of course you don't like me—you regard others as perfect revolutionaries." He was right. I couldn't discuss anything with him even for half an hour. Not because he was less capable than me or knew less. No! He just didn't try to discuss in ways that could lead to collaboration. He just couldn't do it, and I lacked the patience to teach him.

What did I want? I really wanted to work [with someone]. For a long time, both in prison and outside, I had been alone, cut off from the friends. I had learned to work independently and make decisions. I gained experience that gave me some autonomy. This quality surfaced in the leadership work. Sometimes it played a positive role, sometimes it caused trouble, but it wasn't selfishness. For me, the party's interests counted more than anything. There was nothing I wouldn't do for it—all it had to do was let me know. It was supremely important to act purposefully and sustainably at the right time at the right place, using one's skills. In prison, revolutionary practice required setting standards and behaving appropriately. It was the ABC of a dignified life, resistance, and death. Absent this ability, it was difficult to maintain one's balance in political life.

I had a position within the organization, and ethical influence with those around me, and that made me a force. I had a better reputation within the organization than Şener did. Although Şener was the secretary, I had more power. I always tried to protect him in our joint work, and he was acutely aware of it. Many rumors surrounded his behavior in 1984, and the mistrust never entirely disappeared. Neither he nor the other men had forgotten his mistakes, even after they were no longer matters for discussion.

What was needed for the work, and how could we meet this need? In the foreground were Şener's positive abilities. He could discuss events and problems in prison fluently and write about them with ease. That was an important skill, one that the other men appreciated as well. More than anyone else, I wanted him to use his strengths in organized struggle and so eliminate the lingering mistrust. In a way, it was I who had restored Şener's trustworthiness. I gave him cover. I was interested in developing his working capacity in the present. His skills did enchant me, and I did help him make the best use of them, as he worked day and night. Our collaboration was what I'd always wanted.

In the early days, we prisoners paid little attention to each other's behavior. We [women] didn't see the men for years, and there was so much general confusion. But now that things had settled down, we paid more attention to individual behavior. The others noticed that Şener and I spent a lot of time together writing texts and talking. Internal party problems were our main focus. The friends considered my writing to be incidental and criticized me for not spending enough time with other friends. That criticism hit a nerve, so I started communicating with other wards along with Fuat Kav. But the criticism affected me because my attraction to Şener, and my feelings for him, did influence my work and affect my contact with others. It didn't diminish my working pace or distract me—on the contrary, I was ever more motivated to expand the scope of our work. But as a member of the leadership, I dealt with existing problems too superficially and bureaucratically.

Şener avoided using the classic language of love. He didn't talk about it often, and never during work time. He knew he impressed me every day with his way of working, and he adapted his behavior to my feelings, my standards, and my desires. "I think of you when you're not here," he said. If I brought up the subject during work hours, he'd say, "Not now." I liked his attitude, which preserved certain manners.

We didn't name our relationship and set no conditions. Did loving mean working together? For me, this was the most binding aspect of our relationship. I didn't think about what would happen to us in the future, only about our work together. I expressed my opinions forcefully, I was active, and I took the initiative on things because my position as a leadership member required it in this troubled time.

Şener would say, "You're like a saint. No one can commit a sin in your presence." It was a compliment that he confessed that he was afraid of me. "You're an ideal force, you're holy." I didn't see it as an attempt to influence me emotionally. He meant he adjusted his thoughts to my attitude. "The love of an Apo-devotee is sacred," he said. He kept repeating, "I consider it a duty to change myself in order to do you justice. You can't object."

I didn't take his words as flattery. They agreed with my reality. For me, love for a person was no different than love for our struggle. Just as I believed in our struggle and devoted myself to it, so should my love for another human being be so trusting and unrestricted. I wanted a love relationship in which there were no fears or reservations. Both of us stuck to this ideal.

Complications   The tunnel escape plan filled us all with high expectations. But one day we received a message from Hasan Atmaca, on the outside, saying, "I can't take a step [to prepare] because I have to sign in with the police every day." But our greatest hopes lay with him.

On public holidays open visits took place. We were expecting a message to arrive via Ali Kilic's brother, but the message had originally been referred to not as a message but as a "compass." This created a big misunderstanding. Ali Kilic's family was difficult to understand. One of his brothers was suspected of working with the police, or so a brother-in-law of Cahida had told us. It wasn't the first time we'd heard it, and we'd already informed the friends, who evidently ignored our warning. The enemy was trying hard to recruit spies from this family. The matter had to be clarified, but we could hardly do so from prison. For some who visited and were entrusted with important tasks, we didn't even know if they were tied to a family of a prisoner or worked for the enemy.

During this open visit, a guard discovered that a man positing as one of the Kilic brothers was carrying a compass. It was clear that a compass couldn't be smuggled into prison. The visit was stopped immediately. The first group of visitors had already been admitted, including this man. Now he came straight to our ward and said in a panic, "Let's chant slogans at once. The families aren't going to be let in. Outside, it's full of soldiers. The friends out there sent us. Hasan Güllü was here but left when the chaos broke out."

We didn't chant slogans because we knew it was a provocation. I took the man to the 35th ward. Again, the call for slogans was loud. I warned the friends and voiced my suspicions. The warning was immediately circulated throughout the prison. "Who ordered a compass?" I asked. "Nobody. But back when Karasu was here, someone asked for a message, but instead of using the word 'message,' he said 'compass,'" the friends replied. This clarified this question, but we still didn't know what the man's mission was. The enemy continued his provocations. Soldiers occupied the roof. Suddenly we heard shots and screams from the relatives. The friends upstairs watched the action. We tried to keep calm and to understand what was going on. Since it remained quiet in prison, the situation outside normalized. After some delay, further groups of visitors were admitted to prison.

What was the purpose of this provocation? We had no concrete clues, so we could only speculate. The first thing that came to mind was that our escape plan might have leaked. What else would we do with a compass? I didn't know if a compass was really needed for tunneling, but it probably could help keep the digging going in the right direction. Was that all? Or was it something else we didn't know about?

In the following days, we learned that Simon and his group had been arrested in the city center. They'd been in the same apartment for a long time. It was said that Saliha visited this apartment many times. The news infuriated me. That woman turned up everywhere! Couldn't she be sent abroad? She was a constant plague.

Then Saliha, Hasan Güllü, and Sinan were arrested. The news was deeply disturbing. The tunnel construction was almost finished, with only one or two days of work remaining. So much hope was pinned on it, it just couldn't go wrong.

I had a very bad feeling. There were no specific clues, but I got sick, so stressed in my stomach that I needed infusions. Had all the work on the tunnel been in vain?

Gezgör cursed, "They can't even manage to avoid arrest! Now they've got themselves caught! We shouldn't have trusted them in the first place—why did we ever put hope in them?" And he inveighed against Hasan Atmaca: "Ever since his release, he's been sitting around at home because he supposedly can't leave the village!" Gezgör smoked one cigarette after another, pacing nervously.

Şener's brother Ihsan, [his sister] Fatma, and Cahide's sister Nevin were told to leave the area and come back only after the situation calmed down. Supposedly Ihsan knew about the tunnel. A short time later he went to Greece. Nevin disappeared into another city for a while. Of Simon and his group, it was said they went north, but that they weren't directly involved in the escape plans, so that didn't endanger the tunnel.

Exposure   It was early on an October [1988] morning, and we were in the yard of the 35th. Suddenly all doors were shut—we couldn't leave the yard. Special Forces made their way into the ward. It didn't seem like a normal search. It seemed like an attack.

The fact that the administration had said nothing and the Special Forces were in charge showed how serious the operation was. The other wards were searched lightly, but the focus was the 35th. The walls and floor in the toilet room were knocked down with a sledgehammer. It was clear that they'd come because of the tunnel.

"Let's keep chanting slogans, but avoid provocation and extreme behavior," we decided. The friends in the other wards asked by cipher, "Should we do something to distract them?" We said no.

By noon, they'd still found nothing, but our nerves were raw. Gezgör chain-smoked. Since not all the prisoners knew about the tunnel, we weren't allowed to show concern. We didn't yet know what the enemy knew. "Sinan and Hasan know there's a tunnel in the 35th ward, but they don't know the exact location," Fuat said. That gave us a little hope.

All our books and written texts were confiscated. Okay, as long as the tunnel wasn't discovered. "If we're lucky, we'll finally be out of here, I'll definitely go," Gezgör whispered. His hands shook. The situation was maddening.

The search was halted. "They didn't find anything!" we whispered joyfully. But the soldiers were still in the prison. The officer in charge cursed out his soldiers and left the ward with rage. We smirked at his anger.

The prisoners' representatives went to the administration, where Sait demanded a list of the items that had been confiscated. He overheard a telephone call in the next room: *"We haven't found anything … He certainly knows the spot. You have to make him talk. I'm not leaving till I find it."*

Sometime later the soldiers returned to the ward and knocked down more walls with a sledgehammer. Then they saw soil spilling out of a wall. They'd found the tunnel.

We chanted slogans, but why? "To prevent the enemy's attacks," some said. I didn't care. I didn't listen, just sat paralyzed in a corner. I'd quit smoking in 1984—now I asked the men for a cigarette. "Don't do it!" said Fuat. I watched Gezgör pound his fists against the wall.

So much work had gone into that tunnel. Before Hasan Atmaca was released, he had sent me his diary—we women had still been isolated at the time, so I knew a few details. The diary meticulously described the daily work on the tunnel. It was like the movie *The Great Escape*, which I'd recently seen on TV. Our tunnel was much more exciting—it required work, conspiracy, and patience. It was like no other tunnel in the world. Even the enemy was stunned. An escape tunnel—from the fourth floor! How had we made holes in the concrete? The cells were stacked on four floors, with air shafts running between them. At first, there had been small windows in the cells, but they had been filled in for security reasons. The friends had by chance discovered an air shaft and perforated the wall. From there, they descended to the ground floor and dug another five meters into the ground. The tunnel was to end in a house in the Bağlar district. The excavated soil was deposited in the other air shafts. Actually, it was a brilliant plan. But dammit, it hadn't worked.

We stayed in the yard until the evening without food and drink. It got cold. To warm ourselves, we ran back and forth. What would happen now? We had to be prepared for anything. Whining wouldn't help. The only certainty was that there would be transfers. Whether only the 35th ward or the entire prison would be affected was unclear. Most suspected the entire building would be evacuated.

Gezgör was furious: "Who betrayed us? What unscrupulous bastard did this?" It was no big secret, there had been arrests, and the victims had probably not withstood the torture. Maybe a secret betrayal was involved, too. Speculation wouldn't help us, but we had to find out, because this betrayal would require revenge: for the lost time, the work we'd done in vain, the disappointed hopes, the sleepless nights, the humidity, the life-threatening oxygen deficiency, and the rheumatism that had attacked Gezgör's heart.

My dreams of escape had been so nice. How many times had I imagined a friend lying in my bed during roll call, biting his lip to suppress his laughter. I had imagined hiding in the 35th ward, then leaving the prison and going to the mountains. We'd meet the chairman … It would've been so nice to be back with the party and the chairman after all these years.

We paced in silence, sighing, cursing, and raising questions. Night fell. In the next ward, the BBC news was on. Suddenly a racket erupted. "Friends, good news! Esat Oktay has been shot!" someone cried.

Cheers, whistles, *halay* … my God, what a day! It was amazing. If only the escape had succeeded! How wonderful if these two messages had complemented each other: "Forty cadres erupted from prison" and "Esat Oktay shot." It was such damn bad luck!

Still, it was a comfort that Esat was dead, and that would have to be enough! The party had taken this executioner's life and so avenged Mazlum, Pir, Hayri, and the others. And it would continue to take revenge. Oh, if only we had shot Şahin and Yıldırım and the other scoundrels who didn't belong to this earth!

The news so raised our spirits even though we were still mourning the tunnel. Only Gezgör repeated painfully, "Just one or two more days, and the escape would've succeeded for sure." He sighed so deeply, his chest seemed to burst.

At night, back in our own wards, the doors were opened, and we were searched and sent back to our wards. Everyone was depressed. Would we meet again? "See you," we said in parting. The corridors were full of soldiers wearing Special Forces uniforms. The civilian guards and the rest of the staff were conferring anxiously in small groups. Everyone watched us four women as we walked down the corridor between the lined-up soldiers to our ward.

The ward looked like a battlefield. All the books and texts were gone, including *Hawar* and other periodicals. Gezgör had written more than a thousand pages of documentation of the events in prison. It was excellent and significant and contained numerous interviews of us and members of other groups as well. Cahide had typed up the manuscript little by little. There were no other copies. We'd planned to smuggle it outside in several parts and had already sent a small one. We'd hidden the rest, but how were we to get it back now? It was a disaster. Gezgör didn't know about it yet—he'd be devastated. Once again, the result of an enormous effort had been wrecked. It was too much to endure.

Banishment! The administration announced the transfers, to destinations unknown. Not all the prisoners would be transferred, they said, but we had to be ready for anything.

The doors stayed locked the next day—nobody was allowed in the yard. As many as 100 of us were to be transferred. In the evening we were ready. Şener informed me, through the slot in the door, that by majority decision of the leadership, nobody was to go voluntarily. Those who were to be transferred shouldn't step forward, and the prisoners should hook arms to create chains. Create a chain? We laughed—we women were only four! Still, we put on tight clothes. Some of the men managed to say goodbye to us. We wished each other success.

At 10 p.m. Special Forces entered the wing. We heard screams, thuds, and chain rattles from everywhere in the prison, lasting until 4 a.m. The racket was torture. We pounded on the door, chanting slogans and demanding to see the men. Nobody responded to us, which made us crazy.

Our turn came last. When the door opened, we women hooked arms and chanted slogans. Our attackers were Special Forces, and one said he was a police chief. They beat us with truncheons. We resisted. Four or five of them grabbed me. My body was numb from the blows. I kicked, and they gagged me with the cloth I wore around my neck, and they beat me all the way to the car. It was the worst clubbing I'd had in recent years. It took them at least an hour to get us all out of the ward. Finally, they forced us one by one through the rear door of a military van. Morning dawned—no one was around except us. In the van, we resisted being handcuffed behind our backs. They beat us some more. We never stopped chanting slogans.

The alleged police chief snarled, "Shut her up!"

"You're gonna end up like Esat," I said. "You've heard of Esat?"

Livid, he climbed into the back and punched me in the face, barking, "I'll break your nose!"

I felt a terrible pain, as if my eyes were coming out of their sockets. My nose was bleeding, probably broken. That vile fascist dog! He probably wanted to avenge Leyla Akbas. Too bad I never managed to break her nose. "Don't forget what happened to Esat," I repeated.

The police chief said, "Have you heard of Hüseyin Yıldırım? He's from Tunceli, like you. He's split from you, you know that?"

I said, "Aw, he was always one of yours, from the beginning. We always knew it, he was never PKK, just one of your cheap chess pieces. He'll die too—he's a coward, he's probably already dead from fear. The message we sent via Esat was much more impressive." Trying to punch him mentally was all I could do in this situation.

The vehicles got in motion. As we passed the prosecutor, standing at the gate, I called him a fascist one last time. From the prison came slogan chanting, which we joined until we left the city. Judging from the engine noise, we must have been moving in a long military convoy.

Our handcuffs were so tight, they cut off our circulation. It hurt. We pounded the partition to the front of the van and said to the soldiers, "Loosen the handcuffs! Our hands are swollen." "That's forbidden." They yawned. Finally, we managed to loosen the handcuffs with a bobby pin and even pull out a hand. What a relief.

The long ride in a closed vehicle after all the beatings was grueling, but we managed to pull ourselves together. We wrote short texts and slogans on notebook pages, describing how brutally our transfer had gone so far. We couldn't see where we were, but when we felt like we were driving through a village, we pressed them through tiny holes in the van to the outside. "Maybe we can stir up some interest in the people," we told each other.

Before we left, when we'd asked the police where we were being taken. "Yassiada," they'd said. Was it true? Why not? It was a former prison island [in the Sea of Marmara]. The trials of Celal Bayar and Adnan Menderes had taken place there. I thought again of the novel *Papillon* and told the others the story of a prisoner fleeing a prison island on a coconut-shelled raft. His companion had died. The sea was dangerous. "Let's eat a lot of fish—escape will be easier if we can swim," someone said.

"They're taking us to a place so remote, we can't even have visitors. We'll probably be cut off from the outside world entirely. Well, we can always go on a hunger strike or a death fast. To demand a transfer," we said. All the time we remembered the failed tunnel escape plan. The pain of the beatings passed quickly, but the pain of the tunnel failure was far worse than our damaged puffy faces, bruises, and broken noses. That betrayal was unbearable. Who had betrayed us? Who could be so evil?

The car stopped. We saw a wall with a sign "Sivas Closed Prison." Were we to stay here? We had to wait. We asked a soldier to open the door so we could get some fresh air, but his superior denied the request. Then we pounded the door and shouted, "Down with the banishment! Long live the resistance! End the torture!" We chanted more slogans to stay alert. We made a marvelous amount of noise despite our miserable condition. From outside we heard voices. Where were the men? Was there another prison in Sivas? Since our slogan chants could cause trouble, we soon got back on the road.

"Where are our men?" we asked the soldiers. "Are they back in Sivas? We don't hear any more engines."

"They haven't been with us since Malatya. You're alone," came the answer. We literally froze. So we were segregated! Isolated! Curses! The bastards were pulling off what they'd failed to do in May.

I felt like a piece of my heart had been cut away. Only now did I feel sadness at leaving Diyarbakir. As long as I thought I was in a convoy with the men, the pain hadn't sunk in. *Wherever we go, we'll turn it into Diyarbakir.* This thought had comforted me. Now we learned we'd already been alone for hours. Were we the only ones being taken to Yassiada? Maybe other prisoners had already been transferred there.

We asked the soldiers, "Did our friends stay in Malatya?"

"No, they drove on. Last we saw, they were heading for Eskişehir," they answered. Eskişehir! And where are we going? "We don't know," said the soldiers.

They told us their supervisor had collected some of the messages we'd thrown out during the ride. But most of them had fluttered away. They wanted to use them as evidence against us. All their thinking was focused on ways to punish us. Fools! We laughed. It was always nice to annoy the enemy. Don't give him a moment's peace—that was like an oath we'd taken.

After 24 hours we stopped at a gate with the sign "Amasya Closed Prison." Amasya? It was notorious as a place of exile. At the gate a middle-aged man awaited us, standing like a feudal lord with his coat draped over his shoulders. "Are these the savages from Diyarbakir?" he asked with a dirty grin, then laughed like he was drunk. "Now what's happened to them? Let's see what they look like. Diyarbakir was certainly beautiful, but this is Amasya. Have you heard of us? We're not interested in what went on in Diyarbakir. Here we have rules, and we make no exceptions for women!" And he led us into a room.

"Be careful with our belongings—we have fragile items," we said. "They're to be searched only in our presence." This feudal lord type, who was probably the director, said, "Yeah, well, how about that. They show up at our door and give us orders right off. Oh, they're gonna be trouble. What did we do to deserve this plague? I'd rather have a hundred men than these women." He frowned with contempt and distinct unease.

I couldn't hold my tongue. "Who are you? What is your function?"

"What? You're interrogating me? No, first you say who you are!"

Inwardly, I guffawed. How weird he was, a fascist with complexes and affectations trying to intimidate us. Obviously, he was frightened. Since we were women, he disparaged us, but we were PKK from the Diyarbakir dungeon and no docile sheep, as he well knew.

"Oh, just look at the files right in front of you—they'll tell you all about us," I said in my edgy voice. "My name is Sakine Polat, I am PKK in exile from Diyarbakir. I've been in prison for ten years. Now that we're here, you'll be getting to know us, but I can already see who and what you are. We're political prisoners, so don't treat us like common criminals like most of the prisoners here. I don't have anything against them, but we're PKK revolutionaries, convicted by courts of a state that knows very well who we are. You should study up. And respect that our personal belongings are to be searched only in our presence and only by a female guard. We've been tortured and injured, so we need to see a doctor right away. You don't want to be held responsible for our injuries. We'll let the public know, they'll see our situation. If you don't get us the care we need, you could be liable."

"You come in and give orders!" he babbled nervously, and a little more softly. "I'm the director here, Hasan Can. Here we have rules. Books, radios, and TVs are forbidden. The criminal prisoners have a TV they can use at certain times." Then he thought for a moment. "All right, a doctor will come here tomorrow and examine you."

We spent the night in a cell, and in the morning, sure enough, a doctor examined us. My nose was broken. We showed the doctor the marks the batons had left. We didn't want to show him certain places. Our goal was to prevent further physical assaults—and to make clear to the enemy that we weren't the sort to accept everything quietly.

The doctor shook his head in surprise. We told him what had happened: "The administration discovered a tunnel among the men prisoners and used it as an excuse to get aggressive with us. But actually it was because of the shooting of Esat Oktay Yıldıran. He got what was coming to him— he was responsible for the deaths of dozens of our friends in Diyarbakir. These torturers have human lives on their consciences, and no matter where they are, we will hold them to account. You're a doctor, bound by the Hippocratic oath, so you'll do what's right. Doctors aren't torturers, and they don't protect torturers."

Looking panicked, he said quickly, "Of course I'm a doctor and not a torturer." He wrote us a note saying we were sick and prescribing a week of treatment. That was good—we asked for a copy. He gave us medications too. Our directness had impressed him. The guards—some of them obvious fascists—regarded us with amazement.

There were four other women political prisoners besides us. "They're from your gang too," Hasan Can said. He was really a funny guy and I laughed without intending to.

The other women were from TİKB. One was the sister of Aysel Zehir, who had suffered permanent health damage from the death fast in Metris. The women's wings in all E-type prisons were similar. They had an L-shape. We were put in a cell on the side of the first ward. We shared a kitchen, yard, bath, and toilet with the TİKB women. The nonpolitical women were in another ward.

"Visiting day is the day after tomorrow," we learned. We did a two-day warning hunger strike. On the day of the visit, the TİKB women told their families about us, and we sent messages to other prisons announcing that we were at Amasya.

For a long time, several prisons had been planning a simultaneous hunger strike, to protest the transfers, the last brutality in Diyarbakir, and a recent decree on prisons. The action had already begun in Diyarbakir, Ceyhan, Antep, Eskişehir, Malatya, and almost all others that held PKK prisoners. Now Amasya joined. We supported the overall demands but made some separate demands as well, because the prison conditions in Amasya were abysmal.

In Diyarbakir, whenever prisoners did a hunger strike, the families had supported them with demonstrations. But for the people of Amasya, hunger-striking prisoners were something new. The Amasya region was quite reactionary, and so was this prison, which was known as a place of exile. The town of Amasya was small, and the prison was situated far from the center, in a village called Helvacilar. Previous political prisoners here had carried out hunger strikes with just one demand: to be transferred to another prison. They just wanted to get away—they didn't bother to make other demands.

So the prison administration had not had to make any changes, and conditions were even worse than in 1979 in Elazığ, and the methods they used were very primitive. Prisoners at Amasya had no rights at all. Rights that had been won in other prisons years earlier were unknown here. *Cumhuriyet* newspaper and *Notka* magazine were not handed out. Sewing needles and scissors were prohibited. There were still underground isolation cells—Terzi Fikri had been murdered in one of them.

Hasan Can behaved like a feudal lord, and the guards like little pashas. None of the staff were ordinary people just doing their jobs. The young female guards were engaged to police officers, or had officers as friends, or had brothers in the military. They were all cogs in the prison system, in it all the way.

So we had to start from scratch. Along with the general demands of the common hunger strike, we made local demands that were far-reaching. Detention conditions were very bad too in Erzurum, Malatya, and Elazığ—the prisoners there heard little from outside, and repeated hunger strikes had resulted in no noticeable improvements. Since the hunger strike was taking place in many prisons at the same time, the families and others on the outside supported it. It all put the state under pressure. "Our prison was fine until the PKK women arrived and brought anarchy," Hasan Can said.

The TİKB prisoners participated for only a little while. They wouldn't participate in a long-term hunger strike, they said, because their group had decided to protect their cadres. We'd never heard of such a thing. It never occurred to us that cadres had to be protected. We did just the opposite. Even if we had decided to protect certain cadres, it would have been impossible because they would reject special treatment. Were we too tough? It seemed pointless to discuss this issue with them further, so we just told them a joint action plan had been submitted to all groups.

17 Cansız with the three other PKK women prisoners at Amasya, c.1989. *Left to right*: Mevlüde, Cansız, Cahide, and Emine.

We sent each other messages by inserting them into bread balls and tossing them from the roof. We were able to keep each other more or less up to date, even though the bread balls didn't always reach their destination safely. The ward where the men stayed was hard to hit from the roof. Sometimes a message landed on the roof, where the guards would find it. They figured out what we were doing and sometimes secretly lurked in wait and ran to intercept the bread balls. Some messages that fell into their hands became the subject of new charges against us.

The public outside didn't know much about prison realities, and prisoners' resistance was a new topic for them. And because Amasya was so remote, the families barely managed to unite and coordinate their efforts to help us. While the hunger strike was under way, no letters or telegrams from outside were given to us. [Among we four PKK women], Mevlüde never got visits from her family anyway. Emine's family lived far away in Mardin, a long and difficult journey. My parents were in Europe. That left only Cahide's relatives, and they came immediately, bringing the news that 120 of the men at Diyarbakir had been transferred to Eskişehir.

Şener was still in Diyarbakir, they said, along with Fethi, Mahmut Tanrikulu, Cevdet, and a few others. It was good that not all the cadres there had been transferred, as there were many new arrivals, but it bothered me that Şener was still there. The last time we spoke—through the door slot—had he known his name wasn't on the list? Why hadn't he said anything? It gave me a bad feeling. After all, he had been in the 35th ward, and the enemy surely knew he belonged to the group intended for escape. Had they left him in place for a specific reason? Or was it because his trial was still going on? But many others had been transferred whose trials were incomplete. No, the enemy must have a specific purpose, probably to direct general attention back to Şener.

During this hunger strike, I wrote in my journal about the feelings that my banishment from Diyarbakir had unleashed. Leaving had been terrible for me. I loved Diyarbakir. Can you love a dungeon? Astonishingly, the answer is yes. It had been the site of brutal torture and cruelty, and our most valuable comrades had fallen there. But I loved the memory of the pain we suffered there. It was a sentimental bond for me. The friends who read my piece later criticized it as "extremely emotional."

After a while, the hunger strike ended in some prisons, but we continued, as did Diyarbakir, Ceyhan, Malatya, Erzurum, and Elazığ. The newspaper said Karasu and several others [in Ceyhan] were in critical condition. We got public support, and the families went on a hunger strike, too. Some even tried to set themselves on fire in front of the parliament building. The prisoners at Eskişehir took it to a death fast. They were transferred to Aydin, where Hüseyin and Mehmet died. When we heard about it, we chanted: "Mehmet and Hüseyin are immortal! Long live the resistance! Down with torture!" And then we turned our hunger strike into a death fast too. It was the first death fast in Amasya. There were many protests outside, and calls to prevent more deaths. But those two deaths pressured the enemy to finally accept our demands. We got a telegram from Şener in Diyarbakir: "End the action."

The hunger strike had lasted about a month. Soon more prisoners from Diyarbakir were transferred to Elazığ and Eskişehir—obviously the prison was to be "cleaned out."

After the hunger strike ended, I began a lively correspondence, sending letters everywhere. I wrote to Şener, who soon wrote me back with news and musings about his state of mind after our banishment. He included a new poem.

Then in December we got a telegram: "Şener and Mahmut Tanrikulu have been released." I was shocked. *Şener—released? How can that be?* But once my shock subsided, I was glad. Had he managed to reach the friends [in the Beka'a valley or in the Iraqi mountains]? I wondered. Or had the enemy coerced him into military service, before he could reach the party?

When prisoners were released, they rarely had a chance to move around freely. Usually the enemy handed them over to the military for induction. Those who had families were sometimes granted a few days' leave. But unless a released prisoner managed to make his way to the party right away, he would be drafted into the military. It was part of the enemy's strategy.

Many former detainees did not contest being drafted, and quite a few former prisoners did military service. Some even used it as an excuse to avoid going to the mountains. Such cases infuriated us whenever we heard of them. We considered it a betrayal for a former prisoner to do military service for even a single day, after so many years of torture and repression.

Back at Diyarbakir, we had even written an advisory on the subject. Friends who were released, we wrote, had a revolutionary duty to defend themselves against any hostile action that was designed to alienate or control their ideals and identities as a continuation of imprisonment. Friends who held to their convictions in prison, mounted a political defense in court, and declared their support for the party would have to refuse to do service in the enemy's most important fascist and colonial institution—the military.

> As we know, many prisoners after release are drafted. If possible, they must try to prevent this and use the days or even hours that they have to reach the party. If this is not possible and they are drafted, cadres whose political identity is known to the enemy must oppose the enemy's orders and make it clear that they reject military service. As soon as possible, they must desert. No obstacles are valid.

We issued this text to all prisoners and set a clear resolution to the cadres: "Anyone who performs military service is considered a traitor."

After a while, I got a letter from Şener, postmarked Istanbul. Writing under a different name, he hinted that he had evaded military service, which calmed me a bit. He was in a safe place but had been unable to make contact with the friends. "I'm with acquaintances of yours," he said. He didn't say who, but presumably they were people from the Turkish or Kurdish Left.

Then at some point, an article he wrote was published in the TKP journal. It was upsetting that he had written for the TKP at all, but the content was strange too—it lacked his usual incisiveness, and his PKK-style spirit was missing. Şener could write very well, but this article was slanted to satisfy the magazine's publishers. Had he and they become friends in prison? I wrote him that it wasn't right. Was he dependent on these people now? I asked. Was he just using them to help him get out of the country? If so, was it wise to rely on such people? Were we so desperate? For me it was also a question of dignity. "Even if I were stuck here for 40 years, I wouldn't put myself in that position with the TKP," I said.

A local legend The Shahnameh, an epic written by [the eleventh-century Persian poet] Ferdowsi, contains the love story of Ferhat and Sirin. Amasyans claim their story took place in their town, although in reality, this Kurdish legend played out in Kermanshah, and the graves of Ferhat and Sirin are actually in Mount Behistun. But according to Amasya locals, Ferhat was in love with Sirin and carved a tunnel for her through the Amasya Mountains. [Someone falsely told Ferhat that Sirin had died.] He couldn't bear it and killed himself. Then Sirin[, who was still alive,] received news of Ferhat's death. She committed suicide. From the Amasya prison window, you could see the mountain summit where their supposed tombs lie, now pilgrimage sites. "Two roses grow there, and between them are impenetrable thorns, it's a beautiful place," they tell each other. The name Helvacilar, the village where Amasya prison is located, had its origins in this legend. As news of Ferhat's death spread, Sirin's father distributed halvah [Turkish helve]. The sesame candy was handed out for Sirin's death too, and from it the village supposedly got its name.

The rocks of the surrounding mountains had enormous holes, attributed to Ferhat's digging. He had dug his way through the mountains and overcome the greatest difficulties, to get to his beloved. Yet he had been denied happiness with Sirin. Strange—were all great love stories similar? The story made me think: the fulfillment of desire comes at a price. It is unrealistic to regard love as either unreachable or sacred, but it is also not easy.

What was this "sacred love" that Şener spoke of in all his letters? It was a beautiful term, but it raised doubts and worries. I had told him, "Love means struggle." And he had replied, "Love is sacred." But wasn't the fight sacred? My letters, my love, my conversations, all my years had been marked by struggle. The content and the form, cause and effect of this struggle were all important.

A month after the hunger strike ended, we started another one because the administration had failed to fulfill any of the promises it had made after the first. We entered an indefinite hunger strike on almost the same terms as before. In negotiations with the administration, Cahide represented the women's wing, and Sait Korkmaz the men's. The first talks were fruitless, and some of the demands were met with outrage. In discussions with the administration, the way a question was framed was important. But Cahide and Sait lacked the political experience necessary to handle the relentless enemy.

As the hunger strike continued, a group of prisoners from Eskişehir arrived, transferred here. [PKK cadre] Muzaffer Ayata was among them. So was Celalettin Can of Dev-Sol. How strange—the enemy was moving prisoners around, first to Eskişehir, then to Amasya. Didn't he know what to do anymore? It had to be part of the strategy to split the prisoners and bring them under control. The prisoners became occupied with different issues in different prisons. The enemy always came up with new methods.

All the transferred prisoners were in bad health. Muzaffer had stomach bleeding, and his condition was getting worse. I was worried. It seemed wrong to insist on the fulfillment of all our demands—it wasn't worth losing a comrade like Muzaffer. If the issues at stake were fundamental, we'd make every sacrifice. But insisting on the demands meant risking death; unless they were absolutely necessary, it was just wrong. I was ready to take responsibility [for ending the strike].

At the next discussion [among the hunger strikers], I said, "We should work towards resolving the remaining issues right up to the last moment and then end the action." Muzaffer, who participated on my insistence, objected, even though he was doing poorly.

Then we went to talk to the administration. Ultimately, it gave in to most of our demands, and we ended the hunger strike. "Just a few of the less basic demands are left, and we'll put them into effect on our own," we said. Afterward the TİKB and Dev-Sol prisoners criticized us for this decision, and even after we explained our reasoning, they understood. There was always some left-wing sectarianism behind such criticisms. They claimed the right to protect their own cadres, but they were less sensitive to ours. Another cunning move in politics!

Serhildan The Amasya prison had forced us to hold two hunger strikes in quick succession, each of which lasted over a month. Before we could recover, a new wave of repression began.

We had to fight prison conditions. We had to organize our social and political lives, to undermine hostile control mechanisms, and to live up to the struggle being fought outside. The enemy's omnipresence in prison made it especially important. But we were striking so often that even small causes could lead to grueling hunger strikes. Yet hunger strikes and death fasts were our most effective weapons.

Muzaffer was angry.

Isn't there any other form of action we can do besides hunger strikes? We can't always do active resistance. An uprising can have grave consequences—the enemy will risk bloodshed to crush it. Slogans and such don't really help. A hostage taking wouldn't solve anything. Is it really so difficult, or are we just not creative enough?

Letters between us and friends outside prison made clear that we all wished to find a suitable way of dealing with this situation. Yet it was a sensitive topic. We realized that the enemy was attacking us in prison in order to divert our attention from other issues, to siphon off our energy, and to frighten the people outside who might have been attracted to our struggle.

[In March 1990, at the time of Newroz, Kurds in all the southeastern cities protested widely. In Nuseybin, about 5,000 protesters gathered at the funeral of a PKK fighter. Turkish troops fired on them, and over 700 were arrested. In Cizre, about 15,000 protesters clashed with police, and 5 protesters were killed, 80 injured, and 155 arrested.]

But the enemy attacks in the prisons became less frequent, as the Serhildan [popular uprising] developed in Kurdistan. People in villages, small towns, and even in big cities were rising up. Our fight was becoming a mass movement. The joy and pride of the Kurdistan revolution gave strength to many people, as in the Palestinian intifada. The TİKP's magazine celebrated the uprising as a success of their own party, ignoring that it was a consequence of our struggle.

Enthusiastic about the Serhildan, I proposed the optimistic thesis of an armed insurrection, "1990 will be the year of liberation," I predicted. "There will be mass uprisings—the necessary conditions are being developed in Kurdistan and Turkey." The women friends called me a dreamer. Yes, my assessment was inspired by my imagination, but my hope was based on real events. The same hyper-optimism had led me to believe that August 15 had begun the phase of strategic insurrection. But my idea wasn't wholly unrealistic.

Increasingly I found my captivity intolerable. I couldn't stand being confined within prison walls. I passionately desired to share the excitement outside. Every day it inspired me to devise new escape plans, however risky. I went up to the roof to scout possible escape routes. We made a rope ladder by braiding bedsheets and clambered down it to explore the guard situation and the surrounding area. It was exciting, but we kept coming up against insurmountable obstacles. I swung between radiant hope and burning disappointment. Not even Muzaffer, who was known for his patience, could rein me in.

I exercised in the yard. I created an obstacle course using boxes and stools, which I named after mountains. I walked for hours, imagining myself climbing a mountain. I walked in the rain until I was soaked from head to toe. I even walked in snow, so I could feel connected to the life of the guerrillas in the mountains.

Şener becomes a soldier We had expected Şener to go abroad, but to everyone's astonishment, he was captured and drafted into the military. It was upsetting. Why had he stayed so long in Istanbul? He had supposedly been seized at a meeting with Mehmet Eksen and others I didn't know. Who were these new people he'd taken up with? Everything was unclear, and our mistrust grew. We had little information, so we could only guess.

Later, the friends in Diyarbakir reported that he had refused to put on the uniform or follow military discipline, which heartened me. No PKK soldier could wear the uniform of the Turkish army! Şener himself had written a text on this subject and formulated resolutions. Serving in the military as such was a grave offense. It violated our principles. In prison you could protect your heart and mind so they continued to function, but in the military, the enemy had the means to force his will on you.

Sometime earlier I learned about [a former prisoner] Dilaver, whom I had met in Elazığ—he was a good friend of Hamili. Dilaver had been released from prison and was drafted for military service. He fled abroad, but then in 1988 we heard he committed suicide. What had happened?

The lawyer Mahmut completed his military service as a reserve officer, then went abroad—where he was shot. We trusted the party and assumed it didn't err. But why would a person who had been imprisoned for years and then finally reached the party suddenly commit suicide? What could have induced Dilaver to kill himself? I kept wondering. Could Mamak prison have changed him so much? Or the brief military stint? I was mystified. I talked it over with those who had known him personally.

Cantürk, a smuggler who had been in Mamak prison with Dilaver, asked me tearfully, "Sister, I will believe you, but please tell me the truth. Did the party shoot him? He wasn't the type to kill himself. I knew him well."

I answered, "The party certainly didn't shoot him, you can believe me."

Tears streamed down his face. "I just hope it wasn't the party. That would just be too hard." But without more information, our conversations made little sense.

This news added to concern about Şener's military service. How would the enemy deal with someone convicted as a PKK member in the military? Şener must desert immediately or at least resist orders. There was no alternative. I said to Muzaffer: "We have to make his case public—otherwise he'll be shot for sure!" In the Republic of Turkey, resisting the draft was considered unpardonable. We informed our lawyers and wrote letters to newspapers. [Lawyer and journalist] Ilhan Selcuk wrote about the topic in his column.

Underlying my concern, however, was Şener's weak behavior during the January 1984 uprising. When people have passed such a test, you don't have to worry about them anymore—they were so unshakable in the face of the enemy's most insidious intrigues and greatest cruelty that

18 Cansız with Saliha Şener and Muzaffer Ayata at Çanakkale, June 1989.

you need fear losing them only physically. They radiate trustworthiness. But Şener had a weak side that always triggered my reflex to try to bring him back and save him. I felt like I kept pulling him up from the bottom of a well. I hoped he would overcome his weakness. He'd already come a long way, but now he was on his own, and had to steer clear of a deep fall. My optimism about him decisively shaped my relationship with him.

Soon thereafter [Şener's mother] Saliha stopped by Amasya en route to Tokat to visit [Şener where he was stationed]. She had just come from Ceyhan, where she had visited Karasu. Karasu, Saliha told me, had advised Şener to be "reasonable," arguing that an open refusal [to wear the uniform] would make it impossible for him to flee. He advised Şener to lie low until conditions were right for a desertion. Karasu might have advised such behavior for tactical reasons, I thought, but I had trouble believing Saliha.

I wrote a short message to Şener, saying, "Don't put on the uniform. So far you've refused, so don't give in now. We'll publicize your case." I intended to give it to Saliha because Karasu had told her that Şener should wear the uniform so he could escape.

That morning, just as visiting time was due to begin, it was cancelled. The visitors were angry—some had traveled a long distance. We knew that, like every episode of harassment, every arrest, every degrading treatment, this cancellation was an attempt to intimidate the families— he could invent any reason for it. So we protested, "Stop criminalizing the families!"

But why did the enemy cancel visiting time today? What was it about today? It turned out that Saliha had been arrested. What, had a message been found on her again? I choked. I didn't trust her at all. What a huge stupidity, if someone was still using her as a messenger! She stirred up problems wherever she went.

But our protest didn't last long, because the prison director soon said, "We had nothing to do with it." Saliha had been arrested by civilian police and taken to the station. She had been searched and then released. When she arrived at Amasya, she probably expected us to welcome her warmly. She explained, "They searched me from head to toe"—she lifted her skirt—"even the seams! Then they asked where I was going, where I was from, who I wanted to visit." She liked playing the victim, liked to bask in admiration, liked to make a spectacle of herself. My God, what kind of mother had she been? You couldn't really be angry with her, but her insatiable need for recognition was exhausting.

But Muzaffer and I remained cool. "Don't come back here again," we said. "You're old and sick. If they arrested you on the road, nobody would even know."

I didn't give her my message for Şener, just a photo. "Greetings to Şener," I wrote on the back, "who does not wear a suit. Take care of yourself and look out for your health." Saliha took the photo and left.

I couldn't write anything else, lest I contradict Karasu's advice. In the end, Karasu's advice would be decisive, and logically, he was right. It wouldn't be easy, but we had to set new standards about military service. Still, I wished Şener would prove himself. Unconsciously, I was trying to get him to turn his 1984 weakness into a victory.

I told Muzaffer about my relationships with Hamili and Şener. I omitted nothing and prettified nothing. He sat and listened. He was my comrade, and I had no qualms about telling him everything, including my mistakes and weaknesses. I just wanted him to know. In my opinion, a romantic relationship shouldn't be kept secret, least of all if it consisted of nothing more than a mutual promise. Back in Diyarbakir I had wanted to tell Fuat and Samil, but Şener had advised against it: "The friends wouldn't be able to handle it. They'd assume you broke up with Hamili because of it. Or they wouldn't like it." Then he added, "Besides, no one wants to see you tied to a man. I know from my own experience, I didn't want it either."

But I'd always refused to be tied to a man. *This relationship is different,* I'd thought. Different how? I wasn't afraid of love, but Şener was afraid

of my love. He'd said so openly, to which I replied, "You can't be afraid
of love, love doesn't produce fear, so why are you afraid?" For him, my
love was both sacred and frightening. That was a contradiction, a ... I
didn't know, couldn't put it into words. It was just a feeling.

In love there should be no lies or roughness. Yes, I was a dreamer,
prone to illusions. My attitude toward love was utopian. Meanwhile I
thrived on conflict. A moment without struggle was like torture for me.
It was struggle that made life worth living and gave me strength.

I told Muzaffer I had an agreement with Şener, that "our relationship
will be proven in practice. Its only guarantee is our struggle." Besides
that, we had agreed that "whichever of us meets the chairman again first
will be the one to tell him about our relationship. The decision lies with
the chairman."

Muzaffer's blue-green eyes were shining—why? Did he want me not
to belong to anyone either? No, his eyes expressed honest affection and
restraint and deep comradely concern.

During our conversation, we had been holding hands. Now he put his
hands on each side of my head and pulled me close until our foreheads
bumped. "I don't say anything. Blue eyes don't betray feelings, and my
eyes are blue." I sensed he didn't favor this relationship. I wished he had
spoken to me candidly. Afterward we went for a long walk.

I belonged to nobody, but in the person I loved, I was looking for
something of me, of us. When I found it, I protected it more than I
protected myself. Risking, gambling, winning, or losing in love! I never
thought of love in those terms, but I seemed to pursue risks. Was loving
trouble like loving your own murderer?

After a while I got a long, detailed letter from Şener. He was to be
transferred from Tokat to Bayburt. He wrote that he initially refused to
wear a military uniform but then put it on. It was difficult but couldn't
be avoided:

> My sister, I have to admit a weakness to you—as you know, I cannot hide
> anything. I was up against a battalion commander, and at that moment I
> lost control and burst into tears. It wasn't good that he saw me cry. It was a
> moment of defeat, expressing helpless despair.

We discussed it in more letters. I signed mine "Your sister" and sent
them to an address in Europe he'd given me, from where they were
forwarded.

On the way from Tokat to Bayburt, he would pass near Amasya and the prison. Dungeons and military! News of his death would've shaken me less.

I thought of Cahide's father—maybe he could help. Koç Ali had a car. "Drive to Şener and talk to him," I said. "You and he even have the same surname—you can pretend to be a relative. Tell him he must defect from the military—he shouldn't stay there another day." To make sure he'd do what I said, I added, "The enemy will shoot him and claim he was trying to escape." Koç Ali agreed, and we gave him money, and he promised to drive to Tokat as soon as possible.

Soon thereafter I got a telegram from Şener: "I'm sitting in a restaurant with Cemil. It's like a vacation." The telegram had been sent from Antakya. So he had defected! I passed it on to Muzaffer. Everyone was happy. Şener had dodged another bullet—he just couldn't get caught!

Then another letter arrived, angry in tone. Apparently he'd had an argument with Yıldız Durmuş over the phone. She had criticized him for a certain word choice rather than showing understanding for his situation. "If things go on like this, the only thing I'll be able to do is to die. I won't go back to things that are hell on earth for me, even if they try to force me."

What did he mean? Why did he think he was so helpless? On the outside, a person could find a way to leave the country alone. I'd been helpless during my escape in Malatya, but that was different. Besides, he wasn't alone, he had his brother-in-law with him. His attitude was absurd. His panic was a sign of weakness. How pathetic that he was thinking about his own death! I was angry and worried, but most of all I was afraid he might do something stupid. I cried. And I was also annoyed at Yıldız—if only she'd been a little more constructive. I couldn't stop worrying.

Muzaffer got irritated with me. "I know him, he tends to panic, and he makes a racket when he doesn't like something. Don't worry, he's not gonna do anything, he's not a kid!"

After I calmed down a little, I sat down and wrote a long letter and criticized him harshly: "Why do you talk about death whenever things get a little tight for you? Or is that a threat? If you want to go, then go—go to hell!" It was the first time I'd written in such a tone. I thought it was the only way to bring him to his senses.

I sent it to the address in Europe. I don't know if he ever got it. At some point I found out he was in Greece, and in later letters, he described the Acropolis and the beauty of the sea. Then he said he was waiting to travel to the party academy [in the Beka'a valley]. This was the first reassuring news in months.

Planning to escape Amasya The nonpolitical female prisoners were transferred to another ward, a little farther away. On visiting days or on the way to the administration, they used the lower corridor of our section. The guards were responsible for both wards. Usually, they preferred to stay with the other women because they felt more comfortable there. Besides, we'd forbidden them to enter our ward without permission, except for search days. At first, they kept popping in, and we demanded that they not invade our lives. Several times we were able to pressure them to leave the ward.

[When it came to an escape attempt,] Amasya had many disadvantages. But some of the Acil prisoners were from Samsun [on the Black Sea], where there was a state hospital. I asked what they thought [about using it as a means of escape]. With support from outside, they said, an escape might be possible. The Acil comrades gladly promised to help. If the plan worked, it would be a good example of practical solidarity. "Turkish revolutionaries help Kurdish revolutionaries escape from the hospital," the announcement would read. Ah, just the thought was nice.

Getting me admitted to the hospital there was the main problem. I needed an oral surgeon to repair my Diyarbakir-mangled jaw. Doctors at Diyarbakir's military hospital had refused to treat it, but there was an oral surgeon in Samsun. The jaw treatment could justify my admission there.

While I was waiting for a reply, I came up with another plan. The prison director's apartment was adjacent to our ward. Its windows looked out onto the exercise yard, but there was no direct access. The front door led outside.

It seemed possible to dig a hole in the wall of the back cell into the cavity under the stairs to the director's apartment. We calculated the exact location and got to work. First, we removed the plaster from the wall. We had to be extremely careful, because every noise on the wall penetrated directly into the director's apartment and the lower guardroom. The guards meanwhile were used to listening at the walls and the floor to find out if a tunnel was being dug anywhere. We draped a blanket over the hole to conceal it, then a piece of particleboard.

We worked mainly during the daytime, as it was less noticeable. When a popular program was broadcast on TV in the evening, we used those hours. At that time, the series *Maria* was very popular. I seldom watched TV apart from the news, so my absence from the TV room wasn't striking. The TV was in the kitchen area on the lower floor, some distance from the spot where we worked the wall. We ordered art supplies, paint and canvas, so Cahide, with her artistic talent, could paint pictures and design patterns. The female guards were very interested, constantly busy with their own trousseaus, sewing, crocheting, and embroidering.

The cement content in the mortar between the bricks was high, so the mortar was as hard as steel. Apparently, the best cement in the world had been used to make the wall as stable as possible. We used spoons and other small metal objects, but we still felt like we were digging through a mountain with our fingernails. It would take forever. How could concrete be decomposed? We learned from Muzaffer to treat the wall with acid from a syringe but still made only slow progress.

We would need identity cards, and a camera to take our photos and someone to help us. On a visiting day, Yilmaz Dagli arrived from the academy and met us. He brought a short letter from Şener. He was to help us escape by taking care of the IDs. We changed our hairstyles, and he took several pictures. The whole affair was a gamble. We calculated how long we still needed for the wall and asked him to hurry.

One night we were awakened by slogan chants. A raid had discovered a tunnel in the section of the Dev-Sol prisoners. The next day the guards searched all the wards, looking for more tunnels, scrutinizing the floors. Fortunately, our hole was well camouflaged, covered with plaster.

Every day since Diyarbakir, I'd written in a diary. I wrote even during the time of torture, whenever possible, even on tiny pieces of paper, if that's all I had. Writing was both a duty and a pleasure. From time to time, I sent my diaries to Europe, along with my accumulated letters and texts, in large yellow envelopes. Some documents I passed on by hand. Hasan Atmaca and Yıldız were in Europe, as well as Cuma, surprisingly. I wrote hundreds of letters, to more people every day. I wrote to Şener, describing every moment of my life. I was so lonely, I used every chance to talk about the struggle and to connect with people, at least in writing. Hasan joked that the post office was operating solely for me. So as not to attract attention, I mailed my letters from various local post offices. Much later I learned that the enemy always opened my letters and copied them before sending them on, but since they always reached their destination, I'd never suspected.

Every letter I got was precious. Tearing up messages felt like destroying a living organism. If letters had to be destroyed for security reasons, I left this task to others. I liked collecting them. I sent all my correspondence with Muzaffer and the other friends in Amasya to the outside. Muzaffer wrote a lot too, describing our daily life. I wrote to him, to the outside, and to friends in other prisons.

In my journal, I stayed away from political analysis, and I couldn't research specific topics since we still didn't have the books we wanted. I'd hardly read anything for years. The hunger strikes played a role too, so I confined myself to writing about events or my feelings. Writing about prison, without filters, was relaxing. Expressing my feelings openly and unreservedly broke the everyday monotony. It became a daily need. I wrote about my thoughts, illusions, and dreams, my anger at the enemy, and my attitude to current events. In so doing, I resisted the enemy's spatial restrictions on me, his walling us in. I couldn't get enough of writing, it was an outlet for my surplus energy. Physical captivity stimulated my imagination and awakened longings for infinite space.

Contradictions   Newspapers and magazines arrived fairly regularly. *Serxwebun* published a series called "Confessions of Agents." One of the articles inside had previously been published in the TİKP's magazine. Now it was in our magazine, along with a photo of Cihangir on the front page. Underneath was the caption "M. Şener in court." A letter inside, titled "Claim of a Pesengci" [member of the PPKK], said Şener was an agent. It was published without comment. "Şener was punished," the letter said, then noted, "Mehmet Cahit Şener's sister Cahide is still in prison."

Of course, Cahide wasn't related to Şener at all—never mind that. And never mind that the photo showed Cihangir, not Şener. Why were they trying to create confusion? Even when Şener was still in prison, they'd used propaganda against him. Back in 1988, a prisoner from the 35th ward, one entrusted with our paperwork, unexpectedly crossed over to the administration and became a defector. After spending some time there, he changed his mind again and came back to the friends. He said he'd felt very bad about turning on the party and now regretted it.

But he claimed that the administration had told him, "Şener is one of us." We just assumed the enemy was deliberately spreading false rumors about Şener. "He's under criticism anyway," we told ourselves.

Many other groups and some of those who've left us are attacking him. The enemy has certainly heard about it from confiscated articles, and the defectors have surely told the enemy about our internal problems. They want to fuel suspicions about Şener. Why else would they have this guy tell us that Şener was working with them?

It seemed to us the enemy had sent this man back precisely to deliver this message. We were less concerned with his message than with the person.

Around that time Captain Abdullah Kahirman had asked Cahide Şener about her relationship to Mehmet Şener. "You've confessed, haven't you?" he barked at her. Yes, in the early years, under interrogation, her attitude had bordered on betrayal. The enemy kept reminding her of this weakness: "You surrendered a long time ago. Why are you still calling yourself PKK?" He was trying to humiliate her, to get her to cross over to the enemy. Or maybe he thought we didn't know about her problems and was telling us.

But we already knew about Cahide's behavior. Back in Siverek, she had suffered at the hands of the friends there for insisting on her own values in her relationship with Süleyman. The organization isolated her because of it. After she was arrested, the enemy tried to use that relationship for his purposes. Under torture, she had made statements and almost capitulated. But after 1983 she abandoned that behavior, and in court, she had defended herself as a patriot. She worked out her past problems with the Siverek friends in written discussions. She had argued with Yilmaz Uzun the most back in Siverek, but now he self-criticized his "narrow-minded and feudal behavior." Her relationship with the party was officially clarified, and the sanctions against her had been lifted. Her demeanor became increasingly radiant.

"Claim of a Pesengci" added up to an intention to publicly defame Şener. But why? I told Muzaffer and other friends about it. "Bastards! They've found a new way to create confusion." Why were they trying to raise doubts and distrust? It made me especially uneasy, since it coincided with discomfort about Şener that was already lurking in me.

Muzaffer immediately wrote back to me, "These bastards have some intention with this article. Don't worry too much about it." He knew me well. He used to say to me, "You just can't leave things alone—you always find something to be upset about." Once he said, "Even if we handed Sakine an independent Kurdistan on a platter, she'd find something wrong with it." That was an exaggeration, but he was right that I often did worry too much. Extreme emotionality never helped solve problems, as I also knew.

The next time I met Muzaffer, I asked him, what was the intention behind this article? Why did they pay so much attention to the claim of a Pesengite? Şener had left the country and was staying with the party—why was this mistrust being sown? Was it to signal that former prisoners were not to be trusted? Many questions passed through my mind, and I gave voice to them. This time Muzaffer didn't tell me not to worry but listened thoughtfully.

I was profoundly uneasy, writing to Samil, "I couldn't bear it if anything happened to any of you. It would just kill me." I told him the article about Şener had hit me hard. But he just criticized my emotionality, saying it prevented me from assessing reality politically and systematically.

Shortly thereafter, letters we received were full of speculation about who had betrayed the tunnel. The main focus was on Hasan Güllü and Sinan Caynak, who'd known about the tunnel, but supposedly didn't know the exact location.

And some mentioned another suspect: Şener. Apparently, rumors about him were circulating outside. I shared my concern about Şener with Karasu. Rumors had been circulating about him for a long time, I wrote to him, and it had been a mistake to have never cleared them up. All the speculation about Şener had to be stopped, I said. It had a bad effect on him, and I suggested informing the party. "You know him best," I wrote to Karasu, "you know his idiosyncrasies. He has a tendency to withdraw and say, 'If you don't trust me, then I'm done here.' I'll write to him, but that's not enough. You write to him too." I meant well—I'd always tried to protect Şener, to keep him from making mistakes. But if he had an unknown side, it had to be revealed. The most contradictory feelings blazed in me.

Şener and the tunnel! The very idea was horrendous. Again and again I thought about how the tunnel had been discovered that day. I asked the women friends what they remembered, and together we reconstructed the timeline for that day. They wondered why I kept asking the same questions and cared about these details.

"When the Special Forces entered the 35th ward, didn't they look downstairs first?" I asked. "If they knew the location of the tunnel, wouldn't they have gone directly to the fourth floor?" The search had turned up nothing all morning. In the afternoon, after they got new information by telephone, they continued their search and finally discovered the tunnel entrance. Soil had been drizzling from a crack in the wall, and all they had to do was follow this trail. This point calmed me. Even if the enemy had delayed the discovery of the tunnel in order to conceal someone's treachery, he wouldn't have delayed for so long. And we would've seen through the playacting.

I thought of Saliha. That woman really was a witch. I'd never liked her. I was nice to her, called her Mother, hugged her, and let my picture be taken with her, but I'd never liked her. I maintained my connection to her only because of Şener, who was very close to his mother. Sometimes he got annoyed with her and I'd even seen him scold her, but whenever anyone spoke ill of her, it bothered him. "It would be wrong to draw conclusions from the rumors about her," he'd once written to the outside. "She's temperamental and garrulous."

"I do as you advise"   Then a letter from Şener arrived. He began by telling me the chairman had criticized him, but that he also gave him strength.

> The uncle [Apo] provides excellent support, but that's not the point. There are a few things I can't understand or explain. I'm still uneasy and hesitant to speak, but above all, I am sorry I haven't yet fulfilled my promise.

He was referring to our mutual promise that whichever of us met the chairman first would tell him about our relationship. "There have been so many other things that I haven't mentioned it to him yet, but I'll do so at the next opportunity, believe me."

Şener's usual pattern was to bring up a subject, analyze its sociological, psychological, artistic, and aesthetic aspects, and then throw it out for discussion. In every letter he took up a different topic. But this time he wrote that things weren't going well for him. "What does it mean to live?" he asked, then said he identified with the character Pavel in the [Bulgarian] novel *Tabak* [by Dimitar Dimov]:

> If things go on like this, I'll end up like Pavel. Some people seem cut out for this. It's not about whether I can handle it here—that's as easy as walking from one room to another. But there are things that can drive a person into a rage. Without the uncle, I'd go crazy. He supports me the most.

I shared the letter with Muzaffer and asked what he thought. "You know Şener—his sectarian streak must have surfaced," he said. "He likes that role the best anyway. He doesn't know his way around outside and probably never expected to be misunderstood."

In the novel *Tabak*, Pavel belongs to an organization that distrusts him—some aspects of his personality don't fit with its principles, and he is excluded. His brother Boris is a tobacco producer who collaborates with imperialist states, even with German fascists, and is later killed by revolutionaries. Pavel fights in the Spanish Civil War and then returns to Bulgaria, where he takes an active role in the war front. What was Şener trying to tell me? He must have been having serious problems. When I wrote back, I called him out:

> What do your hints about Pavel mean? Why do you always insist on being misunderstood? You're the only one who can change the situation. If the "uncle" really supports you so much, then focus on him and not on the others.

I told him never to write about this again and that I expected to hear from him about more positive developments.

Again and again Şener emphasized how much he needed my letters. I always wrote back to him, but what could my letters, or Karasu's, do? After all, Şener was at the Party Academy. Surely he could identify with Pavel as a right-thinking militant. So why did he always get embroiled in arguments? Why did suspicions always swirl around him? Did any criticism ever get through to him? My doubts wouldn't leave me alone. Şener was being talked about all the time. I made it my mission to get to the bottom of it. Şener's negative side attracted me to him as much as his strengths and abilities. That was a contradiction—and even this contradiction attracted me.

My affection for Şener had developed amid all the contradictions and conflicts of that time. They shaped our relationship. So it was all the more important for me to find concrete evidence that either confirmed or refuted the suspicions about him.

Our relationship was like a mosaic: on one side was an idealization that allowed for no discrepancies and contradictions, and on the other, a reality marked by contradictions and conflicts. I wasn't worried about the future of our relationship. I was worried about Şener himself.

I had developed a warm conversational style in prison that the other prisoners appreciated. I had good standing among them, and I was generally popular. But I was so important to Şener that he adapted to my views on every subject. I was hungry for work and full of energy, and Şener had a rare talent for implementing my plans. "I do what you advise," he said, and he really did. He asked me for advice and made no decision without my approval. In our letters he kissed my hands, and I kissed his eyes, his forehead, and his head. Our relationship gave him a sense of security. It protected him and gave him influence within the organization. He regarded me as a kind of guarantee and had been aware of this benefit from the beginning. He needed me. So it was only logical that he revered me and accepted my standards for love without contradiction. For my part, I was always impressed. He was a force in a difficult environment, engaging in ways that appealed to my feelings, raising the same questions that were at the center of my interest.

Many former prisoners, upon leaving prison, had turned out to be disappointments—they stayed at home or got involved with trivialities. So it was always good news when a former prisoner reached the party and actively participated in the work. Now that Şener was at the academy, my expectations were high. I wanted him to apply his skills to party work and thereby gain influence. I placed great hopes in him and desperately wanted him to succeed.

Once upon a time we'd knitted sweaters for the chairman and sent them to him as an expression of our love for him and our longing to see him. Now I knitted a sweater for Şener and sent it to him along with a letter in which I expressed what our relationship meant to me. I felt no doubts. For me, I wrote, love was synonymous with life and struggle. I had mostly overcome my earlier concerns that I would regret taking this step. I admitted, so to speak, that he had convinced me. I admitted that our relationship was important to me.

Probably the fact that he was at the party academy and thus in direct contact with the party gave me a certain sense of security. Responsibility for Şener now lay with Şener himself, and with the party. My worries hadn't disappeared entirely, but I trusted that the party could solve the problems. My only responsibility was to energize Şener and encourage him in our relationship. My good intentions were not entirely unrealistic. On the one hand, our relationship was boundless and infinite; on the other, I always expected a break. Both expectations reinforced my sense of attachment to him. I never felt closer to him than during this time of intense contradiction.

Love Some of the friends knew about my relationship with Şener and even read our letters. I wrote to Hasan and Yıldız about prison life and urged them both to forward my letters to Şener. I could imagine how much he needed them.

Around this time I told Cahide about it. She was surprised and irritated, saying, "I suspected something like that from him, but not from you." I told her this relationship was different, but she seemed unpersuaded. We didn't talk much about it after that.

By now she'd been engaged to Süleyman for over ten years. He was sincere and unpretentious, and their relationship was intense. She had defended her relationship with him even when it had led to grave consequences in Siverek. During the time of torture, it had given her strength, like a tree branch that she could hold on to. After the period of torture, however, she began to see it through different eyes. She realized that her relationship was one of the causes of her own defeats.

Now she wanted to end the relationship, she told me. In 1988 she had a chance to speak directly to Süleyman, and she told him the relationship was hampering her growth. From Amasya, she wrote critical letters to him. She explained that she'd changed and that it was wrong to regard a relationship as the immutable destiny of a lifetime. Was it love to wear a ring for ten years? Did love play a role in their relationship at all? What was its foundation? She was right, but I felt that her reasoning was influenced by a petty-bourgeois worldview—she hadn't entirely abandoned her childhood values when she started working with the PKK. One cause of her problems had been her selfish, individualized approach to her relationship with Süleyman.

I had had a similar reaction to Gönül. She hadn't been straightforward from the beginning, either about her party work or her love relationship. An unpredictable rage lurked behind her allegedly intimate bond that almost led her to sell the relationship to the enemy. In both cases, her motives were less revolutionary ideals than a petit-bourgeois thirst for adventure. As for Aysel, her approach to love was shaped by her general fatalism and her traditional mindset. Her long deep sighs reflected the reality of a repressed, enslaved woman. For her, love was like the desperation of an orphan clinging to someone who listens to her.

"Tunnel discovered"   The prison administration refused to transfer me to the hospital in Samsun. We were allowed to visit doctors only in Amasya, not in any other province. Hasan Can was a fox, he became suspicious and almost paranoid. Of course, he wasn't entirely wrong, because we constantly stirred up unrest. The cells were searched frequently. "I've run many prisons and there were a lot of women everywhere, but none frightened me like you," he said. Had he noticed something? we worried.

Meanwhile we made good progress on the wall, and the IDs arrived. They were fine. We'd arranged for suitable clothing. The friends around Muzaffer had requested a fashion catalog, which caused a stir. People probably thought that we'd become interested in the latest fashion or were planning a fashion show in the dungeon. The gossip annoyed me, but Muzaffer stayed calm as usual. In any case, Cahide and I would leave the grounds as smartly dressed ladies.

Guests often came and went from the director's apartment. He seemed to hold regular events that were well attended. Our escape would take place on one of those days. We would meet Cahide's father and go to Samsun [on the Black Sea, near Acil]. We had chosen Samsun on the advice of the Acil friends, because it was easier to hide on the Black Sea. If necessary, the Acil comrades would help us.

We worked meticulously on each brick. We had to be careful not to damage the plaster on the outer wall, despite our impatience.

Our last days with Muzaffer and the others were drawing near. Not everyone knew about our escape plan, but tense expectation hung in the air. Muzaffer was glad for us but also seemed depressed. "Don't forget us when you get out," he said. "This damn place is unbearable. There's always a way out, it just has to be found, and the friends have to be pressured a bit to do their part. But whatever Dev-Sol can do, we can do too." He continued, "We'll have to deal with a few fascists. The torturers would be a little more restrained if one or two actions were taken against them." We all knew the targets he meant. We certainly believed in our success and were excited accordingly.

While we were talking, a guard came in and announced to me, "You have a visitor." It wasn't a visiting day—who would it be? Someone from the public prosecutor? Or someone who'd come from far away? Sometimes exceptions were made for them, or for those who had some important reason for the visit. Excited, I rushed to the visiting booth.

Much to my surprise, [my ex-husband] Baki appeared on the other side of the glass. My mood darkened right away.

"Hello, Sakine, how are you? We haven't seen each other for a long time," he said.

"I'm fine," I said. "What are you doing here? What makes you think you have the right to visit me? Did you ask my permission?"

"We're related. You're my uncle's daughter. Surely that gives me the right to come and ask how you are."

"Not even my parents are allowed to visit me against my will! Oh, and why do you write to me all the time? It's very strange, especially since I've never answered you! I read your first letter, then you always wrote the same thing as if you were obsessed. After that I tore up your letters without reading them. There's no connection between you and me. Kinship is not binding for me. Leave now. I have nothing to discuss with you."

Crying, he replied, "I've come so far—let's talk a bit. Okay, maybe I don't mean anything to you, I respect that."

Again I asked him to leave. He refused. Finally, I got up and left the booth. "Don't you have any pride at all? How can you abase yourself so? You know I don't want to see you. I don't want to kick you in front of the enemy, but you've given me no choice."

I returned to the friends and told them what happened. "What a pest!" Muzaffer said. "Where did you find this guy? You've had to deal with this plague for years!" Yes, where had I found him?

Cahide said, "I've been destroying his letters to you without showing them to you. They're unbearable. He's married and has kids, but he's still after Sakine. What a guy!"

I wouldn't have objected to friendly or even familial contact. For me, the end of a relationship is no reason to be hostile. But Baki didn't function at that level. He had long since created a new world, but in his feudal obsession, he returned to the same point again and again.

It bothered me that he didn't consider me human and revolutionary, merely a woman he had been with years ago. He still wanted to revive the relationship with the woman I had been back then. It was disgusting and intolerable. I wouldn't dream of talking to him about it—it made no sense. And I don't like it when someone tries to arouse pity.

One evening while everyone else was watching *Maria* on TV, I was working on the wall. I was hurrying. The longer we waited, the greater our risk of being caught. Emine paced the corridor, keeping watch. Suddenly a guard called her into the kitchen and locked her in there. Another called more guards from the corridor. Loud steps pounded from the stairs. The women in the kitchen hammered their fists on the door and chanted: "Stop the repression!" They were trying to warn me.

I immediately stopped work, covered the hole, and tried to hide my tools. But before I could finish, a horde of guards stormed into the ward like a hungry pack. They pushed the bed aside and kicked the wall. They spotted the hole. I sat in a chair, trying to stay calm.

The director shouted, "So, you wanted to escape! Yeah, we've been waiting outside for you for three days now. It would've been much more fun to nab you that way." Feverishly, the guards searched the entire ward. One pointed to the wall, "Look, director, they've hung pictures of Apo. There are photos of terrorists everywhere—that's forbidden!" He raised his arm to tear down the pictures.

I jumped up. "Don't you dare touch those! If you do, all hell will break loose! Okay, you've raided us and discovered our secret. But that's no reason to act like this. We're revolutionaries, and even in jail, we stay creative. Your job is to stop us. Now you've done your job, so don't get carried away!"

The director gaped dumbfounded. "Oh, it's too much. You're guilty, and yet you still act like you're strong. My employees haven't touched anything, and now you're threatening them."

But my warning had been effective—the guards got more cautious. They discovered tools and overturned a cabinet where we'd hidden some texts. I got scared but managed to distract them through conversation.

The women friends called from below, "Sakine, what's going on? What are you doing, are you all right?"

"Don't worry, I'm fine," I answered.

Now I heard voices coming from the back. Muzaffer and the other men were worried. I deliberately didn't answer, so they would put pressure on the administration. But I wouldn't have been able to make myself understood anyway.

Because although I tried to appear calm, inside my heart was breaking. Once again we'd failed. How had they found out about our plan? *We've been waiting for you for three days*, the director had said. But how did they know? Had they heard us? Maybe they'd been listening in the director's apartment. The walls were thin and all noises went through. If you put your ear to a prison wall, it always sounded like hundreds of people living in a basement vault.

A search log was created: "Tunnel discovered." The women shut in the kitchen threatened, "Open the door now, or we'll set a fire!" They kept up their slogan chants. After the guards finished their work, they opened the door.

I informed Muzaffer. The men felt bad for us and tried to comfort us, saying, "Don't take it to heart."

New legal charges were brought against us because of the escape attempt. Oh, some trial or other was always under way against me. They'd even brought charges against us for the papers we'd thrown out of the transport vehicle en route to Amasya. Each slip of paper was considered a "separatist propaganda pamphlet." That trial was still going on. And now we'd have the "tunnel trial" too.

These trials took place in prison, since the enemy was afraid to take us outside to the courthouse. Four of us were on trial. Our statements were taken. I took the lead: "It was a hiding place. I created it." Everyone laughed. "What did you want such a big hiding place for?" they asked. "I wanted to hide our texts. For the long term. That's why it's so big. We could have kept books there too." Even the men friends burst out laughing. I stuck to my testimony, but of course no one believed me.

How had the enemy learned about the escape plan? Had Koç Ali [Cahide's father] betrayed us? It had been a mistake to bring him in on it. Oh, if only we'd kept our mouths shut! But it was too late—we should have thought of that sooner.

From prison to prison   The year [1989] was almost over. A year had passed since our banishment from Diyarbakir. One day a message ball was thrown to us, saying, "Muzaffer is to be transferred." We erupted into slogan chanting, as we had so many times before. These transfers from one prison to another—how helpless the enemy must be! It took all his might just to stay in control of the prisons! It was like a ridiculous war. We demanded to speak to Muzaffer but were refused. Once I heard his voice through the door flap: "Sakine!" A guard said, "It breaks your heart, the way that blue-eyed boy cries." Muzaffer was transferred without our seeing each other one last time.

Presumably more transfers would follow, and I sensed I'd be one of them. The tunnel would be reason enough. My intuition was confirmed a few days later when I was told I'd be transferred to Çanakkale. Muzaffer had been taken to Antep, in Kurdistan, but I was to go west. The enemy's naked rage underlay this choice, as he sought to punish me relentlessly.

I left Amasya. Maybe I'd find a chance to escape during the transport. I secretly carried my fake ID with me and some money—maybe I'd need it. But I was taken straight to Çanakkale without stopping, a long, arduous journey.

The day I arrived, the friends welcomed me and joked about my transfer: "What's the problem? You'll be with us now." Actually, they

19 Cansız with unidentified women prisoners at Çanakkale, c.1990.

were right. Why was I so fanatical sometimes? I had comrades in all the prisons! Even banishment had a positive side.

There were friends in Çanakkale—I'd written to some of them. From the PKK, Zübeyde was there, Zübeyde was as brisk as ever. She had been in Antep for a while and had been transferred to Çanakkale along with Mürvet of the TİKB. The women's section also had about ten women of the Turkish Left and some nonpolitical prisoners as well.

The Çanakkale prisoners were [politically] diverse. There were about 30 from the PKK, including Celal Özalp (Numan), Cemal Şerik, Burhan, Mehmet Çınar (Resul), Deza (Hamit Kankılıç), Dursun Ali, Can, and Sadrettin. Dursun Ali hadn't changed at all. I'd last seen him in 1977, when I visited him at the prison at Ağri. Now he had crossed the country westward to Çanakkale, with stops in Erzincan and Niğde. These constant transfers were taking us all to so many places in Kurdistan and Turkey! We joked about which of us held the record. Dursun Ali took the prize as our "senior officer," but I outdid him in number of prisons.

I'd met Can during the hunger strike negotiations in February 1988. He had been arrested with Kemal Pir, when they were stopped at a military control. Mahsum Korkmaz (Agit) had been in the pickup truck too, but he escaped by jumping out while it was still moving. Now Can was ill. His brain was damaged during the death fast, and he was being treated medically. The friends said his condition was critical, although when I saw him, he seemed lively enough.

I met Numan, that is Celal Özalp, for the first time. He had been captured in the time of Sabri. I didn't know anybody from this group well. After their brief trials, they'd been sent to various prisons.

Cemal Şerik and Burhan were both Çanakkale veterans. They'd never been transferred and were part of the inventory, so to speak. Cemal looked after the younger prisoners. His brother Hasan Şerik was in Antep. I once visited their family home in Tuzluçayır but met only their sister. I met Hasan during the press service in Elazığ. In Tuzluçayır, Cemal had been the youngest PKK member but now he had grown up, no longer the boy of yore.

Burhan was a grandson of Aga Bakil, who had been killed in Dersim for being an agent. It was true that Bakil had had close contacts with the state, but Burhan said, "He wasn't an agent, at least he didn't deserve death for that reason, he was just shot." Burhan was a quiet and reflective comrade.

Prisoners at Çanakkale had no internal visiting rights. When I told the friends about the setup in Amasya and Diyarbakir, they brightened. "We could do that here too," I said.

Can asked, "How's your relationship with Hamili?"

I answered, "Not good. We'll talk about it later."

We learned that the enemy was cracking down on Eskişehir. The count-off system was to be reintroduced, and two prisoners had already died there. We sorely needed to discuss forms of prison resistance. We needed a binding and overarching policy, one that made our resistance actions consistent with the struggle outside.

We were clear that we would always resist hostile attacks on principles we'd fought for. But hunger strikes and death fasts weren't always the right method. In some prisons, hunger strikes were called even for minor issues, and then other prisons had to follow suit. We criticized allowing the enemy to force us to use these methods. Muzaffer had raised the issue back in Amasya when he'd asked, *Aren't there any other methods, or are we just not creative enough?*

It was a sensitive topic, and suddenly the room was filled with accusations of "right-wing" tendencies. We had to get to the crux of the problem, otherwise the discussion ran the risk of going to extremes. We needed a binding discussion to design a timely and workable resistance plan. We formulated some proposals, and even though communication between prisons was limited, we sent them to Karasu and to other prisons. The sharpest opposition came from prisoners in Aydın—they accused us of being under the influence of the Turkish Left. But their criticism was extreme. The prisoners in Ceyhan generally agreed but believed the Eskişehir system had to be prevented. Antep also agreed with us and made specific suggestions.

Some, in response to our argument, called into question the resistance as a whole, if it was reduced to hunger strikes. But resistance is indispensable to life. Even simple patriots knew that there could be no life without resistance. The PKK struggle had raised this awareness. The matter had to be handled creatively and address all aspects of resistance, its conditions, goals, and consequences.

While we were still discussing the practical implementation, a statement arrived from the chairman on "perspective of the struggle in the prisons." Occasionally, copies of *Serxwebun* or *Berxwedan* arrived, and we were able to read the chairman's analyses. But this letter was extraordinary and of the utmost importance to us. It was addressed to "all comrades who resist in prisons" and was signed "the party leadership." It was also a Newroz message that arrived late because of the recent arrests.

The chairman said, "A decade of significant fighting lies behind us, and at the beginning of the new year, I send you my greetings and use this occasion to point out some developments." He said the prison resistance policy required careful thought. It was not right to constantly resort to hunger strikes and death fasts. Prisoners should definitely resist major attacks on them, but they should focus on strengthening the struggle outside prison and on supporting party organs. We should use art and literature to communicate about prison resistance to a wide audience. In addition, we should contact and try to activate democratic institutions. We might need new forms of organization to frame the political front outside the enemy's control and to involve all social groups in the struggle. Within this framework, any form of self-initiative was conceivable. The letter ended, "I wish you success and send you my love and respect."

We were overjoyed. It boosted our confidence that the chairman's views matched our own. As soon as we could, we forwarded the chairman's letter to the other prisons, including those where prisoners had criticized us so sharply. Some of the forwarded copies arrived promptly, others were delayed. In some places, forwarding wasn't possible, but we at least made sure to convey the content.

Along with the chairman's letter, a text written by Şener arrived, with similar content, addressing the tasks of prisoners. He elaborated on the chairman's views about organized prison resistance. "The chairman must have asked him to write this," we speculated. Of course we were happy about it. I concluded that Şener had become involved in party work.

Around this time, [the former leftist] Doğu Perinçek interviewed the chairman and published the interview in his magazine [Aydınlık]. I didn't trust Perinçek. In fact, I found him repellent, a political showman. Now he was presenting himself as the courageous politician who visited the PKK leader. The Turkish Left denounced the interview, saying it meant the PKK was now somehow aligned with Doğu. "Doğu is a great opportunist with an unclear identity," raged some leftists. "It's incorrect even to talk to him." But the interview had no more political significance than an earlier interview by the journalist Mehmet Ali Birand.

Only Turkish and Kurdish leftists could be so contradictory as to abstain from an alliance with us yet also vehemently condemn our contact with others! They had previously denounced our contact with İsmail Beşikçi [a pro-Kurdish author and human rights advocate]. Beşikçi was a sincere and warm-hearted advocate of the peoples. His views on Kurdistan, our struggle, and the chairman were factually sound, based on friendship and brotherhood. Their attacks on Beşikçi and our relationship with him, in the name of the revolution, said more about them than about him.

The issue of *Aydinlik* with Doğu Perinçek's interview of the chairman also contained an interview with "Camp Commander Metin" (later identified as Şahin Balic). Some of his comments surprised and disturbed us. To Doğu's question, "Is there torture in this camp?" Metin replied, "There's no torture, but sometimes we punch someone in the stomach to find something out."

We were stunned. A friend read the passage aloud and fumed,

> What kind of camp commander is that? This bastard must be torturing people. No PKK revolutionary commander would ever give such a stupid answer—it's gangster talk! We have to write a criticism and pass it on to the party. Such guys shouldn't be allowed to talk to journalists, least of all on such sensitive subjects. That Doğu is a fox—he doesn't ask questions out of the blue. He must know something. His magazine has often claimed that the PKK shoots agents in its own ranks.

We suspected there were discrepancies between the party's understanding and practice in its actions against banditry.[8] The enemy exploited this contradiction. "Some actions even contribute to the spread of banditry," we said. We repeatedly denied that the PKK was responsible for such actions and even condemned them in court. Later, it turned out that agents who had infiltrated our ranks were behind them. They were a big problem for the party.

The chairman, in his analyses, criticized the cadres' practical work. Meanwhile we focused on his expositions of his views and discussed them and sent our critiques to the party. "If we're wrong, the party will tell us," we said. But sometimes our word choices were interpreted to mean that we thought we knew better than the chairman. [And sometimes we got too far ahead.] In 1988 we had denounced Hüseyin Yıldırım's treachery in court before the party issued its statement—it led to speculation that we were representing our own line. We did a self-criticism right away, but we would make the same mistake again in the next period. Some of us did tend to be know-it-alls.

Meanwhile I was relieved to see Şener's face amid others in the photos in Doğu's magazine. It put to rest the negative rumors about him. Can saw my joy and shared it. "Şener's star seems to be rising again," he said. "That's good, and if it works out and he applies himself, he can be of great use." We continued to write letters, and I continued to keep my journal.

Cahide warned me that the enemy inspected everything we'd sent from Amasya. We'd given the guard sealed envelopes, which he'd mailed. Wouldn't the recipients have noticed if the envelopes had been opened? But it was certainly possible to open and reseal envelopes without leaving a trace. Presumably it would be no different in Çanakkale. We could also mail letters via the administration, but there were often delays. And even though we wrote in code, it was difficult to avoid inadvertently disclosing information. In any case, we circulated important news in other ways. If my journal had fallen into the enemy's hands, it could have given him information about my strengths and weaknesses.

Karasu wrote to me, warning that I should pay attention to the wording in my messages.

> We know you and your feelings, but others might misunderstand. You're very open and emotional, but conditions are not the same everywhere, and we have to be careful. Don't get me wrong, I have no problem with it, but you make a very emotional impression on the outside friends, who are more likely to be looking for political texts.

As I read it, I sensed how difficult it must have been for him to write it and how hard he had tried not to hurt my feelings. Although it did hit a nerve, I understood Karasu's criticism of my emotionality and realized I had to be more careful.

In the past, I had asked Yıldız to read my texts and tell me what she thought of them. She once told me that my letters were imitations of Rosa Luxemburg's letters to her lover. I thought this criticism was unfair and based on a misjudgment. My letters all had the same style. I could like and admire people without imitating them. Others' positive qualities sometimes gave me more pleasure than the individuals themselves, but imitation would have been repugnant. How could Yıldız have said such a thing? How could she regard my naturalness as imitative?

20 Cansız with unidentified women prisoners at Çanakkale, c.1990.

Still, I took her criticism seriously and got angry at myself. I stopped
writing in the journal but didn't want to send what I'd written so far to
the outside. I didn't want to destroy it either, so I handed it over to the
men:

> Can you take care of this? I can't. If my words give rise to discussion and
> criticism and I'm accused of a petit-bourgeois imitation of Rosa, I won't
> write anymore. My journals reflect every moment of our lives, and perhaps
> they have no meaningful political content, but they do reflect our emotional
> reality. But some friends seem less interested in this content than in my word
> choices. [As for my letters,] I always write to "my Yıldız" or "my Hasan." All
> my letters end with kisses and hugs, everyone in prison is used to it, but for
> those on the outside, such expression may violate their morality.

The friends replied,

> Not all criticisms are correct. The criticism of your alleged petit-bourgeois
> ideas and the charge of imitation are minor. You do sometimes react with
> too much emotion, and you tend to subjectivism. You were subjective
> when you were analyzing your relationship with your family. But your
> valuations are sometimes too detailed, obstructing your view of the totality
> of a political matter, which can lead to erroneous conclusions.

They were right. I usually formed opinions based on first impressions.
I lacked the patience to connect small events and the big picture in

the right way. I acted and made judgments rashly, without taking precautions or foreseeing the consequences. I lacked the stamina to piece fragments together. Against this criticism, all the positive aspects of my actions faded to the background.

"Internal reckonings" Meanwhile on the outside, every day the newspapers and TV reported on the PKK's guerrilla struggle. The coverage was designed to discredit the movement, but we could see that the Serhildan in Cizre, Nusaybin, Kerboran, and many other places was having a great impact. It was spreading to the big cities and was increasingly anchored in the people. Visitors updated us further. These developments outside gave us a sense of power.

And they affected other groups' views of us. The expansion of our struggle overcame many prejudices. It became normal and even inevitable for people who called themselves revolutionary to look to the reality of Kurdistan. We wanted to have friendly if critical relationships with other groups and to develop a minimal basis for common struggle against the enemy.

Now various political groups were discussing the formation of a united struggle. Programs were drafted, but they were usually rejected before the first practical step could be taken. Then more discussion would follow. We kept trying to be optimistic.

In Çanakkale and elsewhere, different groups often worked together on hunger strikes. But some groups kept their distance from us and still narrowly protected their own interests. Dev-Sol itself closed itself off to us entirely—they considered themselves superior to all other groups. They especially despised our "petit-bourgeois nationalism," although they took us more seriously than other groups did. After [their leader] Dursun Karatas escaped [from prison],[9] Dev-Sol initiated a "new phase" outside that involved "internal reckonings." We saw the frightening effects in Çanakkale.

[Ali Akgün was a Dev-Sol member.] I'd known him back in Elazığ— he'd been called "Gavur Ali" then.[10] He'd been the kind to always stir things up—my impression of him in those days wasn't very good. But he'd been in prison for a long time, and I heard he'd changed a lot.

Gavur Ali came from Kurdistan, so he couldn't be indifferent to the events there. Lately, he'd been discussing the Kurdish question with us. But he was also a senior cadre of Dev-Sol and risked being declared a traitor, so he was careful to confine his discussions. When relatives from Europe visited him, he said it was necessary to adopt the right attitude toward the revolution in Kurdistan.

To us, he frankly expressed his concerns:

> I realize that when I talk about principled contradictions, I make myself a target to certain people. I've officially communicated my thoughts to the party outside and have not yet received an answer. I've been told it will be discussed later.

The PKK men around him, who knew him well, told him, "We respect that you want to formally solve your problem within the organization. But this delay is worrying us. If your suspicions are right, you don't have to stay with Dev-Sol. You can come to our ward."

Gavur replied, "No, I'll stay where I am, no matter what it costs." That was our last conversation with him.

Gavur Ali knew he was going to die, but his pride left him no choice. He was murdered in Çanakkale prison with 11 knife-wounds. It was a cruel reckoning. That day everybody talked only about him and his tragedy. He was buried in Elazığ, the place he loved most.

Analyses from the chairman   Sometimes I complained,

> Resolutions are constantly being made outside, but we don't even get to read the party writings regularly. Even at this point we still have to devise ways to smuggle them into prison. There's a lack of ambition out there, much is just talk. Decisions taken at congresses and conferences are not implemented.

With much effort, we managed to get more analyses from the chairman, and we got verbatim transcripts of his dialogues with friends at the Party Academy. They gave us insights into the problems of practical work. It was obvious that the behavior of many cadres was causing trouble for the chairman and having a negative impact on the struggle. His criticisms were serious and comprehensive, even tough. He dealt with the problems, analyzing the work areas and the individuals, and demanded constructive solutions.

He wrote an important analysis of the period after August 15, in which he criticized the cadres' behavior. "If we'd correctly interpreted the events of 1985," he wrote, "we could have used them to create the conditions for a general uprising, accelerating the victory of the revolution in Turkey and Kurdistan." In our discussions, we tried to understand just what had happened during this period. It was deeply regrettable that the chairman's analysis reached us only now. His critique was understandable and constructive.

One issue he raised was the nature of guerrilla action. The guerrillas had raided villages and taken extreme actions against the village guards. It didn't match our fighting style. We came to the conclusion that such actions harmed our movement. And they extended the basis for the village guards. It put the party under pressure, and the enemy used this for its propaganda. It would have been better—if harder—to attack the enemy's main pillars.

We shared the chairman's texts with prisoners from other political groups, since we assumed they could benefit from them. But apparently no other revolutionary leader dealt so intensively with the errors in the work. They had difficulty grasping the significance of this approach, and the severity of his arguments surprised them. "If we were to criticize each other that way, there'd be none of us left," they said.

The transcripts opened the danger that outsiders or the enemy might use them to discredit us. "When transcribing, the friends could have omitted some of the curses, even if the chairman used them," we murmured. "It would've been better if they'd left them out, as these dialogues will circulate, and many outsiders don't really grasp our reality."

The curse words were regrettable, but what made us angry were the causes of his fury. We were more concerned with their content. Painstakingly, we tried to understand the issues that he raised. The problems were serious, and the criticisms were correspondingly harsh. We had to make a correct assessment.

We carefully formulated our own opinions of the dialogues, and we sent our criticisms and suggestions to the party. We didn't take issue with the content—we meant only to urge the friends responsible for publication to edit more carefully. We sealed our message and labeled it, "Not public, for the uncle's eyes only." We wanted to avoid it being read everywhere and possibly misused. The enemy would use any means to discredit the chairman.

Prison writings   The chairman's writings inspired us to take this kind of work more seriously, to write about our imprisonment. Many of us liked to write, but not everyone was able to describe the Diyarbakir dungeon. Years wouldn't have been enough to write a complete picture, but those who had been at Diyarbakir felt a great responsibility to contribute to a public assessment. So each of us who tried could sketch only a small part of reality.

Prisoners read novels, stories, poems, and investigations. Gezgör was asked for the texts he'd written in Diyarbakir. In Antep, Muzaffer was interviewed by a Dev-Yol prisoner, resulting in a text of a thousand pages. He sent a copy to us in Çanakkale. We read it carefully and sent him our detailed corrections.

Everyone who wrote a text sent it out for publication at their own discretion. But prison writers had obligations. They might reflect the personal opinions of individuals, but they were also about shared events. In addition, we had a party line, and the revolutionary work of publishing literature and art couldn't be arbitrary. Given that pressure, great caution was needed, and we all felt it, but too much worry could lead to self-censorship.

We needed a system that could help make the wealth of texts available to the public and also control the publication of texts from prison. Finally, we decided to found a committee to supervise and edit all writings intended for publication.

Years earlier our fierce resistance to isolation cells had had the result of emptying them—our demand had been enforced. Now prisoners wanted to voluntarily transfer there to write in peace and solitude. Prisoners had paid a steep and cruel price demanding the closing of the cells—comrades had even lost their lives in the struggle. So it was astonishing that writers now wanted to live there voluntarily.

Mehmet Cimen, in Çanakkale, was one of them. He declared himself a writer, although he had yet to produce any work. He grew a beard and styled himself as an intellectual. Living among friends was difficult, and he seemed a bit mysterious. A person who deals with art and literature has a mind marked by beauty, diversity, and creativity—he is attractive and alive. But Mehmet Cimen had certain qualities for which he was criticized. When he asked to work in a former isolation cell, his proposal was judged to contain a desire to avoid life, and it was rejected.

Many prisoners had similar characteristics. One tragic reality of Turkish prison life was that some prisoners turned their back on politics, turned away from the organization and gave up hope. Instead of organizing, they opted for individualism. They manufactured alcoholic drinks from various ingredients, or they proposed to father a child in prison.

Those who gave in to selfish demands and desires in life suffered severe defeats in politics. Their disregard for principles in life had a direct impact on their position in the organization. Mehmet Cimen experienced a nervous breakdown. Trying to hold him and influence him would have been of limited use. Our constant concern was that the enemy could exploit such characters, so we tried to deescalate any issues quickly, even if our solutions hardly met revolutionary standards and were rarely profound or radical.

My conversations with friends often centered on a future outside prison walls.

For me, imprisonment had become unbearable. Never had I so ached to be outside. The mountains, the Serhildan, the chairman's analyses magically attracted me. The idea that the revolution could surprise us while we were in the dungeon was beautiful, as it showed how close we were to victory. But I felt a burning desire to experience this intoxicating development in the movement's nerve centers, places that were in my wildest yearnings. How could I get involved in the ongoing events from prison? Nothing seemed satisfying.

Leyla [Zana] came to visit, saying, "Let's leave the country and go to the party." I said, "That won't work," and explained that Mehdi Zana was furious at us. He had even accused us of stealing Leyla from him. "It's not us," we'd said, "it's the revolution that sweeps her away." The women of Kurdistan had literally awakened to life and joined the revolution in droves, and Leyla was one of them. But "Xalo" blamed us, and certain people spread weird rumors to fuel his anger. So the party wouldn't support her proposal. I tried to explain to her that you just couldn't go to the party at will. "You need the consent of the friends." Afterward when I informed the friends, they denied consent, so Leyla had to stay.

I continued to make escape plans, even though all the attempts so far had been unsuccessful. A successful escape would require help from the outside. Back in Malatya, I had received no external support and only trusted in my luck. It had been much riskier, and my luck had lasted only two hours. Then it had taken me three months to recover from my failure.

Prisoners were being released and making their way to the party. In prison, they'd shared our complaints about this issue, and they knew the situation and what outside support we needed in order to escape. But much to my annoyance, once they were outside, they didn't do anything about it. Still, I continued to watch for opportunities, even if I had little hope of gaining support.

The prison system mainly operated on fear, and the prison employees were no small part of that system. They worried about losing their jobs and their incomes and even about compromising themselves. Yet they also set up a system within the system. Their low salaries were barely sufficient for their livelihood, so they got a side job: corruption, which they carried on audaciously. They'd start by taking small bribes, then quickly learned to enrich themselves by demanding material consideration for everything. Prisons had always been associated with torture and oppression, but in the background was another system of payoffs and corruption.

Corruption was common in other institutions of the ruling system—in prison it was just adapted to specific circumstances. Each prison was a world unto itself. In prisons that held mostly political prisoners, for example, embezzlement was an open secret. Especially in the first years after the military coup, when relatives brought money to their imprisoned family members, it would vanish without a trace. Prisoners' money was used, among other things, to create murals depicting the Turkish flag and Atatürk.

Some employees, in addition to seeking personal enrichment, fulfilled other needs. They could be torturers, money collectors, bootlickers, or even leftists and Kurdish nationalists. They acted as informers, betrayed their colleagues, and kept their hand in the game. Some of the prisoners' favorite guards were also close confidants of the administrators. It was easy to see through these machinations. Of course, there were also honorable and honest people among the employees, but at most one in a thousand. For most guards, playing a double game was part of everyday life.

For a long time, I had had my eye on one guard, N., whose wife was Kurdish. He was well thought of in prison and had no apparent political opinions. He was greedy, caring only about personal gain. I judged that he had been participating in the unofficial employment for years. He took on small jobs such as forwarding messages or purchasing personal necessities for compensation. I tried to lure him by hinting at extra income for him. Later I said openly: "We need some things you could get. It'd be worth your while." At first he was afraid: "I don't want to end up where you are." I dropped it for a while, since I couldn't figure out whether he was just trying to drive up the price. But he finally agreed. Anyway, our job wasn't that dangerous—we needed him to get a wig and an ID, and something else that I didn't want to request immediately.

The men didn't trust N. and kept warning me, "Be careful, don't get tricked, this guy doesn't seem right." I didn't trust him either—it was just a game of chance.

I waited excitedly for the completion of the preparations. For my new ID, photos were taken with a camera smuggled into prison. I gave my letters and some books to the men and sent some to the outside. "This time it's got to work," I said. Although they didn't quite believe I'd pull it off, they didn't rule it out either.

Meanwhile, under our party's leadership, the revolutionary struggle in Kurdistan continued to expand. The guerrilla areas spread every day, and many people were attracted to the fight. The enemy failed to prevent this spread, even using all civilian and military means. The Kurdish question was now a current issue in politics both domestically and internationally.

[In 1987 two Communist politicians, Nihat Sargin and Haydar Kutlu, had returned from exile to Turkey and merged the TKP and TİP, two Communist parties, to found the TBKP (United Communist Party of Turkey).]

The events around Sargin and Kutlu were no coincidence, as it was part of the state's long-term plan to establish a controllable left-wing party. It was a typical Kemalist project, in which the Turkish state exploited the weak points within the revolutionary democratic movement in order to implement Kemalist policies. Individuals and organizations were to be integrated and legitimized into the official state system. In the guise of democratization, the manipulation was intended to prevent a left-revolutionary movement from developing in Turkey. It wasn't the first time the TKP had been used this way—this game already had a 70-year history. Of course, the problem wasn't limited to the TKP. It was also about Kurdistan.

From the information available to us, we concluded that the representatives of imperialism and of Turkey were searching for a concrete interim solution to the Kurdish question. Conceivably the state would allow the establishment of a legal Kurdish state, and for this purpose it sought cooperation partners. Who could they be? There were different guesses. Then the media reported that some ethnic Kurdish deputies stepped forward and offered themselves for it. The state, pretending to be Kurd-friendly, had easily found players who claimed to represent the Kurdish cause.

An interim effort by imperialist forces to suppress the Kurdish question: this was how we assessed the formation of the HEP. We waited impatiently to learn the chairman's view. In the last statement from him that we received, he had predicted that the imperialist forces would form an artificial alliance in the form of a "Kurdish party." We would have to exhaust the legal opportunities on the political front and, if necessary, set up a legal party ourselves. Events proved him to be correct. It quickly became clear what the supposed democratization package of the state meant, but then, it had never been a mystery to us anyway.

Articles 141 **and** 142   During this time, newspapers were reporting that the Constitutional Court was overturning certain convictions. Lower courts had previously convicted the plaintiffs on charges of PKK membership and for making statements in their defense. Now this was found to be a "legal error." Lawyers were reviewing the cases of all prisoners who had been convicted this way.

The repeal of Articles 141 and 142 was also discussed. All PKK members had been sentenced under Article 152, and Article 168 imposed the death penalty. Articles 141 and 142 were used against us only in additional cases in which we had been charged with defending ourselves politically. We had been convicted in separate proceedings. The envisaged change in the law would also involve the criminal proceedings against those who had written articles published in magazines.

[Articles 141 and 142 of the 1982 Turkish constitution had been designed to restrict political activity by communists, fascists, and Kurdish nationalists. Western diplomats pointed out that these provisions restricted individual freedoms, in violation of the European Convention on Human Rights. In May 1990, under pressure from the European Community, Turkey repealed Articles 141 and 142. Prisoners who had been convicted under those articles would be freed.]

Our lawyers examined the convictions being reversed by the Constitutional Court and searched for loopholes and procedural errors in our own trials. They were almost overly zealous because there was now little risk.

I had already served out my sentence for PKK membership, but my detention was still in force due to the other convictions. My case was still in the appeals court. For formal reasons, the case moved back and forth between the courts. I had been convicted in all the side matters, and some proceedings were still ongoing, but due to discrepancies between the courts, a previous verdict had no legal force. Occasionally I received official notifications.

The Constitutional Court relied on the principle that a convicted member of an organization couldn't be convicted again for the same charge. This finding could possibly be useful in my case. The lawyers were optimistic.

But I didn't give up my escape plan. N., the guard who I'd roped in, knew about the lawyers' efforts and prayed for their success because he was afraid of getting in trouble. The real reason for his nervousness, however, was the double game he was playing. He didn't bring the items I requested, and the controls were tightened on visiting days. N. had accepted my money but also informed the administration.

The friends laughed at my rage. "That's the way it is—you always have to expect something to go wrong," they advised me. "But you always get deep into something, and then afterward you're devastated. Don't do that—you have to stay cold-blooded."

Numan added, "I never believed it from the start, but I didn't want to depress you." Cemal made fun of N., and Deza told a long story about people from Siverek. So it went—everyone had something to say about my latest aborted escape plan. This time I felt my failure not as bad luck but as incompetence.

Criticism and self-criticism We held self-criticism platforms. In some prisons they began on Newroz [1990], in others on November 27, the anniversary of the founding of the PKK. In Çanakkale, it was November. I attended many platforms in person, and got a rundown of the others at our weekly meetings. "The escape plan fell through," I said at my self-criticism platform, "so in the future I won't write so many letters. Instead I'll work on something with lasting value." The men friends criticized me, saying I didn't think and act comprehensively enough, given my position. I had to overcome my emotionality, my narrow-mindedness, and my superficiality.

After that, five of us, on the pretext of writing our defense, started writing a text that we called "Women in Kurdistan." Based on examples from my life, we analyzed and explained the specific situation of women in the freedom struggle. The men also dealt intensively with this question: Can, Numan, Cemal, and Dursun Ali asked questions, and I answered. We recorded these dialogues, filling over 50 cassettes with them. At Can's suggestion, I drafted the text on the woman question, drawing material from books and magazines.

While I was doing this research, I still thought about new escape plans. The thought had settled in my mind and wouldn't leave—it preoccupied me more than anything. Surely it wasn't fated that all my attempts would fail. We'd found countless possible ways. We'd informed the friends outside, but they didn't take us seriously enough and hadn't provided the necessary support. We criticized this attitude and sent another specific proposal to Hasan Atmaca. Unknown to us, he was arrested shortly thereafter, and the police found our message in his papers. No one informed us about it, so we kept hoping for a positive response for a long time. Only later did we learn that the message had fallen into the enemy's hands, which also explained the tightened controls in prison.

In Amasya, I'd failed to get referred to a hospital. But now, after much effort, I got a referral to Bursa, due to some elevated blood levels. A few friendly doctors offered to publicize my complaints, but I said no—such publicity always had the danger of being used against us.

Hospitalization always opened opportunities. With high hopes, I set out for Bursa, accompanied by two soldiers and an NCO. We drove through a rural area. A single armed person would've been enough to release me. I got sick in the car, so we had to stop several times, and the handcuffs were even removed then. The opportunity was perfect. But in the end, I wasn't taken to the hospital. I was taken to Bursa prison.

Since there was no ward for female political prisoners, I was put in with others. The first thing I saw was a huge Turkish flag hanging on the wall. I walked over and ripped it down. All the guards on duty attacked me. There was a scuffle with kicking and punching. It made little sense for one person to shout slogans, but I did anyway: "Down with torture! Fascist administration!"

As a result of this episode, another criminal case was brought against me. I was charged with insulting and destroying the Turkish flag as well as resisting state authority. At the hearing, I explained that the administration had deliberately provoked the incident.

I was transferred to Bursa to be treated at the hospital. Instead, fascist guards attacked me in the prison. I didn't damage the flag, I just don't want to be in a place where that flag is hanging. I'm a revolutionary. I've been convicted as a PKK member. My identity is, so to speak, officially recognized. So why is that flag in my face? It's my right to resist it.

Over the course of several hearings, the judges studied my file and were shocked by my years of punishment. Anyway, it was strange to bring charges against a prisoner who actually belonged in a hospital. I demanded to be sent back to Çanakkale and refused any medical treatment after all. To call attention to my demand and to protest the attack on me, I went on a two-day hunger strike. Eventually, I was transferred back to Çanakkale.

When I was next summoned to court for a hearing, I assumed it was for one of my existing cases. But it turned out that while I was working with the men friends on the women's text, a complaint had been filed against me on suspicion that I was preparing to escape.

I didn't care who had reported me. The staff even reported on each other, so it was natural for them to do the same to us. It would have been absurd for the enemy not to suspect we were making escape plans. Prisoners all over had been digging tunnels—in some prisons, several had been discovered. So inspections were constant now—the enemy was on the alert.

Nevertheless, it was unacceptable for them to be constantly dragging us into court. Constantly having to refute ridiculous allegations was itself a form of torture, one that probably affected me the most.

I knew the men were working on their own escape plan, so I didn't want to draw the enemy's attention to them. Despite all these obstacles, we managed to finish the women's text and attend the remaining self-criticism platforms. The men took care not to leave me out. For urgent matters, they brought me in with brief door-slot chats or written messages.

Once again I dedicated a lot of time to writing letters. I wrote to prisoners in Turkey and Kurdistan, and to people in Europe and even Australia. Hundreds of friendly people were interested in me and in prison conditions. Religious organizations and Amnesty International wrote to me. Each letter gave me a new contact, which I nurtured carefully. I wasn't writing to kill time—on the contrary, I always seemed to have too little time.

Over the years in prison, it had been difficult to spend our time usefully. It took a huge effort just to get books approved. We constantly had to resist various forms of repression like being isolated or segregated from each other, or banished to other prisons. In Amasya, the hunger strikes had claimed half the year. We also had our own problems with time management. We rarely succeeded in setting up and maintaining work programs. We hardly wrote any texts that would be of lasting value to the general public. We didn't live up to the party's expectations. In Çanakkale, the work routine was little better, and I increasingly felt the need to concentrate on specific topics in depth—that is, when my never-ending thoughts of flight didn't distract me.

I got another letter from Şener. "Today the uncle gave me your letter. I was glad, it did me good," he wrote. Then he said something that made me sit up and take notice. It was about emotions: "It's beautiful and wild to flow like the Zap. But sometimes it can also be necessary to be as deep and calm as the Tigris." What was he getting at? I'd never seen either the Zap or the Tigris, except maybe on TV, and some of the women friends mentioned them. It's true that my feelings often rushed through me, but I didn't understand if Şener was referring to our correspondence or if something else was going wrong.

Mutual deliverance   The Elazığ group's trial came before the Constitutional Court. Only a few of us were still in prison. The lawyers were looking for procedural errors. They invoked precedents and exploited the discrepancies between different court rulings. All these efforts seemed to me a waste of time and energy, but the lawyers weren't put off by my indifference. Some friendly person had decided to "get his sister out of there," at any price.

One day [in 1991] I was summoned to the administration, along with some prisoner representatives. One of the men friends congratulated me. What did he mean? Was this a joke? Maybe he thought I'd been chosen to represent our ward to the administration, but I hadn't, Dursun Ali was our representative, and he was fine.

"I don't like this. I don't know what I'm doing here," I said to Dursun Ali, who knew why I'd been summoned.

"I congratulate you too," said the director. "We will be freed from you, and you from us."

I still didn't understand. "There's no freedom for me. It's not so

simple. I'll still be resisting in prison even after the revolution comes,"
I said.

Everyone laughed. "Sakine, your sentence has been lifted," said Dursun
Ali. "The state owes you three years. You've served three years too much."

I looked at him incredulously.

"Here's the decision," he said, handing me a document. "Read it
yourself if you don't believe me."

I glanced at it. "You're telling me what—that I'm getting out now?
You're—you're unbelievable! Of all things—how can you be so calm?
In your place, I'd be spinning! When I'm released, I'll be the Radau!" [A
rushing river in Germany.]

I said I'd go to the men friends and then be released in the morning.
The director approved, saying, "Sakine will do what she wants." I went
straight to the men and told them my news through the door slot. At
first they didn't believe me. Then the guard unlocked the door, and only
then could I convince them I wasn't joking.

Our joy was indescribable. But I also felt strangely depressed, as if I
had lost something. I'd never thought I'd really get out of prison.

I didn't stay long—I went to all the wards to say goodbye. Everyone
wished me success. "See you!" I said.

21 Cansız with Dursun Ali and Besna Yüce, at Çanakkale, perhaps on the day of
her release, which was December 26, 1990.

On my last night in prison, people talked about their thoughts and feelings and gave me advice.

The next day Can, Numan, Dursun Ali, and Cemal escorted me to the door of the outer corridor. Never had it been so hard for me to say goodbye. I didn't want to leave them. Sobbing, I hugged them one at a time. Numan blinked hard and said, "Come on, you're gonna make us cry too." The friends tried to stay composed, but in the end we were all sobbing in each other's arms. Even the guards were caught up in it.

It was such a painful farewell. Leaving comrades behind in jail rips you apart—you leave your heart with them. "See you on the outside," I said. "In the mountains! We'll see each other there. Take good care of yourselves!" Then I left.

Can had telephoned Besra to pick me up, and she would be waiting for me at the train station. Before I finally left the prison grounds, I had one last argument at the checkpoint. The officer said my suitcase had to be searched. I had to wait for a policewoman or female guard to be brought out. None came. Finally he gave up and ordered his soldiers to search the suitcase.

Of course I objected: "It's already been searched inside!"

"I've got an order that everything has to be checked again," he said.

We got into a scrap. Finally, a female guard came and confirmed that my belongings had all been searched already and no second search was necessary. The officer dug in his heels. He was a true fascist and wanted to demonstrate his power.

I looked him in the eye and said, "I so hope we meet again under different circumstances."

He returned my gaze. "Are you threatening me?"

"Interpret it any way you like," I answered, then stepped into the street and found a taxi. Even after years of prison, nothing outside seemed strange to me. In my mind, I had always been with the friends. As I put prison behind me, my heart was on fire.

Notes

1 Ahmet Hamdi Akkaya, *The Kurdistan Workers' Party (PKK) National Liberation, Insurgency, and Radical Democracy Beyond Borders* (PhD dissertation, Ghent University, 2016); Basak Gemici Ay, *Dynamics of Collective Action in Turkish Prisons: Comparative Analysis of Mamak and Diyarbakir Prisons Between 1980 and 1985* (MA thesis, University of Pittsburgh, 2016); Arda Ibikoglu, *Incarcerating Politics: Prison Reform in Contemporary Turkey* (PhD dissertation, University of Washington, 2012); Welat Zeydanlıoğlu, "Torture and Turkification in the Diyarbakır Military Prison," in *Rights, Citizenship and Torture: Perspectives on Evil, Law and the State*, ed. Welat Zeydanlıoğlu and John T. Parry (Oxford: Inter-Disciplinary Press, 2009). See also Amnesty International, *Turkey: Testimony on Torture* (London: AI Publications, 1985). For a survivor testimony in English, see Mehdi Zana, *Prison No. 5: Eleven Years in Turkish Jails* (Watertown, MA: Blue Crane Books, 1997).

2 See Sakine Cansız, *Sara: My Whole Life Was a Struggle*, trans. Janet Biehl, Vol. I (London: Pluto Press, 2018), pp. 181–197.

3 See ibid., pp. 246–247.

4 See ibid., pp. 183–189.

5 See "Death Under Torture in Turkey," *Amnesty International Campaign for the Abolition of Torture Monthly Bulletin* 5, no. 2 (February 1978).

6 See Cansız, *Sara*, Vol. I, p. 53.

7 Fatsa is a city in the Black Sea region. On October 14, 1979, the socialist Fikri Sönmez (aka Terzi Fikri) was elected mayor of Fatsa. Under the slogan "The red sun will rise in Fatsa," his People's Liberation Army-Revolutionary Path divided the town into 11 sections and created people's committees, empowered to recall government authorities. They worked against violence against women, poor infrastructure, gambling, and environmentally caused diseases. Fikri was very popular. On July 11, 1980, the Turkish Armed Forces, under General Kenan Evren, entered Fatsa, arrested him and 300 others, and imprisoned them. This operation is considered a rehearsal for the 1980 Turkish coup, also led by General Evren. Fikri Sönmez was murdered in Amasya prison in 1985.

8 Early in the armed conflict, guerrilla groups were often on their own, lacking radio contact. Some feudalistic, undereducated commanders asserted their own power and, in some cases, executed intellectuals. The media labeled these gang leaders "bandit kings" [German trans.].

9 Dursun Karatas (1952–2008), co-founder of Dev-Sol in 1978, escaped from prison on October 25, 1989.

10 Ali Akgün, of Dev-Sol, was accused of being an "agent" and killed in Çanakkale prison in 1989 on the order of Dursun Karatas.

List of people

Agit. *See* Mahsum Korkmaz.

Ali Gündüz: participated in 1978 founding congress; Elazığ group member; betrayer.

Ali Haydar Kaytan (code name Fuat): b. Dersim; participated in 1978 founding congress; chosen for party's central committee; after the 1980 military coup, he fled to northern Iraq, where he led the PKK's education camp (currently a member of the KCK executive council).

Aysel Öztürk Çürükkaya: PKK member; friend of Cansız from Bingöl; married Selim Çürükkaya; arrested on November 27, 1979; imprisoned with Cansız at Diyarbakir. *See* Vol. I, pp. 232–233, 244–245.

Aytekin Tuğluk: PKK member; arrested in Elazığ before Cansız; male prisoner at 1800 Evler.

Ayten Yıldırım: b. Dersim; childhood friend of Cansız; PKK member; married to Hamili Yıldırım; a teacher; arrested with Cansız in Elazığ.

Baki Polat: Cansız's ex-husband.

Cahide Şener: b. Siverek; PKK member; fought in Hilvan and Siverek; imprisoned with Cansız at Diyarbakir and elsewhere. *See* Vol. I, pp. 262ff, 292–297.

Celal Aydın: betrayed the PKK in Elazığ and Malatya; joined Tekoşin; assassinated in Malatya in 1979.

Celalettin Can: b. Dersim, 1956; head of Dev-Genc, associated with Dev-Sol; arrested in Malatya in 1981.

Cemil Bayik: b. Elazığ; participated in 1978 founding congress; prominent PKK cadre (currently still active).

Cemile Merkit: wife of Ali Haydar Kaytan. *See* Vol. I, p. 236.

Duran Kalkan (code name Abbas): participated in 1978 founding congress; PKK leadership cadre (currently still active).

Emine Turgut: female prisoner at Diyarbakir; gave birth to Hêlîn in prison.

Erol Değirmenci: Elazığ group member; betrayer.

Eşref Anyık: PKK member; one of four male prisoners at Diyarbakir who set themselves on fire in 1982 to protest prison conditions.

Fatma Çelik: female prisoner at Diyarbakir.

Ferhat Kurtay: one of four male prisoners at Diyarbakir who set themselves on fire in 1982 to protest prison conditions.

Fuat Çavgun: b. 1954 in Hilvan; brother of Halil Çavgun; PKK member; arrested and imprisoned at Malatya and Diyarbakir. On July 14, 1982, he joined a death fast, from which he suffered brain damage that went untreated.

Fuat Kav: PKK member; male prisoner at Diyarbakir (currently active as a journalist).

Gönül Atay: female prisoner at Diyarbakir; Cansız first encountered her in Tuzlucayir (Vol. I, p. 216); said to be engaged to Rıza.

Gültan Kışanak: b. 1961, Elazığ; arrested in Diyarbakir in 1980, just before the coup; imprisoned with Cansız; later a prominent politician for pro-Kurdish parties in Turkey; was co-mayor of Diyarbakir (currently in prison).

Halil Çavgun: brother of Fuat Çavgun; Kurdistan Revolutionary who organized the poor and landless against the wealthy landowning Süleyman clan; shot dead on May 19, 1978.

Hamili Yıldırım: b. Dersim; married to Ayten Yıldırım; member of Elazığ group; arrested with Cansız; no relation to Hüseyin Yıldırım or Kesire Yıldırım.

Hasan Atmaca: male prisoner at Diyarbakir.

Hayri. See Mehmet Hayri Durmuş.

Hüseyin Yıldırım: served as defense counsel in 1981 to arrested PKK members; arrested in October 1981 and imprisoned at Diyarbakir from November 1981 to July 1982; afterward served as European spokesperson for PKK in the early 1980s, then split from the party; no relation to Kesire Yıldırım or Hamili Yıldırım.

Kemal Pir: b. 1952 in Black Sea Region; participated in 1978 founding congress; prominent PKK cadre; arrested and imprisoned at Diyarbakir; died on July 14, 1982, on the 55th day of a death fast.

Koç Ali Şener: father of Cahide Şener. See Vol. I, p. 293.

Mahsum Korkmaz (code name Agit): b. 1956 in Silvan; member of PKK central committee; played a leading role in organizing the August 15, 1984 commencement of armed propaganda. Killed by Turkish forces, March 28, 1986.

Mazlum Doğan: b. 1955; participated in 1978 founding congress; a leading PKK cadre; arrested in 1979 and imprisoned at Diyarbakir; hanged himself on March 21, 1982, to raise awareness of the inhumane conditions, his suicide inspired hunger strikes and resistance campaigns among other prisoners.

Mehdi Zana: b. 1940; socialist; mayor of Diyarbakir, 1978–1980; husband of Leyla Zana; arrested and imprisoned at Diyarbakir.

Mehmet Hayri Durmuş: b. 1955; participated in 1978 founding congress; prominent PKK cadre; arrested November 1979 in Hilvan-Siverek area; imprisoned at Diyarbakir; died in July 1982 in a death fast, protesting prison conditions.

Mehmet Karasungur: b. 1947; prominent PKK cadre.

Mehmet Şener: participated in 1978 founding congress; imprisoned at Diyarbakir.

Metin (Meto) Cansız: brother of Sakine Cansız; imprisoned at Diyarbakir.

Mevlüde Acar (Bêse): female prisoner at Diyarbakir (currently active in HDP).

Mustafa Karasu: b. Dersim; prominent PKK cadre; imprisoned at Diyarbakir (currently a member of KCK executive council).

Muzaffer Ayata: b. Siverek, 1956; imprisoned at Diyarbakir (currently active as a writer).

Rıza Altun: b. Kayseri; founding member of PKK in 1978; male prisoner (currently a member of KCK executive council).

Şahin Dönmez: b. Dersim; participated in 1978 founding congress; betrayer. See Vol. I, pp. 183–189, 245–247.

Saliha Şener: mother of Mehmet Şener.

Selim Cürukkaya: husband of Aysel Cürukkaya; imprisoned at Diyarbakir.

Süleyman: b. Dersim; married to Cahide Şener; imprisoned at Diyarbakir.

Yıldırım Merkit: b. 1956 in Dersim; PKK founding member; arrested in late 1979 (declared a traitor at Second Congress in 1982; killed in Romania in 1994).

Yıldız Durmuş: sister of Mehmet Hayri Durmuş; early female cadre.

List of political names and acronyms

PKK-related organizations

ARGK (Artêşa Rizgariya Gelê Kurdistan): People's Liberation Army of Kurdistan; armed unit established at the PKK's Third Congress in October 1986; previously called HRK; in 2000 the ARGK would become the HPG.

HPG (Hêzên Parastina Gel): People's Defense Forces; military organization of the PKK since 2000.

HRK (Hêzen Rizgarîye Kurdîstan): Kurdistan Liberation Units; armed wing of the PKK until 1986.

PKK (Partiya Karkerên Kurdistan): Kurdistan Workers Party founded in 1978.

UKO (Ulusal Kurtuluş Ordusu): National Liberation Army; precursor of PKK until 1978.

Other groups and parties

DDKD (Devrimci Demokratik Kültür Derneği): Revolutionary Democratic Culture Association.

Dev-Sol (Devrimci Sol): Revolutionary Left; Marxist-Leninist party founded in 1978.

Dev-Yol (Devrimci Yol): Revolutionary Path; Marxist-Leninist group founded in 1977.

HEP (Halken Emek Partisi): People's Labor Party; pro-Kurdish political party founded in 1990; banned in 1993 for promoting Kurdish cultural and political rights.

HK (Halkin Kurtuluşu): People's Liberation; Turkish leftist party founded in 1976.

Kawa: Kurdish leftist party founded in 1976.

KDP (Partîya Demokrata Kurdistan): Kurdistan Democratic Party.

KUK (Kürdistan Ulusal Kurtuluşçuları): Kurdistan National Liberators; Kurdish leftist party.

Kurtuluş: a Kurdish leftist party.

MHP (Milliyetçi Hareket Partisi): Nationalist Action Party.

Özgürlük Yolu (Kurdish *Rîya Azadî*): *Freedom Road,* journal of the 1970s TKSP (Socialist Party of Kurdistan Turkey).

PDA (Proleter Devrimci Aydınlık): Proletarian Revolutionary Enlightenment; Turkish leftist party founded in January 1970.

PPKK (Partiya Peseng Karkeran Kurdistan): Founded in 1975 as an appendage of the DDKD; in Europe it published an organ called *Peseng bo Sores.*

Rizgarî (Kurdish for "Liberation"): Kurdish leftist party founded in 1979.

Tekoşin (also Kurdish for "Liberation"): Kurdish party established separately from UKO in Antep, Maraş, and Dersim; following the death of Haki Karer in 1977, UKO considered Tekoşin a continuation of Stêrka Sor (which had killed Karer) and thus a target of violence.

THKO (Türkiye Halk Kurtuluş Ordusu): People's Liberation Army of Turkey; Turkish leftist group founded in December 1970.

TİKB (Türkiye İhtilalci Komünistler Birliği): Union of Revolutionary Communists of Turkey; Turkish leftist party founded in 1979.

TİKKO (Türkiye İşci ve Köylü Kurtuluş Ordusu): Liberation Army of the Workers and Peasants of Turkey; armed wing of the TKP/ML.

TİKP (Türkiye İşçi Köylü Partisi): Workers and Peasants Party of Turkey; a Maoist party founded in 1978 and chaired by Doğu Perinçek; terminated after the September 12, 1980, coup.

TİP (Türkiye İşçi Partisi): Workers' Party of Turkey; a socialist party founded in 1961.

TKP or TKP/ML (Türkiye Komünist Partisi/Marksist Leninist Hareketi): Communist Party of Turkey/Marxist-Leninist, founded in 1976.

Timeline

1978: Kurdistan Revolutionaries attack large landowning clans (*aghas*) in Siverek and Hilvan. These clans dominated the local economy and were allied with the state and the police.

1978 November 26–27: PKK founding congress in Fis village, in the Lice district of Diyarbakır province.

1979 May: The Turkish state's first arrest wave of PKK members, including high-ranking cadres, begins in Elazığ. On May 7 Cansız, Hamili Yıldırım, and Ayten Yıldırım are arrested in an Elazığ apartment.

1979 July: In Siverek, PKK units fight the powerful Bucak clan.

1979 July: Abdullah Öcalan flees Turkey for Syria.

1979 late in year: In Turkey's southeast, tens of militants and founding members are arrested.

1979 November 27: In a car on the road to Urfa, Mazlum Doğan is arrested, along with Aysel Çürükkaya and Yıldırım Merkit.

1979 late in year, to early 1980: In Lebanon, first PKK militants get basic military training.

1980 summer: Gültan Kışanak is arrested and detained in Diyarbakir prison.

1980 August 20: Cansız attempts to escape from Malatya prison.

1980 September 12: A junta of five generals stage a military coup in Turkey and declare martial law. It abolishes the parliament and suspends the constitution. It bans political parties and trade unions. It arrests leaders, members, and sympathizers of opposition groups, especially socialist and Kurdish ones. It tries them in military courts and detains them in military prisons. The coup marks the emergence of a far more authoritarian political system in Turkey.

1981 January 4–12: At Diyarbakir prison, PKK cadres begin the first hunger strike, to show they will not obey new military rules. It lasts eight days.

1981 *c.* March 1: Cansız and the rest of the Elazığ group arrive at Diyarbakir prison.

1981 March 4: At Diyarbakir prison, the PKK leadership starts a second hunger strike or death fast with 14 others from the Ward 35; they are protesting Esat Oktay's brutality and violence.

1981 April 13: The main trial begins, including the Elazığ group; the death fast continues.

1981 April 16: The death fast ends after 43 days. Some hold out till May 24.

1981 summer: At Helwe camp in the Beka'a Valley in Lebanon, the PKK holds a conference that decides to prepare for guerrilla warfare in Kurdistan.

1982 January: In Europe, the monthly ideological journal *Serxwebûn* (Independence) is launched.

1982 March 21: On Newroz, Mazlum Doğan hangs himself to protest prison conditions.

1982 May 17–18: The Night of the Four. Four male PKK militants immolate themselves by fire to protest prison conditions.

1982 June: PKK leadership cadre enter a death fast.

1982 July 14: On the 55th day of the death fast, Kemal Pir, Mehmet Hayri Durmuş, Akif Yilmaz, and Ali Çiçek perish.

1982 August 20–25: Second PKK Congress, held in a Palestinian camp in Syria, near the Jordanian border. Afterward trained militants in Lebanon are sent to the mountains of northern Iraq to set up bases for guerrilla warfare.

1983 September: Esat Oktay is removed from Diyarbakir prison.

1983 September 5: At Diyarbakir, a hunger strike begins, with broad participation.

1983 October 2: After 27 days, the hunger strike ends.

1983 November: In Turkey, military rule officially ends. The new civilian government requires all imprisoned insurgents to wear uniforms by the end of 1983.

1984 January 1: At Diyarbakir, the uprising begins: prisoners initiate a hunger strike against the mandatory military uniforms.

1984 August 15: In the Kurdish-populated southeast, guerrilla units attack the towns of Eruh and Şemdinli. The organization announces the start of the "people's war" against the "colonial and fascist" Turkish state. It calls on the Kurdish people as well as the revolutionary Left to join forces and fight dictatorship. By announcing these revolutionary goals in this period of armed propaganda, it hopes to recruit supporters. August 15 marks the beginning of the PKK's protracted armed conflict with the Turkish state.

1986 March 28: Death of Mahsum Korkmaz, leader of the August 15 attack on Eruh.

1986 October 25–30: Third PKK Congress, held in Helve Camp (renamed Mahsum Korkmaz Academy), in the Beka'a Valley, Lebanon.

1988 January: In Europe, arrest wave of PKK members there begins.

1988 October 22: In Istanbul, Esat Oktay is murdered by a former prisoner; at Diyarbakir prison, the tunnel is discovered.

1988 October: Cansız and other women are transferred to Amasya prison.

1989 December: Cansız is transferred to Çanakkale prison.

1990: March: In the Kurdish southeast, the Serhildan (uprising) begins. Kurds who tried to bury 13 guerrillas killed in the Savur district of Mardin are brutally attacked by state forces in Nusaybin and Cizre. Mass attendance at guerrilla funerals spreads throughout Kurdistan.

1990 May: Turkey repeals Articles 141 and 142.

1990 November: At Çanakkale prison, PKK holds self-criticism platforms.

1990 December 26–31: Fourth PKK Congress, in Haftanin, South Kurdistan (Iraq).

1991: Cansız is released from Çanakkale prison.

Index